Manipulating
Public Opinion

Essays on Public Opinion as a Dependent Variable

Manipulating Public Opinion

Essays on Public Opinion as a Dependent Variable

Edited by

Michael Margolis
University of Pittsburgh

Gary A. Mauser
Simon Fraser University

Brooks/Cole Publishing Company
Pacific Grove, California

Brooks/Cole Publishing Company
A Division of Wadsworth, Inc.

Printed in the United States of America

10   9   8   7   6   5   4   3   2   1

Library of Congress Cataloging-in-Publication Data
Manipulating public opinion/ Michael Margolis, Gary A. Mauser,
   [editors].
       p.   cm.
   Includes index.
   ISBN 0–534–11121–1
   1. Public opinion—United States.   2. Electioneering—United
States.   3. Political socialization—United States.   I. Margolis,
Michael.   II. Mauser, Gary A.
HN90.P8M29   1989
303.3′8—dc19

Sponsoring Editors: *Leo A. W. Wiegman and Cynthia C. Stormer*
Editorial Assistant: *Mary Ann Zuzow*
Production Manager: *Ann Cassady*
Production Editors: *Carol Schoen and Penelope Sky*
Typesetting: *Compset Inc.*
Printing and Binding: *Malloy Lithographing, Inc.*

We dedicate this book to our children:
Mathieu, Kendrick, Kele, and Jesse;
Karen, Jenny, Abby, Max, and Nicky

PREFACE

This book grew out of our discussions at a panel on public opinion methodology at the 1985 meeting of the American Political Science Association in New Orleans. Our discussions became so animated that we adjourned to Delmonico's, where we began studying French wines, and continued talking late into the night. We found that both of us were disappointed by the current state of research on public opinion and democratic government. The focus of research in public opinion was far too limited by the over-reliance upon "representative" survey methods. Researchers, however sophisticated their methodology, were letting their tools determine the problems they studied. We felt that all too often they failed to study the most important questions. Too many researchers presumed that opinions given in response to survey questions determine—or at least set strict limits for—public policies. Few were attempting to trace the origins of those opinions.

We thought that the prevailing research orientation generally gave short shrift to the problem of managing 'r manipulating public opinion, and tended to place the burden of responsibility for unpopular policies upon the mass public, not upon political decision-makers or other elites who, arguably, are more powerful. We decided to write a book predicated upon the notion that public opinion could be viewed more fruitfully as a dependent variable. *Manipulating Public Opinion: Essays on Public Opinion as a Dependent Variable* is the result. There is no other book like it; it defines its own niche.

In this book we demonstrate that any analyst who seeks to account for public policy decisions is well advised to begin by examining the preferences of elites rather than the "state of public opinion" as measured by survey studies. *Manipulating Public Opinion* covers three types of problem areas: (1) short-term studies of opinion formation during election campaigns; (2) short-to-medium-term studies of the development of selected public policies; and (3) medium-to-long-term studies of the process of political socialization. This book can be used as a main text or supplement in undergraduate courses in political science or communications. It includes empirical studies of hypotheses about the abilities of political elites to manage public opinion in each of the three topic areas. It is of particular relevance to courses on the role of the mass media in modern democracies, such as public opinion, campaigns and elections, political communications, mass media, journalism and politics, public policy, political sociology, and political marketing.

While American politics provides the impetus for this book, several chapters touch on politics in countries as various as Canada, France, and Ethiopia. Our contributors include academics and practitioners from Canada as well as the United States, who specialize in political science, communications, economics, marketing, and rhetoric. We are confident that *Manipulating Public Opinion* will have a strong cross-disciplinary appeal.

General readers should also find this book of interest. We have tried not to use the turgid prose that permeates too many professional books, and we worked with our contributors to develop a coherent style without sacrificing academic rigor. We provide introductory and concluding chapters that state succinctly our view that public opinion acts more as a dependent than as an independent variable. Every chapter is conceptually tied to the central theme of the book, and we provide brief introductions to each chapter, showing how the author develops aspects of our theme. As an aid to the serious researcher, we have included a names index, a subject index, and a bibliography.

As originally conceived, this book demanded a greater span of knowledge and effort than we possessed between us. To help us flesh it out, we enlisted some of our colleagues who were actively conducting important research in related areas. In June 1986 we began to commission the original essays for this book. We sought out colleagues who could write essays with two complementary goals: to summarize the major findings in public opinion and to break new ground. This project has gradually taken shape over the past few years. Interim reports were delivered at the annual meetings of the American Political Science Association (1986); the Northeast Political Science Association (1986); and the Midwest Political Science Association (1987).

Acknowledgments

No book springs full-blown like Minerva from the brow of its creator, and *Manipulating Public Opinion* is no exception to this rule. We have benefited from the gracious assistance of many people, among them our colleagues who generously read and criticized early drafts of our manuscript. In particular, we thank Mark Wexler and John Richards, Simon Fraser University; and Bert Rockman and Fred Whelan, University of

Pittsburgh. We also thank the readers who evaluated the first submission of the book and who now are willing to break their cover of anonymity: Allan J. Cigler, University of Kansas, and Gregory B. Markus, University of Michigan. They provided valuable criticism and suggestions that, despite our initial protestations to the contrary, greatly improved the final version.

We also acknowledge our respective universities, not only for the secretarial and scholarly support, but for the use of their computer centers' international communication networks. Without Bitnet, Netnorth, and Autonet we could never have maintained the almost daily contact over "e-mail" that was necessary to complete this project. Special thanks to the Department of Political Science at the University of Pittsburgh, and to the Faculty of Business Administration at Simon Fraser University in Burnaby, British Columbia. Gary Mauser also thanks Stanley Shapiro, Dean of the Faculty of Business Administration, and other members of his faculty for being so supportive of his work on this book, despite their wondering perhaps just what such a project had to do with marketing. Finally, we owe thanks to our secretaries and manuscript typists, who provided advice about word processing systems, modems, and telecommunications protocol as well: Anita Mahony and Betty Chung at Simon Fraser University; and Donna Myers, Michelle Pupich, and Josie Raleigh at the University of Pittsburgh.

Leo Wiegman, formerly political science editor at the Dorsey Press (now at Peacock Publishers), deserves special recognition for negotiating and coordinating the complex contractual arrangements, and Penelope Sky deserves a rose for pushing the book through production on schedule after Brooks/Cole inherited the project.

Finally, we express our gratitude for the loving support our families have shown us throughout the many months we have worked on this book. Ede particularly, and our children, have made numerous sacrifices, giving up plans for family outings, dinners, and even romantic evenings alone, in order to allow us to work on what must have seemed like an unending project. We hope that they, and you, will find the result worthwhile.

Michael Margolis
Gary A. Mauser

ABOUT THE EDITORS

Michael Margolis (Ph.D., Michigan) is professor and director of graduate studies in the department of political science of the University of Pittsburgh. He has served as visiting lecturer in politics at the Universities of Strathclyde (1965–67) and Glasgow (1973–74). His books include *Viable Democracy* (1979) and *Political Stratification and Democracy* (co-author: 1973). Articles and chapters he has written have appeared in academic journals, including *American Political Science Review, American Journal of Political Science, The Annals of the American Academy of Political and Social Sciences, Polity, The Journal of Mathematical Sociology, The Journal of Irreproducible Results,* and in books published by Cambridge and Indiana University presses. His popular pieces have appeared in the *New York Times,* the *Pittsburgh Post–Gazette,* the *Scotsman,* the *Washington Post,* and other newspapers and journals. A consultant on survey research and electoral analysis, he has worked for Pittsburgh radio and television stations, and for local governments, candidates, and interest groups.

Gary A. Mauser (Ph.D., California, Irvine) is associate professor and marketing area coordinator in the Faculty of Business Administration at Simon Fraser University, Burnaby, British Columbia. He has served as visiting professor in marketing at the Université Laval, Québec (1979–80), and at the Institut d'Etudes Commerciales, Université de Grenoble (1971–74), and in politics at the Institut d'Etudes Politiques, Université de Grenoble (1973–74). He spent a year as a Postdoctoral Fellow at the Language–Behavior Research Laboratory at the University of California, Berkeley (1970–71). He is the author of *Political Marketing, A Strategic Approach to Electoral Analysis* (1983). Articles and chapters he has written have appeared in academic journals, including *Public Choice, Journal of Consumer Research, Journal of the Marketing Research Society, Journal of Marketing, Revue Française du Marketing, Relations Industrielles,* and *Tourism Management,* and in books published by Wiley, Seminar Press, and NuWest Press. He has conducted marketing surveys for political parties, television stations, and other private clients in the United States, France, the United Kingdom, and Canada. He is currently working with Patrick Smith on a study of electoral redistribution in British Columbia entitled *Justice or Gerrymandering in BC?* to be published by Detselig Press (Edmonton, Alberta), and on a study of Canadian attitudes toward gun control and self-defense.

ABOUT THE CONTRIBUTORS

Lance Bennett is professor of political science at the University of Washington. He has written extensively on political communications, public opinion, political culture, and political language and rhetoric. His work on mass media news and popular perceptions includes *News: The Politics of Illusion* (2nd ed., 1988) along with numerous articles in political science and communications journals.

Robert E. Burtt is a Ph.D. student and teaching fellow in political science at the University of Pittsburgh. He has also co-written "The Impact of Industrial Decline: Braddock, North Braddock, and Rankin," which appeared in *Steel People: Survival and Resilience in Pittsburgh's Mon Valley* (1986).

Christopher J. Bosso is assistant professor of political science at Northeastern University. Among his recent publications is *Pesticides and Politics: The Life Cycle of a Public Issue* (Pittsburgh, 1987), while his current research centers on the role of Congress in policy formation.

Randall G. Chapman is associate professor of marketing at Boston University. His publications include *College Choices of Academically Able Students* (co-author, 1987) and *BRANDMAPS: The Competitive Marketing Strategy Game* (1988). His articles have appeared in *Journal of Marketing Research, Marketing Science, Journal of Consumer Research, Journal of Retailing,* and *Management Science.*

Benjamin Ginsberg is professor of government at Cornell University. His most recent publications include *The Captive Public* (1984) and *The Consequences of Consent* (1982). Ginsberg is presently at work on an analysis of the politics of the Reagan era.

John Hurwitz is assistant professor of political science at the University of Pittsburgh, specializing in political behavior (public opinion and voting). He has published articles reflecting his current interest—foreign policy attitudes—in journals such as the *American Political Science Review* and the *American Journal of Political Science*.

Xandra Kayden is a research fellow at the Institute of Politics, Harvard University. She has written two books: *The Party Goes On* (1985) and *Campaign Organization* (1978), and contributed a number of chapters to other works on parties, interest groups, and campaign finance. She is currently working on a book entitled *Surviving Power*.

Michael Johnston is associate professor of political science at Colgate University. His research and teaching interests include ethical issues in politics, and the political uses of the mass media. He is co-editor of *Corruption and Reform: An International Journal*.

David B. Magleby is associate professor of political science at Brigham Young University. He has written *Direct Legislation: Voting on Ballot Propositions in the United States* (1984), on the initiative and referendum process; and co-written *The Myth of the Independent Voter* (1988).

Michael Margolis is professor of political science at the University of Pittsburgh, a lecturer, and a survey research consultant. His publications include *Viable Democracy* (1979), *Political Stratification and Democracy* (co-author, 1972), and numerous articles in professional journals and periodicals.

Gary A. Mauser is associate professor of marketing at Simon Fraser University. He is a professional marketing researcher and has conducted strategic surveys for political parties in Canada, France, and the United States. He is the author of *Political Marketing* (1983), and has published articles in *Journal of Consumer Research, Public Choice,* and *Revue Française du Marketing*.

Benjamin I. Page is Gordon Scott Fulcher Professor of Decision-Making at Northwestern University. He has written or co-written a number of books and articles on public opinion, the mass media, elections, and policy making, including *Choices and Echoes in Presidential Elections* and *Who Gets What from Government*.

Kristian Palda is professor of business at Queen's University in Kingston, Ontario. His latest articles on the effects of campaign spending appeared in *Public Choice* and *Canadian Public Policy* (1985). His latest book, *In-*

dustrial Innovation (1984), is critical of government intervention in industry.

Michael Parenti is a political scientist, author, and lecturer. His publications include *Inventing Reality: the Politics of the Mass Media, Democracy for the Few* (now in its 5th edition), and *The Sword and the Dollar: Imperialism, Revolution, and the Arms Race*.

Terence H. Qualter is professor of political science at the University of Waterloo. He is the author of five books and several articles in academic journals. His major research interests are in the fields of public opinion, propaganda and the mass media, and English political theory.

Robert Y. Shapiro is associate professor of political science at Columbia University. He is also a researcher at the University's Center for the Social Sciences. He has published numerous articles on public opinion and the policy making process in professional journals and, with Benjamin Page, he is currently completing a book entitled *The Rational Public: Fifty Years of Opinion Trends*.

Theodore Otto Windt, Jr. is associate professor of political communication at the University of Pittsburgh. He is editor of *Presidential Rhetoric: 1961 to the Present* and co-editor (with Beth Ingold) of *Essays in Presidential Rhetoric*. He is a communications consultant and has also served as a speech writer.

CONTENTS

SECTION TWO
Public Policy   137

SECTION THREE
Long-Term Influences   251

Manipulating Public Opinion

Essays on Public Opinion as a Dependent Variable

CHAPTER 1

Introduction: Public Opinion as a Dependent Variable

Michael Margolis

Gary A. Mauser

HOW SHOULD WE STUDY PUBLIC OPINION?

All governments, from the most dictatorial to the most democratic, find it valuable to secure the support of the general public. Indeed, as recent events in the Republic of South Africa, South Korea, Poland, Afghanistan, and the Philippines have demonstrated, even dictatorial regimes find it difficult to prosper without the good opinion—or at least the acquiescence—of most of their citizens. The costs of using naked force to maintain power over a recalcitrant majority can become unacceptably high.

In all modern governments, public opinion serves to legitimate governmental institutions and to determine in greater or lesser detail the limits of public policy. While this is true for dictatorships as well as for democracies, modern democratic governments distinguish themselves by claiming that public opinion also plays an important role in determining the content or direction of public policy. Consistent with this claim, political scientists and pollsters, particularly Americans, have devoted considerable effort to surveying the opinions held by representative samples of citizens and to comparing the extent to which public policies tend to correspond to popular opinions.

The critical assumption underlying this survey effort is that public opinion not only "matters" in modern democracies, but that it serves as a guideline, an indicator of people's interests and desires that elected representatives and other political decision makers are supposed to take into account. In democracies, decision makers normally are granted considerable discretion to act in the people's stead between elections. But in the end, the decision makers are responsible to the people for their policy choices; in the interim, public opinion polls can provide current information about people's views on pressing problems of the day.

How realistic is the critical assumption that political decision makers

1

in societies we call democratic attempt to formulate policies that conform to the public's wishes? To what extent do these decision makers strive to bring public opinion into conformity with their own personal wishes? And if the latter efforts are extensive, then what is distinctive about the role of public opinion in democratic societies?

As Samuel Kernell has recently documented, American presidents and other "issue entrepreneurs" have learned to use technological developments in communications and transportation to "go public" to promote themselves and their policies. The ultimate object of going public is to stimulate mass support for the entrepreneurs' policy preferences in a manner that impresses targeted political decision makers, such as members of Congress. This leads Kernell to ask: "Do the fixed preferences of the public motivate and direct the strategic activities of politicians, or conversely, do politicians shape the preferences of the public, at least those that are effectively communicated to Washington?" (Kernell 1986: 221).

After reviewing three "grass-roots" campaigns: the "flat-tax" movement of the late 1970s that led to the Reagan income tax reforms; the Mothers Against Drunk Driving (MADD) push for federal drunk-driving legislation in the early 1980s; and the popular groundswell against the Internal Revenue Service's (IRS) proposed regulations in 1983 that would have required banks and savings and loans to withhold a portion of depositors' interest for taxes, Kernell concludes that it is by no means certain that the public acts on its own volition. In all three of the above-mentioned cases, certain politicians and organizations with the financial resources to use communications technology effectively played key roles in generating the campaigns. Even though recent examples of failed public campaigns abound, such as the Alliance for Energy Security's efforts to secure deregulation of natural gas prices, the emerging pattern of successful policy-making calls for the president and others to act as issue entrepreneurs, creating demands and channeling their expression toward legislators or other relevant policymakers (Kernell 1986: 222).

Indeed, focusing upon public opinion as though it were an autonomous force behind public policy formulation has produced rather paltry results. In a critical review of the state of scientific research on public opinion, Richard Niemi (1983) noted the dearth of theories that employ public opinion as an independent variable. He found this rather troubling, especially in light of the relatively large portion of political science research budgets devoted to sample surveys that measure public opinion. Was all this investment worthwhile?

> If by "public opinion" we mean the ideas of an amorphous group of opinion leaders, being public in the sense that it is not always the same, concentrated elite, then I readily concede that public opinion is important. But if that is

what we mean, then why conduct surveys that are representative of the population at large? If, on the other hand, by public opinion we mean what we measure in representative surveys, then the answer is more problematic. . . . Perhaps what is most important about public opinion in a broader sense is that people are willing to acquiesce in what a small set of leading individuals say. But the fact of such acquiescence is a lesson learned long ago, and continual rediscovery of this fact does not justify an extensive investment in representative samples. (Niemi 1983: 18–19)

Niemi's point is well made, but it also seems to beg a previous question: why presume that public opinion should be studied primarily as an independent variable? Why not adopt the more entrepreneurial approach suggested by Kernell? Our view is that we can achieve richer theoretical and explanatory results from research that treats public opinion essentially as dependent. To the extent public opinion is independent, we suggest that it acts primarily to set limits on the range of public policy choices; public opinion rarely dictates policy decisions to governmental elites. As Niemi pointed out, opinion surveys of representative samples that aim to discover positive influences on policy have produced (and most likely will continue to produce) largely disappointing results.

We believe that many of our disappointments with public opinion research arise from focusing too narrowly upon responses to sample survey questions as though they represented the driving forces behind public policy decisions. We suggest that focusing upon the opinions and policy agendas of political elites and then linking them with those of the general public is a more fruitful strategy. In our view, opinion surveys are better used to measure the extent to which established elites—the leaders of major business, religious, educational, or governmental institutions, for example—succeed in gaining popular acceptance of their policy preferences, and to discover the limitations, if any, that public opinion places on the adoption and implementation of those preferences. In short, we argue that analysts who seek to account for public policy decisions normally should begin by examining the preferences of elites, not the "state of public opinion" as measured by pollsters.

This book represents an effort to pursue public opinion research from this latter viewpoint. The authors of these essays consider the extent to which public opinion in diverse circumstances is subject to manipulation by political elites. They also examine what role the mass media play in linking elites and the public. Readers will find a variety of views expressed about the nature of elites in democratic societies. The principal differences among these views concern the extent of homogeneity thought to exist among elite groups. Before discussing the specific content of these essays, however, let us consider why public opinion polling and its concomitant emphasis on the independent nature of public opinion has become so prominent in this field.

SCIENTIFIC METHOD AND
PUBLIC OPINION RESEARCH

Since World War II, research in public opinion, more than in most other subject areas of political science, has been affected by three developments: (1) the establishment of national polling organizations that regularly solicit the opinions of representative samples of adults on issues of public concern; (2) the adoption of scientific methods that seek to develop systematic theories of political behavior; and (3) the introduction of modern computers that has enabled researchers to collect and analyze enormous quantities of data. Modern researchers have access to vast compilations of data representative of the distribution of opinions on issues of public concern among various national and subnational groups. Moreover, appropriate sample selection and question wording allow researchers to evaluate statistically the accuracy of sample estimates drawn from the data.

These developments, combined with popular notions of liberal democracy, have led some commentators to treat the results of surveys not merely as data that help inform governmental decision makers, but as mandates, violations of which require explanation and justification. Public opinion analysts, both academic and popular, have a sophisticated understanding of the shortcomings of the mechanisms of direct democracy when applied to mass societies. However, they have often focused upon the extent to which the development and maintenance of public policies have corresponded to the changes in patterns of public opinion. Some have even suggested that a high correspondence between changes in popular opinion and changes in public policy is the mark of a successful democracy (Gallup 1939: 14–15; Monroe 1975: 6; Ippolito et al. 1976: 13–14; Burstein 1979: 158).

The common thread that runs through these survey studies is the treatment of public opinion as an independent variable, which either directs or severely constrains public policy. When their authors compare public opinions and public policies, they generally restrict their efforts to correlating survey data with public policy decisions, and they generally assume that public opinions are causative or at least constraining factors in the development of those policies. Their common problem is their authors' reliance on survey research data to provide the primary observations for their correlational analyses. This reliance precludes direct examination of the means or manners by which opinions are linked to policies. As we know, correlation alone does not demonstrate causation.

The upshot of such developments has been the emergence of a sophisticated but unsatisfying body of findings about political attitudes and opinions. We know a great deal about how children acquire party loyalties, how particular groups claim to view one another, and how people view particular policies and issues. We also know about how some bundles of opinions consistently relate to other bundles or opinions and about how certain of these bundles relate to the act of voting. But that summarizes the extent of the knowledge we have gained. Voting is the only political behavior that public opinion polling has consistently explained. Yet voting itself is a notoriously inefficient way to express policy preferences: it tells us little about how, if at all, public opinion is linked to public policy (Margolis 1977; Asher 1988: chap. 4).

If we are interested in measuring the extent to which public opinion determines public policy, then examining the policy process in subject areas of interest would seem more promising than examining the survey archives for questions about those subject areas. The critical concerns then become the location of policy initiatives and the observation of their consequences, not the mere correspondence of public opinion with public policy. Which individuals or groups set the policy agenda? What are their avowed aims? How do they go about mustering support for those aims? How well do they succeed?

The primary research methods needed to answer these questions would involve the direct observation of behavior, the examination of records or documents regarding resource utilization, and the use of directed interviews with opinion leaders regarding their motivations, aims, strategies, and expectations. Attention should also be paid to the means— mass media, interest groups, political parties, public demonstrations, direct communication—by which information is exchanged between the elite and the general public, and also to the institutional context within which those exchanges take place.

Public opinion polling plays a less prominent role here. Instead of perusing polls and then looking for subsequent correlations with policy, we investigate the policy process and then look for (or conduct) polls as one measure of public response. In point of fact this process broadens our view of democratic politics. Instead of examining the mere correspondence of opinions and policies, we also examine the opportunities for regular and fundamentally unrestricted political participation, for expression of a variety of political views, and for minority dissent. We expect that public opinion will normally turn out to be reactive or dependent, but nothing in these methods precludes our recognizing elite responses to popular initiatives. And even if, as expected, popular initiatives are not common, we can still seek evidence of democratic control by attempting to locate the limits of permissiveness, the opinion dikes, so to speak, within which policymakers are constrained to stay (Key 1961: chap. 21; Flanigan and Zingale 1987, chap. 5).

If the above-described research strategy is as straightforward and sound as we suggest, then why has so much work in the field of public opinion focused on polling representative samples of the general population? At least four explanations seem plausible.

First, studies that employ survey research to collect their primary data have a greater aura of science, a greater ostensive objectivity. For any given level of risk, survey research can guarantee that the values of the variables measured represent accurate estimates of the true values among the general population to within any specified range of error. Studies that begin with selected policy areas face the difficulty of establishing the "representativeness" of those policy areas. After all, correlational analyses have demonstrated that the correspondence between policy and opinion varies by subject area (Miller and Stokes 1963; Friesema and Hedlund 1981).

Second—and more troubling—may be a distaste for the potential results. Studies of policy opinion linkages that begin with policy areas rather than survey archives have a greater potential of uncovering findings that fail to comport with the popular image of liberal democracy to which most of us have grown accustomed. Scratch beneath the veneer of academic sophistication of most American political scientists, and you will find middle-class Democrats and Republicans, who have accepted most of the political values to which they were socialized. As a discipline, American political science has not been particularly receptive to "unrepresentative" studies alleging that public policy is ordinarily determined by or made in the interests of powerful elites who control vast economic resources. Books like *The Power Elite* or *Who's Running America?*, despite wide readership, have never been accepted interpretations of American government (Mills 1956; Dye 1986; see also Margolis 1973). Indeed, to accept such allegations might be tantamount to admitting that the American political system is fundamentally undemocratic. Over and above its claims as a science, then, public opinion polling has become a symbol of faith in mass democracy in America. And as other countries have adopted American practices regarding polling, they have tended to adopt polls as symbolic of mass democracy as well.

Third, empirical survey studies are convenient for the discipline to do. Such studies are conceptually simple, while technically challenging, and they fit comfortably into graduate research programs. The relative simplicity of the research questions makes survey studies amenable to individual research efforts, particularly for advanced graduate students; more complex problems would require teams of researchers working together, which would be difficult to organize in the graduate schools of American universities in the 1980s. It is much easier to work with a single data base, however complex, than it is to study the interrelationships among two or three distinct types of data bases. For example, concatenating analyses of interviews with political actors, content analyses of news reports in the media, and statistical analyses of standard survey data, is far more difficult and costly than working with survey data alone.

Fourth, and perhaps the most threatening to democratic governance, the present research paradigm serves the interests of powerful elite groups in our society. The assumption that public opinion should be treated as an independent variable places the responsibility for unpopular policies upon the mass public, not upon elites. Potential criticism of policy decisions is thereby diverted from the political elites to the general public.

There are other difficulties that stem from relying upon survey research as the primary source for data. Despite the claim of greater objectivity, the questions asked in "representative" sample surveys may not be the unbiased selection of policy alternatives that pollsters assert. Moreover, the model of mass democracy implicit in many public opinion studies based on these surveys is not the only possible model of mass democracy.

To begin with, the criticism of the unrepresentativeness of studies of selected policy areas can be turned on its head. A perusal of archives of public-opinion polls taken in the United States turns up many questions about issues and policies of the day, but few about "nonissues," that is plausible alternative policies that never seem to reach the public agenda (Bachrach and Baratz 1962 and 1963). *Is the economy in trouble?* There are many questions about tariffs, import quotas, government loans, and labor costs; there are few about socialist alternatives, for example. *Is there a governmental scandal?* We find plenty of questions about the honesty and integrity of politicians, but hardly any about the extent to which the political system encourages selfishness and greed. *Is poverty a problem at home or abroad?* Polls are replete with questions about industrialization, productivity, job training, birth control, and abortion; not much can be found about the redistribution of wealth or the validity of the capitalistic system (see, for example, Gallup 1972; 1978–85). Similar lacunae are evident for many other questions about the foundations of the existing order: few questions are posed concerning popular support (or lack of it) for the legitimacy of government authority. If pollsters look for empirical regularities within a presumably democratic system, might they not end up limiting their survey inquiries to questions about minor adjustments to established policies? Might they fail to recognize—let alone analyze— alternatives that governmental decision makers and established interest groups choose to ignore, even alternatives that may well have popular support? (See, for example, Richards et al. 1988.)

The idea that popular opinion is normally reactive or dependent is not necessarily antidemocratic. On the contrary, from ancient Greece to the present we find a strain of democratic theory that accepts the idea of elites deciding policy, and the public or its representatives judging afterward. Pericles, for instance, boasted that Athenian citizens were sound judges of policies, though not originators (Cohen 1972: 540); Burke argued for the independence of elected representatives from the day-to-day opinions of their constituents (Cohen 1972: 436–37); Mill suggested that a properly constituted legislature would confine its policy concerns largely to responding to initiatives proposed by the executive (1962: chap. 5); Lippmann blamed many of the policy failures of modern democratic governments on politicians who attempted to follow rather than lead public opinion (1962: chap. 2); Schumpeter redefined democracy as an institutional arrangement allowing for periodic free elections of policymakers (1942: 269–73); and Schattschneider argued that competitive political parties provided the means for realizing such a democracy (1942: chaps. 1 and 9).[1]

We stress that our conception of the dependent role of public opinion is neither radical nor new. Much of the work on public opinion prior to the ascendancy of public opinion polling in the 1960s concerned not only the proper linkage of popular opinion and policy in a democracy, but also the extent to which such opinion could be manipulated. With regard to the former concern, analysts commonly pointed out the now-familiar moral and logistical problems of conforming public policy to popular opinion in mass democracies, even if one granted the dubious assumptions that most citizens have the wit and interest to develop rational opinions about those policies (Lippmann 1962 [orig. 1922]: pts. 1 and 6; Dahl 1956: chap. 2). With regard to the question of manipulating opinion, analysts were much impressed with the abilities of governments and private interests to employ newfound technologies to influence public opinion. The rise of Bolshevism and Fascism in the aftermath of World War I made "propaganda" a major focus of concern:

> Propaganda, in the sense of conscious attempts to manage the minds of others, either by means of symbols, conditions, or events, has always played an important role in the exercise of sovereign power. Moreover, the practice of propaganda by official agencies of government is not and never has been peculiar to dictatorial forms of government. (Childs 1972: 3)[2]

In retrospect, the idea that public opinion as expressed by the masses ought to be a major determinant of specific public policies seems rather naive. Only a handful of theorists have taken this stance, and most have restricted the application of their theories to smaller polities, such as communes or city-states (see Rousseau 1950 [orig. 1762]; Kropotkin 1909

---

[1]See also in the Bibliography: Committee on Political Parties, American Political Science Association (E. E. Schattschneider, Chairman), 1950.

[2]First published in 1936. See also Childs 1935; Chakotrin 1940; Katz et al. 1954.

[orig. 1899]; Dahl 1970; Schumacher 1975). Before the rise of representative opinion polls, the more accepted stance of American political theorists was that governmental decision makers, within broad constitutional limits, should lead rather than follow public opinion (Madison, Hamilton, and Jay, esp. no. 10; Hofstadter 1973). De-emphasizing the importance of popular preference polls for determining the origins of public policy, therefore, falls squarely within the democratic tradition. We return to this argument in the concluding chapter.

IMPLEMENTING THE RESEARCH STRATEGY

A research strategy is easier to recommend than to implement. Having convinced ourselves of the general advantages of treating public opinion as a dependent variable, we face the more difficult task of applying this perspective to our research. Three types of studies seem feasible: (1) short-term studies of particular elections; (2) short- to medium-term studies of the development of selected public policies; and (3) medium- to long-term studies of the process of political socialization. For all three types of studies, we want to take seriously various claims and hypotheses concerning the abilities of political elites to manage public opinion.

Looking first at elections, we find that a major change since the 1960s has been the improved ability of campaign organizations to direct appeals to target groups via appropriate mass media. The computerization of registration lists, census returns, and data on radio and television audiences and on newspaper and magazine readership has created enormous new data bases. This, combined with the growth and specialization of computerized mail and the use of sophisticated survey research by telephone, has made it feasible to market candidates in ways that were impossible 25 years ago. Electors can be sorted by partisan predispositions, by demographics, by habitual use of particular media, by attitudes toward certain candidates or electoral issues, or by degree of political interest, and the appropriate messages can be directed toward those individuals or groups predisposed to receive them favorably. Similar methods can be used to discover characteristics and policy themes that have the broadest appeal among relevant constituencies, and these characteristics can be emphasized in general advertising and in public appearances that are likely to be covered by daily newspapers, television, and radio. Indeed, as the Bush/Dukakis election campaign of 1988 illustrated, the thematic content of public appearances and paid advertising can be coordinated so that each one tends to complement the other.

While political scientists have taken note of these changes and of the increased costs of campaigning that have accompanied them, the discipline has devoted surprisingly little attention to measuring the actual impact of particular campaign strategies or tactics. Indeed, most recent work on the effectiveness of campaign strategy or tactics has been done by journalists, marketers, and campaign consultants, rather than by academic political scientists who specialize in studying electoral behavior (see Mauser 1983; Meadow 1985). And their findings have appeared more frequently in journals like *Campaigns & Elections, Journal of the Marketing Research Society,* or *Journal of Advertising Research* that emphasize applications than in the theoretical journals of political science. Moreover, theoretical work outside of political science, in other fields of academic inquiry, such as psychology, marketing, and operations research, have made some progress in the past decade in understanding mass communications and persuasion, particularly advertising, selling (or purchasing), and campaigning. Political scientists desiring to understand the general nature of campaigning (electoral or commercial) may well be rewarded by reading more theoretical journals in other social science disciplines, such as *Behavioral Science, Journal of Consumer Research, Journal of Marketing Research, Management Science, Psychological Bulletin,* or *Psychological Review.*

The essays in Section One of this book attempt to remedy this by examining various facets of political campaigning. Gary Mauser, Theodore Windt, and Xandra Kayden look at recent developments in the management of political campaigns, and they take serious and systematic note of various claims regarding the success of political managers and consultants. David Magleby examines the diverse influences on public opinion regarding referenda, and Randall Chapman and Kristian Palda look into the impact of campaign expenditures, which have increased at double the rate of inflation since 1964 (Alexander 1984: 11; Federal Election Commission 1985).[3]

Mauser, a marketing researcher and academic, explains how the techniques of modern marketing are employed to sell candidates and ideas. His chapter sets the stage for this part of the book. Mauser shows how marketing techniques aid political candidates to identify strategic opportunities in electoral contests and to position themselves to their best advantage. He presents the strengths and, importantly, the limitations of these techniques; he evaluates their impacts on electoral outcomes in specific political contests; and he comments on the implications for democratic electoral politics of the increasing use of marketing techniques by candidates. In Mauser's view, marketing acts primarily to clarify the existing conflicts among political elites.

Windt moves the discussion from overall strategies of marketing can-

---

[3]It may be instructive to note that Magleby is the only author in Section One who earns his living principally as an academic political scientist.

didates and ideas to the role that technicians, such as speech writers, play within the modern political campaign. "Speech writer" these days is something of a misnomer, for, in accordance with marketing practices, candidates' messages are delivered mostly via 30-second advertising spots. The speech writer often ends up preparing position papers—which the campaign may publish and distribute to appropriate target audiences, and which the candidates may draw from when making public statements. Windt argues that the influence speech writers exert over campaign strategy varies more with their personal relationships with the candidates and their staffs than with their skills as rhetoricians. Windt's essay, as does Mauser's, highlights the importance of securing sufficient funding to enable candidates to purchase the technical expertise required by modern political campaigning.

Xandra Kayden points out that, contrary to popular impressions, the adoption of new techniques for marketing candidates has not destroyed the political party organizations in the United States. Instead, American political parties have grown more centralized and technologically sophisticated. They are alive and well and far stronger than ever in Washington, D.C., and in many state capitals. The traditional patronage-based local or county party organizations, however, have declined in strength and importance, as the state and national parties have assumed larger roles in major state and federal election campaigns. Nevertheless, Kayden argues that the resurgence of central party organizations offsets the decline of local parties and promises to revive public involvement in American politics.

In David Magleby's essay the primary focus shifts from voting for candidates to voting for policies through initiatives and referenda. Magleby demonstrates how the lack of relevance of party loyalties to most of these policy questions leaves voters more open to pressures of campaigns. Lacking party guidelines, voters make up their minds later regarding ballot questions than they do regarding candidates, and they also are relatively less well informed about the alternatives. It follows that campaigns can influence not only which alternatives are favored, but, more important, the very definition of the questions that are decided in the minds of the electorate. In Magleby's view these circumstances generally provide an advantage to well-financed business elites faced with challenges from public interest groups. By mobilizing their superior resources, such elites can usually overwhelm the efforts of those who favor greater public control—by defining the referendum question to their own best interest.

In the last essay of the first section, Randall Chapman and Kristian Palda use a generalized econometric model to evaluate the relative influence of various campaign factors on turnout and partisan choice. They show that campaign expenditures have positive payoffs for increasing turnout and determining partisan choice. Moreover, the model allows them to compare the relative impact of campaign expenditures, socioeconomic variables, and partisan loyalties. The essay demonstrates the power and elegance of econometric models in highlighting the various advantages of incumbents and the importance of money for aiding challengers to overcome those advantages.

The essays in Section Two look at attempts by leaders to sway public opinion regarding selected issues of public policy. It goes without saying that elites are very much interested in gaining public acceptance of their favored alternatives. They not only maintain institutionalized contact with public officials for purposes of lobbying, but, increasingly, they are taking a more public role in nominating and electing those officials (Salisbury 1984; Ferguson 1983; Sabato 1984).

In attempting to go beyond electoral contests, to study public policy issues, our research strategy brings us up against some serious resource problems. The primary problem is the challenge of selecting an unbiased or representative set of public policies for study. Not only is it difficult to conceptualize the problem of sampling from a universe of policy issues, but, even if one could successfully draw a representative sample, where would one find the resources to actually conduct such an immense study?[4] Still other resource problems arise from the fact that in contrast to electoral campaigns and referenda, public opinion polls, election results, and other measurements of public response are not routinely available concerning most public policy issues. In fact, policymakers may seek to involve the general public as little as possible, for as Niemi indicated, established interests require only public acquiescence, not active support, for their policies (see Brewster 1984: 117–23). Finally, we must also consider devoting additional resources to investigating the extent to which elites act to prevent certain alternatives from reaching the public agenda, that is, the investigation of what we have called nonissues. This means facing squarely the methodological and ethical questions inherent in studying ongoing organizational decision processes.

While we do not pretend to have solved these problems, the essays in the second section certainly deal with important problems, which can hardly be dismissed as a biased sample chosen simply to illustrate elite control. Indeed, the findings here are far more complex.

Terence Qualter's essay on the role of the mass media sets the stage for the chapters in this section. Qualter argues that the media, not the events themselves, determine what makes news and which issues occupy

---

[4]Of course, the same type of argument can be levied against the selection of questions in "representative" sample surveys. But even if we agree that the question selection process is biased, that does not vitiate the criticism that any particular set of public policies we select is biased also.

the public agenda. Indeed, he argues that the mass media have an independent role in fixing the priorities given to public issues and in defining the terms of political discussion. While Qualter is impressed with the "agenda setting" power of the mass media, he is careful not to exaggerate the dangers. He points out that despite their tremendous power, the mass media are limited by the other independent sources of political information that compete for people's attention.

The next two chapters examine cases that demonstrate the mass media's powerful role in shaping the public agenda. Christopher Bosso shows how America's discovery of the Ethiopian famine, and its subsequent disappearance, were choreographed by the mass media. Bosso builds upon Qualter's notion of the media's penchant for drama to help account for the sudden discovery of the issue, and he draws upon Anthony Downs's concept of the "issue-attention cycle" to help explain the issue's equally quick demise. This essay demonstrates the conditions that determine when the mass media will go outside the normal channels that typically filter foreign news to promote "newsworthy" causes.

Michael Margolis and Robert Burtt chronicle how the Denominational Ministry Strategy's (DMS) protest activity has been geared constantly to garnering maximum coverage in the mass media. Margolis and Burtt demonstrate that the DMS succeeded in drawing public attention to its cause, but most of the publicity it received was unfavorable, and it failed to mobilize significant public support. This failure, however, cannot be attributed merely to the mass media. The authors use a theory of political protest developed by Lipsky and others to show how the DMS failed to act in a politically effective manner. This case demonstrates how the mass media set requirements that protest groups must master to enhance their chances of influencing public opinion.

Michael Johnston's study of the political potential of television evangelists demonstrates the difficulties of translating coverage in mass media into political action. Although the "televangelists" have millions of viewers and (they claim) millions of contributors, they have had great difficulty in mobilizing sufficient support to carry out their political goals in the public arena. When right-wing ministers try to move from religion to politics, they encounter many of the same difficulties that hinder other interest groups. Johnston points out that the difficulties televangelists find mobilizing a favorably disposed audience suggest there are severe limits to using the media's power to manipulate the public-at-large.

The president of the United States receives the most thorough and continuous mass media coverage of any elective political office in the world. Modern presidents have not been shy about using this circumstance to help set the public agenda and to mobilize public support. Jon Hurwitz attempts to estimate the willingness of citizens to support the president in several hypothetical—yet plausible—situations. His evidence suggests that presidents, no less than televangelists, face severe limitations in attempting to mobilize support, even among those who are favorably disposed to the president or his policies.

The essays in Section Three involve medium- to long-term influences over public opinion, that is, the process of political socialization. These issues tend to involve broad questions like the philosophy and content of public education, the standards of public morality, or the inculcation of political ideologies. While the line between these and shorter-term issues can be indeterminate at times, the latter tend to concern more narrow and specific public policy decisions.

Michael Parenti argues that the ostensibly neutral American news media actually propagate a conservative ideology. The railings of the far right notwithstanding, the mainstream news media present a picture of reality that supports powerful groups and established causes. Thus whites, males, management, and officialdom are favored over blacks, females, labor, and protestors; and established causes such as private enterprise, capitalism, national chauvinism, and militarism are supported over socialism, communism, internationalism, and disarmament. Parenti points out that there are limits to the media's domination of the popular consciousness: the internal contradictions of Western society force the media to criticize elements of the established order, and an alert citizenry can exert a sufficient skepticism to maintain its independence.

Benjamin Ginsberg takes up the question of the long-term implications of public opinion polling for the management of popular attitudes. He argues that polling transforms the expression of opinion from a powerful group behavior into a manageable individual phenomenon. In essence, polling domesticates opinion by shifting the responsibility for raising issues from the mass public to the elites who *formulate* the questions. Ginsberg argues that the actual effect of ostensibly democratic polls is not only to enhance the powers of those who formulate the questions, but to systematically undermine certain pressure groups, notably unions and dissenting elites like the NAACP.

Benjamin Page and Robert Shapiro show that even though public policy is typically congruent with public opinion, the latter is often misled or manipulated through false or biased information. The biases result from competition among privately owned mass media, government control of certain sources of information, and the disproportionate resources held by business and other established interests. Opinion manipulation has its limits, however. Page and Shapiro demonstrate that at least in the short run the public can be remarkably resistant to persuasion. The key task is to specify the circumstances under which policy responds to genuine public opinion, to what extent opinion is ignored, and to what extent it is misled or manipulated.

W. Lance Bennett points out that the common dichotomy between manipulation of and responsiveness to public opinion is overly simplistic. Using the Reagan administration's efforts on behalf of the Contra rebels in Nicaragua as a case study, Bennett demonstrates a third alternative that he calls the "marginalization" of public opinion. When the administration's attempts failed to win public support for aid to the rebels, they adopted a strategy that effectively ignored public opinion. By an adroit use of classical "carrot and stick" techniques, which included the virulent red-baiting of congressional opponents in anticipation of the 1986 elections, the administration managed to have its viewpoint dominate both the debate in the Congress and the coverage in the mass media for the critical period necessary to pass its bill providing $100 million in aid for the Contras. Bennett suggests that this case illustrates a set of general conditions under which decision makers can ignore popular majorities in formulating policy with impunity.

LOOKING AHEAD

Having argued that public opinion ought to be studied primarily as a dependent rather than independent variable, and having outlined the theoretical and empirical advantages of adopting such a focus, we invite readers to judge how well we and our contributors have carried through our research scheme. While the essays below concern a variety of subjects, they share the common trait of looking first at the political elites who attempt to initiate or suppress particular actions or policy changes. Public-opinion polling occupies a secondary role here. It becomes a way of gauging the impact of these actions; it no longer determines the range of questions the authors may choose to consider.

In each of these essays, readers should take note of how the authors describe the role of the mass media in communicating political ideas and the overall influence of political elites. Specifically, what are the powers of the mass media described in each essay? Their limitations? Do the authors view the political elites as a homogeneous force or as a collection of diverse groups? What are the constraints upon the powers of the elites? How do the processes described in each essay differ from those we might expect in nondemocratic regimes? What are the implications for democratic theory if public opinion plays a dependent rather than an independent role?

While no guarantee can be made that adopting this viewpoint will produce the explanatory theory that is lacking in the field of public opinion, we believe that the strategy these studies exemplify holds more promise for accurately identifying and explaining the linkages between public opinion and public policy than do studies based primarily upon correlating the results of opinion polls with the adoption of public policies. By focusing upon the initiatives of political elites, monitoring the exchanges of relevant information between elites and targeted subgroups, and assessing the consequences of those exchanges, these studies provide an empirical foundation for developing a theory of the role of public opinion in modern mass democracies.

In our concluding chapter we pull together our contributors' findings and evaluate their importance for determining the role of public opinion in mass democracies. We also assess how treating public opinion as a dependent variable serves to provide valuable theoretical and empirical insights. Finally, we present the outlines of a democratic theory of public opinion that builds upon these findings, and we suggest the directions of research needed to further develop and refine it.

SECTION ONE

Electoral Politics

CHAPTER 2

Marketing and Political Campaigning: Strategies and Limits

Gary A. Mauser

INTRODUCTORY NOTE

The conduct of major political campaigns has changed radically since World War II. Where contact between candidates and voters used to be mediated almost entirely by parties and interest groups, the advent of sophisticated communications technology has facilitated the direct exposure of voters to candidates' messages. The skills needed for using electronic and other specialized media to communicate a candidate's message effectively to selected target groups have many elements in common with those needed for marketing a consumer product to potential customers. This has led to the emergence of the profession of political manager, as political parties have come to recognize that skills in marketing and communications technologies are vital for election campaigns. Indeed, political managers, along with professional pollsters and communications experts are replacing the old-time party leaders or "bosses" as the chief planners or strategists for many of these campaigns.

In this chapter Gary Mauser explains how sophisticated marketing techniques are now being used to help political candidates garner popular support. He argues that marketing offers practical solutions to problems inherent in communicating with mass audiences. While there are many similarities between marketing candidates and commercial products, he points out that contrary to popular belief, candidates cannot be marketed as easily as toothpaste. To be effective, strategies for marketing political candidates must accommodate the values of the general electorate. Determining how voters perceive candidates and issues is a key requisite for developing a strategy for "positioning" a candidate favorably vis-à-vis his or her opponents. As marketing must cast arguments within familiar, simple images, public opinion can be seen as setting firm constraints that, while flexible, require elites to rationalize their actions in terms of commonly shared values.

Even though some critics have suggested that applying marketing strategies to political campaigns increases the opportunities for elites to manipulate mass opinion, Mauser is careful to point out the limitations of such strategies. He also notes that marketing technology is available to any candidate or political group who desires to use it. In contrast with other authors in this book, he argues that there is a wide diversity among contemporary elites (including quasi-elite groups such as labor unions and Common Cause). Therefore, the introduction of marketing technology does not tend to exploit the public for the benefit of "the elite," but rather tends to aid those elite groups who can best make use of marketing to "sell" their ideas and values to the public. Moreover, despite their sophistication, modern marketers, no less than old-fashioned bosses, sometimes make mistakes. The important considerations for the conduct of democratic politics concern the abilities that nonspecialists such as politicians develop to work with, and to control, communications specialists.

The Editors

There are three ways for a politician to ruin his career: chasing women, gambling, and trusting experts. The first is the most pleasant, the second the quickest, but trusting experts is the surest.

Georges Pompidou

An army may be likened to water: water leaves dry the high places and seeks the hollows; an army turns from strength and attacks emptiness. The flow of water is regulated by the shape of the ground; victory is gained by acting in accordance with the state of the enemy.

Sun Tzu

Marketing ideas and techniques have been filtering into electoral politics for many years. Despite nervous criticism from some observers, political candidates have increasingly turned to commercial marketing for practical methods of dealing with the day-to-day tasks that face them in running for office. This has been true at least since the 1930s, when F.D.R. and Huey Long pioneered the use of radio in their election campaigns. Television spot advertisements were first introduced to presidential politics by Eisenhower, while John Kennedy popularized the use of sophisticated polling techniques in his successful effort to gain the White House in 1960. Later in the 1960s, spatial models were first used to identify strategy for political candidates. The 1970s saw the introduction of automated dialing to political campaigning. For example, in 1970 the Republicans telephoned all registered voters in California to deliver a recorded message by Ronald Reagan, who was then running for his second term as governor. These trends have not been limited to the United States: Most major political parties in Europe and North America rely upon advertising and marketing firms in mounting national campaigns. In all likelihood, marketing will play an even greater role in political campaigning in the 1990s with the powerful and still growing importance of the mass media in politics.[1]

The rapid diffusion of sophisticated marketing research and communications techniques has been guaranteed since the early 1980s by the widespread availability of powerful microcomputers. The most advanced techniques, formerly limited only to well-heeled presidential candidates, are now available to political candidates at all levels of government. Many firms in both the United States and Canada now offer inexpensive software packages to assist candidates in a wide range of campaigning analysis and communications tasks. In Canada, for example, it is growing more common for members of federal and provincial parliaments to rely upon microcomputers to target individual segments in their constituencies with specially tailored appeals.

The past few decades have also seen impressive changes in marketing technology, which has become ever more powerful. In the early 1960s, spatial models were first used to identify strategic opportunities in commercial markets (Green and Carmone 1970; Stefflre 1968). A few years later, conjoint analysis was introduced as a method for designing new products to position where strategists desired (Green and Srinivasan 1978; Johnson 1974). In the 1970s and 1980s, researchers developed integrated packages that combined marketing research techniques and simulation models to guide the development of new products from the initial screening of potential concepts, through test marketing, to the national roll-out (Stefflre 1986; Urban and Hauser 1980). In the 1980s, these powerful techniques are frequently seen in political campaigns (Mauser 1983).   .

---

[1]An indication of the importance of marketing notions for political campaigning can be seen in the growth of trade journals, such as *Campaigns and Elections,* which focus on new developments in campaigning technology and eschew the traditional concerns of political science. For example, a perusal of such journals documents the explosive growth in the past few years of firms offering computer software designed to assist political campaigners. The recognition of political management as a profession has led universities such as Florida, Kent State, and George Washington to initiate new degree programs. In addition, the New York State Board of Regents chartered the Graduate School of Political Management in October 1986. The independent school, located in New York City (and housed in Baruch College), offers a master's degree in political management. It graduated its first class in 1988.

First I will compare political campaigning with commercial marketing. Here I argue that the driving force behind the growing use of marketing in politics is its utility for solving problems that political candidates and office holders face in addressing mass audiences. Like marketing managers, political candidates need a framework to assess their problems and opportunities and to determine campaign strategy, and marketing offers a managerial technology for influencing mass behavior. As such, marketing offers both a pragmatic framework for thinking about political campaigning and a professional approach to mass communications. However, the differences between the two domains are so great that marketing cannot be thought of as a source of proven formulas for success (alas!). At best, it is a source for potentially useful concepts and campaigning techniques that enterprising candidates can employ in attempting to garner support.

Next, I evaluate the extension of sophisticated marketing techniques, (originally used to identify opportunities for new products in large commercial markets) to the *strategic analysis* of political campaigns. This approach relies upon sophisticated multivariate methods and mathematical decision models (Shocker and Srinivasan 1979; Stefflre 1986; Urban and Hauser 1980). As has been done with new products, multivariate methods have been used to map the electorate's perceptions and preferences, and mathematical decision models identify and evaluate strategic opportunities for political candidates or parties (Mauser 1983). The multivariate methods employed in this approach are similar to those used by political scientists in analyzing elections (e.g., Weisberg and Rusk 1970). The potential and the limits of this approach as a campaigning tool are illustrated by its use in campaigns where I have been personally involved. Most of these examples are drawn from elections outside the United States.

In the conclusions I evaluate the implications of the increasing use of marketing technology in political campaigns. This technology offers politicians greater ability to strategically position themselves by improving their capacity to communicate with, and to respond to, voters. By increasing their knowledge of their strategic opportunities and threats, and by improving communications with constituents, marketing permits politicians to achieve their goals more effectively. Such improvements enhance efficiency and need not introduce a corrupting influence into politics, since, in my opinion, the use of marketing technology in political campaigning acts to clarify the situation rather than to corrupt it. The use of a tool is dictated by the user, not the tool; cynical politicians no doubt will use marketing to deceive constituents, while ethical politicians will not. Improved communications technology, in effect, acts to shrink the distances between political leaders and the governed, much as they are in a small town or village. Such an increase in intimacy is not necessarily corrupting. Certainly it is difficult for generalists to learn how to manage specialists, but this does not imply that specialists are evil. This problem is universal. Politicians, being generalists, must learn how to use wisely the new marketing specialists (e.g., pollsters, marketing advisers, or professional political managers) just as their constituents must learn how to deal with lawyers, doctors, and garage mechanics.

MARKETING AND CAMPAIGNING

To some, marketing conjures up images of cynical salesmen, interested only in profit, selling dangerous, or at least unnecessary, products to a gullible public. Feared or admired, such images suggest that marketing contains all-powerful tools for manipulating people. Such a view is both too flattering and too severe. Certainly, the aim of marketing is to influence and persuade, and unabashedly so, but so is any form of leadership. Marketing is hardly as powerful as is often imagined; there are strict limits upon what marketing can and cannot do. For example, marketing is helpless if individuals are not already favorably predisposed in some way to what is offered. In modern democratic societies, individuals possess a considerable degree of freedom to decide among the alternatives facing them; all marketing can do is attempt to persuade. The high failure rate in launching new products demonstrates that marketing is not all powerful (e.g., New Coke).

The extension of marketing to politics may be Machiavellian, but it is not evil. Marketing, like Machiavelli, is reviled, not because of any intrinsic wickedness, but because marketing dares to make public what political leaders would prefer to keep private. All politicians use marketing techniques and ideas, and have since antiquity, but very few wish to admit it publicly. The tactical value of hypocrisy should not blind us to the strategic utility of marketing concepts and techniques.

Unfortunately, marketers have a reputation of relying on superficial tricks or gimmicks. To a certain extent, this stems from occasional misguided attempts to introduce marketing into politics. Commercial marketing technology cannot be imported *holus-bolus* into the political realm. Techniques which are appropriate in marketing toothpaste may not be appropriate in other domains. While there are similarities between commercial marketing and democratic politics, there are profound differences. The successful introduction of new ideas or techniques into politics requires that innovators be sensitive to the fit between the marketing notions and the new situation. With adequate adaptation, I feel that marketing offers more than just gimmicks; it offers a professional approach to assessing and managing political campaigns.

Marketing may be seen as a managerial technology for influencing mass behavior in competitive situations (Capon and Mauser 1982).[2] As a managerial technology, marketing focuses on those variables that can be manipulated by managers to achieve their goals. It does not concern itself with such variables—however important or powerful—as sociodemographic factors or economic conditions, that are not amenable to control by the marketing manager (or the campaign manager). Marketing is not seen as including all methods of influencing mass behavior but is uniquely identified with voluntary methods, that is, change methods that allow individuals the freedom to choose among competing alternatives. The emphasis upon individual choice means that marketing takes individuals basically as they are, relying upon market forces to generate beneficial results. Marketing thus explicitly rules out coercion and violence as legitimate marketing tools, thereby distinguishing it from legal or administrative approaches to behavioral control.[3] This is not to say that coercion or violence has never been used in marketing commercial products, (e.g., as IBM is alleged to have done in the early years), but merely asserts that such methods do not characterize marketing, as they do administrative and legal methods of influencing behavior.

Because individuals are to be left fundamentally intact, marketing necessarily limits its purview to making only relatively marginal changes. It cannot, nor does it attempt to, change any individual's basic goals, values, needs, or interests; such efforts are better left to more powerful change technologies, such as psychotherapy, brainwashing, or religious conversion, which do aim to make basic psychological changes. Marketing's goals are much more modest: aiming, for example, to influence (a) people's knowledge or their perception of the alternatives facing them, (b) the relative importance accorded to social or political problems, or (c) the salience of the criteria used by people to evaluate alternatives (Assael

---

[2]This definition was inspired by that of Rados (1981) and differs from his in that it specifically limits marketing to competitive situations. As might be expected, there are various definitions of marketing, all of which have adherents. See Hunt (1976), Kotler and Levy (1969), and O'Shaughnessy and Ryan (1979) for discussions about the nature of marketing. One alternative to Rados' definition is that of the American Marketing Association: "Marketing is the performance of business activities that direct the flow of goods and services from producer to consumer or user" (American Marketing Association 1960). Another somewhat similar definition is that of McCarthy (1960) who defines marketing in terms of the managerial control functions, "the four P's"—price, place, promotion, and product. A more abstract and inclusive position is taken by Kotler (1972) who defines marketing as "the set of human activities directed at facilitating and consummating exchanges."

[3]This may appear as a somewhat bloodthirsty way to characterize legal and administrative forms of influence, although the state typically arrogates to itself the exclusive right to murder or imprison people within its legal boundaries. For a similar definition see Lasswell (1951).

1981). Such efforts are not trivial, for small shifts can alter election outcomes; but marketing certainly should not be seen as involving anything
more than relatively small changes. Consider a few election campaigns as
examples of the scope provided for changes in popular perceptions or
beliefs where marketing may be seen to have had an important role to
play.

First, in the 1984 Canadian federal election, two of the three national
parties found themselves with new and relatively unknown leaders at the
opening of the election. Within the past year Brian Mulroney had wrested
control of the Progressive-Conservative Party away from Joe Clark in a
long and bitter fight, and John Turner had narrowly defeated Jean Chré-
tien to capture the leadership of the Liberal Party. Indeed, Turner had
formally been inaugurated as prime minister only days before he decided
on July 9 to call the election for September 4, 1984. Neither man was well
known, so the election campaign would be crucial in creating the electorate's perceptions of the two new leaders and, to a degree unknown in
the United States, determining the shape of the next government. Both
men recognized this and their campaigns reflected their efforts to come
to grips with public ignorance about themselves and their policies in the
brief span of a Canadian electoral campaign: there is less than two months
from the time the writ is dropped until election day. For example, the
leading parties readily agreed to hold a series of televised debates early
in the campaign. The debates played a crucial role in shaping the electorate's perceptions of the two new leaders and their proposed policies,
because this was the first time many Canadians had a chance to compare
the new Tory and Liberal leaders (Fletcher 1985).

In such a situation, political marketing can play a powerful role.
First, marketing concepts were primordial in laying out the campaign
strategy for the two major political parties. Their advisers relied upon
polls to identify strategic opportunities that they could exploit during the
campaign. Secondly, marketing techniques were central to the television
debates that were so important in shaping how the electorate saw the two
new leaders. Polls were used not only to identify issues of concern to
strategic segments of the electorate but also to fashion campaigning styles
for candidates. Given the importance of the electorate's attitudes towards
party leaders, it could even be argued that marketing was the most important factor in this political contest.

Contrast this situation with that of France in 1981, where François
Mitterrand and Valéry Giscard-d'Estaing also held televised debates during the presidential election. Here there was much less scope for influencing the electorate, since this contest was to a large extent a rerun of
the 1974 presidential election: the same political groups were represented
by the same candidates. The electorate's knowledge of the leaders and
their programs was already quite well established, so there was very little

opportunity for political campaigning to make any major change in voters' perceptions. Politics in the Fifth Republic seemed deadlocked between the political formations on the right and on the left, as it had been since de Gaulle's death. No new issues were raised in this election, no new faces emerged; the tableau appeared immutable. Nevertheless, the 1981 presidential election resulted in a novel outcome: the election of the first Socialist president since the founding of the Fifth Republic in 1958. Yet only minute changes in the electorate's beliefs or perceptions were noted by political observers, during this election campaign (*Le Monde,* 1981). Not much change was required, given the delicate balance that then existed between the political blocs supporting the two presidential candidates; hence the potential scope for marketing was much more limited in this case than it was in the 1984 Canadian elections. Nevertheless, marketing still played a crucial role in deciding the outcome, because the election hinged on small shifts in voting behavior.

Marketing is characterized by two distinct methods for changing behavior: (*a*) persuasive communications, and (*b*) adaptation of the offering to fit existing patterns of behavior (Rados 1981). Translated into marketing jargon, we have, respectively, the "sales concept" (persuasion) and the "marketing concept" (adaptation). Adaptation plays a powerful role in changing people's behavior in both marketing and politics. An example of the use of adaptation by a political party to gain political power may be found in recent Canadian politics. While in opposition, the Progressive-Conservatives found it convenient to adopt conflicting positions on many issues in order to appeal to voters in both English and French Canada. One such issue was bilingualism. In the West, where resentment of "the East" runs high, the P-Cs strongly opposed the then-Liberal government's bilingualism policy, whereas in Quebec they ran francophone candidates, who if elected would, by their very election, reinforce the bilingual character of Canada.

Marketing concepts and techniques will be useful in political campaigning to the extent that there exists a structural similarity between commercial marketing and electoral competition. If we adopt a managerial perspective, we find that the problem facing the political campaigner is strikingly similar to that facing the typical marketing manager. First, in both domains there is a set of organizations (companies or political parties) competing with one another for the support of the members of a target audience (consumers or citizens) by fielding various alternatives (products or candidates). Each organization (company or political party), in order to command a significant share of the market (vote), must develop a *comparative advantage* over its competitors.

In both marketing and politics, there is a wide variety of competitive situations that elicit different levels of interest or involvement on the part of consumers or citizens in selecting among the alternatives they confront. Some elections (e.g., presidential elections in the United States), like some product classes (e.g., vacations or automobiles), elicit a high degree of involvement; other elections typically do not (e.g., city councils, county boards, or even state legislatures). The psychological processes that determine voting behavior in a presidential election may resemble more those of a consumer deciding where to spend precious annual vacation time than the decision process of the typical citizen selecting among alternative city councilmen (Ray et al. 1973). These similarities suggest that students of either politics or marketing might profit by studying work in their sister discipline.

Second, consumers and citizens have virtually identical roles to play in each of their domains: that of individual decision maker. Both are called upon to select among the alternatives presented to them on the basis of available information and in the light of their personal needs and interests. In each case, choice implies some degree of commitment to the alternative selected. Moreover, the same basic psychological and sociological processes (e.g., perception, decision making, diffusion of information, and socialization) occur in both domains. The similarity between consumers and citizens is especially striking in large political systems. Researchers use nearly identical methods of studying and modeling voter behavior as they do consumer behavior.

Third, the channels of communication that are available to candidates in most Western democracies are basically identical to those used in modern marketing. They range from personal selling (e.g., door-to-door selling, doorstep canvassing, direct mail, and telephone soliciting), to mass communications (e.g., television, radio, newspapers, and magazines). Moreover, these channels of communication offer both paid (e.g., advertisements, billboards, direct mail) and unpaid vehicles (e.g., news programs, electronic and print editorials, word-of-mouth) for reaching their targeted audiences.

Large modern democracies require sophisticated methods of marketing and communications in order to function. In small communities, such as the archetypal New England village, political leaders could identify citizens' concerns, and attempt to elicit support from them, simply by meeting them face to face. Not so in nation states that span continents and whose leaders claim to represent the wishes of over 250 million citizens. It is impossible, even for most legislative candidates, in modern democracies to attempt to campaign for or to hold political office without the use of modern marketing technology. Without modern methods of communication, politicians would be required to rely upon intermediaries, such as pressure group leaders and lobbyists, for information and communication with their constituents. Modern marketing methods encourage direct democracy by facilitating direct communications between citizens and their leaders.

Particularly intriguing in the context of this chapter is the extension of new-product development technology to political campaigns. The increasing use of marketing in political campaigns implies a dramatic change in the technology of communications in politics. Introducing technological change into any domain almost always frightens people. For those directly involved, it may mean a loss of power or status if younger experts, skilled in polling or in dealing with the mass media, supplant older advisers not skilled in the new technology. Obviously, the self-interest of such traditional elites dictates that they oppose the introduction of any new technology that threatens their privileged position. Others, like the Luddites in 19th-century England, may be frightened by the general uncertainties introduced by any technological change.

The two domains of commercial marketing and politics are not so identical that concepts or techniques can be blindly transferred from one domain to the other.[4] That would be folly. Every marketing concept or technique adopted for use in politics must prove its usefulness anew. Many marketing techniques are situation specific. Not only is it impossible to sell political candidates like toothpaste, but one cannot sell used cars or banking services like toothpaste.

There are some very important differences between commercial marketing and political campaigning. First, commercial markets typically support many business firms, while most political systems tolerate a very limited number of political parties. For example, the United States has only two national parties; the United Kingdom and Canada have three national parties, and France, with a somewhat different political tradition, still has only four major political factions. More important, the number of candidates elected in any given political contest is much fewer than the number of viable products in a typical commercial market. For example, in countries using a "first-past-the-post" rule, only *one* candidate can win in any given election (e.g., a U.S. congressional race or a British-style parliamentary contest). Political campaigns may therefore be more pitiless than commercial markets, since the alternatives are so stark.

Second, campaigners have much less control over their attempts to reach their target audiences than do commercial marketers, since the

---

[4]Much marketing technology tends to be extremely situation specific. This caveat holds when borrowing marketing concepts or techniques between commercial domains as well as between domains that are more apparently different, such as marketing and political campaigning. For example, it is not very practical to attempt to market banking services using the same aggressive tactics that are effective for selling used cars or cold cereal. Nor are the marketing research methods, such as survey sampling, that are indispensable in studying consumer markets, of much practical use in small industrial markets, where there may not be more than 50 potential customers.

news media play a much more important role in filtering communications to the general public in politics than they typically do in most commercial markets. This is primarily due to the greater importance of "free" media exposure (e.g., news and editorial coverage) over "paid" advertising in political campaigns, compared with commercial markets. This lack of control implies a greater uncertainty for all candidates and for the electorate during election campaigns about what each candidate represents. Concomitantly, the media enjoy a greater power to shape public perceptions in politics than they have in commercial markets. Because of the power of the media in political campaigns, extremely complex games have developed between candidates and the media for getting greater favorable coverage in the media (Joslyn 1984; Salmore and Salmore 1985).

Third, political campaigners typically operate under more severe budgetary constraints (both time and money) than do commercial marketers. Campaign organizations therefore tend to rely heavily upon volunteers, rather than paid employees, for many routine tasks, and to be much more ad hoc than business firms; they may even have to be created from scratch prior to each election. Tight fiscal constraints, among other factors, suggest that political organizations are, at the very least, less professional than are business organizations, with all that implies for recruitment, management style, and effective accomplishment of organizational goals. Political amateurs may be at once more naive, ruthless, and error-prone than are their more professional cousins in commercial marketing.[5] However, the increasing professionalization of the national party organizations, particularly presidential campaigns, may act to mitigate this difference (see Kayden, chap. 4 in this volume).

Given these differences, I would argue that the driving force behind the increasing use of marketing concepts and techniques in politics is that marketing offers *practical solutions* for the problems facing politicians in communicating with mass audiences. Marketing offers a professional approach to analyzing large audiences and to managing campaigns. Marketers routinely deal with problems of strategic analysis and campaign management, and they have developed considerable knowledge and expertise in analyzing and persuading large groups of people. With appropriate adaptation, many of these procedures may be extended to politics.

The introduction of new marketing research techniques offers considerable opportunities for political candidates. In developing strategy, it is crucial for prospective candidates to identify the strengths and weaknesses of their competition and to understand the wishes of the electorate.

---

[5]There are still other important differences between commercial marketing and electoral campaigns. The limits of this parallel are discussed more fully in Mauser (1983).

To the extent that the parallel holds between commercial marketing and electoral competition, marketing can be used to identify strategic opportunities. Particularly important in this regard are the sophisticated methods that are used for identifying strategic opportunities in commercial markets and for positioning new products to take advantage of these market opportunities. The next section of this chapter evaluates the extension of these modern marketing techniques to political campaigning.

Once candidates strategically analyze their political situation, they still must assemble the elements of the analysis in order to determine their campaign strategy. This is the most crucial step, for only a gifted and experienced campaigner with a sense of "how it all fits" can put all the elements together in an effective campaign. However, methods developed recently for marketing new products can help candidates empirically test alternative positioning strategies (Mauser 1983; Urban and Hauser 1980). For example, candidates, like commercial marketers, can use this technology to identify the most effective campaign position before going public. Despite the real advantage marketing techniques offer political candidates, I think marketing may be overrated by opponents and proponents alike. Marketing cannot offer formulas for success, for there are none. All marketing can offer is heuristics, that is, useful procedures that may help to solve problems but contain no guarantees. Marketers routinely deal with problems of strategic analysis and campaign management for commercial products, so that they can bring some of this expertise to bear when they are called upon to help out in political campaigns.

There are strict limitations to marketing's power. First, marketing is not always successful even in commercial markets (examples abound: the Edsel, New Coke, IBM's recent string of failures in the microcomputer market—the PC Jr, the PC Portable, the PC Convertible).[6] Some of these mistakes are due to failures in marketing analysis, others to failures of the organization to deliver a product that met customers' expectations (Hendon 1986). Second, there are no guarantees that techniques that worked elsewhere will be equally effective in a particular political campaign. The key to identifying a winning strategy—with or without marketing—lies in the intuition of the individual asking the questions and analyzing the answers. Marketing cannot offer proven formulas for persuasion; all it can offer are potentially powerful concepts and techniques that may help pol-

---

[6]The annals of commercial marketing are littered with spectacular failures. See Hartley (1976) or Ricks (1983) for a list of some of the more uproarious marketing flops during the past few decades.

iticians garner support. Despite its limits, marketing is increasingly used in politics because it offers practical solutions for the practical problems involved in communicating with mass audiences.

STRATEGIC POSITIONING

In this section, I evaluate the extension of sophisticated marketing research techniques, originally used to identify opportunities for new products in large commercial markets, to the strategic analysis of political campaigns. This approach relies upon multivariate methods and mathematical decision models (Shocker and Srinivasan 1979; Stefflre 1986; Urban and Hauser 1980). Multivariate methods are used to map the electorate's perceptions and preferences, and mathematical decision models to identify and evaluate strategic opportunities for political candidates or parties. I will briefly discuss the strengths and weaknesses of this approach as a marketing and campaigning tool, drawing illustrations from campaigns in which I have been personally involved.

In the past decade, marketing researchers have developed and tested powerful new tools for exploring commercial opportunities for new products. Particularly important for political campaigners are the recent developments in generating and assessing concepts for new commercial products. Analytical approaches have been developed for understanding the criteria used by consumers in evaluating alternative product concepts so that management can build products that will position where management has targeted. The introduction of consumer input at the earliest stages of managerial decision making permits management to take advantage of consumers' natural abilities to react to alternatives (rather than to create them). These analytical approaches typically represent products and brands abstractly in spatial models where the axes are related to consumer evaluation criteria. Recent developments in modeling how individuals translate evaluation criteria into purchasing decisions have made these models more amenable to use by marketing managers. These approaches can be used to generate plausible new concepts—either through subjective judgment or systematic search—that can then be subjected to independent empirical tests in subsequent rounds.

As adapted to political contests, this approach contains four basic steps in identifying strategic opportunities: (1) use multivariate techniques to map the electorate's perceptions and preferences; (2) generate hypotheses about the strategic alternatives to be evaluated; (3) empirically evaluate the strategic alternatives and test hypotheses about which attributes govern individual preferences; and (4) assess the alternatives and make strategic recommendations.

The first step is to map the electorate's perceptions and preferences in order to gain an overview of the competitive situation, which is invaluable in identifying strategic opportunities and threats. A wide range of multivariate methods (e.g., multidimensional scaling, factor analysis, and discriminant analysis) are used to map aggregate perceptions and preferences (Shocker and Srinivasan 1979). These spatial models are used routinely by marketing managers as maps of the competitive market in identifying strategic opportunities for new products (Urban and Hauser 1980). This analytical approach has been extended to electoral politics and used to identify strategic opportunities in American and French elections (Mauser 1972, 1980). These structural models resemble the spatial models of elections developed empirically in political science (e.g., Weisberg and Rusk 1970). The principal differences stem from their contrasting objectives: in marketing, the models are designed to generate and to test hypotheses in order to facilitate managerial decision making, rather than to develop explanatory theories of aggregate processes, as in political science.

In determining strategic positioning, marketing managers have found aggregate measures of perception and preference particularly useful (Shocker and Srinivasan 1979; Schmalensee 1986). Political scientists have made extensive use of these types of measures, although they have only infrequently played the central role in studies of changes during an electoral campaign (Converse 1966; Mauser 1983; Patterson and McClure 1976; Weisberg and Rusk 1970). Strategic decisions of many kinds are shaped by explicit or implicit assumptions about: (a) patterns of candidate or partisan competition, (b) the features of the candidates and parties that lead to patterns of competition, (c) the position a new candidate or party will occupy in the old competitive structure, and (d) the position an old familiar candidate or party will occupy if certain features are changed. Such an approach is particularly compatible with analyses of multicandidate contests, which are more common outside of the United States. Most general elections in the United States contain only two principal candidates, while primary elections involve larger numbers.

Next, hypotheses about strategies must be generated and evaluated. It is important to test hypotheses about a wide range of strategic alternatives. Not only does this give the candidate needed flexibility to be able to deal with unexpected events later in the campaign, but it also provides a method for including diverse factions within the campaign strategy committee. As any campaigner knows, strategy development begins with a hard-headed evaluation of both the opposition and of personal strengths and weaknesses. This is largely an intuitive process: all any strategist can do is to rely upon "how it feels" in formulating strategic concepts. However, too many naive candidates commit themselves prematurely. For best results, candidates should consider a wide variety of strategic options. A number of techniques can help campaigners generate potentially fruitful hypotheses: brainstorming, focus groups, as well as polling (see Windt, chap. 3 in this volume).

The third step is to empirically evaluate the strategic alternatives and to test the hypotheses about which factors in the campaign are most important in determining voters' preferences. A number of criteria can be used to screen the hypotheses (e.g., the "fit" between issues and the candidate, the attractiveness of particular positions—either to the electorate as a whole or to particular segments). I have found the degree to which the issues "fit" the candidate to be at least as important in garnering public support as the intrinsic attractiveness of an issue position. Candidates need to keep in mind that their goal is not simply to win the next election, but to build a political career. Finally, the alternatives that have survived preliminary screening must be assessed and strategic recommendations decided upon. (This process is described more fully in Mauser, 1983.)

Several factors severely limit the power of this particular approach to political campaigning. These constraints fall into four main categories: (a) the limits to the spatial metaphor as a model for aggregate phenomena, (b) the limits to the abilities to predict how the electorate will react to campaigning efforts, (c) the limits to the abilities of candidates and their campaign organization to act on the strategic recommendations, and (d) the communications difficulties inherent in the role of the adviser.

First, the limits of the spatial metaphor. As others have already observed, spatial models (like all models) are a frustrating compromise between simplicity and accuracy, as any model must be simultaneously simple enough to be tractable yet rich enough to be accurate (Ordeshook 1976; Stokes 1963). One such limitation is that the spatial model, by definition, must represent an average viewpoint. The value of such an average will be restricted if there is considerable variation within the electorate it is supposed to represent. This problem will be exacerbated if distinct subgroups exist within the electorate (e.g., Democrats versus Republicans, left versus right), each with a distinctive point of view. If so, such variation must be recognized. It may even be necessary to model each such subgroup separately.

Even more restrictive is the presumption that the spatial metaphor is something other than a statistical convenience for representing aggregate data. To what extent can it be said that the spatial model represents how individual voters process political information? Do voters have "multidimensional spaces" in their heads or do they use other, nonspatial, structures for representing their understanding of the political landscape, such as discrete categories or hierarchical tree structures? If so, simple spatial models may not reflect these realities.

Models of party competition need not be limited to spatial assumptions, but may be based upon discrete combinatorial structures similar to those developed in linguistics, psychology, and anthropology.[7] Indeed, models of party competition must take into account the nature of human perception and information processing, as do models of consumer behavior in marketing, in order to realistically reflect political phenomena (Stefflre 1979).

Second, there are limits to the strategists' abilities to predict how individuals will react to campaign efforts. Even if we had an accurate model of how the electorate conceptualizes politics, we would still need to understand electoral dynamics. Campaigns are very complex situations, involving competitive efforts to influence the electorate in a variety of ways. To predict the effectiveness of any campaigning effort, either in marketing or in politics, is more difficult than many care to admit. Much more empirical study needs to be undertaken before social scientists can say they have a firm understanding of these influence processes. Because of this uncertainty, marketing strategists urge that strategic options be empirically tested before adoption. For example, in new-product development, marketing researchers routinely test several variations of each product prototype or advertising themes before committing themselves. In this way, researchers lessen the chances of costly mistakes. And even this is no guarantee against spectacular failure.

Third, and perhaps surprisingly to some observers, are the limits to the flexibility of candidates and their organizations that restrict their ability to adapt to the electorate's expectations. Candidates (and their organizations) have individual personalities that are only so malleable. The hectic nature of the typical campaign forces candidates to let their personalities show to some extent, no matter how much they would like to keep their "warts" and peccadilloes secret. While paid political advertising allows considerable control over what candidates present about themselves to the public, in most democracies no single candidate has a monopoly over the media. The opposition has the opportunity to present a different—and perhaps more convincing—story to the electorate.

Fourth, there are limits inherent in the role of a campaign adviser. The marketing researcher is only one voice on the campaign strategy com-

---

[7]Cognitive anthropologists have traditionally used discrete combinatorial structures to "map" the relations found in kinship systems or other systems of cognitive categories based upon semantic networks (Tyler 1969; Berlin et al. 1974). Linguists also use discrete combinatorial models to describe phonemic structures in human languages (Jakobson et al. 1963; Fodor and Katz 1964) and grammatical structure (Chomsky 1957). Cognitive psychologists also have proposed similar systems to understand human perception and memory (Miller 1956; Minsky 1975; Tversky and Sattath 1979).

mittee, and as such, must compete for the attention of the candidate along with the other advisers. In my experience, all strategic recommendations are subject to stiff debate. Few marketing consultants enjoy the luxury of having full control of a political campaign; some do not even sit on the strategy committee and may have to report to an adviser who does. Organizational considerations such as these obviously limit the power of the marketing strategist to control campaign strategy. Much depends upon the initial reputation of the marketer and how he initially became involved with the campaign. (For a discussion of the limits to the role of a political adviser, see Windt, Chapter 3 in this volume.)

Even when the marketing specialist has the ear of the candidate, effective communication may be problematic. Political candidates, being generalists, often have difficulty in knowing how to work effectively with campaigning specialists (e.g., pollster, marketing researcher, or media consultant). On the other side of the fence, specialists, too, have difficulty in effectively dealing with clients, just as M.D.s, perhaps the most prestigious of specialists, often complain about their inability to get their patients to follow prescriptions. Which decisions properly fall into the purview of the specialist and which are legitimately the responsibility of the candidate? Should the specialist be given complete control or kept on a short leash? Occasionally, if the campaign is simply handed over to the specialist, this confusion works to the specialist's advantage.

This situation parallels the difficulties we all face in our personal lives in dealing with specialists (e.g., lawyers, M.D.s, garage mechanics). How much of the responsibility for decisions affecting our personal health should be borne by one's family doctor (for example, to smoke or to drink)? Such decisions are rendered even more complex due to the financial involvement that the specialist typically has with the decision—lawyers, for example, make more money if one decides to contest a suit than if one does not. Not all specialists are equally impartial or trustworthy. While legislation may be inevitable, the only true long-range solution is for candidates to learn how to manage the kinds of specialists that appear to be required to run modern political campaigns.

California

The first example I want to discuss involves the 1970 gubernatorial election in California. The late Jess Unruh, then speaker of the Legislative Assembly, was attempting to unseat Ronald Reagan, the incumbent governor. Early in July of that year, I was contacted by one of Unruh's principal advisers and asked to participate on the campaign strategy committee to help them identify the major thrust of the campaign (Mauser

1980). When I arrived, the campaign committee was split over the strategy to take in the coming campaign. One camp wanted to adopt the conservative issue positions that they thought were necessary to attract "the undecided voter." They argued that the preferences of those voters who already supported the candidate should be ignored, since such voters had no one else to support. Moreover, it didn't matter what issues the candidate had supported in the past, the only important goal was winning the election. The candidate should say what was necessary to win the election. Since Reagan and his conservative positions had a strong appeal to the political center, Unruh should mouth the same positions in order to compete for this crucial segment of the electorate.

Opposing them in the electoral strategy committee, another group, less concerned with electoral victory, countered that elections should be more than just popularity contests, arguing that the candidate should speak his mind regardless of the consequences. Since Unruh had a reputation as a populist and as a liberal, he should use the election campaign to speak out on those issues he thought were the most important. In this way, even though he might not win, he would build electoral support for his political position as well as fulfilling his commitment to the liberal activist groups that traditionally supported him and the Democratic Party. Both groups took for granted the traditional one-dimensional model of the American electorate that shows the bulk of the electorate, as moderates, occupying the middle of the political spectrum, relegating political activists, who typically have more extreme positions, out in the "tails of the distribution."

I pointed out that this dispute hinged upon an overly simplistic analysis. The political world wasn't one-dimensional. They had created a false dichotomy: the strategic alternatives were more complex than choosing between parroting the opposition in order to win the election and self-destructive purity. I thought it would be possible to find issues that appealed to both committed partisans and "undecided voters." I argued that a survey of the entire electorate should be mounted to evaluate empirically the alternative positions that Unruh was considering. If the electorate was multidimensional, the survey would identify appeals that could simultaneously attract both committed partisans and undecided moderates.

The candidate and his staff endorsed my proposal for a series of surveys to be conducted during August and early September of that year. Rather than deciding the campaign strategy arbitrarily, the committee agreed to put the alternatives to an empirical test. Both camps in the debate contributed "thematic statements" that stated their positions, which were then evaluated in a survey of the general electorate.

FIGURE 2–1   Political Landscape in California (1970)

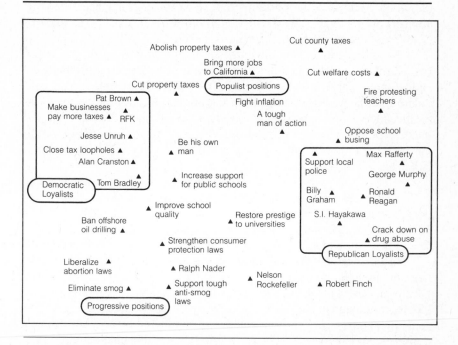

The surveys found that the political perceptions were indeed multi-dimensional (see figure 2–1).[8] At least two dimensions were required to describe perceptions of the electoral contest: social issues and economic issues. Several issues were found to appeal to Democratic partisans and the general electorate simultaneously. Indeed, two divergent strategies were possible: the candidate could take "populist" stances on economic issues (for example, opposing big business and reducing taxes for home-owners) or the candidate could take more "progressive" positions (such as supporting consumer and environmental protection, and increasing financial support for public education). Both of these strategies drew on traditional Democratic support as well as attracting significant interest from uncommitted voters. Neither of these strategies required the candidate to ape the positions of his opponent, nor to adopt a quixotic purity.

---

[8]These spatial models were built empirically using multidimensional scaling. For further details the reader is urged to see Mauser (1983) or Schiffman et al. (1981).

Marketing, by increasing the candidate's knowledge of the electorate, had identified effective issue positions that were closer to his heart than his advisers originally thought possible. Poor information can lead candidates to overlook powerful opportunities.

The spatial model identified areas of latent support for the candidate that could be occupied in order to outflank the opponent. Given the fiscal and temporal constraints during an election, it is not possible for any candidate to either move very far from his original location in the model or to introduce a new dimension into the model (Mauser 1983; 257–67). All that the Democratic candidate in this contest could do was to attempt to outflank his opponent by stressing positions that appealed to voters on either his left or right flanks.

After receiving my strategic recommendations, the Unruh campaign saw its way clear to shift its approach closer to the direction I had proposed. The response of the electorate was immediate: Unruh's support began increasing rapidly. Reagan's lead was cut from 20 percentage points to less than 10. Unfortunately, the change in direction came too late. Unruh did not win, but he was more successful than had been predicted. Reagan barely won re-election. I believe that the strategy I identified for Unruh in these surveys was very powerful; I believe he could have won this election had he adopted my recommendations earlier.

Interestingly enough, this study was conducted before the revolt of California taxpayers against heavy property taxes that culminated in 1978 with the passing of Proposition 13, the famous Jarvis-Gann initiative that forced a reduction in the state property tax. Economic populism, which wasn't capitalized successfully by the Democrats in 1970, was picked up by populist leaders on the political right a few years later.

France

The next example is from the 1974 French parliamentary elections. French politics is strongly polarized and has been since the Revolution of 1789. Despite numerous political parties, the National Assembly is clearly divided into two hostile blocs. During the 1970s, when I was in France, the principal division in French politics was between the *gauche,* those who supported the Common Program, a historic agreement among the major parties of the left, including the French Communist Party, and those who opposed them, the *majorité,* a coalition of groups that tended to support General de Gaulle and his policies since the founding of the Fifth Republic. Each bloc contained several factions that were continually jockeying for power, forming electoral or legislative coalitions, breaking up, and then regrouping into new coalitions depending upon perceived

advantage. Despite the intense polarization, the political center perenni-
ally attracts opportunists and idealists alike. While the opportunities of
many such coalitions proved to be illusory, one such grouping that appeared at the time to have a particularly strong chance to unite the political center was the reformist movement (*movement réformateur*) led by
Jean-Jacques Servan Schreiber. This organization was a bold coalition of
centrist groups that, due to the delicate balance between the *gauche* and
the *majorité,* promised to play a pivotal role in French politics.[9]

Prior to the 1973 parliamentary elections, I was asked to conduct a
comprehensive strategic survey for one of the major political groupings
(Mauser 1983: 167–88). The objective of this survey was to evaluate campaign strategies for candidates in selected constituencies across France.
The client wanted to identify: (1) which issues were most important in the
minds of voters, (2) which campaigning efforts were most effective, and
(3) which local candidates vying for the endorsement of the national party
had the most popular support. With the aid of my analysis, the client
could decide which candidates to support in the first round of voting, as
well as coordinate more effectively local efforts in each constituency with
the national campaign.

The task of identifying strategies was complicated by two interrelated
problems. First, I had to identify effective issue-positions for both rounds
of voting, but the competition would differ drastically in each round. In
the first round, my client's candidate had to outpoll the other candidates
in his bloc, in order to make it into the next and final round. Positions and
postures are required that are effective against rivals within as well as
between political blocs. This problem is not unlike the hurdles facing
American candidates who must first win a primary election before entering the November general election. In France, however, the problem is
more challenging since only one week separates the two rounds of voting.
During the Fifth Republic, the second round usually consists of a two-
way contest between the *gauche* and the *majorité.* But in this election,
the *réformateurs,* due to a sudden upsurge in support, threatened to be
crucial in an unprecedented number of three-way contests. A second
complicating factor lay in the necessity to coordinate the national campaign with the diverse local campaigns in the country. Positions that are
politically expedient in one region may not be consistent with those required in another region or with the party's national strategy. Such problems are typical in any parliamentary election campaign.

---

[9]For a good introduction to French politics during the early 1970s, the interested reader
should see Ehrmann's excellent depiction in the fourth edition of his book (1976).

Early in January 1973, we selected our target constituencies and began interviewing. Constituencies were chosen based on their strategic value to our client; typically this meant either constituencies that presented difficult problems for our client or where the national party wished to aid a particular candidate or faction. In each of the targeted districts, small but representative samples were drawn; respondents were interviewed concerning their political perceptions and preferences. Two types of questions were central in evaluating campaign strategy. First, political preferences were collected for over 20 strategic positions and postures. Spatial models were constructed, at the national level as well as for each constituency, to gain a comprehensive view of the political terrain (Mauser 1983: 167–211). The spatial models were complemented by asking respondents a series of open-ended questions about the benefits and risks associated with each of the major political blocs attaining political power. Comments were analyzed separately for each of the three blocs of voters.

The detailed analysis helped clarify the strategic options facing my client's party at both the national and local level in the parliamentary elections. However, most of these recommendations were quite specific and hence irrelevant to the purpose of the present paper. Here, I will content myself with evaluating the role of spatial models in assessing the impact of the *réformateurs* (see Figure 2-2).

FIGURE 2-2   Political Landscape in France (1974)

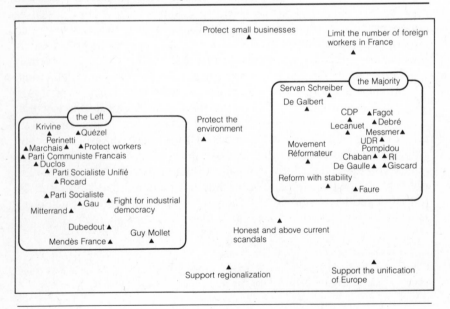

The *réformateurs,* at the time of this survey, did not fit neatly into the polarized mold of French politics. Many of their issue positions appealed to voters on the left, while their leaders remained closely associated with the *majorité.* As such, the *réformateurs* had the potential to draw from both factions. For example, voters who were reluctant supporters of the left were attracted to the *réformateurs* by their promises of reform, while respondents who had supported the majority were attracted by the promises of continuity. Nevertheless, their greatest opportunities came from the *majorité,* and not the left as many political observers had expected. The greatest drawback of a government by the *réformatuers,* as perceived by the electorate, was their strong association with the unstable and inept governments of the Fourth Republic.

The positioning of the *réformateurs* in the spatial model demonstrates the difficulty of attempting to change the nature of the political structure. Neither the tremendous volume of press attention that they had received during the years preceding this election, nor the provocative stands taken by Servan Schreiber, could modify the electorate's perceptions of the political landscape to any significant degree. The *réformateurs'* efforts to position themselves between the two major blocs did not succeed: all they could do was to distance themselves somewhat from the *majorité,* but they still remained firmly anchored to that coalition in the minds of most French voters. My study showed that, while they primarily threatened the *majorité,* this varied considerably across France, depending upon the particular constituency in question. Both the spatial model and simulated electoral contests showed that, overall, the *réformateurs* were most likely to draw votes from the *majorité.* These predictions were verified by the results of the 1973 parliamentary elections, when the *réformateurs* doubled their membership in the National Assembly, capturing 16 new seats, primarily at the expense of *majorité* candidates (Mauser 1983: 167–88).

Canada

In 1988, as this was being written, Canadians were expecting an election call, which could come at any time. The Progressive Conservatives had been in power since 1984 when Brian Mulroney defeated the Liberal Party, led by the lackluster John Turner. Since taking office, the Tories blundered from scandal to scandal, quickly squandering their initial popularity, so that during the summer of 1988 they languished behind the Liberals in the public opinion polls, with only 31 percent of the adult population across the nation admitting to support them. Despite being the Official Opposition, the Liberals have not been able to capitalize fully on the blunders by the Conservatives under Mulroney. The Liberals remain demoralized and dispirited almost four years after their drubbing at the hands of the Conservatives. Instead, for most of 1987, the New Democratic Party, a traditionally small, third party ran neck-and-neck with the Liberals in the polls (even outdrawing them for much of the year), while Ed Broadbent, the leader of the NDP, often acted more like the leader of the Official Opposition than did Turner.

Will the Liberals be able to recover from their problems, as they have so often before in Canadian history, to recapture the government in the next federal election, or will they, like centrist parties in other countries, be squeezed out between the Tories and the NDP? Two factors suggest that Canada may be at a watershed in its history. First, Quebec, traditionally a Liberal stronghold, can no longer be taken for granted. The collapse of the *Parti Québecois,* and the weakness of the Liberals under an anglophone such as Turner, have given both the Tories and the NDP the opportunity to build strong new political organizations in Quebec. Second, the Liberals, never strong in the West, must now face a revitalized NDP drawing primarily from potential Liberal support.

In late 1987, the questions uppermost in the minds of political strategists concerned how the Liberals might be able to regain power. To answer some of these questions I conducted a small survey in British Columbia. While the study itself is proprietary, the general results can, I would think, be discussed without disclosing any confidential information. Preliminary results suggested that the Liberals under John Turner were seen by many voters as having moved too far to the right to mount a credible opposition to the Tories. The Canadian public believed that Turner and Mulroney agree on most of the major issues that have faced Canadians recently: e.g., the recent constitutional amendments (the Meech Lake agreement) and the death penalty. The only issue that seemed to divide them was free trade, where Turner had damaged his credibility by reversing the Liberal's traditional stance, to oppose Mulroney. In contrast, Broadbent was seen by the general public as more honest, more trustworthy than either Turner or Mulroney. The question remained, however, was there any way for Turner to recover? Must the Liberals dump Turner in order to mount an effective opposition? As long as public attention focused on honesty or leadership style, the NDP had a natural lead over the other parties.

However, the NDP was seen as vulnerable on issues. As can be seen in Figure 2-3, many of the NDP's positions deviate widely from those held by the majority of Canadians. Preliminary results suggested that the issues for the Liberals to focus upon were the NDP's far-left stance, such as their position that Canada should pull out of NATO and NORAD. Another possible line of attack for the Liberals would have been to argue that the NDP is the puppet of organized labor so that it could never govern responsibly if it came to power. But could the Liberals under John

FIGURE 2–3   Political Landscape in Canada (1987)

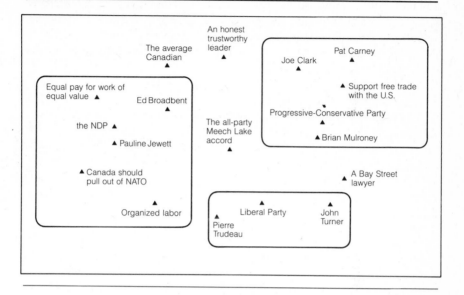

Turner capitalize on these weaknesses of the NDP? On the basis of this survey, I argued that Turner's best strategy was for him to forcefully oppose the free trade agreement with the United States that has been proposed by Mulroney. And that is exactly the tack that he took.

CONCLUSIONS

Political campaigners are increasingly using marketing concepts and techniques. The 1988 presidential election in the United States is a case in point. The goal of this chapter was to assess the powers and limits of marketing as a source of influence on the citizenry during election campaigns. I argued that despite the significant advantages that marketing offers political candidates, such advantages tend to be overrated by proponents and opponents alike. Marketing was defined as a managerial technology for influencing mass behavior in competitive situations; a technology that, because it leaves individuals fundamentally intact, must limit its objectives to making only relatively superficial changes in individual psychology. Unlike legal or administrative change methods, marketing eschews the use of force. Unlike more powerful change technologies, such as psychotherapy or religious conversion, marketing does not attempt basic changes in goals, values, or needs. These comments, I hope, do not leave the reader thinking I believe that marketing concepts and techniques cannot be used to bring about important political changes, for such is not the case. In close elections, superficial changes are all that may be needed to help one candidate triumph over another.

In this chapter I observed that marketing could be characterized by two distinct types of change methods: persuasive communications and adaptation of the offering to fit existing expectations. Neither of these two change methods, however, are foreign to democratic politics. Politicians have used variants of them for hundreds, if not thousands, of years. The difference, perhaps, lies in the impressive technologies that have been developed recently for implementing these classic change methods; and secondarily in the implication that marketing is primarily interested in short-term benefits rather than the long-term, so that marketing tends to focus upon satisfying short-term customer wishes rather than long-term individual or group needs.

Marketing's principal contribution to politics lies in its professional approach to analyzing and managing political campaigns. This essay briefly described sophisticated new methods that have recently been introduced into electoral politics from marketing that were originally designed to position new products in commercial markets. Such techniques rely upon mathematical models of aggregate perceptions and preferences and are reminiscent of the spatial models that are familiar to political scientists. These methods were briefly described in the preceding sections of this chapter.

This new technology has been shown to be able to aid candidates identify strategic opportunities and to position themselves in electoral campaigns to their best advantage. Despite the power of marketing research techniques, several factors place severe limits on this particular approach to political campaigning. These constraints fall into four main categories: (1) the limits to the spatial metaphor as a model for aggregate phenomena, (2) the limits to any researcher's abilities to predict how the electorate will react to campaigning efforts, (3) the limits to the abilities of candidates and their campaign organization to act on the strategic recommendations, and (4) the communications difficulties inherent in the role of the adviser. While these factors act to limit the power of marketing technology in influencing the public, it is still important to ask what the impact of this technology will be on democratic politics.

It is my contention that the use of marketing technology will act to clarify the nature of electoral politics rather than to reform or to corrupt the process. It is understandable that many people fear change. The introduction of marketing concepts and techniques to electoral politics means that the old guard will have to adapt to the sometimes sizable changes involved and perhaps yield power to younger people skilled in the new methodologies. However much these changes may frighten or displease those currently in positions of power, such changes do not necessarily corrupt democratic institutions. To a certain extent, marketing simply means more direct communications links between the electorate and politicians, which increase the abilities of politicians to respond to their constituents in large modern constituencies. How any technology or tool is to be used depends primarily upon the motives of the individuals who employ it.

Moreover, the genie is out of the bottle. Any temporary advantage enjoyed by one party will be swiftly erased in the following election when the opposition also adopts the marketing concepts or techniques found to have been useful. To a large extent, marketing is simply a logical extension of the mass communications technologies required for effective functioning in large-scale modern democracies. The candidate who wishes to mount a modern political campaign involving mass communications, finds that to use such technology effectively virtually requires a professional approach.

Effective communication in any situation requires immediate and pertinent feedback. This is true in education or politics, as well as in normal conversation between any two persons. A speaker needs a detailed understanding of what his or her listeners know, and what they do not know, in order to decide how to present what he or she wants to say to them. Moreover, once a dialogue has begun, continuous feedback from the listener(s) is required for the speaker to effectively communicate. In normal human conversation, this is done so naturally we hardly recognize it. Similarly, in small towns or villages, where the size of the electorate is much smaller than in large modern democracies, political campaigners can get the necessary feedback by simply listening to the people they meet face to face. However, this is impossible when the electorate includes tens of thousands of persons. Modern communications technology is required for such large electorates. Political surveys, both marketing research and traditional political polls, provide this necessary feedback for political campaigners.

Despite the importance of feedback in human communication, it is possible for a speaker to be overconcerned with the audience's reaction. Too great a preoccupation can inhibit a speaker; or, even worse, can lead to demagoguery or sycophancy. This is as true for political candidates as it is for all of us in everyday conversation. But such a possibility does not negate the value of feedback, nor by the same token, does it negate the value of marketing research for political candidates.

Marketing research technology, by providing feedback about the electorate, acts primarily to clarify the situation rather than to corrupt or to reform it. This technology simply aids political campaigners to achieve their goals, and does not restrict or shape their goals in any way. Its use reflects, and perhaps intensifies, the a priori motives of the political actors. All candidates must decide for themselves what they wish to do with the feedback they receive. Marketing research, like political polling, has the potential of helping candidates cynically find appealing promises that dupe an unsuspecting electorate. On the other hand, marketing research can also encourage candidates to provide greater leadership, to take bolder stands, because it can provide empirical support for a wider range of strategic opportunities. The lack of good information about the electorate's reactions can cause candidates to overemphasize lobbyists' concerns, or their own fears, and to unnecessarily restrict themselves to vague general campaign themes for fear of displeasing a critical segment of the electorate. Better strategic information can enable political candidates to identify opportunities that are more in accord with their personal preferences, and thus avoid being forced to choose among less desirable alternatives.

To summarize, this technology offers politicians much greater ability to position themselves strategically by improving their abilities to communicate with, and to respond to feedback from, the electorate. By improving the knowledge of politicians about their strategic opportunities and threats, and by improving communications with constituents, marketing permits politicians to achieve their goals more effectively. Such changes represent improvements in efficiency and need not introduce a corrupting influence into politics. The introduction of marketing technology into political campaigning acts primarily to clarify the situation rather than to corrupt or to reform it. Just as the use of a tool is primarily dictated by the user, not the tool, so then cynical politicians will use marketing to deceive constituents, while ethical politicians will not. Improved communications technology acts to shrink the distances between leaders and citizens in large constituencies to approximate the proximity found in a small town or village. Such an increase in intimacy is not necessarily corrupting. However, the price of this increased intimacy is that politicians must learn how to work with communications specialists. Certainly it is difficult for generalists to learn how to manage specialists (e.g., pollsters, marketing advisers), but this does not imply that specialists are evil. Politicians, being generalists, must learn how to use marketing specialists wisely, just as their constituents must learn how to deal with lawyers, doctors, and auto mechanics.

CHAPTER 3

Speech Writing in Campaigns for Governor

Theodore Otto Windt, Jr.

INTRODUCTORY NOTE

When we think of famous political speeches, formal statements such as George Washington's Farewell Address, Abraham Lincoln's Gettysburg Address, or William Jennings Bryan's "Cross of Gold" speech are apt to come to mind. In modern times, however, the importance of formal speeches, both as electioneering and policymaking statements, has diminished as electronic media, especially television, have assumed greater importance for communicating a politician's message directly to the people. Television news, in particular, is not normally suited to formal speech making. Stories tend to be no more than a minute or two in length, and they usually focus on circumstances that involve action, where dynamic visuals, rather than "talking heads" can be presented.

In response to these new circumstances, the role of the "speech writer" has changed—though not necessarily diminished. Instead of preparing formal presentations, the speech writer has become part of a team of media consultants. Formal speeches are still written "for the record," when a candidate or officeholder wants to set forth details of a policy or program. But most of the time politicians are concerned with getting coverage of selected ideas that can be effectively summarized in a 90-second news story. Thus, the speech writer's task often becomes the presentation of ideas or programs as a set of minispeeches, which then can be excerpted as "sound bites" for the evening news.

In this chapter, Theodore Windt contrasts the role of the modern speech writer in political campaigns with the "myths" that surround it. He points out that while speech writers can be valuable members of a campaign team, they are nonetheless dispensable. Their value depends upon whether the circumstances or strategy of the campaign calls for statements of policy "for the record," and whether such statements have a high enough priority to justify expenditures that might otherwise be spent on alternative forms of communication—such as direct mail or advertising. To illustrate his points Windt presents a case study of the successful campaign of Richard Thornburgh for governor of Pennsylvania in 1979, in which Windt served as a speech writer.

The role of the speech writer is part of the new communications technology that modern candidates must learn to master if they wish to get elected. Modern candidates must also learn how to deal successfully with mass media—television, radio, newspapers, and magazines. Candidates need both resources and knowledge: money, an understanding of the media, and management skills for working with a campaign organization. With money, candidates can buy the necessary talent, such as speech writers, who can help them portray the image that is most useful strategically. In a properly managed campaign, speech writers can help candidates bridge the gap between the worlds of the professional politician and the ordinary voter by helping candidates find the most effective language for formulating their appeals.

Windt and Mauser's characterizations of modern electoral campaigns, in this and the previous chapter, raise some important collateral questions regarding the conduct of democratic politics. To what extent do the complexities and costs of modern campaigning shift the locus of influence away from the electorate to established elites? What are the implications of modern campaign technologies for the organization of political parties? Would these changes work in favor of centralization or decentralization? What type of person would tend to gain and to hold power within a political party? Do such conditions influence the type of candidate (e.g., lawyer rather than physicist)? The type of social class from which they are drawn? The political interests that they tend to defend?

The Editors

In the spring of 1796 as President Washington prepared for his final leave of office, he began to prepare his farewell to the American people. He dusted off a draft of a farewell address that James Madison had written four years earlier and that Washington had planned to use when he retired after one term in office. He rewrote that draft, changing it considerably, and brought it up-to-date by adding new ideas and topics. Once he had a completed draft of his farewell address, he enlisted Alexander Hamilton's help in revising it. Hamilton, as was his nature, even went so far as to prepare a main draft of his own for use by Washington, but the president found it unsatisfactory. But between the two of them—Washington and Hamilton—a final version was completed. This collaborative effort produced Washington's Farewell Address, one of the most revered state documents in American history (Flexner 1972: 292–303; Paltsits 1971).

Hamilton's collaboration with Washington is just one famous example of a president using someone to assist in the preparation of formal speeches. Andrew Jackson used Amos Kendall; Andrew Johnson relied on George Bancroft; and both Warren Harding and Calvin Coolidge enlisted the services of Judson Welliver. In each of these cases as well as a variety of others that could be cited, presidents employed others for speech-writing assistance. But it was Franklin Roosevelt who began the institution of presidential speech writers by making extensive use of a speech-writing–adviser team that he called the Brain Trust. Since his time, every president has used some kind of speech-writing team, and such an institutionalization is now taken for granted (Spragens 1984: 78–84; Hall 1965: 168–76; Safire 1975; Price 1977; Denton and Woodward 1985: 234–73).

Despite the widespread use of speech writers by presidents, few others are willing to admit that they rely on someone to assist in the preparation of speeches. William Safire says that the reason why only the president, among political figures, can admit to using a speech writer is because he is the only political figure whom the public recognizes as being too busy to write all his own speeches (Safire 1978: 257). Perhaps this reticence is also due to the negative attitudes among the public about politicians using professional communication consultants, be they television consultants or speech writers. Since there is a dearth of information about speech writers except about those who have written for presidents, much misinformation and a number of misconceptions have arisen about what speech writers actually do in politics.

In this essay, I want to address the issue of speech writing in election campaigns for governors. Almost all my information will be based on personal experience, either from my experience as a speech writer or from speech writers I have worked with in campaigns. In order to manage this subject, I will divide it into three sections: (1) myths about political speech writing and speech writers; (2) sources of ideas for speeches in a campaign; and (3) a case study in speech writing for a gubernatorial candidate. I believe it important to begin with the myths because there are so many about what speech writers actually do.

FOUR MYTHS ABOUT POLITICAL SPEECH WRITING

Myth Number One.   Speech writers are the alter egos of political candidates. This myth might appropriately be called the Theodore Sorensen myth. Sorensen had that kind of relationship with John F. Kennedy, and it spawned the belief that all speech writers have special relationships with the people for whom they work.

In the scenario of this myth, when a speech has to be delivered, the candidate and the writer kick off their shoes, sit down, and begin pounding it out together. The relationship then is a personal one of give-and-take between the candidate who has something important to say and the writer who works hard to make certain that the message is well said. This myth presumes that the writer through a long and close association with the candidate has learned to think as the candidate does and thus to write and speak as the candidate speaks. It also presumes an advisory role for the writer and makes the writer a near equal partner in an ongoing decision-making process. Certainly, Sorensen appeared to have been a confidant of Kennedy and had this unique relationship with him. But it was unique, and rarely do professional political speech writers have such a relationship.

Instead, when speech writers are hired for a campaign, they are usually professional employees, only sometimes personal friends. Normally a writer is a supporter of the candidate because it is difficult to write effectively for someone one does not support. The role that writers play in campaigns depends on their prestige and their particular skills. If the candidate knows the writer is politically sophisticated about campaigns and is trustworthy, the candidate may use the speech writer to "sound out" or even assist in developing communication strategies as well as to write speeches. If the candidate knows a writer is knowledgeable in particular policy areas, the candidate may solicit or even rely on the writer's judgment in formulating policy speeches in those areas. If a writer has sufficient prestige and the trust of the candidate, the writer may have a direct working relationship with the candidate rather than having to rely on staff members for information about speeches. However, even in the best of circumstances, writers seldom have much time with candidates due to the rush of campaigns. They find themselves dealing primarily with campaign staff members, fighting for a few minutes with the candidate and seldom getting it, and thus ending up relying on experts within the campaign for information and advice, or on their own research or experiences, as a guide to writing campaign speeches. Speech writers are professional writers, most often former journalists, and they are seldom policy advisers. What advice they may give usually concerns the presentation of the message, not the message itself.

Myth Number Two.   Speech writers hand finished manuscripts to candidates who then present the speech as prepared for them. This myth seems to underlie most of the controversy about speech writers (Borman 1961: 262–67; Nichols 1963: 35–48; Einhorn 1981: 41–47). It makes the speech writer a ventriloquist, and the candidate his dummy. It presumes that speech writers are extremely important figures in political campaigns who are given the power to prepare scripts for candidates who dutifully deliver the lines crafted by the writers. Perhaps, some speech writers do have this power and position in campaigns though I have never seen anyone given that kind of authority and power.

It is more realistic to think of speech writing as one of many interdependent processes within a campaign. That process includes participation from a variety of different staff and nonstaff people.

In a sophisticated campaign with a large staff and budget, that process goes something like this. The candidate decides he or she has something so important to say that it has to be said in a formal, written speech. The candidate then outlines the central thrust of the speech, other ideas that should be included, and what the candidate wants to achieve with the address. Sometimes the candidate conveys this information directly to the writer. Sometimes a trusted assistant conveys the information. The speech writer prepares a complete draft of a speech. Before its submission to the candidate, the draft is submitted to a variety of different gatekeepers for review: political review, press review, and legal review. As the draft is reviewed, it is also revised, sometimes by the gatekeepers, sometimes by the candidate, but usually by the speech writer. Like all other kinds of writing, speech writing is essentially rewriting. Eventually, the candidate and perhaps the staff agree on a final draft of the speech for presentation. In sum, the speech writer does not hand a finished copy to the candidate. Instead, writing major speeches for a candidate is a process that includes as many members of the campaign as the candidate believes are necessary to develop effective speeches. The writer contributes by focusing ideas that were previously fuzzy or not completely thought out, by organizing ideas, and by lending precision to positions—all of which have to be approved by the candidate, and in many cases, by the staff as well.

Myth Number Three. Speech writers are part of a team of professional communication and media consultants who map out a campaign, manufacture an image, create issues and positions based on polls, and then direct the candidate to follow the game plan. By calling the speechwriting effort a process, one might naturally be led to believe this third myth. And it is one favored by many social scientists who want to find organizational structure and intentional strategy programmed into a campaign. Like all myths, this one has some truth to it. Campaigns do have professional consultants, pollsters, and media experts who try as best they can to map out a reasonable campaign based on the amount of money available, the political circumstances of the campaign and the candidate, and the other resources available.

However, the difference between what is planned and what actually happens is as great as the difference between any theory and its application. Circumstances change, and unforeseen events occur. Equally important, after the initial strategy outlines are developed, it may be exceedingly difficult for people in the communication section of the campaign to get together again. The media consultants are often creating those all-important television commercials from a distance, and the first time some members of the staff may see them is when they are completed. At the same time, speech writers may be working on speeches without any knowledge of the specific content of the commercials that are being created. Instead of collaboration, the actual process often results in communications people working in their own discrete areas of responsibility and then submitting their work to the senior political staff for approval. This does not mean that broad outlines of communication strategy are not worked out in advance of the campaign or that writers do not attempt to follow that strategy as faithfully as they can. But campaigns do not act like well-behaved social science models. They are far too messy and unpredictable. The original consultants may quit or be fired after the primary election, and a new team with new ideas may take over. It is also not unheard of for a consultant or writer to quit in the middle of a campaign thus requiring the candidate and managers to search quickly for replacements.

Above all, candidates are suspicious of communications consultants. Candidates recognize that such consultants are necessary to modern electronic campaigns, but they remain suspicious anyway because they think these professionals may try to change them or present an inaccurate portrait of them to the public. Thus, the candidate is sometimes a reluctant participant in some of the communication strategies and activities of the campaign. The key words for the candidate and the communication consultants are *accuracy* and *credibility*. Candidates demand that, and consultants attempt to meet those standards. Any communication effort in a campaign is a collaboration between the candidate and the communication consultants, be they media consultants or writers. The exact nature of the collaboration varies as the people in the campaign and the structure of the campaign varies.

Myth Number Four.   Speech writers are essential to any successful election campaign. In presidential campaigns, this is probably true. But in other campaigns, it is rare to find a professional speech writer on the staff. In local or county campaigns, candidates cannot afford to spend precious money on speech writers. In campaigns for governor or the U.S. Senate, candidates usually have enough experience speaking in public that they do not need someone to write speeches for them. They have basic stump speeches they themselves refine over the course of campaigns. That renders speech writers superfluous, except on those occasions when candidates want to present ideas precisely as part of the public record. On such occasions, a professional may be brought in for that speech, but usually someone or a group of people in the campaign work on the speech.

The most important development in campaign speech writing is that the role of formal speeches has changed radically. Prior to the emergence of television, speeches were the major means for candidates to get their messages to the public. Television and sophisticated campaign technology have changed that. The primary means for communicating with the public are through television commercials, free and generated television appearances, press conferences, direct mailings, and public meetings with organized interest groups or political groups. It is only in this last instance that formal written speeches may be needed. Usually, such appearances are limited during the course of the campaign.

In modern campaigning, the changing role of speech has changed the nature of formal speeches. In this age of media politics, rarely is a gubernatorial candidate's speech published or televised in full. Eloquence is not a prerequisite for election success. Instead, 30–45 second summaries of major ideas within the speech are needed because that is what television news will excerpt from the speech and that is what gives candidates the free television time on the evening news that all vie for.

Furthermore, many of these developments have come about because technology has changed audiences. Who wants to sit and listen to a formally written speech delivered by a candidate? One should remember that in the days before radio and television speech making was a form of entertainment as well as enlightenment. Today, people have better forms of entertainment available to them. Seldom are people willing to take several hours off from work or leisure time to go someplace to listen to a formal, half-hour or forty-five minute speech. Usually, an audience gathers or is assembled because it wants to hear specifically what a candidate plans to do on an issue important to that particular interest group. It is on these occasions—when speeches "for the record" are made—that a formal speech is required.

Knowing that formal speeches will have to be delivered to important constituency groups, candidates would be well advised to hire a professional for those occasions if not for the entire campaign. A professional writer becomes useful if the candidate has to give, say, an announcement of candidacy or a speech to an organized interest group or political group. However, it is not unusual for a campaign manager to decide that money that might be spent on a professional writer can be spent more effectively elsewhere. In that case, someone on the staff can usually be conscripted to prepare a draft for the occasion. If necessary, an outsider can be brought in to do a particular draft for a particular speech to a particular audience. Thus, speech writing has often been relegated to a lesser role within the overall structure of the communications of the campaign. Technology and sophisticated methods of communication now make formal speeches a unique addition to, rather than an integral part of, campaigns.

By presenting these four myths about speech writing in political campaigns, I hope to place the subject of this essay in a realistic context. And the most realistic element of that context is money: money the candidate has for the campaign, and money the candidate hopes to raise for the campaign. It is money that determines what kind of campaign one will run, and what kinds of people can be hired to make it run effectively. Generally speaking, a speech writer is not a high priority item in the budget for gubernatorial campaigns. However, in a campaign with sufficient financial resources, a speech writer may be a valuable addition and may provide a unique service. If that is the case, then the questions become what do speech writers do and how do they do it?

SOURCES OF IDEAS FOR SPEECHES

The campaign gets ideas for speeches, policy papers, even campaign strategy from anyone or any source it can enlist in its effort. This ranges from the candidate's basic beliefs, to polls, to expert research on issues, to local political figures who know the politics of a particular ward, district, or county. In other words, the campaign will draw upon whatever resources are available. For speech writers, ideas come from four basic sources: (1) candidates and their advisers; (2) research; (3) polls; and (4) discussion groups (either formal or informal groups).

Candidates and Their Advisers

Candidates always bear responsibility for the major issues that they are going to emphasize in campaigns. Insofar as possible, they attempt to set the agenda for the campaign. They usually do this in consultation with major advisers or the campaign team. If a series of speeches are scheduled for the campaign, this team decides on the issues for these speeches. Since candidates usually have public records of positions on major issues, some of these choices are easy to make. After all, candidates cannot radically change the history of those public records. Furthermore, if they are Republicans, they are generally going to hew the Republican line on some issues. The same attitude is true of Democrats. On new issues that may have emerged just prior to the campaign or developed during the course of the campaign, the campaign team certainly will consult political advisers and polls. When issues are of importance only to one county or section of the state, similar consultations occur before a decision is made by the candidate.

For single speeches, the audience usually dictates the subject of the speech. A speech before a group of educators will be concerned with education and the candidate's position on educational issues. An address to a major union will deal with issues of concern to the union and its members. The same relationship will be true of addresses to women's groups, senior citizens, civic groups, religious organizations, and so on. The important part of a campaign is not only adjusting positions to audiences and audiences to positions, but choosing which audiences to address. In every campaign, candidates are deluged with invitations to speak.[1]

If a decision has been made to give a series of major speeches on issues, then choosing which invitations to accept becomes important. This choice is usually determined by the issues that the audience is most interested in, and by the influence that the group has or is presumed to have within the electoral process. There are natural constituencies that one cannot ignore, and there are constituencies that one wants to get support from. At the same time, candidates may want to speak out at length on certain pre-chosen issues and may look for an appropriate symbolic audience to address on those issues. The important question for the campaign when deciding whether to give a major speech is: What do we have to gain by giving a formal speech on this issue to this particular audience? After all, television and other media offer a variety of means for publicizing positions on particular issues that are more efficient means of reaching the public than devoting a considerable amount of time and energy to preparing and delivering a major speech.

In sum, the sources of ideas for speeches are varied, but the candidates bear the primary responsibility for those ideas. It is their campaigns, and their futures, that are on the line. They may seek all the advice they can from polls and aides, but the candidates must make the final decisions.

---

[1]There may be some confusion on this point since I observed earlier that people are reluctant to come out for a formal political speech. However, different organizations are constantly requesting candidates to speak to their groups. Even though only a handful of people may actually show up to hear a speech, the campaign may decide to address a particular organization for strategic purposes. Thus, the nature of the speaking occasion has changed from pre-television days. The campaign may choose to speak to an organization for symbolic purposes, that is, to use that occasion to say something about issues important to such an organization. The real audience for such a speech is media because they can disseminate the ideas of the speech more widely than the actual people present. The people who show up for the speech create an environment for the occasion, but they are not the major audience. In a campaign, media are always the major audience.

Research

If not enough money is available for people whose primary responsibility in the campaign will be research, speech writers often double in that role. Two kinds of research are important to speech writers. First, they need accurate and up-to-date information on major issues. The information has to be accurate because formal speeches are for the record. When candidates are speaking extemporaneously and make mistakes, the press secretary can correct them later or say the candidate "mis-spoke." The public and journalists usually accept such an explanation because candidates are speaking in informal settings, and mistakes are inevitable in such circumstances. But one rarely has that luxury in a formal, written speech. In fact, the major reason for giving a written speech is to put the candidate on the record on an issue or series of issues. And in writing such speeches, the writer has to know that the prepared speech is one important standard by which the candidate will be held accountable in the future. In such a speech the factual material has to be as current and as accurate as possible. If it isn't, the speech writer will have to take the blame within the campaign, and if using inaccurate information becomes a pattern in speeches, the speech writer will soon be in search of other employment.

Second, speech writers need accurate and up-to-date research on "minor" issues. By minor issues, I mean those that affect only a small segment of the electorate or are important in only one small area of the state. Even though such issues are minor, candidates are expected to have positions on each and every one of them. Obviously, candidates do not know about every little highway problem in every little town and hamlet throughout the state, but the voters in those little towns and hamlets expect candidates to know the problem and have a policy to deal with it. Therefore, extensive research, usually with the aid of local supporters in those areas, is necessary into area issues and peripheral problems. These issues can be woven into the fabric of major issues or themes of the campaign as candidates stump in those areas. Equally important, using these minor problems as examples of overall problems facing the state allows candidates to appeal on a specific level in different areas of the state.

Polls

Before discussing the uses of polls in the process of speech writing, a brief explanation about their uses in the campaign is necessary. Polls have become so sophisticated and accurate that serious candidates do not enter campaigns without at least one. The campaign relies not only on its private polls, but on public polls—such as those conducted by news organizations—as well. In a campaign, the private polls may be so important that only some among the staff are privy to them. For example, in one campaign in which I worked as speech writer, I never saw any of the private polls. In another campaign in which I was writing the television commercials and did have access to polling data and the interpretation by the pollster, the candidate asked me not to reveal that information to his own campaign manager for awhile. He asked me not to say anything because the candidate's low standing in the polls was depressing. Although polls are a major basis for mapping out strategy and doing a variety of other things, the information they contain is jealously guarded within the campaign. Pollsters work on a confidential basis with candidates, and candidates are the only ones who decide who else will be given access to the pollster and the polls.

For speech writers, the "benchmark" poll is the most important. It identifies the major issues in the campaign, and it identifies the major values of the public. Usually, members of the campaign have already decided upon what they believe ought to be the major issues, and the poll then confirms, modifies, or denies those choices. If polls confirm the choices already made, there is a jubilant celebration of the intuitive political knowledge of the candidate and the staff about the public and its opinions. If the polls conclude something very different about those choices, there are long soul-searching discussions about how to reconcile the choices already made with the polling results. Additionally, the benchmark reveals the degree of intensity that the public feels about those issues. The stronger the positive attitudes toward an issue, the greater prominence that issue will be given in speeches and the more likely that it will show up in other speeches on other topics. The benchmark also tells one what the public knows or does not know about the candidate. This information is important in determining how much personal and professional background material has to be included in speeches. In a campaign, people vote for a person. The public's perception of the personality of the candidate is essential to the success of any campaign. Humanizing speeches—both in content and in style—becomes an important task of the speech writer. To decide to vote for one candidate rather than another, voters need to know the candidate as a person and as a professional capable of assuming the office that is sought.

Finally, the benchmark reveals the basic values of the electorate. For speech writers this information is invaluable in constructing certain kinds of arguments to support positions. In every campaign one is trying to relate the candidate and the issues to the basic values of those constituencies that either comprise the candidate's base or comprise target constituencies for the campaign. Furthermore, the primary themes of the campaign are created by blending the values of the candidate with those of the electorate. Candidates run on themes, or at least ought to. Themes, rather than issues, provide consistency in a campaign. In speeches, disparate issues can be united through these themes. Thus, in a speech, a variety of issues can be discussed coherently by relating those issues back to the candidates' basic beliefs and to the primary themes of the campaign. (See the essay by Mauser in this volume.)

During the course of a campaign issues may change, but the basic values of the electorate do not. This underscores the importance of the benchmark because it revealed the electorate's values and beliefs.

"Tracking" polling is more important to the political strategists in a campaign than it is to speech writers. However, having said that, it is true that results from tracking have some particular uses to speech writers. The results can tell the campaign if the themes and issues are "playing" with the public. They can sometimes reveal a new issue that interests the public that has not been given prominence previously. They can reveal weaknesses to be exploited in an opponent's stand on issues. In these days of statewide television debates between candidates, the results of polls can be especially important in deciding what issues and themes to stress in the short opening and closing statements for the debates.

In sum, polls provide precise information that is essential to an effective campaign. As one consultant remarked to me: "Without a poll, we don't know what to do." His statement was an exaggerated jest, but it does point to the important role that polls now play in campaigns. But polls are guides for developing the campaign, not absolute controls of a campaign. For speech writers, polls provide one kind of useful information that helps in constructing persuasive arguments to support the contentions and policies of the campaign.

Group Discussions

There are a variety of different kinds of group discussions that aid in developing strategies for campaigns. For example, the campaign may assemble a group of 15 to 50 politically active people who gather to brainstorm about public perceptions: perceptions of the candidate; perceptions about the office the candidate is seeking; perceptions about issues; perceptions about values; perceptions about other matters pertaining to the campaign. Since these people are politically active, their conclusions may be more sophisticated than those that might have been reached by a randomly sampled group. Nonetheless, as politically active people often are opinion leaders, their informed suggestions about specific candidates, offices, and campaigns are important.

Another kind of group that can be assembled is a sample group of "typical" voters. Such groups are called "focus groups." These groups, like groups of politically active people, are asked to discuss their perceptions of the candidate, the office, and the campaign. What such a group lacks in political sophistication, it gains in representativeness.

Discussion groups—be they politically active or sample groups—are important when candidates have little name recognition in the polls. If the electorate does not know the candidate very well, the pollster's questions about the candidates may produce vague or not very reliable information. Discussion groups may fill in needed information. Furthermore, since these brainstorming or focus group sessions may last for hours, they provide more extensive information about public perceptions than polls can. For speech writers, these sessions supplement the information received from other sources and help to expand on the results from polls.

Thus, as speech writers prepare for campaigns, they draw from each of these sources for their material. This information is used in combination and in a variety of ways—everything from stylistic niceties to primary themes and substantive arguments. But knowing the candidate's political beliefs and knowing the characteristic ways in which those beliefs are expressed by the candidate are imperative and essential to the speech writer.

Perhaps the best way to understand how all these matters may come together in the speech-writing process is to use a case study. The example I have chosen is Richard Thornburgh's 1978 campaign for governor of Pennsylvania. I chose it because it was a well-run, professionally organized campaign where the process of speech writing played a significant part; because I worked as chief speech writer during the primary phase of the campaign; and because—above all—it was a successful campaign. Richard Thornburgh was elected governor of Pennsylvania in 1978 and reelected in 1982.

THE THORNBURGH CAMPAIGN:
A CASE STUDY IN SPEECH WRITING

Having served two terms, Governor Milton Shapp of Pennsylvania could not succeed himself. Therefore, in 1978, both the Democratic and Republican nominations for governor were contested. Richard L. Thornburgh, former U.S. attorney and assistant attorney general of the United States, was one of several seeking the Republican nomination.[2] Although he had never been elected to a major political office, Thornburgh was very popular and highly respected in western Pennsylvania for his vigorous work as U.S. attorney.

The campaign Thornburgh ran in 1978 was a reflection and an extension of the man himself. He wanted a professionally run campaign with competent, reliable, and politically sophisticated people working for him. Thornburgh expected each person with a major position in the campaign to carry out his or her responsibilities with enthusiastic professionalism (Darr 1978). The senior staff consisted of: Jay Waldman, campaign manager; James Seif, assistant campaign manager; Paul Critchlow, press sec-

---

[2]Among those contending for the Republican nomination was Arlen Specter, now U.S. senator from Pennsylvania.

retary; and Richard Stafford, director of research and issues.[3] Thornburgh's decision to have a senior staff member responsible for research and issues reflected his intention to run an issue-oriented campaign. Thornburgh's passion for politics was a passion for policies and policy-making.[4] He intended to run his campaign on specific issues, and he intended to present those issues persuasively during the course of the campaign.

Sometime in December 1977, Richard L. Thornburgh and his senior advisers decided not to issue a formal platform for Thornburgh to run on in his quest for the Republican nomination for governor of Pennsylvania. Instead, they decided upon a series of position papers to be delivered as formal speeches periodically during the course of the primary election campaign. This approach had distinct advantages. First, Thornburgh could set the issue agenda for the campaign by selecting and emphasizing what he considered to be the most important issues facing the Commonwealth. Second, using a series of speeches would allow more time to work out details of each proposal. Third, each speech could be used as a "substantive media event," thus generating free media attention at various

---

[3]These were the formal senior staff members on the organizational chart. The candidate undoubtedly consulted informally with friends he trusted and with his wife, Ginny, who was a full partner in the campaign.

[4]After serving two successful terms as governor of Pennsylvania, Thornburgh became director of the Institute of Politics at Harvard University. In 1988, President Reagan appointed him to succeed Edwin Meese as Attorney General of the United States.

[5]I want to distinguish between what I think are "pseudo events" and "substantive media events." Pseudo events, the description coined by Daniel Boorstin, are events such as going to a supermarket to denounce the high price of food. Such events are staged for the primary purpose of gaining free media time on the evening news. Every campaign stages such events. A "substantive media event" is one in which firm announcements of policy are made for which the candidate wants maximum media coverage. The Thornburgh campaign sought maximum coverage for its policy proposals by delivering a series of speeches on the issues of the campaign.

But it also sought to solve another problem confronting candidates who run on issues. Campaigns "happen" in the media, especially television. However, television rarely has time to publicize issues, especially in primaries when there are numerous candidates. Issuing a series of position papers might be reported in the print media, but probably not in the electronic media because this would not provide visuals for television or live voices for radio. Since an important aspect of the Thornburgh campaign was the particular policies he wished to propose, the idea of using formal speeches to announce policies seemed to be an effective solution. The speeches would provide stories for both print and electronic journalists and at the same time gain the widest possible publicity for the proposals the candidate wanted to advance.

Unfortunately, the idea was only partially realized. The pressure of the campaign and of traveling across the state did not allow sufficient time to select symbolic audiences and settings for delivery of these speeches in the best media markets. Therefore, several of the speeches were never delivered formally to an audience. Instead, a symbolic setting was chosen, the speech was handed out to the journalists, and the candidate made a few remarks for the microphones and cameras that summarized the most important points he wished to make on that topic.

times for the candidate and his policy proposals.[5] Finally, when taken all together, these speeches would form the platform on which Thornburgh would run in the general election, once the nomination was won. The rhetoric of the campaign, then, reflected Thornburgh's commitment to presenting policies persuasively to the public and one standard by which he wished to be held accountable to the public.

The candidate and staff decided on seven speeches. The first speech, of course, was the announcement speech. Not only did it announce Thornburgh's candidacy, it also laid out the issues and themes for the campaign. Each of the other speeches developed one of these issues and continued the themes set in the announcement speech. The topics for these six speeches were: "The Role of the Governor"; "Facing Up to the Highway and Bridge Crisis in Pennsylvania"; "Creating a Climate for Jobs in Pennsylvania"; "Education: An Investment in Pennsylvania's Future"; "The Challenge of Crime in Pennsylvania"; and "Growth, Opportunity, and Security: Commitment to Pennsylvania's Human Services." In a long memorandum I had written Thornburgh, I recommended that the first major speech after the announcement be concerned with the political role of the governor. This speech would outline the opportunities available to a Pennsylvania governor to exert leadership, but equally important, would also discuss the limitations on the office within which the new governor would have to govern. The speech would attempt to place the office in a realistic context of what could be expected from a governor and what should not be expected. This speech was intended to establish a credible context for the proposals Thornburgh would present during the course of the primary campaign—by elucidating the parameters of gubernatorial leadership. This was the only specific speech topic that I recommended. The candidate and his staff approved it and selected the topics for the other five speeches. When all were completed, they formed the platform for Richard Thornburgh's campaign. Later, they were bound together and distributed under the title *Position Papers Issued by Richard L. Thornburgh, Republican Candidate for Governor, Primary Campaign, 1978.*

To understand how speech writing developed within the campaign, one must understand the structure of the decision-making process and how the writing process worked. First, in this campaign I was a speech writer, not a policymaker. That is important to remember. I had initiated contact with Mr. Thornburgh and expressed my interest in his campaign because I thought he was the best and most capable candidate in the field. At a meeting with him and several of his supporters, he asked me to prepare a memorandum about how a speech writer might be used in his campaign, which I did. This long memorandum became the basis for my role in the campaign. In it, I limited the role of speech writer to preparing drafts for a series of policy speeches on major issues in the campaign, which turned out to be consistent with the candidate's thinking about how he would run his campaign.

My responsibility was to work directly with Stafford in developing drafts of the speeches. With the other staff members, I had minimal contact. I had no responsibility for stump speeches, nor was I consulted about them. Political decisions were made by the candidate and the staff and handed down. The candidate made policy based on advice from his senior staff and others he trusted. However, because of my academic and political background, I felt quite free to voice my opinions on the substance of a variety of issues, most particularly relating to the speeches on the role of the governor, and on education. And like any other member of the campaign, I said on occasion what I thought about political strategy, issues, and priorities. But that was independent of the job of speech writing.

Second, it should be noted that no one person can claim to have written any of the speeches. The process is more complicated than that, as I shall soon make clear. My major responsibility was to prepare drafts with Stafford that would accurately reflect Thornburgh's speaking style, accurately explain his position on issues, and persuasively present Thornburgh's message to the electorate. The word *reflect* is absolutely crucial here. Speech writers should no more impose a style on the candidate than they should presume to make policy for the candidate. Those who would write for another must subordinate their style to the style of their principal. If they do not, they are more hindrance than help and probably do not belong in the speech-writing business.

To achieve the goal, the resources I drew upon were varied. I had heard Thornburgh speak on several occasions before the campaign began. I had talked with him at length on two occasions (but, once he announced his candidacy in January, I did not have the opportunity to speak with him again until the night of the primary election). In addition, Stafford provided me with copies of a number of speeches Thornburgh had delivered while U.S. attorney and later while assistant attorney general. From these sources, I filed away in my memory distinctive word choices and syntactical usages characteristic of the candidate. For example, in one conversation, Thornburgh talked about the suspicious mood of the people toward government and talked about their being "seduced by cynicism." I thought that phrasing particularly apt, and several months later found an appropriate place to work it into one of the speeches. Once the campaign began, Paul Critchlow sent me bits and pieces of phrasing that seemed to work on the stump.

The most important source, however, was Stafford. He provided the research for speeches, relayed the candidate's positions on issues, and answered all the questions I had while developing the drafts. I had no *direct* access to polls in developing the policy sections of speeches. However, information from Stafford about polling data became useful in deciding about emphasis in certain sections of speeches. My responsibility as speech writer was to absorb all the information—both policy and political information—and structure it so that I could produce the draft.

How, then, did the actual process work? When a speech was scheduled, Stafford would provide me with a binder of background information and research on the topic. This binder might be as long as 200 pages. Stafford would outline the major issues, the positions Thornburgh had decided to take on the issues, and direct me to the most important areas of research. I then began to absorb the material, and once I believed I had it under control, I would begin writing the first draft usually in Stafford's office so we could confer with one another quickly.

When an initial working draft was completed, Stafford would go over it for accuracy. Together, we would look to shadings and emphasis, to adding or deleting sections, to expanding or contracting a discussion of a particular part of the speech. We would argue over some of these points: he from a political or policy standpoint; I from a rhetorical or structural standpoint. He won some. I won some. In the end, the candidate and his senior staff would make the final decisions. At this time, the real work began: rewriting. The time it took to rewrite could vary greatly, depending on the problems encountered with the first draft; that is, on my ability to get it right. For example, the speech on education took only two drafts, and we completed it in one 10-hour writing session. Primarily, the speed with which it was finished was due in part to my familiarity with the issues involving education in Pennsylvania. On the other hand, the speech on highways and bridges required more than a week's work and more drafts than I care to remember. Part of the delay was due to my unfamiliarity with the issues; part was due to serious omissions in the research. One of Stafford's research assistants who had worked on the issues had to do additional research to provide the information we needed to complete the speech. That is not uncommon in campaigns. In fact, that frequently happens because one does not know exactly what information will be needed for a speech until one begins writing it.

When Stafford approved my working draft, he took it to other members of the senior staff. They would examine it, refine or revise it, and finally give it their approval. In particular, they looked for additional political nuances that we may have missed, for parts that could be excerpted for press releases, and for a myriad of other things. Each apparently suggested other things, including stylistic changes. Finally, the candidate received it for final revisions and his approval. If all of us had done our jobs well, the draft would require very little editing by the candidate. Once he made his changes and approved the speech, the campaign organization printed copies of the speech for distribution to journalists and voters. The process I have described is standard in any professionally managed campaign. To work effectively, it depends on each staff member performing his or her job professionally.

Of course, the candidate is the focal point of any effective communication strategy in a campaign. For someone trained in classical rhetoric, as I was, that is a commonplace of rhetorical theory. Aristotle wrote that *ethos* is the most potent force in persuasion. In a political campaign that is undoubtedly true. Leadership is always the central issue in any campaign for executive office. What Aristotle called *ethos* is generally what political scientists call "image making." *Ethos,* the character of the candidate and the public's perception of his or her character, is an integral part of any campaign because the candidate is a person, and people vote for a person they believe they can trust. It is one thing to advocate sound policies. It is another thing to persuade voters that the candidate is the trustworthy person to carry through on those policies and promises. Thus, our purpose in these speeches was not only to present policies, but more important to persuade people to vote for the leadership Thornburgh offered and to give persuasive reasons why his leadership was now needed in Pennsylvania.

Emphasizing *ethos* or image in a speech is different from doing it in television commercials. In commercials one can film "visuals" of the candidate in a variety of settings relating to people: the candidate with his or her family; the candidate among various representatives of constituencies; and so on. A voice-over can be used to tell the viewer what kind of person the candidate is. Or, a commercial can use testimonials from well-known figures or "people on the street." Testimonials allow these surrogates to say positive things about candidates that candidates might find embarrassing or unseemly or politically counterproductive to say about themselves.

But a candidate giving a public speech cannot rely on all the devices available to the media consultant in preparing political commercials. Of course, in a speaking situation, one can depend on the person doing the introduction to stress the attractive qualities of the candidate in the typical "I give you a person who . . ." introduction. But the candidate's speech has to be written to present and exhibit those qualities rather than preach about them. There are three essential means for doing this: through personal experiences or through expressions of personal concerns or through themes. The first two are self-explanatory; perhaps the third needs elaboration.

In the Thornburgh campaign, three themes were struck: integrity, competence, and compassion. Even before the campaign was put together, it was clear that integrity would be a central theme. During the previous administration, more than 60 people had been charged with crimes relating to their conduct in office. Several cabinet-level people had been forced from office for criminal convictions or allegations of serious wrongdoing. In addition, the speaker of the House, the chairman of the Senate Appropriations Committee, and the state senator who would have become majority leader had been convicted of serious federal offenses.

And all of this came on the heels of the Watergate scandals. Juxtaposed to these events was Thornburgh's long experience as a U.S. federal attorney and his stint in the Ford administration as assistant attorney general. The theme of integrity was a natural choice, and one Thornburgh could present with absolute credibility. The benchmark poll apparently confirmed this choice. I was told that the poll revealed a greater intensity among the electorate about this issue than had been imagined. According to the poll, integrity or some variation of that theme was the overriding concern of the public, far outdistancing everything else.

Competence for office is always a part of speeches and campaigns. In this campaign, it had a special place for two reasons. Thornburgh had held only one *elected* position prior to the race for governor, and that position had not been an executive office: he served as an elected delegate to the 1967 constitutional convention in Pennsylvania. Furthermore, I was told the benchmark poll showed that he was well known in the western part of Pennsylvania, which was his home base, but that he had a low name identification in other parts of the state, especially in the critical area of eastern Pennsylvania around Philadelphia. If voters do not know who the candidate is, certainly those same voters are going to be in the dark about the candidate's ability to handle the office of governor. In their overall effect and in specific sections, speeches had to stress the competence of the candidate.

Compassion is a standard theme among most candidates. And certainly every candidate has issues that arouse his or her compassion and that demonstrate his or her compassion for people.

How, then, were the speeches put together to integrate policies with themes?

As I mentioned before, a consistent structure for the speeches was created. Each speech opened with the candidate stressing his personal concern about a particular problem, always emphasizing the human dimension of that problem. For example, the speech on creating jobs in Pennsylvania began:

> As I have travelled throughout Pennsylvania, I've listened to people deeply worried about their economic future.
> Factory workers worry that employers may relocate in another state.
> Elderly persons try to scrape by on a fixed income in a time of rising inflation and soaring energy costs.
> And young families search for ways to budget for the present and plan for the future.
> None of these worries can be resolved while our state's economic situation is confused, and in some cases, chaotic.
> Frankly, I'm worried too.

Following this introduction, the candidate would launch into a discussion of the problem and its ramifications and then begin describing various proposals he would advocate to solve them. Usually, he would stress the need for cooperation among different segments of the population and stress the value of that cooperation. One way in which this was done was to stress his experience as a delegate to the constitutional convention where he had "learned first-hand how representatives of both parties can work together for the public good when effective leadership is exercised." Or he might stress common interests by saying:

> We are, after all, a *Commonwealth*. We have more in common than we often admit, and surely we have a wealth of untapped talent and resources. We need a Governor who recognizes these mutual interests and who will provide the vital leadership to direct such a coalition for the public good.

Each speech also combined the issues of integrity and competence by citing his experience in running a large bureaucracy (the Criminal Division of the U.S. Department of Justice), experience that would enable him to manage the executive office with efficiency. Or he would propose a public integrity unit for his administration to enforce conflict-of-interest standards. For example, in his speech on the role of the governor, he stated:

> As U.S. Attorney for Western Pennsylvania for 6 years, I was the first to blow the whistle on corruption in the Shapp administration and among the leadership in the General Assembly—and to do something about it through successful prosecution. As Assistant U.S. Attorney General, I established a Public Integrity Section, the first unit in the history of the Justice Department specifically designed to focus on official corruption and conflicts of interest.

Each speech included sections such as these, sometimes extended if the topic warranted (as in the speech on crime), sometimes contracted (as in the speech on education). The responsibility of the speech writer was to weave these themes of integrity, competence, and compassion into the narrative of problems and proposals, and to find every conceivable way to stress them repeatedly.

Finally, each speech concluded with a summary of major ideas in the form of a series of parallelisms, each phrased in personal terms:

> But today, the people of Pennsylvania are worried and dissatisfied with the state of the economy. And I'm dissatisfied too.
>   I'm not satisfied when I see good workers leaving because we can't provide jobs for them.
>   I'm not satisfied when I see young families struggling to pay their monthly bills and finding themselves unable to plan securely for the future.
>   I'm not satisfied when I know we are not making the fullest use of both our natural and our human resources.
>   I'm not satisfied with a transportation system that delays rather than speeds delivery of goods and services.

I'm not satisfied because I know we have not provided leadership to get our state moving once again.

I think we can do better. I know we must do better. I believe vigorous leadership in the Governor's office, a partnership among leaders in industry and labor, among citizens of all walks of life, and a clear planning for the future will create a new spirit in Pennsylvania. And that new spirit will lead us out of the darkness of recent years into the light of a growing, thriving Pennsylvania.

Or the conclusion might take a more positive approach by making the parallelisms positive rather than negative. In either case, the extended personal concern of the candidate highlights that a *person* is running for office, a *person* who is concerned about these problems and intends to do something about them. But this type of conclusion also serves another function. It "plays" well on television. It summarizes the main ideas of the speech. It is vivid and personal. And it takes no longer than 40 seconds to deliver.

Anyone who works in statewide campaigns knows that the campaigns "happen" in media. Speeches and position papers can be handed out for the print media. But for the electronic media, special accommodations in speech writing have to be made.

Radio and television stories rarely run longer than one minute, thirty seconds. Therefore, internal summaries of ideas and proposals have to be sprinkled through the address. Internal summaries are no longer than 45 seconds, and usually run 15 to 30 seconds. They are striking phrases or minispeeches that encapsulate an idea and take the form of a story by having a beginning, a middle, and an end. They must be vivid, personal, and dramatic because the electronic media are vivid, personal, and dramatic. Given the time constraints of electronic media, the 45-second limit is absolutely imperative and optimistic. (Usually, electronic reporters only take a 5- to 15-second sound bite, although radio is sometimes more generous with time.) A good television or radio reporter will pick out these minispeeches quickly because they provide the "visual" or "actuality" that the reporter needs for the story. Every speech writer has to take this into account when writing political speeches. A speech filled with long arguments, regardless of whether they are skillfully reasoned or rambling, may be rendered ineffective for radio and television if the reporter cannot excerpt a 15- to 45-second segment from it. Generating free media time is essential to any electoral campaign.

In 1978 Richard Thornburgh won both the Republican primary election and the general election. In the primary campaign, speeches were used to set the issue agenda. They were also used to present the specific policies that Thornburgh intended as his platform for the general election and that he intended as the standards by which he would be judged once he became governor. By using a limited number of major policy speeches, he was able to focus the policy discussion of the campaign consistent with his belief that an election should be focused on a choice among issues as well as candidates.

SUMMARY AND CONCLUSION

Because the means for communicating with voters has changed with the advent of mass communication, the role of speeches has also changed. Formal written speeches are now given only when candidates want to present precise proposals to the electorate or when a formal occasion calls for a formal speech. But when candidates make formal speeches, they create a public record of their promises to the electorate. Such speeches then become the standard by which they will be held accountable. Almost any other utterance during the heat of a campaign can be explained away if it becomes embarrassing by shifting the blame to someone else. Candidates can dissociate themselves from television commercials that backfire. Aides can explain that the candidate mis-spoke himself or herself during a press conference or an extemporaneous speech. But a candidate cannot do that with a formal speech, formally delivered and printed. Such a speech becomes a standard by which to hold candidates accountable not only in the campaign, but also in office. And the men and women who hold executive political offices are held to a higher standard of accountability than almost anyone else in American society. It is at these times that a professional speech writer can render valuable assistance to the candidate by helping to organize and shape a speech into an organic, persuasive, and responsible whole.

Speech writers are hired on the basis of the needs of the campaign and the reputations of the writers. Besides the writing skills necessary to speech writing, the most important quality one must have is political reliability. By that I mean knowledge of how campaigns work, the politics of a particular campaign, and discretion.

Speech writers function within the overall political and communication strategies of the campaign. It is their responsibility when writing speeches not only to reflect the style and substance of candidates, but also to make certain that their writing blends with the rest of the campaign. In many cases, speech writers have other responsibilities. They may be part of the political or communication staffs, and thus may assist in developing those strategies for the campaign. In any case, they must maximize candidates' strengths and minimize weaknesses in a manner similar to developing a legal case in a courtroom. Persuasion is at the center of a campaign, and the purpose is to win.

On the technical side of speech writing, there are three basic rules: the writing must reflect the ideas and style of the candidate; the speeches must be consistent; and the speech must be written to be spoken. Let's take these one at a time.

By definition, speech writers write for other people, not themselves. The purpose of writing effective speeches is to reflect the ideas and style of the candidate, not to present one's own ideas or to create a style for the candidate. That means one has to observe the candidate as much as possible to begin not only to talk as the candidate does, but to think as the candidate does. Developing a sensitive ear for verbal idiosyncrasies, paying particular attention to the kinds of proofs (examples, statistics, quotations, and so on) the candidate typically uses, and knowing what the candidate believes are essential starting points for preparing to write for another. The speech must be written so the speaker can speak it easily and naturally. The speech must flow with the natural rhythms, emphases, and cadences of the candidate's oral language.

Second, each formal speech must be consistent with the speech that came before it and the one that comes next. Furthermore, formal speeches must be consistent with the extemporaneous speeches given by the candidate on the stump. The campaign cannot afford to have a candidate who speaks one way in a formal speech and another way in impromptu situations.

Third, speeches are written to be understood instantly. Writing speeches is different from writing pieces intended to be read. When one is reading an essay or a report, one can pause to reread a sentence or a paragraph or even the entire piece, if one does not immediately understand what has been written. That luxury does not exist for a speaker. Each word and each section of a speech must be instantly comprehensible to the audience. This requires an economy of language, precision in word choices, and attention to the nuances of oral language.

It is unfortunate that candidates give so few formal speeches in campaigns, and equally unfortunate that the public demands so few. Formal speeches allow candidates to present ideas and proposals with detail and nuance. They allow candidates to put themselves fully on the record on a variety of important issues facing the electorate. They create one standard by which the public can later hold elected officials accountable. And finally, they provide an indispensable means for educating the electorate about issues, candidates, and prospects for the future. In sum, formal speeches complete the compact with the people that is truly the essence of a democratic society.

CHAPTER 4

Alive and Well and Living in Washington: The American Political Parties

Xandra Kayden

INTRODUCTORY NOTE

If, as Mauser's and Windt's chapters suggest, professional political managers are replacing the traditional party bosses, how has this affected political party organizations? In this chapter, Xandra Kayden argues that in both the Republican and Democratic parties the locus of power has shifted from city and county organizations, traditionally the balliwicks of party bosses, to the state and (especially) national organizations, where professional managers have assumed prominent roles.

This has come about not only because of the complexity of modern campaign technology but also as a result of legal and socioeconomic trends over the past several decades. Reforms made during the Progressive Era weakened local parties by eliminating most local patronage and by instituting nonpartisan elections in many constituencies; the New Deal's expansion of the national government's responsibility for citizens' welfare replaced many of the charitable activities and services that local parties once provided; the Federal Election Campaign Act of 1971 and its subsequent amendments had the effect of encouraging a concentration of party resources at federal and state levels rather than with local party organizations. Parallel changes in the nature of the American economy and society—e.g., two-income families and increased levels of education—have brought about a decline in the availability of (mostly female) volunteers who served as local party functionaries, and a decline in the value and prestige of blue-collar jobs that remain as political patronage exempt from the Progressive's civil service reforms.

Despite these changes, Kayden argues that the new national parties are not only "alive and well," they are vigorous and effective. She presents evidence that the revitalized state and national party organizations play an increasingly important role in recruiting, campaigning for, and electing candidates for state and federal office. By providing candidates with campaign services and materials that tend to stress common themes, the central party organizations increase their potential to influence public opinion, both directly and indirectly. Not only do common campaign themes and advertising impact upon public opinion directly, they have the indirect effect of providing winning candidates with common positions to propagate, once they assume office. Finally, Kayden suggests that the emergence of strong state and national party organizations may help to reverse the trend toward political independence among the electorate and to revive public involvement in American politics.

The Editors

The American party system has gone through a metamorphosis in the past decade, changing from a weak, decentralized structure to a strong centralized organization possessed of new resources in money and technology. Although there is still considerable debate about the consequences of these changes (ranging from the death of democracy through the loss of intermediary institutions and the uncontrolled rise of candidates and ideologues to a rebirth of political commitment and order out of the chaos of an interest-dominated politics), it is my view that the new system represents a dramatic change from the past and that it is a positive step in bringing the processes of politics into line with the communication and opinion formation of a modern technological society. The new system is capable of recapturing the traditional functions of political parties: control of nominations and resources, and influencing public opinion and public policy. That the rebirth has coincided with turbulent political tides and a widespread contention that the parties are dying, if not already dead, has obscured the picture of what they are and what they might portend for our future. One task, therefore, is to describe them; and a second is to consider their meaning—assuming that the new form comes out of new needs and serves new functions. What is the role of the party: as an organization, as a vehicle for expressing and influencing opinion, and as a participant in political life?

The rebirth may not have been inevitable, although an argument could be made that if the parties did not exist, they would have to be created, for they are an inherent characteristic of the modern democratic state. The circumstances that encouraged the current rebirth were: changes in campaign finance regulation (effectively limiting the participation of other participants in the process) and the increased complexity and cost of modern campaign technology (requiring resources that only a permanent organization such as the party could sustain). We must also credit leadership in both parties for recognizing what had to be done and making the tough decisions to do it. Finally, the remaining causes of party change must lie in the changes in the practice of politics and government.

THE NEW ORGANIZATION: A DESCRIPTION

For several years it has been accepted wisdom that the national Republican Party has become a strong, centralized organization. Doubts have persisted about the ability of the Democrats to catch up, but it is apparent to this writer, at least, that the path is clearly marked and that the world's oldest political party is well along it. For our purposes, however, we will use the GOP as the model, making comparisons with the Democrats as warranted.

Both national parties consist of three committees: the national committee (which is composed of representatives of the states and is supported by a professional staff) and the campaign committees for the House and Senate. Until the mid-1970s the national party existed principally for the function of organizing a national nominating convention to select its candidate for the presidency, and secondarily as a clearinghouse for political appointees.

In recent time, the influence of the national party has declined in the actual selection of presidential candidates—giving cause to the cry of the demise of the party—but it has *increased* in the selection of all other candidates for party office at both the federal and state levels. All three committees in both parties raise money, recruit and support candidates, develop data and techniques to affect the outcome of elections, and participate in policy debates. The strength of the committees rests in their staffs who do the work and who, in more instances than is generally recognized, influence the selection of candidates and issues upon which they will stand. The professional organization is the core of the modern party.

The decline in the role of the convention as a decision-making body reflects the decline in influence of local party bosses, rather than a weakness in the national organization. Indeed, there is little question that local parties are in danger of disappearing in many places, leaving vestiges of their structures with few volunteers willing to devote the time and energy necessary to their sustenance. The decline of local party volunteers is due to a variety of causes. These include the loss of a major function due to nonpartisan local elections, the accompanying decline of party control of patronage that promised future rewards for volunteers, and changes in lifestyle that do not permit as much time for volunteer efforts, particularly by women. The loss of volunteers also reflects a decline in partisan identification in the electorate—the second measure of the weakness of the parties usually relied upon by political observers. Whether the loss of partisan support is a permanent situation, however, remains to be seen because recent polls suggest a small but marked resurgence in partisan identification.

The national committees have used their increased resources to enhance their role in the selection and election of candidates and to create super campaign committees. Few candidates can afford to run for federal office today without the backing of the national party. The Federal Election Campaign Act (FECA) permits the party to spend an average of two cents per voter in an election district for federal office (the regulations regarding the presidential candidate are more complex, but do permit party spending during the general election when all other groups are prohibited from making campaign contributions). The money, while greater in amount than any other group can contribute, is minor compared to the services the party can provide in research, polling, advertising, fundraising expertise, and legal and accounting help. The Republican Senatorial Campaign Committee raised $90 million in 1984 (a presidential year) and $83 million in 1986. During the presidential campaign year it spent the maximum of $25 million on Republican candidates, paid off a $3.5 million debt, and ended the campaign season with $6 million in the bank for the 1986 election cycle. The rest—$55.5 million—went for overhead. Overhead expenditures include staff sent out around the country equipped with computer linkages back to the home office, "genre" advertising advocating the election of Republicans in general, expensive polling research which could be sold to Republican candidates at very low rates, issue research provided free of charge to candidates, and so on (Kayden and Mahe 1985: chap. 3). The 1986 campaign also included rather controversial bonuses to the staff, amounting to $225,000 after the election (Berke 1987: E5).

The national party trains candidates, campaign managers, and fundraisers, and provides technical assistance in just about every phase of an election, including detailed information about the opposition and the voters. It has the capacity to contact registered party members, independents, and registered Democratic voters who live in districts that voted Republican in previous elections. The finely tuned message, while not as personal as a neighbor canvassing his or her block on behalf of the party, can be made more accurate and more informative than any ever before directed to American voters.

National/State Relations

The national parties used to be financed by a tithe placed on each state party. Their activities were, not surprisingly, limited. The FECA changed this. The national parties moved from dependence on the states to reliance on direct funding from millions of small contributors and thereby changed the relationship within the party organization. Today, the national party supports the state parties with funds, staff, and a multitude of other resources. The congressional campaign committees are now almost entirely responsible for supporting their respective candidates, freeing the other committees to use their resources elsewhere.

Besides helping state parties (and in the Republican case, those at the county level as well), both national parties recruit candidates for office. Although many still think of our system as candidate-centered, i.e., that the candidates are self-selected and independent of the parties, the reality is that very few candidates for federal and important state offices run without expecting and receiving significant aid from the national party in the form of money, advice, research on issues and the demographics of the voting district, staff and organizational support in registration and get-out-the-vote efforts, help in soliciting political action committee (PAC) and individual support, and assistance in federal and state compliance procedures. No other individual or group can contribute anything closely approximating it. In many instances, it is the party which makes the first approach. Since 1976, the Republican National Committee (RNC) has supported its recruits in primary elections, although recent changes in party rules now require the approval of the state committee before RNC intervention. The rule does not apply to the House and Senate campaign committees, and they are free to participate as much as the law permits in primary elections (the federal law limits the contribution a party can make in a primary to $5,000—the same as a nonparty committee). But direct contribution is only a small part of what the party has to offer. Besides the multitude of campaign services which can be made available at or below cost, the party name can provide legitimacy, which can be of tremendous value in a primary election.

Another area of national party activity, which grows out of the new resources and professionalism, is the activism of the party in policy debates. The influence of the party varies from presenting candidates for office with issue positions (including proposed press releases and speech outlines) to lobbying Congress, and even to publishing views which differ from the official party platform adopted at the nominating convention. The issue positions that come from the party during the election period cover a wide array of topics. They serve not only to influence public opinion but they also have the indirect effect of providing elected officials with public positions developed and enunciated by the party proper before they ever get to Washington. Although it is improbable that candidates will rely solely upon the party on every issue, it certainly increases the chances of agreement within the party's congressional delegation.

The Party in Washington

Debates about party influence must inevitably blur the lines of participants. On one hand, this discussion has been based on the professionalism of party staffers. On the other hand, the growth of party influence in Congress includes the increased power of House and Senate party leaders. Their influence is due in large measure to the increased resources they can provide for the next election, and whether they are holding a carrot or a stick, it is true that voting within Congress has become markedly more partisan in the last few years.

The range of national party activities beyond campaigns and policy debates in Washington includes general recruitment; appeals to special segments of the population to increase the party's base; voter registration and get-out-the-vote efforts; and support at the regional, state, and local party levels.

For the first time, both major national parties own their headquarters in Washington. These buildings on Capitol Hill are more than symbols of the new institutional strength of the parties: they are the bases of ongoing activity by individuals who have devoted themselves to party building for several years. Most of the staff in both parties are young, well educated, and well versed in modern technology. They are partisan, but they have developed the outlook of professionals and since 1980 (when several academic conferences brought them together following the presidential election), they have maintained communication with each other. As professionals they seem, in fact, to have more in common with each other stylistically than with many of their adherents out in the field. As one party worker noted in an interview, "We tend to be three-piece wool-suiters dealing with the polyester crowd." They are yuppies. They are organizers. They are not ideologues for the most part (Broder 1980; Kayden 1978).

THE RESOURCES OF STRONG
NATIONAL ORGANIZATIONS

The sources of national party money are twofold: large donors (a traditional but less important source in recent years), and small donors whose participation is solicited through the mails. It is the direct-mail fund raising which has turned out to be the key to the new strength, and ultimately, to the nationalization of the parties. The shift to direct mail began paying off for the Republicans in 1974, when the FECA went into effect. The process is well suited to the law's requirements to gather information about those who contribute to federal elections. Although it took several years to build and refine the lists, both parties entered the 1980s with large groups of committed direct-mail donors.

It should be noted that direct-mail fund raising by the parties does not come as an isolated phenomenon in American political life. Issue groups and individual candidates have led the way, helped in turn by the intensity and scope of the media. Television brings issues to the public mind and thereby enables activists to seek support. Although many observers have criticized the trivial nature of media communication, the fact that it focuses attention makes possible the more comprehensive mail appeal. The attention also brings about the nationalization of issues, and that process strengthens the nationalization of the parties.

As more and more decisions have been made at the national level, more and more interests have established themselves in Washington to serve constituents in the rest of the country. National interest groups interact with other national power brokers and the parties are no exception. Interests make appeals to the parties, and parties seek their support as part of their coalition for winning and governance. Although it always seems to some that the interests are in danger of dominating the parties, they never do in the end. Interest-group participation may affect the outcome of individual elections, but they must share their role with others. What generally happens is that, in time, the parties co-opt interests in the course of building their coalitions. Organized labor has probably been the most successful to date in coming close to co-opting a party, but even its relationship with the Democrats is marked by frequent periods of perceived insensitivity and lack of attention.

The parties are most successful making appeals for funds on issues for which there is no standing constituency. It is hard, for instance, for the Democrats to solicit support in opposition to Republican environmental policies because there are already too many national groups out there with refined lists soliciting for themselves. Democrats have done best on Social Security because that issue has been identified with them since the New Deal, and because activist groups among the elderly are only recently developing the kind of organizational strength it takes to sustain a direct-mail list. Republicans did best during the Carter years by opposing the Panama Canal Treaty and the role of U.N. Ambassador Andrew Young, two issues which again had no active organizations preceding their emergence as topics of concern.

Direct-mail appeals tend to be negative: opposing some policy, person, or action in which the appealer is in the minority. Those who view themselves in the majority are less apt to get angry, less apt to be concerned, and less apt to feel they must do something to change things or defend the status quo. Those who give large donations usually expect to gain access and the possibility of influence in return for their gift; those who give small amounts of money cannot realistically have such expectations; hence what motivates them is the sense of moral satisfaction which comes from participating in the battle. The success of the New Right in the early 1980s in raising money to use for opposing abortion and bans against prayer in public schools, and the host of other issues which fall under their banner, is testament to the success of this strategy.

Party appeals are more constrained than those of single-issue groups but the direction is similar. One example was a letter mailed in England, written on the letterhead of the George V Hotel in Paris. The writer described the tear gas wafting in the breeze outside his hotel window—a consequence of riots resulting from a socialist government in France—and warned his readers that such things could happen in America if the Republican Party did not maintain control of the Senate (Kayden and Mahe 1985: 82).

Fund raisers have known for a long time that commitment follows money. Once you make a donation, you tend to believe more fully in the cause. Giving to the party, therefore, helps intensify partisan commitments, and the GOP, which began its direct-mail program more than a decade before the Democrats followed suit, has tried to inculcate among its supporters the habit of giving to the party. The effort has had mixed results, and the Republicans now spend a great deal of money prospecting for new contributors. The Democratic direct-mail strategy is to reach out beyond the traditional liberal base of Democratic contributors to increase both the funds and the commitment of the more ideologically neutral Democratic majority (interview: Frank O'Brien 1985).

The impact of national party direct-mail fund raising extends beyond the funds brought into party headquarters. It increases the sense of loyalty to the national party itself, extending participation in its affairs (at least in the form of direct communication) to far larger numbers than ever before. In the 1984 presidential year, there were between 3 and 4 million GOP contributors (interview: Wyatt Stewart 1984). If everything we know about the relationship between giving money and loyalty is correct, it suggests that partisanship may be increasing in intensity among larger portions of the population.

How much we can account for intensity of belief because of active commitment (giving money) or because of the politics of the day is a moot point. The issues of the last two decades have been more ideological than was once thought to be normal in American politics (Nie, Verba, and Petrocik 1979: chaps. 7–10). Whether the increased ideology is a consequence of instability often associated with realignment, or whether it is the result of a better-educated, more widely informed populace remains to be seen.

NATIONALIZATION: THE CAUSES

Local Decline

Local party organization—the structure we usually associate with strong parties—is now the weakest link in the system. While it has not disappeared, it has certainly changed in importance and, in many instances, in the kinds of activities it undertakes.

There are many explanations for local party decline. The most important include the following:

- The reforms of the Progressive Era, principally the growth of non-partisan elections and civil service reform, which were intended to eliminate the influence of party bosses, succeeded in doing so.

- The New Deal and the assumption of governmental responsibility for the well-being of the citizenry eliminated many services and rewards that the local party customarily offered members as incentives for belonging.

- The increased levels of education and access to employment by many in the population made the old material incentive for participation less valuable.

- The women's movement not only encouraged the women most likely to be local volunteer activists to seek full-time employment but also affected their sense of how to spend leisure time, e.g., more on family-centered and health-related activities.

- The economy itself has forced both spouses to work in order to maintain an adequate standard of living.

- The complexity of modern campaign technology has placed greater emphasis on the centralization and professionalization of politics and less value on volunteer activity.

- The sheer complexity of the FECA and its amendments became an active discouragement to local party participation in federal elections.

Parties were required to maintain separate accounts for federal and state candidates (because many states permit corporate contributions that federal law does not), and were required to report all income and expenditures on behalf of their candidates for congressional elections. There were, and are, limits as well on how much the party can spend in presidential elections, especially during the general election, which is otherwise publicly financed.

Even though many observers blamed the decline in local party activity directly on the law, it soon became clear that while the law placed some burdens on the party, it placed greater prohibitions on others, and the cumulative effect was to enhance the role of the central (national and state) party in all campaigns. I believe the passage of the law was only one factor in the decline of local party activity. Because of the newness of the law, and because of the increased interest in campaign behavior following the revelations of Watergate, we looked more closely and saw more clearly that local parties were already all but dead in the water. Congress amended the law in 1979 to address some of the obvious limitations on local parties, and by 1984 there were even signs of local party rebirth, but the prognosis remains somewhat guarded.

Resurgence of local parties is not likely in the immediate future. For our purposes, the question is not whether or not the local party is weak, but what caused the organizational decline and what—if anything—is likely to bring about a change.

All but the last two explanations of party decline (the technology and the law) can be summed up by saying that the incentives which maintained the organization in the past no longer do so, and that other incentives will have to replace them if the local party is to survive. There are, according to Peter B. Clark and James Q. Wilson, three kinds of incentives: material, solidary, and purposive (Clark and Wilson 1961). The local parties in the past were maintained principally by material incentives, with solidary benefits coming in an important second, especially in the late 1950s and early 1960s (Wilson 1962; Eldersveld 1964).

Purposive incentives appear to have become more important as the 1960s progressed, with conservative Republicans challenging the Eastern liberal establishment, and liberal-to-radical Democrats seeking to unseat Lyndon Johnson and to redirect the party to the values of the civil rights and peace movements. There can be something of a conflict between solidary and purposive incentives (solidary incentives being those which provide a sense of camaraderie and fellowship associated with group participation, and purposive being those which motivate individuals because they seek the attainment of a worthwhile cause) (Wilson 1973: 34). Ideas, and especially idealism, can divide people as well as unite them. As the ideologues sought control of local parties in the 1960s, they frequently drove out those who enjoyed the camaraderie. But since the ideologues were motivated principally by national concerns, their intrusion into the activities of local parties often meant a diminished commitment to local parties. Not infrequently, the new activists were involved with national issues first and the local party organization second.

The National Impetus

Local party decline and the nationalization of issues were important dynamics in the restructuring of party organization, but perhaps the most important factors were the nature of modern campaign technology and the reform of campaign finance laws. One reason politics provided solidary benefits was because it was a labor-intensive operation. Campaigns needed people to stuff envelopes, knock on doors, engage in a multitude of research activities, and so on. Some of the work was essential to the campaign; some of it was "make work," designed to allow volunteers to make a contribution without letting them interrupt the development and implementation of campaign strategy. Most research activities by volunteers fell into the latter category. Nonetheless, campaign headquarters were rather free-wheeling places where individual entrepreneurship counted as much as anything, and creativity and energy were usually rewarded.

Today's campaigns are dominated by professionals. Research has become a highly focused and important part of campaign strategy. Polling data are available to test the attitudes of voters to candidates, issues, and campaign tactics. Complex computer analyses now provide tremendous amounts of information about the characteristics of the voting population and about the opponent: voting records, public utterances, backers, etc., all bear scrutiny. The computer has gone a long way toward alleviating the uncertainty so characteristic of past elections. (See essays by Mauser and Windt in this volume.)

We may not yet have reached the stage where total manipulation of the population is possible, but we can at least measure the impact of campaign advertisements and events in 24-hour tracking polls. That level of sophistication leaves little room for volunteers who want to test their political sensibilities. It requires money, complex equipment, and persons who know how to compile and analyze the data. Much of the background information on issues, voters, and opponents requires years to amass and ongoing efforts to maintain. It is usually beyond the ability of the temporary campaign organization created by a challenger, and often beyond the ability of an incumbent. Individual campaign consulting firms are more apt to maintain the skills than the data because they cannot be sure which campaigns they will run. That leaves only the party because it is a permanent organization, and because it has the resources in money and accumulated hardware and software.

As campaigns have become more technical so the consultants have become more specialized. Typically, separate firms are hired to develop the advertisements, write and send out direct-mail solicitations for funds and support, and even to run phone banks, which can be done by computer if not paid workers. If volunteers are no longer available to walk their precincts, the campaign has gotten around that failure in communication by relying more heavily on radio, television, telephones, computers, and the mails. It may be less personal, but it is frequently more informative because the message is not filtered through an intermediary who may or may not be knowledgeable about the candidate's positions on a spectrum of issues.

Along with the communication stemming from the campaign has come *party* communications: advertisements suggesting that people vote Republican or Democratic. "Genre" advertising has grown in importance because the ads are usually good, because the parties can target them where they will have the most impact, and because the money to run them is charged to the candidate's spending limitations imposed by law. There is also an economy of scale that comes into play. When the party speaks, it reaches down below Senate and House races to state legislative contests as well.

Party activity also includes efforts to mobilize volunteers for the traditional activities of registering voters and getting-out-the-vote. In the 1980 and 1984 presidential elections, the national parties (particularly the Republicans) spent millions of dollars to organize such grass-roots efforts. The 1984 election was more intense on both sides because of the highly publicized campaign organized by the Rainbow Coalition on the Democratic side and a counter effort by the GOP that claimed to have registered 4 million new voters, double the original goal (Republican National Committee 1984). The activity may be local, but it is fueled with national money and professional advisers who are frequently trained and certified by the party.

Campaign Finance Legislation

Three main features of the FECA and its amendments had an impact on the nationalization of the parties: the disclosure provisions; the limitations on contributions to campaigns placed on individuals and interest groups; and the special provisions favoring party participation. The complexity of the law was also a factor because it forced many to turn to the national party for advice—these included campaign managers, political action committees, and local parties. The national party, particularly the RNC, was able to maintain a staff of lawyers who, over the years, have developed an expertise that few can match.

Disclosure.   The law requires that all income and expenditures be reported in timely reports, which increase in frequency as the election draws near. This can be extraordinarily burdensome for a temporary campaign organization, and was so for smaller campaigns in particular, until the Federal Election Commission (FEC) simplified the forms in 1979. The reports require that contributors provide not only their names and addresses, but also their places of business.

Contribution Limits.   The contribution limit of $1,000 for an individual per campaign and $5,000 for a PAC means that records must not only be kept but checked in order to ensure that the limits are not surpassed. Because they are publicly financed, presidential campaigns are bound by limitations not applicable to congressional races. Matching grants for contributions from individuals of $250 and less are provided for in presidential primaries, and the total financing is provided from public funds during the general election, unless the candidate opts not to accept it. (Since 1976, only one candidate has chosen to forego public funding: John Connally, a Republican candidate from Texas in the 1980 primaries.) Along with the funds come limitations in campaign spending by state and in the aggregation of all expenditures during the primary period. Again, the reporting of contributions and expenditures requires sophisticated professional assistance. A presidential campaign is usually well equipped to handle the job, but most federal election campaigns rely to some extent on the national party for help. Republicans have been more than willing, and able, to provide campaigns at the presidential level with fundraising lists, as well as software, computer time, and other relevant support.

The greatest impact of the contribution limits, however, has been to leave the political party as the largest single participant in the political process. The closest competitors, in terms of money spent, are those groups which make independent expenditures (expenditures made for or against a candidate for office without consultation with either the candidate or his committee). The National Conservative Political Action Committee (NCPAC), which was by far the largest group making such expenditures, spent $9.7 million independently, advocating the reelection of Ronald Reagan in 1984. This made it the largest single spending group, but the money pales in contrast to what the national party contributed in funds and services (Federal Election Commission, "Independent Expenditure Index" 1985). According to Michael J. Malbin, 85 percent of NCPAC's expenditures went to direct-mail programs, which, though not irrelevant in terms of educating voters, are clearly directed more toward fund raising than influencing public opinion and voting behavior (Malbin 1985). Independent expenditures, and the groups making them, are a controversial topic in their own right, somewhat beyond the scope of this essay, but they have yet to prove themselves significant in the outcome of elections, or in long-term relationships with those in office. What is germane is the relationship of these large-spending groups to the parties in general, and the national parties in particular, a subject we will come to shortly.

The political parties are typically permitted to spend the equivalent of two cents per voter on federal elections. In addition, they can—and do—provide a host of services to the campaigns at or below cost, which far exceed the contributions of any other single group. The most realistic competitor to the services are those organizations with a membership they can turn out to work for a candidate at the local level. Organized labor and the Moral Majority are good examples, but their participation is usually directly, or indirectly, in support of particular candidates rather than the party slate. This may change with the adoption of independent spending by more traditional interests. According to the "Independent Expenditure Index," published by the Federal Election Commission in March of 1987, the 1986 congressional election marked the first time the top independent spenders were *not* the ideological New Right groups, but traditional "special interest" PACs representing such groups as the American Medical Association and the National Association of Realtors.

Party Participation.   In 1976, when the FECA first made its impact both national parties discouraged local party committees from participating in federal elections because the complexities of the law required separate accountings of allocations among candidates and spending in the various races. The 1979 amendments exempted the local parties from reporting requirements for expenditures under $2,000, but the way back toward significant participation proved to be difficult for many reasons, not the least of which was the weakness of the local parties. The RNC spent several million dollars in the 1980 presidential campaign to generate a grass-roots effort, but they did not consider it a success (Campaign Finance Study Group 1982). In 1984 the RNC focused on selected county organizations around the country and believed it to be a more successful effort.

Another easement in the law was a postal subsidy passed in 1978, which enabled the parties to send their mail at the lower rate available to tax-exempt organizations, a rate frequently used by the ideological groups. Given the shift in both parties to direct-mail solicitation, the provision turned out to be an important benefit to the national parties particularly.

The passage of the federal campaign finance law was not directly intended to help the parties. Its main objective was to curb the undue influence of special interests: the eternal goal of political reform. After the first two election cycles (1976 and 1978), when it seemed that the law was hurting the parties, Congress sought to correct the perceived imbalance, again in the interests of limiting the influence of other groups. Although as a nation we have always been ambivalent about the value of the parties, most observers decried the apparent party decline and applauded legislative efforts to forestall the decline. What is interesting is how difficult it has been to reach a consensus on the consequences of the changes that have taken place in the past decade and a half. Most journalists, political scientists, and even politicians believe the strength of the parties ranges somewhere from dead to dying. A minority—generally those scholars who do research in Washington or in the states by talking to politicians and party leaders—have reached a far more optimistic assessment of party strength, but they are still divided on whether or not a strong central party is a good or an evil development. Political life is so complex and depends on so many variables that it encourages the coexistence of antithetical views. For those, like myself, who have been interviewing political activists since the early 1970s, the increases in strength of the national parties between then and now are truly startling.

Judicial Decisions on Party Membership

In the last two decades, the courts have repeatedly held in favor of the national parties over the rights of states and state parties to determine criteria for party membership, primary participation, ballot access, and delegate selection (*William v. Rhodes*, 1968; *Obrien v. Brown*, 1972; *Kusper v. Pontikes*, 1973; *Cousins v. Wigoda*, 1975; and *Democratic Party v. Wisconsin*, 1981). (See Adamany 1984: 71–75.) The impact of these decisions has been to return to the parties much of the autonomy they held prior to the Progressive reforms in the early part of the century. But the autonomy has been returned to a revitalized national party that barely existed in the pre-Progressive era.

NATIONALIZATION: THE IMPLICATIONS

The national parties are essentially professional organizations. They are well financed, mostly through millions of small individual contributions. The law, the technology, and the nature of national politics support the activities of the parties in candidate selection, use of resources to win elections, and, as a result of candidate dependency, using resources to influence public policy. These activities are traditional functions of a party, although for many years American political scientists have tended to emphasize only the parties' role in elections.

Underlying these activities are the coalitions that make up our politics: broad segments of the population and special interest groups. Since the 1960s the political environment has appeared fragmented: candidates were self-selected; interests were all-powerful. The development of strong national parties has brought some measure of cohesion to the scene, but the order that exists is hardly uniform.

The Party versus Candidates: Who's Boss?

In 1976 the Republican National Committee began to intervene in primary elections in support of the candidates it had recruited for office. The behavior of the national party was a departure from the past and marked a turning point in the relationship between the parties and their candidates. Since 1980, the RNC has been prohibited by party rules from intervening unless invited in by the state party, but most national participation has been taken up by the House and Senate campaign committees for Republicans and Democrats. Although somewhat circumscribed by the FECA (a party can contribute no more than the $5,000 that a nonparty committee can contribute during a primary election), the legitimacy and resources these committees provide in federal elections make them the single largest actor in a campaign. The money raised and spent by the Republican Senate Campaign Committee (see page 73) is only a superficial indication of the value of other resources it provides, such as staff or research.

Although the Democratic Party has not been as active in recruiting as the GOP (as the majority party, recruitment is somewhat less critical to the Democrats), in recent years its resources have grown to the point where it, too, has something to offer candidates. In 1984, for instance, the Democratic National Committee actively participated in elections in Nebraska and Idaho (interview: Charles Manatt 1985). This modest effort set a path-breaking precedent for the DNC.

The result of this increased activity has directly and indirectly affected the relationship of the party to its candidates. Political observers have noted an increase in partisan voting in Congress in the past few years. While this increased partisanship could be attributed to the effects of President Reagan's popularity and ideological conservatism, it could also be recognized as the result of increased dependence on party coffers by incumbent members of Congress in both parties.

Under the leadership of Representative Anthony Coelho of California, the Democratic House Campaign Committee became a significant power in campaigning and in congressional decision making in the 1980s. In 1983, Coelho threatened to resign his post if he (and his successors) were not granted a formal role in strategy and legislative decisions. His position was accepted and his success as a fund raiser (moving the committee to direct-mail solicitations and making a strong play for corporate PAC money) has been widely recognized (Farney 1983).

While Coelho's leadership had a major impact on Democratic fund raising and on the Democratic agenda in the House (enabling him to move directly into the House leadership after the 1986 elections), the Republican national party has been even more influential. It spends more money than the Democrats; provides more resource for its candidates; and with its president in the White House, it has had a clearer policy agenda to promote. In 1981, for instance, the GOP spent several million dollars on a public campaign urging people to write their congressmen in support of the Reagan tax plan. Such an active role was unheard of ten years ago.

The consequence of the increased role of the party in the election of candidates and on their behavior in office is that the era of self-selected candidates is coming to a close. Since the federal law places no limitations on how much candidates can spend on their own behalf, wealthy candidates willing to spend large sums (frequently in excess of $1 million) are still around, but now the party can make a choice, and the importance of such party choices grows. The new circumstances have sometimes led to party censure (the case of former Democrat Phil Gramm—who, chastised by the party for lack of support, resigned his seat and ran as a Republican—was the most extreme) but more usually have led to candidates acting as "team players" rather than prima donnas.

The Party versus the Interests

As the late California Democrat Jess Unruh once said, "Money is the mother's milk of politics." It can come from the candidate himself, individual supporters (now limited to $1,000 contributions per election), from the party, and from the interests. The age of candidate-centered politics coincided with the perception that the interests were king and the parties dead. The bulk of a federal candidate's funds came from individual donations. According to Gary Jacobson, the percentage of House candidate funds from *individual contributors* has declined from 73 percent in 1974 to 63 percent in 1982, and for Senate seats increased from 76 percent in 1974 to 81 percent in the 1982 election (Jacobson 1984: 39).

To some extent, the proportion of individual contributors may be skewed because some percentage comes from direct-mail solicitation, and the list for such appeals is likely drawn from either an interest or the party. We cannot tell, however, how much comes from which source. *PAC contributions* during the same period ranged from 17 to 31 percent in the House and 11 to 18 percent in the Senate (Jacobson 1984). But this, too, is somewhat deceiving because of the role of the party in directing PAC contributions to candidates. [According to FEC reports, PAC contributions in 1986 grew to 44 percent of all funding for House candidates, and 26 percent of funding for Senate candidates. On average, incumbent House members received more than 7 times more PAC money than did their challengers.—*Eds.*]

Jacobson's figures on *party contributions* range from 4 to 6 percent in the House and from 1 to 6 percent in the Senate, but do not include party expenditures on behalf of candidates, and even Jacobson draws attention to the changing role of the party: "The most striking departures in the financing of the 1980 and 1982 elections are not captured by an analysis of contributions given directly to candidates. They lie, rather, in the unprecedented amounts of money spent by political parties (particularly Republicans) and in the sharp increase spent by groups independent of any campaign" (Jacobson 1984). *Independent spending* at the congressional level doubled, in fact, between 1980 and 1984, going from $2.3 million to $4.5 million (Kayden and Mahy 1985) but we will come to that later.

Clearly, the numbers reported do not tell the whole story. The dramatic changes are to be found in the nuances of these proportions and in the evidence we can compile in interviews and observation.

The participation of interests in politics is not new. What is new is that campaign contributions are disclosed, and we can get some sense of the proportionate relationship one candidate has to some interests vis-à-vis another candidate's relationship. Some observers are appalled by the process (Drew 1983). Others argue that the disclosure provisions of the law have simply opened our eyes to what probably went on before (Malbin 1985). The fear is that the interests are more powerful than the parties: there are more formally organized interest groups today than there used to be (Schlozman and Tierney 1983); they are centralized; they have more funds and greater sophistication in their use of funds; and they can act in concert. Some believe they have all but replaced the party by engaging "in broader forms of political activity, including political education, grassroots lobbying, coalition building, and electoral funding through political action committees" (Conlan 1985).

The evidence used to support these conclusions typically depends on the published data from the Federal Election Commission. But as Jacobson points out, it is a mistake to rely on the figures alone because of the nonmonetary (and unreported) contributions from the party. Another problem is that it does not show the relationship between the party and the PACs. Both major parties actively encourage political action committees to make donations to candidates they are apt to find sympathetic to their interests. In the mid to late 1970s—early days in the campaign finance reform era—the GOP devoted resources to mobilizing corporate PACs, only to discover that they tended to give as much, or more, to Democrats as they did to Republican candidates: the majority of such PACs simply wanted to back likely winners, most of whom were Democratic incumbents. (See the essay by Chapman and Palda in this volume.)

Even at the state level, which I would argue is similar organizationally to the national party (lacking only in the degree of resources), one state legislative leader described the parties as "clearinghouses" for PAC contributions (confidential interview: April 1985). According to state campaign finance expert Ruth Jones, political parties have played a traditional role in electoral campaigns by aggregating and articulating multiple interests and providing party-nominated candidates with the resources necessary to wage campaigns. Although the contemporary role of parties has been the subject of considerable debate, the concept of *party* remains central to state elections, and political party organizations are certainly involved in the electoral process (Jones 1984). It does not take much imagination to project the state experience to Washington, the home of both the national interests and the parties.

Parties, almost by definition, seek to form majorities capable of sustaining credibility for governance. Interests rarely, if ever, represent majorities. Some may be more dominant than others, but the impetus to organize comes from fear that the majority voice will dominate. Coalitions of interests which would make a majority are difficult to mount and sustain over a period of time because of the narrowness of their goals and the changing saliency of their concern in the public mind.

The most effective recent coalition has been the New Right, which has brought together those concerned with abortion, prayer in the schools, the Panama Canal Treaty, and so on. It appears to be one of the laws of political life that any conscious change begets unexpected and, usually, unattractive consequences. The strongest of the groups which make up the New Right were originally organized by Republican Party professionals. They were concerned that the Watergate scandals had so decimated their ranks that the GOP would have no weapon to counter labor's support of the Democratic Party. They organized groups such as NCPAC and started them on the way (interview: Stewart 1984). At least since 1978, chairmen of the RNC have been wary and often hostile to these groups, although the New Right would appear to have achieved, in money at least, what its founders wanted: it spent as much money in the 1984 presidential election year on behalf of Republican candidates as labor spent on behalf of Democratic candidates.

The problem the GOP faces with the New Right is that its activities may place a higher priority on issue purity than winning elections. It is a conflict inherent in politics based on firmly held beliefs. Several years ago, the Moral Majority "took over" the Republican party in Alaska, and it appeared as if the danger existed of similar actions elsewhere. But party takeovers per se are characteristic of American politics. We frequently look to the quadrennial presidential election as the time for such actions, as the advocates of various candidates vie for position within the state parties—as a preliminary step to the national nominating convention. The Young Turks of one election provide new blood to the party organization and frequently stay to become the Old Guard of the next election. Whatever relationship there is between a presidential election and the health of the parties, there is no question that the interest and excitement it generates play a critical role in party revitalization. It would be difficult to distinguish the revitalization of the parties due to candidate allegiance from that due to issue allegiance, especially in the long run.

The main objective of a political party in our system is winning elections. Those who would place any other goal above that either tend to drop out, or to change their views, becoming more conciliatory toward others. Continual losses at the polls leave the party leadership ripe for another takeover, especially if there is a chance that another candidate might win. Parties which are so much in the minority that they do not stand a chance of winning may be able to afford the luxury of retaining their issue purity; however, both major parties have become more competitive around the nation in recent years and a contest is likely to draw them toward the middle as victory is sensed within reach.

The New Right appears to have been in trouble since 1985. It does not have the vast amounts of money it once did, and it has not succeeded in capturing the Republican Party. On the contrary, the GOP appears to have tamed it, at least to some extent, although RNC Chairman Frank Fahrenkopf still kept at arm's length from their leaders and acknowledged meeting the Reverend Jerry Falwell (leader of the Moral Majority) only once (interview: April 25, 1985). Because the New Right is essentially antiestablishment in nature (compared to organized labor, for instance), coming into the Republican fold will be fraught with difficulty as long as the ideology comes first. But as they become socialized to politics, it seems just as likely that those who became active through the New Right will switch their loyalty from the interest to the party because, in the long run, what motivates politicians is power, not specific issues.

NATIONALIZATION VERSUS FEDERALIZATION

Some argue that the Republican Party has become a national organization because of the tremendous resources in Washington that have forced the rest of the party to accept its authority along with its money. The Democrats, in contrast, have developed a more federal structure because of their delegate selection rules and "national character" (Wekkin 1984: 1). There appears to be little controversy surrounding the first assertion about the GOP. Wekkin cites several political scientists who have expressed similar views, including John Bibby, David Adamany, and M. Margaret Conway. With the possible exception of those in the field who are still decrying the death of the parties and the age of self-selected candidates, most serious scholars who have looked at the numbers have accepted the fact that all that money must make a difference.

The more interesting debate, then, surrounds the Democrats. According to the advocates of the federalist position, the delegate selection and party charter require "intraparty interactions," and therefore it is at least a more federated structure than that found in the GOP and than what we would consider a nationalized system (Wekkin 1984).

The arguments may not be inconsistent with each other. The major difference between the two views is that those of us who are looking at the professional party—the resources, the staffing, the programs of outreach—see a national system, and those who are looking at the activist party (a group usually more visible in the Democratic Party) see interaction and federalism. The reason the Democrats do not appear to be nationalized is that they have not had the funds or the professional staff to compete with the Republicans. The reasons the Republicans do not appear federalized is that their professionalism is so splashy and they do not always have the volunteers—or the interest groups which could provide volunteers—at the grass-roots level.

If this line of argument is correct, the perceptions would change if the Democrats had the money possessed by the Republicans. And that, according to the prediction of their direct-mail director, is precisely what will happen by the end of this decade (interview: Frank O'Brien 1985). They still have a long way to go: the RNC raised $83 million in 1986, compared to $17 million raised by the DNC that year (Edsall 1987).

Under the leadership of the Democratic National Committee Chairman, Charles Manatt, the Democratic Party took giant steps toward becoming the kind of organization found in the GOP. Programs were emulated (a Republican effort to attract young community leaders was called the "Concord Program" by Republican National Committee Chairman Bill Brock in the mid-1970s; a similar Democratic effort was called the "Lexington Program" by Manatt a decade later) (Schram 1982). Technological applications were emulated, and in some cases improved upon; and for the first time since this writer has been interviewing party personnel, a sense of professionalism pervades the headquarters.

It is difficult to overstate the dramatic nature of this change in the DNC. In the Carter years, there was a 100 percent staff turnover during each of the first two years of his tenure. Carter was probably the most antiparty president we have had since George Washington, but the average previous tenure was probably no more than two years for most of the staff. Party staff appointments were typically made on the basis of patronage for those who did not quite qualify for federal appointments. Each new chairman swept house, bringing in a whole new set of longtime personal associates and friends.

It was not until Manatt borrowed the money to invest in a direct-mail program that would put the party on an equivalent financial base to the GOP—and hired people who knew something about direct mail and modern campaign technology—that things changed. Perhaps most significant of all, a good portion of the staff survived the next change of chairmen. Most of the administrative staff, and many of the key professionals, remained in place under the next chairman, Paul Kirk.

Since 1980, the ratio of money raised between the parties has generally declined from 1:12 to 1:3, rising to 1:4 in 1986 and falling again to 1:3 ratio in mid-1987, when federal reporting suggested the impact of the Iran/Contra scandal and the revelation of large consulting contracts to party fund raisers probably weakened Republican fundraising efforts (FEC 1985; Edsall 1987). The ratio is only part of the financial story because the differences in campaign spending were always more apparent than real. Democrats usually outspend Republicans in congressional elections; it is just that most supporters give their money to the candidate and not to the party. Republicans have traditionally relied far more heavily on their party than Democrats have on theirs. Without going into the arguments for and against the giving pattern in the past, it is sufficient to note that the current political environment (law, technology, etc.) makes it more efficient to give to the party, and that is beginning to be seen even in the Democratic Party.

If the argument is made that national parties are those with the resources to overwhelm every other segment of party structure, then the case can be made that both parties are, or will be, national in nature by the end of the 1980s. How intrusive or coercive such nationalism will be remains to be seen, but parties test their credibility with elections at least every other year. In the end, a national party system will survive if it wins at the polls.

The emergence of national parties comes at the same time as the decline of local parties, but is not causal in the decline. It could be viewed as an organizational adjustment: a restructuring of the organization to fit the current need. Whether the system remains "nationalized" or "federalized" will probably depend on the ultimate source of its power. Most of the causes of national party growth (including the nationalization of issues and communication) would suggest the maturity of this party system will be national.

NATIONAL PARTIES AND PUBLIC OPINION

The party system described in this chapter represents a marked change from the past in terms of organizational structure. The ultimate question any student of party politics must ask, however, is "So what? Does party organization make a difference in how anyone believes or behaves?"

It used to be—in the halcyon days of the 1950s and before—that, if asked, an American would define him or herself by listing religion, ethnic background, region or state, and party identification: "I am a German Lutheran Democrat from Indiana." The response provided information about the values, political orientation, and often the class of the speaker. From it, one could predict a certain amount of behavior, barring extraordinary circumstances. Much of that predictability has declined in the past quarter century; and now, some believe, political predictability (and, by implication, political stability) extends only as far as the next election: "I am a Democrat" means the speaker will probably vote Democratic in November.

Political scientists believe that one of a party's principal functions was providing the framework for understanding political events. Party members were inclined to view the world through the prism of partisanship and believed their views corresponded with the party line. The complexity of political issues and communication being what it is, pollsters frequently discovered that the views were not as compatible as asserted, but, what is important for our purposes, is that the respondents *believed* they were.

As the decline of partisanship was measured through the 1960s and 1970s, that other American virtue—independence—asserted itself and a growing portion of the population described itself as not being bound by a party. "I vote for the man, not the party" was the common cry. Deeper analyses suggested, however, that many of those who described themselves as independents leaned toward one party or the other, and that these "leaners" tended to be as consistent in their voting behavior as party identifiers.

The parties reached their nadir in the late 1960s and early 1970s, as the proportion of independents grew. Confidence in most of our institutions declined, although party identifiers were likely to be more confident than their neighbors (Lipset and Schneider 1983: 101–04). The situation with regard to confidence changed in the 1980s, however, and both partisan identification and confidence increased, at least until the end of the decade when political scandals began erupting in the Reagan administration.

Although the issues of the day are a significant determinant of the confidence, political identification, and partisan strength in the electorate, it nonetheless makes sense to suggest that a strong national party that spends a good part of its resources communicating to supporters and potential supporters will have an impact on public opinion. The political reforms of the past were aimed at the destruction of the power held by party organizations at the local level. To the extent that the reforms were directed at local party machines, they succeeded in irradicating them. At the national level, however, there never had been a strong party organization. This new phenomenon in some ways fills in for the loss of local volunteers (who have disappeared for many reasons beyond "reforms") and in other ways increases the accuracy, if not the intensity, of the communication throughout the structure.

We can trace the rise and fall of organizational resources. We can measure activities and observe crises. When it comes to political opinion formation—including how and why people vote the way they do—we can only speculate. I would argue that the increased communications ability of the parties, particularly to supporters and potential supporters through the mail, telephone, media advertising, and professional staff at the national, state, and sometimes local levels, has an impact on public opinion.

The positions on issues expressed in these communications are, in fact, considerably clearer than what ordinarily came from a local party representative in the past. The messages are more direct, going from national and state party to the voter, and they are finely tuned, addressed to everything market research can tell the party about the economic and social status of the recipients. They are meant to have impact. The communications account, in part, I would argue, for the greater issue coherence among Republicans, particularly when it comes to foreign policy and defense issues.

If we cannot measure the direct correlation between party activity and opinion formation, we can borrow from the experience of fund raisers in other areas who aver that belief follows money: if you can get someone to contribute money to a cause by whatever strategy (e.g., personal appeal from a friend or community leader or at a social occasion) his or her commitment to the cause will increase after the donation. Opinion, in other words, will be formed and focused by the contribution and the attachment the donor has to the contributing act.

The one thing we know with certainty about party activity and growth in the past two decades is that the number of contributors has increased dramatically. The contributors, in turn, will increase their commitment to the party and to the issues described by the party to motivate the contribution in the first place, and each contributor is likely to have an impact on the opinions of those in his or her circle of family, friends, and associates.

There are times when some issues are more divisive than others, and although parties normally seek to assemble coalitions and represent large, uncontroversial segments of the population, if the issues are significant, in time, one or the other party (in a two-party system) will move to adopt a position. These periods of political upheaval, which we like to think are reflected in significant voter realignments, clearly have a more dramatic impact on public opinion and party identification than does the less sensational work of party loyalists. But such diverse issues are not always in evidence, nor are they necessarily clearly divided up by the parties. In their absence, the work of the parties in opinion formation is the most probable cause of growth in party identity as a first step, and opinions about political issues as a second step.

A recent poll of political attitudes, conducted by the Gallup Organization for Times-Mirror Publications, suggests that Republicans are more issue-coherent as a group, and that they are less likely than Democrats to owe their partisanship to their parentage and historical ties (Gallup 1987: 95–101). This study concludes that "issues seem to play an important role in the movement between parties. In fact, the gains that Republicans have made among white Southerners (the group that has shifted the most) may be partly explained by the issue differences that exist within a single Democratic group—the New Dealers" (i.e., those over 60).

There are many explanations we can offer for this conclusion, not the least of which is the significance of the social issues particularly to this segment of the electorate. But added to the assumption of linkage must be the efforts made by the Republican Party, particularly, to reach out directly to voters on these issues in fundraising appeals through the various communications techniques available to them. In 1987 the Republican National Committee estimated that it received contributions from almost 540,000 donors (this does not include those contributing to the two congressional campaign committees). If these partisans behave the way most donors to causes behave, it suggests that they, in turn, probably represent several million more individuals (family, friends, and associates) who are likely to be influenced by them. The larger the core of true believers, the greater the following.

This is not to say that other factors—the things polls can measure quite accurately—such as socioeconomic status, religion, and ethnicity, are not strong predictors of opinions and partisanship. My argument is only intended to be stretched far enough to make the case that party strength has increased, when measured by organizational resources and behavior, and that one consequence of the improved organizational ability is, and will continue to be, an increase in the impact of parties on public opinion.

CHAPTER 5

Opinion Formation and Opinion Change in Ballot Proposition Campaigns[1]

David B. Magleby

INTRODUCTORY NOTE

Referenda differ from elections of candidates in that the positions of political parties are not explicitly associated with the questions on the ballot. Indeed, the parties themselves often do not take official positions on the

[1]Many of the data analyzed in this paper were provided by private polling firms who conducted surveys for media clients or one side in a campaign. I appreciate the willingness of these individuals and firms to permit me to use their data. Data were provided by the following sources:

California: The Field Institute, *The California Poll,* provided by the State Data Program, Survey Research Center, University of California, Berkeley; the *Los Angeles Times Poll,* provided by the Roper Center, University of Connecticut, Storrs; and the Rand Corporation, Santa Monica.

Colorado: Research Services Incorporated, Denver; the *Denver Post*/KCNC Television Tracking Polls, provided by Talmey Associates of Boulder—a random statewide telephone sampling of registered voters from October 6–November 2, 1986.

Florida: Florida State University Poll, Policy Studies Program, Florida State University, Tallahassee.

Massachusetts: The Massachusetts Poll, provided by the *Boston Globe* and Research Analysis, Boston; Becker Polls, provided by the *Boston Herald-American* and Becker Research Corporation; and the WBZ-TV Poll, provided by Decision Research Corporation, Wellesley Hills, Mass.

Michigan and Ohio: Market Opinion Research, Detroit, Mich.

Utah: KBYU and Utah Colleges Exit Poll, Department of Political Science, Brigham Young University.

The original collectors of these data are, of course, not responsible for the analysis or interpretations presented here.

Research support for this project was provided by the College of Family, Home and Social Science of Brigham Young University. Research assistance was provided by James Lyon, Greg Matis, Brad McLaws, and Martin Nichols. Don Norton, Malia Howland, and Candice Nelson read and commented on the manuscript.

questions. In such circumstances, voters are forced to make decisions regarding the questions at hand without knowing the stand of the political organizations with which most still identify. Consequently many are left without an adequate framework for understanding or making up their minds about the questions at issue.

In this chapter David Magleby explores the implications of such circumstances by reviewing recent ballot questions in several states. To begin with, Magleby finds a pattern of "drop off": that is, fewer electors express their opinions in referenda than vote for candidates when the same election includes both ballot questions and candidates. Furthermore, those who do vote in referenda report making up their minds later than they normally do regarding votes for candidates. Finally, Magleby argues that by dint of superior resources, particularly money for advertising and research, the opposition can usually defeat a proposition by defining the issue negatively or by creating enough confusion to trigger a negative reaction.

Voters' opinions are by no means infinitely malleable. Magleby points out that on certain questions, such as the public opinion regarding capital punishment, there are "standing opinions" that are virtually impervious to change. Nonetheless, he concludes that, because of the greater number of initially "undecided voters" in referenda, the campaign is far more important for determining the outcome of ballot propositions than for contests among candidates for public office.

The Editors

When and how public opinion is translated into public policy and electoral choice are important questions to political scientists. In many cases where efforts are undertaken to change public opinion, however, there is no direct effect on public policy or electoral choice. But in initiatives and referenda there is a direct and immediate consequence.

Ballot propositions can be placed on the ballot by the state legislature or as a result of direct legislation. All the states except Delaware require that constitutional changes be ratified by the voters in a referendum. But 26 states go beyond this requirement and permit voters to circulate petitions seeking enactment of a new law or constitutional amendment (the initiative) or the overturning of an action by the legislature (the popular referendum). The initiative can take one of two forms: the *direct initiative* permits citizens to draft laws, and in some states constitutional amendments, and then place those directly on the ballot if they can generate sufficient signatures. Among the states most identified with the direct initiative are California, Colorado, and Michigan. Each of these states has examples of opinion change which will be examined in this chapter. A smaller number of states provide the *indirect initiative;* here citizens may circulate petitions regarding laws they seek to have enacted. Once sufficient signatures have been gathered, these proposals must be submitted to the state legislature. Only if the legislature does not enact the proposed law can the petitioners then gather additional signatures and place their measure on the ballot. The state most often identified with this form of indirect legislation is Massachusetts, a state for which we will also examine opinion change on ballot propositions. In this chapter I will examine primarily initiatives because these measures have generated more survey data.

IMPORTANCE OF BALLOT PROPOSITION VOTING

Americans vote more often and for more offices than voters in any other democracy. With so many candidate contests, it is not surprising that elections are generally thought of in terms of such contests. But the United States is also among the countries that vote on ballot propositions most frequently (Magleby 1985). Every general election year, Americans decide scores of ballot issues.

Voting on ballot propositions is also important because it can set the agenda of American politics. The most visible issue decided by voters in recent memory was California's Proposition 13, the Jarvis/Gann property-tax reduction initiative of 1978. The vote on this initiative stimulated speculation that America, not just California, was facing a tax revolt. Proposition 13 helped spur a variety of movements that proposed constitutional amendments to set federal spending limits, require a balanced federal budget, or index the tax brackets; and voters passed judgment on 33 tax-cut or spending-limitation measures in the next two years, 14 of which were adopted.[2]

Ballot propositions have not been limited to taxes and government spending. In recent years voters have cast ballots on topics as diverse as the Equal Rights Amendment, the nuclear freeze, the safety of nuclear power, legalized gambling, abortion funding, and state lotteries; permitting nondentists to fit dentures (Idaho, 1984); permitting self-service gasoline stations (Oregon, 1984); designating English as the official state language (California, 1986; Florida, 1988); and regulating cable television decency (Utah, 1984). Since the mid-1970s, there has been a resurgence in use of the initiative process and a greater awareness of its importance. This trend has accelerated since 1978.[3]

---

[2]During the 1978 and 1979 legislative sessions, 37 states restricted sales tax collections; income and sales tax cuts alone surpassed $4 billion (Tax Review: 1979).

[3]The 1978 California vote generated interest in the initiative process as well; virtually every state that did not have the process had legislation introduced to establish it.

PUBLIC OPINION AND VOTING BEHAVIOR IN THE CONTEXT OF REFERENDUM VOTING

Voting on ballot propositions places voters in a distinctive decision-making role. Effective participation requires them to be aware of the proposition and to have or to form an opinion on it. *Issue awareness* and *opinion formation,* as will be demonstrated, require more information and involvement than does voter decision making in a candidate contest. This chapter will also clarify patterns of *opinion change.* In particular, I will examine why voters who have formed opinions tend to change from a position of support for a proposition to one of opposition. Finally, I will examine the circumstances under which *opinion reinforcement* occurs; that is, when the campaign serves to strengthen or affirm voters' initial opinions. In most elections, partisanship and public opinion on candidates have been found to play more significant parts in the decision-making process than have opinions on issues (Campbell et al. 1960; Abramson 1983: 72–73). On ballot propositions, however, candidate appeal is irrelevant, partisanship is less important, and public opinion on current public policy issues assumes greater significance (Magleby 1984: 173–79). In this context the vote can be presumed to reflect the public opinion of the voters on the ballot question as the voter understands it. Voting on ballot propositions also differs from answering conventional public opinion polls, for turning out to vote on a measure requires more effort and thus presumably entails more serious consideration than does responding to a survey interview.

Nonetheless, the fact remains that the results on ballot propositions reflect public opinion only on what the voters understand the question to be. A proposition ostensibly on nuclear power-plant safety may in fact be more a measure of public opinion on jobs and energy; or a proposition restricting smoking in public places may measure opinion on government regulation. The typical ballot question is worded so technically that few are able to read and understand it without advanced education (Magleby 1984: 118–19). Thus the question is generally defined by the news media, and more importantly, by paid advertising (Magleby 1984: 130–39). This fact only underscores the importance of the campaign as an effort to shape or change public opinion.

The study of opinion formation, reinforcement, and change on ballot propositions thus affords a politically relevant and theoretically interesting context in which to study public opinion and voting behavior. In this chapter I will examine which voters have opinions on ballot measures, and I will assess the extent to which opinions on ballot issues change during a campaign. Are there issues where opinion change is less likely? Does opinion change normally occur in both directions, "yes" to "no" and "no" to "yes"? Or is it disproportionately unidirectional? Using data on recent propositions in California, Colorado, and Michigan, I will test alternative explanations for opinion change. I will also contrast opinion change on ballot propositions with that found in statewide candidate contests. We are fortunate to have ample survey data with which to evaluate public opinion and opinion change in these contexts.

AWARENESS OF BALLOT PROPOSITIONS

Writing some years ago, V. O. Key (1961: 47) said, "For most Americans, issues of politics are not of central concern." Others have come to the same conclusion (Pomper 1972: 415; Campbell et al. 1960: 400). While these studies have explored the topic of voter interest generally or in the context of candidate elections, relatively few studies have been done on how interested the voters are in ballot propositions (Magleby 1984).

In an important study of local (city and county) ballot propositions, Howard Hamilton (1970: 133) concludes that "manifestly most of the public paid little attention to the campaign." Hamilton's study is helpful in demonstrating the broad contours of public interest in a proposition election, but he does not address the question of what kinds of citizens are interested in this mode of politics. Are the same citizens who are more interested in candidate elections—the well educated, those of high socioeconomic status, and partisans—also more interested statewide propositions? Using data on Florida elections I examined these issues and found:

> Persons who are interested in one form of election are also interested in the other; almost all of those who are very or somewhat interested in one type of election are very or somewhat interested in the other. Voters who are not interested in candidate elections are also not interested in ballot propositions. (Magleby 1984: 125)

The Florida data also demonstrate that the less educated, non-white, and socioeconomically less advantaged strata are more interested in candidate contests than either in propositions or politics generally. Indeed, a distinguishing feature of many proposition elections is the comparatively large proportion of voters who drop off—turn out to the polls but do not vote in all candidate races or on all ballot propositions (Magleby 1984: 83–90).

An indication of the comparative interest levels most voters have for candidate and proposition elections becomes evident when they make up their minds about how they will vote. Table 5–1 compares the time of the vote choice for two candidate elections and two proposition elections.

Voters are much more likely to decide on their votes early in the campaign for candidates, including candidate primary elections. Over 60 percent of those who voted in the June 1980 primary election reported that they knew their candidate choice for president six months before, and almost half the voters had decided their gubernatorial vote months

TABLE 5–1   Time of Voting Decision for California Candidate and
Proposition Elections

	Vote for Candidates		Vote on Issues	
	1978 Governor General Election	1980 President Primary Election	1978 Proposition 13 Property Tax	1976 Proposition 15 Nuclear Safeguards
Election day or last weekend	11%	8%	14%	25%
Past week	11	5	15	13
2–3 weeks	11	9		18
4–5 weeks	12	8	26	14
2–3 months	8	4	44	21
4–6 months	7	3		6
6 months +	31	63		4

SOURCE: CBS News, *Los Angeles Times* Poll no. 6, June 6, 1978; *Los Angeles Times* Poll no. 12, November 7, 1978; *Los Angeles Times* Poll no. 30, June 3, 1980; and the Survey of Attitudes on Nuclear Power, Rand Corporation, Santa Monica, Calif., May–June 1976.

before the 1978 general election. In contrast, proposition voters decide much later. One-fourth of all June 1976 California voters decided their vote on Proposition 15, the nuclear safeguards initiative, on the last weekend.

To take some other examples, over one-third of Utah voters in 1982 indicated in a statewide exit poll that they had decided their vote on Proposition 1, a legislatively initiated taxation measure, over the last weekend or on election day, and 19 percent decided their vote on election day. This compared to 7 percent who decided their U.S. Senate vote on election day. In 1982, Michigan voters decided three controversial ballot proposals regarding public utilities. Despite a multimillion dollar campaign, more than 40 percent of those who voted on two of these measures had not made up their minds about how to vote until election day or a few days before. On all these measures, fully four out of five Michigan voters had not decided how to vote until October or later, something quite uncommon in partisan candidate contests.

Because ballot propositions often deal with complex issues, it is important to differentiate between voter knowledge about the broad issue involved and knowledge about the proposition itself. Even with widespread coverage during the course of the campaign, very few voters will become knowledgeable about a subject as complex as nuclear power during the course of an election campaign. For instance, in their analysis of voting on California's Proposition 15, the nuclear safeguards initiative, the Henslers (1979: 70) estimate that only "between 10 and 33 percent of the voters were well enough informed to make educated judgments about the advantages and disadvantages of nuclear power." Just as voters may not know the broad subject area of the proposition, they may also not know or understand the specific provisions of the measure. What they may know about is how the proposition has been presented in the media, especially through television advertising, often an incomplete and inaccurate representation of the proposition. On propositions that generate little media coverage, such as California's 1972 Proposition 2, a health sciences bond, one-third of those who turned out to vote did not remember having heard anything about the proposition before the election. This was true despite the fact that all registered voters had been mailed the *Voter's Handbook* describing the proposition and arguments for and against it.

Expecting voters to be minimally aware of a proposition is another matter. One measure of voter awareness is the response to this question: "Have you heard anything about an initiative, Proposition X, that will be on next month's statewide ballot having to do with _____?" Table 5–2 presents the proportion of registered California voters who indicated they had heard of propositions in preelection polls from 1978 to 1986.

In the first poll, typically taken about three months before the election, an average of 36 percent of the registered voters interviewed reported that they have seen or heard about the proposition; by the last preelection poll, the average is up to 70 percent. The figures in Table 5–2 display this upward trend. On some propositions, however, the last survey, taken a few days before the election, reveals that more than half of the registered voters still had not heard of the proposition. Even on very controversial or highly publicized propositions, large proportions of the electorate report not having heard anything about the proposition. For example, data from a September survey on Colorado's 1986 Amendment 4 show that only 24 percent of the registered voters were aware of the amendment; and among those who indicated they were very likely to vote, the number rose to only 30 percent.

Education best explains awareness of the proposition, with only 8 percent of those with less than a high school education aware of the measure, compared with 43 percent of those with schooling beyond the bachelor's degree. The same strong relationship between education and awareness is found in an October survey on this amendment. By this time, 19 percent of those with less than a high school education were aware of the proposition, but 61 percent of those with graduate work were aware. Overall, the relationship between education and awareness is strong and statistically significant.

The California data lead to similar conclusions. Education is strongly

TABLE 5–2   California Voter Awareness

Propositions	Time of Awareness				

1986 General	*August*	*Early October*	*Late October*
No. 65 Toxins	35%	54%	78%
No. 64 AIDS	46	56	76
No. 63 English	65	77	76
No. 62 Local tax	8	11	47
No. 61 Salaries	43	50	77

1986 Primary	*March*	*Early May*	*Late May*
No. 51 Pockets	28%	75%	90%

1984 General	*Early September*	*Early October*	*Late October*
No. 36 Property Tax	55%	80%	84%
No. 37 Lottery	63	85	93
No. 39 Reapportionment	27	46	67
No. 38 English	57	63	73
No. 40 Camp spending	29	28	49
No. 41 Public assistance	12	40	62

1984 Primary	*Early February*	*Early April*	*Mid May*
No. 24 Legislative reform	33%	34%	38%

1980 General	*Mid July*	*Early September*	*Mid October*
No. 8 Canal		73%	69%
No. 10 Smoking	65%	56	93

1980 Primary	*Early April*	*Mid May*
No. 9 Income tax	78%	82%
No. 11 Surtax	48	49
No. 10 Rent	49	58

1978 General	*Mid August*	*Mid September*
No. 5 Smoking	72%	95%
No. 6 Homosexual teachers	65	84
No. 7 Death penalty	48	59

1978 Primary	*Early May*	*Late May*
No. 8 Home tax	63%	93%

	Early February	*Late February*	*Early April*	*Early May*	*Late May*
No. 13 Property tax	58%	51%	76%	94%	99%

SOURCE: California Polls, Field Research Corporation, San Francisco, Calif., provided by the State Data Program, University of California, Berkeley. Question: Have you heard anything about an initiative, Proposition X, that will be on next month's statewide ballot having to do with ———?

associated with voter awareness of ballot propositions. On some measures, the range is as wide as or wider than that found in Colorado. A September 1984 poll shows that 34 percent of those with schooling beyond a bachelor's degree were aware of Proposition 39, a reapportionment proposal, while only 6 percent of those with less than a high school education were aware. The late October survey on the same proposition shows an 83 percent awareness for those with schooling beyond a bachelor's degree, with an awareness of only 45 percent among those with less than a high school education. Although age is also positively related to voter awareness—the September 1984 poll on ballot proposition 38, the English language initiative, shows awareness at 91 percent among those 65 and above, while only 64 percent for those aged 18 to 25—the relationship is weaker after controlling for the effects of education.

On some ballot propositions, like the California vote on open housing in 1964 (Wolfinger and Greenstein 1968) and the 1978 vote on property taxes, Proposition 13, there was a very high level of voter awareness. The better educated were more confident that they knew about the measures. The question of voter informedness was put directly to Colorado voters, who were asked in a survey, "When you vote on ballot issues, in general do you feel very informed, somewhat informed, or not too informed about the specifics of the issue?" More than three in four Colorado voters considered themselves either somewhat or not too informed about ballot propositions. Among the less educated and lower-income voters, most felt they were either not too informed or not at all informed when voting on ballot issues. These findings are consistent with the conclusion that direct legislation is a political process best understood and used by those voters who are better educated or better off financially (Magleby 1984: 103–19).

The importance of education to awareness was confirmed using a categorical model.[4] In the seven 1984 California propositions we exam-

---

[4]We used CatMod in SAS, a widely accepted tool to assess the relative importance of several categorical independent variables. The table below summarizes the significant *p*-values for the independent variables in each of the seven propositions.

Categorical Modeling Significance Scores
for Demographics and Awareness

Aware	Education	Income	Party	Age	Race	Sex	Religion	Time
APROP24	.0126			.0001	.0120	.0001		.0001
APROP36	.0417	.0001		.0001	.0048	.0060	.1087	.0001
APROP37	.0098	.0268			.0519			.0001
APROP38	.0001	.0086		.0001	.0153			.0001
APROP39	.0001	.0012		.0001	.0005	.0001		.0001
APROP40	.0153			.0001				.0001
APROP41	.0287	.0936		.0380			.0702	.0001

ined, time is the most significant determinant of awareness, strongly supporting our previous conclusions that awareness rises over time. Among the demographic variables, however, education ranked first with respect to awareness in each. Moreover, education has a linear relationship to awareness. Age also was significantly related in all but one case, but age appears to have a quadratic or logarithmic relationship to awareness. Awareness is highest among older people, but drops off among the very old. Religion, race, and gender were less frequently related to awareness, and party had no statistically significant relationship at all.

Having an Opinion on Ballot Propositions

A necessary precondition of having an opinion on a ballot measure is awareness of the issue. But among those who have seen or heard about a proposition, not everyone will have an opinion. The extent to which voters are undecided is a second factor in understanding opinion formation and opinion change. Data provided by Market Opinion Research on the 1982 Michigan elections reveal that voters were consistently more likely to indicate that they were undecided on ballot propositions than on the candidate races for governor and U.S. Senate. In the late September polls 11 percent indicated that they were undecided in their vote for U.S. senator (Riegle [D] versus Ruppe [R]), and 14 percent were undecided in their vote for governor (Blanchard [D] versus Headlee [R] and Tish [I]). In contrast, 78 percent were undecided in their vote on Measure D, and more than 90 percent were undecided about Measures G and H. (See the Appendix to this chapter for a description of these propositions.) In the last preelection poll, conducted only two days before the election, 10 percent were undecided in the U.S. Senate race, 11 percent in the race for governor; in contrast, 34 percent, 51 percent, and 60 percent were undecided on the respective ballot propositions. These comparatively high proportions of undecided voters are even more dramatic when one considers the large sums of money that had been spent on the referenda, especially by those opposed to Proposition D.[5]

Voters in candidate elections can use the simplifying device of party labels, which allows them to act where party cues are available without fully knowing the particulars of an election. But on statewide propositions the party cue is absent. Moreover, in candidate elections, voters can use

---

[5]The total campaign spending on Proposition D was $4,439,265, of which 99 percent was spent on the "no" side. This amount far exceeded the total spending in the U.S. Senate race, $2,586,108, or the total spending in the governor's race, $2,453,454. In the candidate races the spending was much more evenly divided.

candidate name identification and a more generalized judgment of the candidate in deciding their vote. Voters face a more complicated task in deciding how to vote on propositions because parties rarely take stands on propositions, and elections rarely focus on the individual attributes of proposition advocates. In short, information costs are much higher for voters in the ballot-measure context. As a result, when it actually comes to voting, as many as 25 percent of those who turn out fail to vote on some ballot propositions (Magleby 1984: 83–95).

In California, cross-sectional data on vote intentions exist over a much longer period of time, permitting more systematic analysis of patterns of decision and indecision on ballot propositions. Since 1960 there have been 48 ballot propositions in which the California Poll has asked comparable questions about awareness and voter intentions in at least two preelection polls. In roughly three out of four ballot measures studied (38 of 48) the pattern of voter decision making is one of growing indecision as the campaign proceeds, with a precipitous drop in the proportion of undecided only near election day. This tendency is not limited to any segment of the population, but rather appears to occur across all segments of education, age, party, race, or gender. This pattern is very different from that found in most candidate races where the proportion of undecided voters changes far less, and in fact tends to decline as election day approaches. The difference is explained in large part by the fact that from the beginning voters can use partisan and candidate cues to simplify their candidate voting choice.

The finding that the proportion of "undecideds" rises for most ballot propositions may be the result of a phenomenon of instant or snap opinions. Perhaps because California voters are called upon to decide as many as 20 or more ballot measures in both the primary and general elections, they are used to giving instant or snap responses about them. But even though people are willing to state an opinion on a ballot proposition several weeks or months before an election, these opinions are not deeply rooted. What typically seems to happen is that as the campaign starts up and media coverage begins, information for and (especially) against the measure surfaces, and voters become uncertain or undecided in their opinions. This only underscores the opportunity for opinion formation, reinforcement, and change present in this electoral context.

Awareness of ballot propositions is correlated with education, and to a lesser extent, age, and gender. Because of the complexity of the issues and the nature of the campaigns, it is not surprising that less educated, younger, and minority (especially Hispanic) voters, do not fully participate in this process. Having an opinion or intended vote on ballot propositions, however, appears to have no correlation whatsoever with any of the aforementioned demographics. Having laid this foundation we can now turn to the topic of opinion change.

PATTERNS OF OPINION CHANGE

There are two quite different patterns in the stability of voting intentions on ballot propositions. The first pattern, which I have previously
called *standing opinions* (Magleby 1984: 170–73), refers to propositions
on which the aggregate of voters' opinions changes very little throughout
the campaign (see Table 5–3). Voters seem to have their minds made up
on such issues as the death penalty, legalized use of marijuana, and En-

TABLE 5–3   Ballot Propositions with Standing Opinions

Proposition	Yes	No	Undecided/ Dropoff	Number of Respondents
California 1972 General Proposition 17: Death penalty				
10–14 August	65%	27%	8%	471
29 Sept.–7 Oct.	62	26	12	1,113
30 Oct.–1 Nov.	62	31	7	1,355
Actual vote	63	30	6	8,595,950
California 1972 General Proposition 19: Marijuana legalization				
10–14 August	31%	63%	5%	471
29 Sept.–7 Oct.	32	58	7	1,114
30 Sept.–1 Nov.	35	63	7	1,334
Actual vote	32	63	5	8,595,950
Massachusetts 1986 General Question 1: Equal Rights Amendment				
Pre–Labor Day**	63%	13%	24%	500
Early October*	75	15	10	600
October*	59	12	29	500
Actual vote	56	37	8	2,594,262
California 1986 General Proposition 63: English as official language				
August	72%	22%	6%	1,028
Early October	74	17	9	1,023
Late October	66	25	9	701
Actual vote	67	25	8	7,617,142

SOURCE: California data are from the California Poll, Field Research Corporation, San Francisco,
California, and the State Data Program, University of California, Berkeley. Massachusetts data
marked by an asterisk (*) are from the Massachusetts Poll, and where marked by (**) are from the
WBZ-TV Poll; all other Massachusetts data are from the Becker Polls.

glish as the official language. Propositions on these subjects pass or fail on the basis of voters' standing opinions on the issues. Using the California Poll data since 1960 I found standing opinions in roughly 14 percent of the propositions with at least two preelection polls. In another 12 percent both the "yes" and "no" sides rose during the campaign; opinions here were not as stable, but the shift in opinion was consistent with the initial distribution. Part of the explanation for this phenomenon was the unusual occurrence of the proportion of undecided voters declining over the course of the campaign.

But on most propositions for which we have data over time, there is an instability in opinion and a demonstrated pattern of opinion change. Excluding the cases where there were standing opinions, the California Poll data reveal that in roughly three out of four cases there was a pattern of "yes" votes falling and "no" votes rising. This tendency can result in a reversal (53 percent); a decline in "yes" support but not enough for a reversal (12 percent); or a divergence of "no" from "yes" votes if the "no" side started out ahead (12 percent). There were three unusual cases (6 percent) where the "no" side declined during the campaign, either resulting in a reversal or in convergence.

Further substantiation of the pattern of opinion change described above was found when we performed logistic regressions on the proportion of "yes," "no," and "undecided" voting intentions on the California propositions over time.[6] The logit analysis supports the finding that "yes" votes fall ($p < .02$) and "no" votes rise ($p < .006$) as election day approaches (see Table 5–4). However in the final preelection polls and in the actual voting the proportion of undecideds drops as the election nears. Because preelection polls are different from actual voting situations in that the actual voting situation seems to preclude the undecided option, we tested to see whether there was evidence that the "undecided" moved more in the direction of a "no" vote than a "yes" vote. We found that the rate of declining "yes" vote is constant, but the slope of the "no" vote rises, meaning, we assume, that at the last minute, undecideds shift overwhelmingly to "no" votes.

We tested for differences between primary and general elections. There is no significant difference in the pattern of "no" votes rising in these two contexts. In primaries the "undecided" vote rises faster and the "yes" vote falls more slowly than in general elections. This difference is statistically significant and is explained, we speculate, by the different decision-making context of general elections.

---

[6]The logistic regression models on proportions of "yes", "no", and "undecided" over time were specified for each of these propositions. Details of the analysis are available from the author upon request.

TABLE 5-4   Ballot Propositions with Opinion Reversals

Proposition	Yes Vote	No Vote	Undecided/ Dropoff	Number of Respondents
California 1972 General Proposition 14: Tax reduction				
10–14 August	67%	26%	7%	561
29 Sept.–7 Oct.	40	20	40	1,113
30 Oct.–1 Nov.	24	51	25	834
Actual vote	31	61	8	8,595,950
Massachusetts 1976 General Question 5: Handguns				
June	55%	39%	6%	1,000
Labor Day	58	31	11	500
October**	51	41	8	1,000
October*	40	44	17	600
Actual vote	29	64	7	2,594,262
California 1978 General Proposition 6: Homosexual teachers				
12–28 August	61%	31%	9%	1,049
17–24 September	47	41	12	1,075
30 Oct.–1 Nov.	37	58	6	1,375
Actual vote	40	56	5	7,132,210
California 1984 General Proposition 40: Campaign spending				
Early September	59%	17%	24%	1,021
Early October	39	32	28	1,022
Late October	27	43	31	1,022
Actual vote	31	56	13	9,796,375
California 1986 General Proposition 61: Public salaries				
August	49%	40%	12%	1,028
Early October	18	48	34	1,023
Late October	21	56	23	701
Actual vote	31	59	10	7,617,142

SOURCE: California data are from the California Poll, Field Research Corporation, San Francisco, California, and the State Data Program, University of California, Berkeley. Massachusetts data marked by an asterisk (*) are from the Massachusetts Poll, and where marked by (**) are from the WBZ-TV Poll; all other Massachusetts data are from the Becker Polls.

It would be a mistake to overgeneralize from the propositions included in the California Polls since 1960. First, the data on California ballot propositions may not be typical, (even though similar tendencies were also found in the Massachusetts, Colorado, and Michigan data).

Second, the sample of propositions included in the California Poll are typically ones around which there is some controversy. It is possible that the generalized pattern of declining support for propositions may not apply to the scores of propositions which are not controversial.

If, however, there is sufficient interest and controversy around a measure so that it is included in the California Poll, the prevalence of the declining "yes" vote and rising "no" vote is dramatic. First, it must be underscored that the switch from "yes" to "no" appears to be indirect for many. Voters initially switch from "yes" to "undecided" and then from "undecided" to "no." The "normal" California tendency appears to be that voters will state an initial preference, largely an instant or snap opinion, and usually in favor of the propositions. Thus the initial poll on some measures is as much as two-to-one in favor of the proposition. As the campaign progresses, the voters discover that there are two sides to the issue and that it is not necessarily as good an idea as it initially seemed. Rather than indicate that they are opposed to the measure, however, they simply indicate they are undecided. Finally as election day approaches and a decision on the measure must be made they tend to vote "no." The data in Table 5–4 illustrate this pattern for five controversial issues.

OPINION CHANGES AND BALLOT PROPOSITIONS

Public opinion on many ballot propositions changes during the course of a campaign.[7] Commenting on this phenomenon, Mervin Field, the respected California pollster, has said, "Voters seldom have clearly defined opinions about ballot measures" (Baker 1977: 13–14).

The issues on which substantial opinion change occurs are impressive in their diversity—tax reduction, electric utility rates, homosexual teachers, handguns, nonsmoking sections in public buildings, and campaign spending. Unlike propositions on which voters had standing or un-

---

[7]Substantial changes in the aggregate voting intentions that occur during many proposition campaigns almost certainly reflect a degree of measurement error. Some respondents, when asked about their intended vote, will indicate a positive or negative preference even though they know nothing about the proposition. This is the problem generally referred to as nonattitudes (Converse: 1964, 1970). The number of nonattitude, or inaccurate, responses should decline as election day approaches.

There is a second methodological issue of considerable importance to this study. My analysis of the changes in opinions toward ballot propositions and voting intentions on them is not a study of the changes experienced by any single individual or group of individuals but a comparison of representative samples of all voters taken at several points in time. Thus what is being studied here are changes in voting intentions among the population of likely voters. To study change in individual voting intentions would require panel data, which unfortunately do not exist.

settled opinions, here there was a uniform shift from "yes" to "no" opinions. In some cases the degree of opinion reversal is remarkable. On the precursor to California's Proposition 13 of 1978, the antipoverty tax Proposition 14 of 1972, opinion shifted from 67 percent for the measure to a "no" vote of 61 percent. An even more dramatic shift occurred on the Massachusetts flat-rate utility measure, a shift from 67 percent supporting the measure to a "no" vote of 69 percent. As previously noted, the California Poll data permit us to examine opinion change in both candidate and proposition contests over a longer period of time. Table 5-5 summarizes the degree of opinion change in California contests included in the California Polls from 1960 to 1986.

Substantial opinion change can also occur in candidate elections, but it is much more likely to happen in a referendum. Significant aggregate opinion changes were more than three times as likely in California proposition campaigns since 1960: there were widespread fluctuations in only 14 percent of the statewide candidate races, in this period, while 48 percent of the proposition campaigns exhibited widespread fluctuations. While there was little change in voting intentions in 74 percent of the candidate contests, this was the case in only 30 percent of the proposition campaigns. These findings are consistent with earlier research on this subject (Magleby 1984: 170–73). Roughly half of the proposition races included in the California Poll since 1960 have seen opinion reversals. In addition, more than two-thirds of all California measures studied showed the "yes" to "no" trend, with 68 percent of those cases resulting in opinion reversals.

The finding that voting intentions of the electorate change more on ballot propositions than in candidate races is consistent with the findings that voters on propositions are less sure of their voting intentions, less knowledgeable about the proposition contests, and probably more sus-

TABLE 5–5   Stability of Voting Intentions in California Candidate and
Proposition Elections, 1960–1986

| Change in Voting Intentions | Type of Election | |
	Candidate	Proposition
Little*	74% (32)	30% (15)
Moderate†	12 (5)	22 (11)
Significant‡	14 (6)	48 (24)

SOURCE: California Polls, 1960–1986, Field Research Corporation, San Francisco.
*Roughly the same margin of preferences persisted throughout the campaign.
†There were significant differences in the margin of preferences, but the side that led all along won.
‡There were significant changes in voting intentions as the campaign proceeded; the side that at one time had been behind won.

ceptible to campaign appeals. In candidate contests, party identification acts as a standing decision and a simplifying device. In contrast, only a few issues found in ballot propositions have the kind of standing decision so typical of candidate contests.

Even more precise data on opinion change exist in the Colorado and Michigan cases. Here frequent tracking polls were conducted which permit us to monitor opinion change more closely. The change in voting intentions on Colorado's 1986 Amendment 4 (see the Appendix) appears to reflect a nearly across-the-board drop in support from September to October. Republicans favored the measure 65:29 in September and Democrats favored it 59:32. By October those proportions had fallen to 36:39 for Republicans and 35:47 for Democrats. The most notable exception to this widespread drop in support is education. In the September poll all but those with advanced degrees supported Amendment 4. Among those with less than a high school education the proportion of support to opposition was 76:14. Only among those with schooling beyond the bachelor's degree did a majority oppose the amendment, 37:60. By the October survey, however, support for the measure had dramatically declined among all but the best educated, who, as noted, were already strongly opposed.

But education is not the only predictor of opinion change; lack of strong partisan and ideological attachment also seem to be important. California data confirm my earlier finding, that "to a surprising extent ideological self-classification appears to determine voting behavior" (Magleby 1984: 176). The tendency toward greater awareness of propositions and stronger attachment to an intended vote by strong conservatives and strong liberals means that it is the less ideological and less partisan voters who reverse their opinions.

EXPLAINING OPINION CHANGE ON BALLOT PROPOSITIONS

The 1986 Colorado vote on tax limitation is an example of the ability of the opponents to define the issue in terms favorable to their side and to achieve a reversal in the distribution of public opinion on the measure. On this measure, the September benchmark poll found that 75 percent of Colorado registered voters were unaware of the measure; and among those who indicated they were very likely to vote, the proportion who were unaware of the measure was 69 percent. High levels of voter ignorance of an issue makes the campaign even more important, because it can define the issue for the voters without being encumbered with prior perceptions. On the Michigan Measure D campaign, the opponents had a similar opportunity, because in late September 80 percent were undecided about how they would vote on the measure. In both of these cases, much of the explanation for the defeat of the measure came therefore from opinion formation rather than opinion reversal.

In the Colorado campaign, opponents of the measure succeeded in defining the issue as extreme and potentially dangerous to Colorado's economic development and ability to respond to emergencies. This message was presented by former Republican Governor Love. In a widely covered press conference he reminded Colorado voters that during his term he had sought and obtained an emergency tax increase to respond to problems resulting from flooding. Former Governor Love was joined in opposing the measure by numerous other elites, including the current governor, Dick Lamm. Instead of making Amendment 4 a referendum on taxes, opponents defined it as extreme and dangerous. As the evidence presented above indicates, this message apparently worked. The opponents had a major advantage beyond their dominance of elite endorsements—money. Fully 71 percent of the spending on this measure was by the opponents.

This was also an advantage of the opponents of Michigan's 1982 Measure D. This measure would have required hearings for rate increases by public utilities. The utilities, understanding that they were not very popular, sought to deflect opinion from the issue of public utilities, instead focusing on the slogan "D is Dumb." The utilities and their allies clearly dominated the media, spending 99 percent of the more than $4 million spent on this measure. In this case there was not an opinion reversal, but as the "undecideds" made up their minds, they more often than not decided to vote against the proposition. The utilities' strategy is typified in the title they gave themselves as opponents of the measure: Citizens for Jobs and Energy. If the issue is jobs and energy, and Measure D is not good for jobs and energy, then it is not surprising that as that message was successfully communicated, more Michigan voters opposed than supported the measure.

One factor that leads to uncertain or changing opinions on ballot propositions is the tactic often used by opponents: confusing the issue or raising serious doubts about its impact. The initial strategy is to raise doubts about the need, implementation, or impact of the measure. This may result in persons shifting from "yes" to "no," or it may mean that voters shift from support to indecision and then later respond to the appeal—"When in doubt VOTE NO." The California Poll data on propositions with opinion reversals confirm this.

CONCLUSIONS

Voting intentions, in the aggregate, can change dramatically during the course of a ballot proposition campaign. This chapter has demonstrated that decision making on ballot measures differs from that in candidate elections. Voters tend to decide later how they will vote on ballot propositions and in some cases larger proportions of voters have not seen or heard about statewide ballot questions until the last few days of the campaign. Voters' choices about candidates are more stable over time.

The explanation for this more unsettled opinion on ballot measures is that the simplifying cues of partisanship and candidate recognition and appeal are absent. The information is less understandable and often not integrated into a standard political framework. As a result, the cognitive task of forming an opinion on a ballot proposition is more difficult and time-consuming.

There is an exception to this finding: on some ballot issues voters have started out aware of an issue and formed a standing opinion on it. Issues like the death penalty are ones upon which voters have standing opinions and there is remarkable stability in voting intentions throughout the campaign. Issues upon which votes have standing opinions are often highly charged and contentious. Voters have been found by the visibility and centrality of the issue to have considered it and decided their personal position on it.

Voters are not as certain of their opinions on most ballot propositions, and are more susceptible to the influence of the campaign. The 1978 California property tax vote, Proposition 13, differed from other tax-cutting propositions before and after in that an opinion reversal did not occur. The Jarvis forces were successful in keeping the issue focused on dramatically rising property taxes and the unwillingness of government to respond.

About half of the ballot measures included in the California Poll in 1968 had opinion reversals. Here the pattern is predictable and the role of the campaign in defining the issue is very important. Ballot propositions generally sound like a good idea to most people. But once the opposing side joins in the campaign, presents its arguments, solicits elites to oppose them, and spends money on advertising, the patterns of opinion change described tend to occur. Most often the cross-sectional data suggest that the shift is from "yes" to "undecided," and in subsequent surveys the "undecided" category declines and the "no" category grows, until on election day the measure is defeated by a large margin.

On these measures the campaign is critical. The strategy is often to raise doubts, create confusion, and trigger a negative reaction to the proposition. With sufficient money for advertising, careful research on what parts of the issue voters would not like, and effective commercials playing to these themes, the "no" side can usually prevail (Magleby 1984: 167–68).

As discussed previously, in 83 percent of the California propositions in which voters did not have standing opinions there was an observed pattern of declining support and growing opposition to the proposition.

Hence the key task for the "yes" campaign: stem the tide of growing or potential opposition.

Opinion change can often be misunderstood. To those who only heard that California voters in 1978 rejected an antihomosexual teachers proposition, the conclusion might have been that Californians were supporting the gay lifestyle. In fact, the issue was defined by the "no" campaign as a civil liberties measure where government could punish innocent people based on hearsay evidence. Had California voters' opinions changed about homosexuals or homosexual teachers? Not likely. That is not what voters understood the measure to be about. They were opposed to a proposition they thought unnecessary, extreme, and potentially unfair. This same dynamic happens again and again in ballot proposition politics.

Public opinion is directly related to voting behavior on ballot propositions. In cases where standing opinions are involved, the votes are generally an expression of opinion on the underlying issues. But on most other measures, the issues being voted on are up for grabs, open to definition by one or the other side of the campaign. Observers must therefore be careful about assuming that the vote on a ballot proposition is an expression of opinion on the subject of the ballot measure. The critical point is that the campaigns themselves influence how voters perceive the measures. This highlights the importance of campaigns for deciding the outcomes and helps to explain why voting intentions can change so dramatically.

Appendix

CALIFORNIA

Proposition 6, 1978 General, "Homosexual Teachers"

Initiative which prohibited the hiring or required the dismissal of teachers who encouraged or promoted homosexual acts, public or private. Sometimes called the Briggs Initiative.

Proposition 13, 1978 Primary, "Property Tax Limitation"

Initiative which set the maximum property tax rate at 1 percent of market value, reducing those taxes on residential and business properties by at least one-half. Often called the Jarvis/Gann measure.

Proposition 14, 1964 General, "Open Housing"

Initiative overturning California's open housing law, reestablishing the ability of homeowners to discriminate against racial minorities in the sale of residential housing.

Proposition 14, 1972 General, "Property Tax Reduction"
Initiative lowering property taxes and limiting its uses while also raising sales, use, corporate, cigarette, and liquor taxes. Sometimes called the Watson Initiative.

Proposition 15, 1976 Primary, "Nuclear Safeguards"
Initiative establishing restrictions on nuclear power plant construction, and requiring effective safety and waste disposal systems.

COLORADO

Amendment 4, 1986 General, "Tax Increase Elections"
Initiative which would require a referendum for any tax increase at any level of government. Such elections could only be held every two years during the statewide general elections.

MICHIGAN

Measure D, 1982 General, "Utility Rate Hearings"
Initiative requiring hearings on all utility rate increases.

Measure G, 1982 General, "Elected Public Service Commission"
Initiative establishing an Elected Public Service Commission.

Measure H, 1982 General, "Utility Regulation"
Legislative alternative to Measure D, sponsored in part by the utilities. Included less far-reaching rate hearing reform than Measure D and a prohibition on state legislators' working for utility companies for two years after leaving office.

CHAPTER 6

Econometric Models of Voting and Campaigning

Randall G. Chapman
Kristian S. Palda

INTRODUCTORY NOTE

Jess Unruh, the late speaker of the California State Assembly, once observed, "Money is the mother's milk of politics." Without money, candidates find it extremely difficult to campaign effectively. In the 1988 American presidential primaries, lack of funds was cited as the major reason why several candidates had to withdraw from the race: Bruce Babbitt, Albert Gore, Alexander Haig, Pat Robertson, and Paul Simon, to name just a few.

Yet how important is money? Certainly its importance is assumed in almost every one of the chapters in this volume. But how do we know this assumption is true? Is it not possible that its importance has been exaggerated? How do we know that more money for campaigning actually improves a candidate's chances of winning office? Hearsay, mostly. To remedy this, Chapman and Palda in this chapter set out to evaluate empirically the importance of money in political campaigns.

Chapman and Palda use an econometric approach which involves two basic steps. First, they formulate a regression model that takes account of theoretical considerations; then they assess the relative weights of the model's coefficients for selected political contests. While such an approach may look somewhat forbidding to the uninitiated, econometric models offer certain advantages over the more familiar cross-tabulations of survey data.

To begin with, in contrast to cross-tabulations, regression equations permit several variables to be considered simultaneously without running into problems of unreliability that arise from the diminished numbers of cases in each cell of a multivariate table. Second, by dealing with official tabulations of votes—"revealed preferences," as opposed to reported choices—Chapman and Palda increase the validity of their data: they measure how people really voted, not how they individually rationalize their behavior in response to a question on a survey. But there is a price to pay: the increase in validity sacrifices some of the richness in interpretability of survey reports, since it is purchased by moving from individual-level data to aggregate-level measures.

Nonetheless, the regression model enables Chapman and Palda to analyze Canadian federal election results to demonstrate the extent to which a candidate's spending increases his or her share of the vote. Moreover, the model also permits a precise evaluation of the usefulness of each party's campaign spending, the impact of past electoral success, and the value of incumbency. Finally, the results have some surprising implications: they suggest that contrary to the expectations of many reformers, imposing ceilings on campaign spending would most likely redound to the advantage of incumbents, not challengers.

The Editors

In a democracy, members of the public may express their opinions on the issues of the day in a wide variety of private and public ways. Individuals may: discuss issues with family, friends, and acquaintances; write to their elected representatives; participate in individual or collective public demonstrations; write "letters to the editor"; contribute funds and volunteer efforts to candidates and groups with parallel interests; join a political party; express their individual opinions by voting for specific candidates; and, even run for elective office. The right to not do any or all of the above is perhaps the greatest litmus test of a democracy. Opting out is possible, although presumably those who choose to do none of the above appreciate that others' opinions and actions will generally carry the day.

The act of voting in elections is special within this broad range of possible expressions of public opinion. It is a citizen's ultimate and final summary measure of public opinion. As such, the study of voting behavior and the determinants of voting outcomes is crucial to the understanding of the broad spectrum of public opinion. The determinants of voting outcomes are many, however. One fact seems clear: money has a notable role to play in electoral activities.

Cicero, in a famous speech, said "no place is so strongly fortified that money could not capture it" (Guterman 1966: 52). This may be a rhetorical exaggeration, but it is clear that money has an important role to play in elections, where it essentially serves to lubricate the machinery of information transfer. Information transfer moves in both directions—

from candidates to voters by means of personal appearances and news media exposure, and from voters to candidates by direct contact or via opinion polls.

Where money is involved, economists are not far behind with their analysis and advice. Economists have proposed several interrelated theories which are supposed not only to explain but also to predict certain phenomena accompanying political campaigns. Being among the social scientists who are perhaps the most addicted to quantification, they have drawn upon econometrics to buttress their theory and model-building efforts.

In this chapter, our aim is to illustrate the application of economic theory and econometrics to the analysis of political campaign activities and outcomes. We wish to demonstrate the need for sophisticated statistical analysis and also to describe some typical kinds of models and associated empirical results. Our goal is not to describe all existing results in the published literature, but rather to highlight representative models and findings. We will devote considerable attention to the interpretation of various econometric modeling efforts. Using data from sources, we hope to demonstrate that econometrics, or the application of statistics to measure relationships among economic variables, can usefully contribute to the understanding of some political phenomena.

A thorough examination of the determinants of voting outcomes requires that all of the interrelationships among voting, campaign spending, campaign funding generation, and voter participation be studied. It is just not sufficient to examine correlations between pairs of variables. As we hope to show in this chapter, considerable progress has been made over the last two decades in studying voting-outcome determinants from an economic perspective. Of course, this is not the only point of view from which voting might be studied. (See Newman and Sheth [1987], for example, for an alternative view of the study of political choice behavior.)

The second section of this chapter is designed to review the basic statistical tools that might be used to analyze electoral phenomena. We then describe an economic theory of voting and campaigning, and associated econometric techniques. The building of an econometric model, a step necessarily preceding econometric estimation, is guided in its choice of variables and proposed relationships by theoretical considerations. Accordingly, in the third section of this chapter, we summarize some of the economic theory with respect to campaigning and voting. We then draw on this theoretical framework in the fourth section to build and estimate all of the components of an election model, with accent on the role played by money. Some implications of existing empirical findings for the management of political campaign efforts are also discussed. This chapter concludes with a discussion of some managerial issues.

STATISTICAL ANALYSIS OF ELECTORAL PHENOMENA

We begin by substantiating the need for the use of sophisticated statistical techniques, well beyond simple descriptive statistics, to analyze electoral phenomena. To accomplish this, we will discuss an example at some length.

Consider an election with 400 electoral districts. Suppose that there are three parties, A, B, and C. Assume that each party had active candidates in each of the 400 electoral districts. Basic questions that might be posed regarding this (and any) election would include: what role did party affiliation, incumbency, and campaign spending have on voting outcomes? Cross-tabulation analysis may be employed to attempt to find answers. It is important to remember that cross-tabulation analysis (and, in general, any correlational analysis procedure) is only associational in nature, not causal. Furthermore, cross-tabulation can become quite messy if we attempt to include the influence of several variables simultaneously.

For purposes of discussion, some results are displayed in Table 6–1. Let us begin by examining the influence of party affiliation. It appears to have had a major influence on the election outcome. Party A won 70 percent of the election contests, with the B and C parties being successful in 25 percent and 5 percent of the districts, respectively. Clearly, being a

TABLE 6–1   The Influence of Party Affiliation, Incumbency, and Campaign Spending on Voting Outcomes: Illustrative Cross-Tabulation Results

| | Party Affiliation | | |
	A	B	C
Winners	280 (70%)	100 (25%)	20 (5%)
Losers	120 (30%)	300 (75%)	380 (95%)

| | Incumbency Status | |
	Incumbents	Challengers
Winners	300 (75%)	100 (25%)
Losers	100 (25%)	300 (75%)

| | Campaign Spending | |
	Spent the Most	Did Not Spend the Most
Winners	240 (60%)	160 (40%)
Losers	160 (40%)	240 (60%)

member of the A party seems to have had a major positive influence on winning. Turning to incumbency status, we see that 75 percent of incumbents across all three parties won reelection. Incumbents apparently had a 3:1 advantage over challengers in this election. Regarding campaign spending, high levels of spending are associated with improved chances of winning: 60 percent of the candidates who spent the most in their electoral district were ultimately elected.

These simple cross-tabulations have the potential to hide many things. For example, it is possible that all or most of the incumbents were affiliated with party A. So, the apparent degree of success of party A representatives in the election may actually have been disguised by the impact of incumbency. Incumbency may have been the crucial determinant of success, with party affiliation being only an incidental factor. This would be revealed if finer cross-tabulations were conducted. For example, a cross-tabulation of party affiliation and incumbency status by electoral success (winning versus losing) could be developed. The results of such multiway cross-tabulations become difficult to interpret when many factors are considered simultaneously. The interpretation of a cross-tabulation of party affiliation, incumbency status, rural versus urban, and high- versus low-income levels by electoral success (winning versus losing) would be problematic. Multiway cross-tabulations may also become unreliable, since they become based on fewer and fewer numbers of observations as more and more factors are simultaneously considered.

Based on the results displayed in Table 6–1, another question arises: which of party affiliation, incumbency status, or campaign spending was most important in influencing the outcome of the election? Experimentally derived data are really required to answer this question. In such an experimental environment, some candidates of each party and each incumbency status (incumbent and challenger) would be randomly assigned to spend various amounts of money on their campaigns. Then, in principle, it would be possible to assess the separate and distinct influences of party affiliation, incumbency status, and campaign spending on electoral performance. For obvious reasons, such experimentation is rarely found in real election processes.

The cross-tabulation analysis described above requires all relevant variables to be categorical in nature (e.g., win versus lose; party affiliation of A, B, or C). However, campaign spending is a continuous variable, as are many other electoral variables of interest. While we could categorize continuous variables (e.g., "spent less than $10,000," "spent $10,000–$50,000," etc.), this seems a somewhat artificial requirement. Also, as more and more variables of interest are examined, the cross-tabulation analysis procedure becomes burdensome and unreliable. Another approach exists, fortunately.

We might cast the general problem being discussed as follows:

Election performance = f(party affiliation, incumbency
status, campaign spending, other
relevant factors)   (1)

where f(.) is interpreted as "is a function of" (depends on). This kind of model could then be analyzed by appropriate statistical procedures. In particular, regression techniques could be employed to determine the implicit weightings of the independent variables (e.g., party affiliation, incumbency status) in the determination of electoral success. Using regression procedures, we would simultaneously determine how the independent variables (e.g., party affiliation, incumbency status) jointly relate to the dependent variable (election performance).

In estimating a regression model of the form:

$$Y = a + bX + cZ = \ldots + \text{error}$$

we seek estimates of the weights (the parameters "a," "b," "c," . . .) that will best predict occurrences of the dependent variable (Y) based on the variation in the independent variables (X, Z, . . .). Econometric (regression) analysis techniques will provide the "best" (in a statistical sense) set of weights to explain the observed variation in the dependent variable. The form of this model lends itself to the interpretation that a unit change in X leads to a change in Y of "b" units. This is true, however, only if the independent variables are uncorrelated with themselves. With high correlation patterns (say, for example, between incumbency status and campaign spending), the estimate of the *individual contribution* of each independent variable to the prediction of the dependent variable may be suspect. However, the regression technique still yields the best *joint* set of weights, even if individual effects may be problematic to interpret. Of course, cross-tabulation technology suffers from exactly the same problem. In extreme cases, highly correlated variables may be grouped together to form a common factor (using factor analysis techniques, for example). In regression studies, it is important to examine the correlations among the independent variables to ensure that no extreme correlations are present.

To operationalize this model in equation (1), we must define precisely what is meant by "election performance." Several possible definitions immediately come to mind: probability of winning, votes received, or vote share received. Each of these possible selections of dependent variables will influence the choice and form of independent variables in the model. The various independent variables would also need to be quantified. Campaign spending might be defined in dollar terms, or possibly in terms of dollars per registered voter. Or, perhaps different kinds of campaign expenditures (in different media, for example) would be included as separate variables in the model, to assess the possibility of a difference in their productivity. Several variables might be needed to capture all aspects of incumbency status: single-time incumbent or not, multiple-time incumbent or not, etc.

The choice of variables to include in a model such as that described in equation (1) should be based on theoretical considerations. The ad hoc inclusion of variables in such models typically leads to extensive statistical manipulations that are likely to result in highly idiosyncratic rather than generalizable findings. We therefore discuss next the contribution of economic theory to the building of such electoral models.

ECONOMIC THEORY AND THE ROLE OF MONEY IN CAMPAIGNING AND VOTING

There are two fundamental concepts that economists use when analyzing political phenomena. The first, ingrained in the economic view since the 18th century but spelled out in a detailed fashion only 30 years ago, is that voters are "rational": they evaluate available alternatives in light of their benefits and costs, and implicitly employ a decision calculus based on maximizing utility (Downs 1957: 260). Costs and benefits, in this context, would be defined quite broadly. Time and money costs would be relevant, as well as voters' perceptions of the various benefits (e.g., patriotic, economic) associated with participating in the electoral process.

The second concept is that of the government as an exchange process in which taxes are the *quid pro quo* for services received (Buchanan 1975). Citizens, who are also taxpayers and voters, are endowed with essentially the same preferences and informational requirements as public sector consumers as when they act as consumers of privately supplied goods. But, in the role of public sector consumer, the individual's opportunities and constraints are critically shaped by the nature of political institutions and processes (Deacon 1980). In our context, the critical process is the election.

We envisage, then, the economically self-interested voter approaching an election with some demand for a bundle of publicly supplied, and publicly financed, goods and services. These are to go with and to enhance the voter's enjoyment of privately acquired goods. On the municipal level, for instance, the voters–taxpayers require police protection for their domestic bliss; on the state level, road facilities on which to ply their automobiles; and, on the federal level, a judicial system to enforce their private contracts. This demand for publicly provided goods is manifested openly at election time, when voters choose what are literally their purchasing agents. It is through these elective agents that consumers–tax-payers have a chance of signaling their preferences in the "government exchange" process.

On the supply side of that exchange process, we imagine two phases. In the first, eager candidates for political office vie for votes with promises of packages of publicly financed goods embodied in their election platforms. In the second phase, those actually elected compromise on achievable provisions of those goods and exact a tax price for them.

While we have now spelled out, in true economic fashion, the underlying demand–supply configuration of the exchange process, we will now zero in on the interaction of voters and candidates, and on the enabling role that money plays therein. We start by describing the voters' decisions.

Before settling on the candidate of choice, voters must resolve whether to cast their ballots at all. While the two decisions cannot be strictly divorced, it is of interest to examine the turnout issue separately and first. The rational Downsian voter turns out at the ballot box only when the returns (benefits) outweigh the costs of voting. This decision calculus may be summed up in compact form as follows (Frohlich et al. 1978):

$$U = p_1|D| + p_2L - C \qquad (2)$$

where:

U = Net value (expected utility) an individual associates with the act of voting

p_1 = Subjective probability of an individual's vote affecting the final outcome of the electoral contest

D = Expected utility "income," broadly defined, offered by the difference between the winning and the second-place candidate (or party)

p_2 = Subjective probability that an individual's vote will make a difference in the long-run survival of the democratic political system

L = Long-run value of participation in elections

C = Costs of voting

In equation (2), p_2 and L are the long-run components of the participation decision. There is no consensus yet among economists how they might be operationalized (i.e., by what available economic variables they might be approximated). Of course, the sociologically inclined student of the political process can ask direct questions in a survey of voters. The economist professionally distrusts survey data, preferring to rely on statistics issuing from overt observed behavior (such as actual turnout and votes) rather than stated measures of intention, preference, attitude, or perception.

In equation (2), the easiest two determinants to operationalize are p_1 and C. The probability of affecting the outcome can be approximated by both the (ex-post) size of the winning majority, or electoral margin, and the size of the voting population. Turnout is expected to be higher in districts with narrow margins and less numerous voters (Barzel and Silberberg 1973). Note that, in this context, the cost of voting includes not only the actual time spent in going to the polls on election day, but also all the time and other costs related with registering to vote and the efforts required to learn about pertinent campaign issues and to decide on candidates.

Subsequently—or more likely, concurrently—with the participation decision, the voter, acting as a buyer of publicly supplied goods and services, will take account of the availability and persuasiveness of information presented by candidates regarding the offerings and implied tax-prices of such commodities. It seems clear that, regardless of the type of platform offered by the candidate, an abundance of information presented will make it easier for voters to make their choices. The diffusion of information regarding a candidate—whether a challenger or an incumbent—reposes squarely upon monetary expenditure. Since politicians never seem to have enough money for this type of information-dispensing activity, we may assume that they believe it to be beneficial to their quest for election or reelection.

Just like voters, political candidates are assumed to be rational utility maximizers who shape their platforms in competition with one another. In developing campaign platforms, candidates take due regard of the voters' preferences, conveyed to them by opinion polls and face-to-face political meetings. Since polls and campaign meetings are not free goods, money must be raised for those activities, as well as for the diffusion of information toward the electorate via mass media undertakings.

Rational candidates will not spend, or raise, money carelessly. If their chances of election are excellent or very poor, giving them an expected (positive or negative) margin of votes that is large, they will tend to spend less. Contributors to a campaign presumably weigh the chances of the candidate's election or reelection, and the potential services that may be rendered to them if the candidate is successful, when deciding upon the extent of their monetary support.

These comments suggest that we have established the basic building blocks of a comprehensive model of the electoral process from suggestions offered by economic theory. Voting and campaigning activities must be accounted for in this model, as well as the all-pervasive role that money plays throughout the electoral process.

ECONOMETRIC MODELS OF ELECTIONS

Let us sum up our view of the election process. The eligible voter has two principal decisions to make: whether to vote at all and for whom to cast the vote. In the latter decision, voters are certainly influenced by the amount of information about candidates and issues that has been conveyed by the candidates' communications efforts, financed by campaign funds, or while the candidate (incumbent) held office.

After designing the basic features of their election platforms, candidates will estimate how much money they need to convey their promises efficiently to the voters, given the expected competition from other politicians. Candidates' spending decisions will be moderated by the amount of funds they can raise and, should they be elected, by the price their contributors will exact.

Many other elements will be at work, as well. For instance, the socioeconomic characteristics of the electoral district will, in part, determine the tendency to vote for a party. Turnout at the polls may favor one party more than another. Much of this has to be taken into account in the structure of a full-scale electoral market model, yet the model itself is constrained by the availability of the data one would ideally wish to process to estimate its key characteristics. At this point, it is appropriate to highlight a distinction that must be made between the data that an economist prefers to work with and the data that a political scientist will routinely employ.

The political scientist is accustomed to having heavy recourse to individual-level survey results: intentions to vote, respondents' reports on how they actually voted, information about voters' (self-reported) socioeconomic characteristics, and voters' beliefs and perceptions about political issues. The economist usually relies on what can be called "revealed preference" behavior data (actual turnout, actual votes cast for candidates) and census-type or other official statistics (e.g., electoral district average income, candidate expenditures filed under electoral law requirements) that tend to be free of sampling errors, while being somewhat less rich in interpretability. Of course, the economist's data are typically aggregate in nature, rather than being the individual-level observations available to political scientists who survey voters directly. With such census data, recency (have any changes in population characteristics occurred between the most recent census and the election?) and appropriateness (are the census data correctly aggregated into electoral districts?) are important considerations.

Based on this discussion, we now present in detail a comprehensive election market model. Two of the model's equation blocks represent the behavior of voters and two the behavior of candidates.

The Turnout Block

We already presented a theoretical model of the determinants of voting participation in equation (2). With nonsurvey official statistics (statistics that cannot report, for instance, on a voter's degree of preference for a candidate), only some parts of it can be operationalized and estimated:

$$\text{Turnout} = f(\text{probability of affecting outcome, cost of voting}) \quad (3)$$

In one of our attempts to explain a part of the variation in voting participation figures, we used data from the 1973 provincial election staged in the 110 electoral districts of Quebec (Chapman and Palda 1983). Table 6–2 presents the ordinary least squares (OLS) regression estimates of the turnout model.

The R^2 (corrected for the size of the sample, $n = 110$, and the number of variables in the regression model) indicates that the independent variables accounted for about 93 percent of the variation in votes cast in electoral districts. All coefficients (with the exception of the intercept) are statistically significantly different from zero at the conventional 0.05

TABLE 6–2   Turnout Model Estimates for the 1973 Quebec Provincial Election (OLS Regression)

$$\text{CAST} = \underset{(2.429)}{1.698} + \underset{(0.035)}{0.838} \text{ REGVOT} - \underset{(1.074)}{2.402} \text{ CLOSE} - \underset{(0.519)}{1.507} \text{ INC}$$

$$+ \underset{(0.047)}{0.194} \text{ ED} + \underset{(0.669)}{1.473} \text{ TOTEXP/REGVOT} - \underset{(0.035)}{0.074} \text{ FEMPAR} - \underset{(0.082)}{0.254} \text{ U}$$

$$n = 110 \qquad R^2 = 0.93$$

Notes:
1. Standard errors are in parentheses.
2. All coefficients, except the intercept, are statistically different from zero at the conventional 0.05 level, at least.
3. All variables are defined at the level of an electoral district.
4. Definitions of variables in this model:
   - CAST   = Number of votes cast (in 000s)
   - REGVOT = Number of registered voters (in 000s)
   - CLOSE   = Difference between vote share of winner and vote share of the runner-up
   - INC   = Average per capita income (in $000s), from the 1970 Canadian census
   - ED   = Percent of population over 15 years of age with at least complete high school education, from the 1970 Canadian census
   - TOTEXP = Total reported campaign expenditures of all major party candidates (in $000s)
   - FEMPAR = Proportion of employed females in labor force, from the 1970 Canadian census
   - U   = Percent of unemployed workers in labor force, from the 1970 Canadian census.

level. In this turnout modeling effort, we used CAST rather than the more traditional CAST/REGVOT (ballots cast as a proportion of registered voters) for various statistical reasons. The choice of CAST/REGVOT as the dependent variable effectively interacts REGVOT with all right-hand side independent variables. As well, CAST/REGVOT is constrained to lie between 0 and 1, a complication that would violate one of the standard assumptions in ordinary least squares regression analysis. Given the use of CAST as the dependent variable, it was necessary to correct for the size of the district (number of registered voters) by including REGVOT among the independent variables.

The coefficient on REGVOT, 0.838, indicates that (holding all other factors constant) registered voters had, on average, about an 84 percent chance of turning out in this election contest. This may be thought of as a prior probability of participation. The other factors in the turnout model (CLOSE, INC, ED, TOTEXP/REGVOT, FEMPAR, and U) will, of course, modify these prior probabilities.

CLOSE, the actual "closeness" of the electoral outcome, serves as an indication of the voter's probability of affecting the election result. Its coefficient, 2.402, shows that for a 1 percent decrease in the difference between the vote shares of the winner and the runner-up, 2,402 votes more are cast on the average (holding all other independent variables constant). This is a powerful indication of the initiative that close elections give voters to go to the polls. This finding is consistent with the Downsian view: the potential benefits of participation are greater when an individual's vote has a greater chance of actually influencing the election outcome.

The rest of the variables, with the possible exception of unemployment (U), are stand-ins for various aspects of the opportunity cost of voting. Higher-income voters may find that activities other than voting and the gathering of campaign information are economically more attractive to them. On the average, where the electoral district's mean per capita income rises by $1,000, the results in Table 6–2 indicate that participation of voters decreases by 1,507. However, a more highly educated electorate, one likely to process campaign information efficiently and so at less cost, tends to participate more vigorously. The regression coefficient on ED (education) indicates that turnout increases by 194 votes, on average, for each 1 percent increase in an electoral district's population which has completed high school or better.

The income–education correlation phenomenon is a perennial problem in voting turnout studies. One cannot hold the influence of income constant while evaluating the impact of education on voting participation, since education and income are related. In our particular example, however, collinearity is not severe enough to widen the standard errors of the regression coefficients sufficiently to make the coefficients not significantly different from zero. This is due to the large size of the sample (110 electoral districts) and to the substantial variability in the sample data, a combination which mitigates the usual high correlations found between education and income.

As the coefficient of TOTEXP/REGVOT indicates, a $0.01 increase in spending per registered voter leads to an additional 14.73 votes being cast in an electoral district, on average, other variables held constant. In this particular election, the average electoral district had 34,219 registered voters. Thus, a $0.01 increase in per capita spending would represent an increase in campaign spending by all major party candidates of $342.19. The cost per unit of increase in voting participation is estimated to be $342.19/14.73, or $23.23 per voter. This positive effect of aggregate campaign spending on turnout is a usual finding in turnout studies. An implication of this finding is that efforts to limit campaign spending (to reduce the chance that a "deep purse" will dominate elections) may have an unintended and undesirable side effect: voting participation may be reduced.

Female participation in the labor force would seem to leave less leisure time available to households to digest campaign information and to actually go to the polls. This is confirmed by the negative coefficient on FEMPAR. The unemployment rate, U, is a variable which was brought into the analysis due to its sociological rather than its economic significance to participation. Its negative coefficient, -0.254, is suggestive of the possibility that the unemployed feel less a part of the political system than do other voters.

The results of nine additional Canadian provincial elections analyzed in Chapman and Palda (1983) confirm, on the whole, the soundness of the Downsian model of voting participation, estimated with econometric procedures. The economic model of voting participation stands up rather well under careful empirical scrutiny.

The Voting Block

From our previous theoretical discussion, it follows that we wish to make the transfer of information from candidates to voters, financed by campaign expenditures, the fulcrum of our modeling efforts. We can envisage one particular representation of a voting model, as follows:

$$SV_n = f(EXP_n, REXP_n, STRENGTH_n, C_n, \underline{Z}) \qquad (4)$$

where:

SV_n = Share of votes of party n
EXP_n = Campaign expenditures of party n

$REXP_n$ = Expenditures of all rivals of party n
$STRENGTH_n$ = Historical strength of party n
$\quad C_n$ = Candidate-specific characteristics (such as incumbency)
$\quad \underline{Z}$ = Electoral district-specific characteristics (such as turnout, income level, education level)

The electoral district–specific characteristics, $\underline{Z}$, are denoted as a vector (by the underlining) in this model, since they represent a potentially large number of possible elements. All variables have an implicit subscript denoting an electoral district.

The impatient reader may have asked where the party's or candidate's electoral platform, and its influence on votes, is taken into account. In equation (4), we see that, with the exception of $\underline{Z}$, all variables are related to specific parties. By having a separate equation for each party, we permit party effects to fully interact with all other variables in the equation. One interpretation of the constant term in such a model is that it represents the net effect, positive or negative to the voters, of all electoral platform and policy positions.

In Canada, there are three major parties in most political jurisdictions. In Table 6–3, the results of estimating this voting model using ordinary least squares techniques for one of the three, the Liberals, are

TABLE 6–3   Voting Model Estimates for the 1984 Canadian Federal Election for the Liberal Party (using Province of Ontario data only)

LSHARE = Constant + 0.11 LEXP − 0.04 NDPEXP − 0.05 PCEXP
$\qquad$ + 0.63 LSHARE80 + 0.04 LCANINC + 0.39 TURNOUT

$$n = 95 \qquad R^2 = 0.78$$

Notes:
1. All coefficients, with the exception of PCEXP, are statistically significantly different from zero at the 0.05 level, at least.
2. All variables are defined at the level of an electoral district.
3. Definitions of variables used in this model:
   - LSHARE $\quad$ = Vote share of the Liberal party
   - LEXP $\qquad$ = Liberal party campaign expenditures per registered voter
   - NDPEXP $\quad$ = New Democratic party campaign expenditures per registered voter
   - PCEXP $\qquad$ = Progressive Conservative party campaign expenditure per registered voter
   - LSHARE80 = Vote share of the Liberal party in the preceding election (1980)
   - LCANINC $\;$ = Liberal party candidate incumbency status: equals 1 if the Liberal party candidate was incumbent, and equals 0 otherwise
   - TURNOUT = Number of votes cast in the electoral district divided by number of registered voters (i.e., TURNOUT = CAST/REGVOT)

shown (Chapman and Palda, 1987). Given the different platforms and different skills with which these were communicated, as well as the performance in office of the Liberal party, the estimates of the coefficients for the other two parties in that election are quite different.

For the Liberals, the results in Table 6–3 indicate that a $0.01 increase in per-registered-voter campaign expenditures brought about a 0.11 percent increase in vote share in an electoral district, on average, holding all other variables constant. A $0.01 increase in per-registered-voter campaign expenditures of the New Democrats would, however, lower the Liberal vote share by 0.04 percent. Since its coefficient was not statistically different from zero, the Progressive Conservatives' campaign expenditure did not seem to have a direct competitive effect on the Liberal vote. An implication of this is that the Liberals and New Democrats appealed to similar electorates, with the Progressive Conservatives appealing to different voter segments.

We also note the usual allegiance of an electoral district to a party: the current share of the Liberals goes up by about five-eighths of a percent for every percent increase in the Liberals' 1980 vote share. As expected, an incumbent candidate enjoys an advantage. Liberal candidates running as officeholders received about 4 percent more in vote share than nonincumbent Liberal party candidates, holding all other factors constant. We interpret this advantage as being, in part, due to all the information made available about Liberal party incumbent candidates to the voters over the four years incumbents were members of parliament. Finally, we note that TURNOUT is positively related to Liberal vote share: a 1 percent increase in turnout leads to a 0.4 percent increase in Liberal vote share. If known ahead of time, such a result would, of course, be supportive of election day efforts to get the vote out.

The results reported in Table 6–3 are typical of such voting models. What policy or managerial implications can be drawn from these results? Here, we draw upon earlier observations made in Chapman and Palda (1984).

The principal result is that political expenditures backing candidate communications to voters have a measurable influence: a candidate's campaign spending increases the votes cast for him, rivals' expenditures detract from his vote, and combined outlays for all candidates in an electoral district stimulate turnout. The principal policy implication is that political campaign expenditures ought not be discouraged, since they tend to lower voter information cost, and fuel competition.

The implications for campaign management by candidates and parties are better left to discussion after the presentation of the campaigning blocks.

The Contribution Block

On the American political scene, campaign spending is intimately bound up with fund raising (Jacobson 1980). Fund raising by candidates and parties is, in turn, closely linked to the expected vote-getting performance of the candidates. This interdependence, much less intense in Canada where there is generous public financing of campaign expenses, is so crucial that we shall return to it after completing the explanation of the contribution block model. In the meantime, we turn our attention to the representation of the electoral fund-raising process designated as the contribution block.

Candidates exchange implied future legislative support for cash gathered from major contributors or groups of contributors, and for cash raised from small donations by party or platform supporters. There are obvious demand and supply elements at work behind this exchange. Candidates have a demand for funds to finance their campaigns, but this demand is, in part, limited by the price they are willing to pay in implied support for the legislative requirements of the contributing groups. Special interest groups, in turn, will supply campaign contributions on the condition that a candidate is both likely to win and to support their legislative agenda. It has proved to be quite difficult to disentangle these supply and demand elements to develop an operational model of campaign contributions for American campaign settings.

Giertz and Sullivan (1977), for instance, point out that a higher probability of winning would likely increase the willingness of groups to contribute (a supply effect), while possibly decreasing the candidates' willingness to accept contributions (a demand effect). In this case, the theoretical prediction concerning the effect of the probability of winning on contributions is clearly ambiguous.

Welch (1981) cut this Gordian knot by focusing on the supply decision exclusively. He postulated that contributors and candidates are best viewed as making reciprocal gifts rather than engaging in an exchange. Such gifts are not conditional on receiving a specific good in return. Interest group contributions are made to receive favors whose nature and timing are unspecified, otherwise they would be bribes. In such a view, there is no decision to be made by the candidate except to accept the contribution. The candidate's role in the model is merely implicit.

The explicit part of the contribution model is shaped by the contributors' supply decisions. Welch makes a distinction between three categories of contributors: ideological groups, interest groups, and small individual contributors. In the 1972 U.S. House of Representatives election he analyzes, approximately 14 percent of contributions came from the first, 14 percent from the second (mostly PACs), and 60 percent from the third category, with the rest undetermined.

Welch suggests that ideological interest groups, reasonably sure of the candidate's persuasion, will support politicians in close races to maximize their chance of winning. Economic interest groups, on the other hand, will tend to contribute to likely winners (probability of winning more than 50 percent, but not overwhelming), taking election chances as given and trying to influence the future legislative behavior of the candidate. Regarding the small individual contributors, Welch reasons that their giving will also depend on their income and its dispersion, and on their education. Education, as we have seen, encourages voting participation and may also stimulate broader political participation, including monetary support for candidates. Greater income dispersion implies more wealthy families in the electoral district, and higher amounts contributed to various candidates.

Welch's complex but close reasoning leads him to propose the following model of contributions:

$$\text{Log RE} = b_{20} + b_{21} \text{ Log RV} + b_{22} \text{ Log } (100 - \text{RV})$$
$$+ b_{23} \text{ Log Y} + b_{24} \text{ Log G} + b_{25} \text{ Log ED} \qquad (5)$$

where

"Log" refers to natural logarithm and:
    RE = Republican candidate campaign expenditures (which are presumed to equal contributions in the 1972 House race)
    RV = Republican percentage of the two-party vote
    Y = Median family income
    G = Gini coefficient (a measure of income dispersion)
    ED = Median years of schooling

All variables in equation (5) are defined at the level of congressional districts.

Welch finds all coefficients to be positive and statistically significant, with an $R^2 = 0.46$ (so, almost one-half of the variation in Log RE is explained by the independent variables in this model). b_{21} is significantly larger than b_{22} which, as he documents, suggests that the majority of the funds comes from contributors who prefer to support likely winners in exchange for future political favors. The ideological groups would have been shown to have been preeminent if $b_{21} = b_{22}$, that is, where the probability of winning made no difference to campaign contributors. The significance and sizes of the coefficients of the three socioeconomic variables estimated by Welch clearly document the role of the individual small supporter.

The reader should note one reservation. As Welch pointed out: "we theorize about contributions, we regress expenditures." This, so far perhaps the most sophisticated of economic analyses of the contribution mechanism in the United States, relies on the assumption that all contributions are fully spent in the current election campaign. Such reasoning implies that expenditure data may be used in lieu of contribution data, if contribution data are missing.

In recent papers, Palda and Palda (1985) and Chapman and Palda (1987) were able to estimate separate contributions and expenditures submodels, using data from the 1980 and 1984 Canadian federal elections. More is said about this below.

The Campaign Expenditure Block

On the American scene, it is quite plausible to assume that all campaign contributions will be spent. However, this is not necessarily so in other political jurisdictions. For example, on the federal level in Canada, candidates receiving at least 15 percent of the vote and spending a certain minimum are reimbursed by the public treasury for up to 50 percent of their campaign expenses. (There are also campaign expenditure ceilings in effect.) Thus, the spending decisions of Canadian federal-level candidates, while still influenced by the availability of contributions, must nevertheless be modeled separately from the contribution generation mechanism. The expected margin of victory or defeat plays a decisive role therein: when the outcome is expected to be close, any activity that may influence the voter (including communication expenditures) will be pursued to its limit. Using the actual election margin, rather than the unobservable expected margin, the relationship between the size of the margin and the candidate's outlay is hypothesized to be inverse.

Palda and Palda (1985) estimated a campaign expenditure model based on the 1979 federal election in Ontario, in which 285 candidates of three parties presented themselves in each of the 95 electoral districts. Their results, which account for 72 percent of the variance in campaign expenditures, are displayed in Table 6–4.

As hypothesized, expenditures of candidates in close races were significantly higher. On average, a decrease in expected margin of 1 percent (0.01) is related to an increase in spending of $184.33. With regard to contributions, 12 cents out of every dollar of additional contributions was spent in the election. Candidates expecting to be reimbursed for half of their campaign outlay (expectancy measured by the actual event) spent, on average, $5,068 more than those with little hope of reimbursement.

We conclude that the economic assumptions of a candidate's rationality and of the basic operation of demand and supply processes lead to workable models. These models explain a substantial proportion of the

TABLE 6–4   Expenditure Model Estimates for the 1979 Federal Election
                in Ontario

$$EXP_i = -3371 - 18433 \text{ MARGIN}_i + 0.12 \text{ CONTRIB}_i - 952 \text{ INCI}_i +$$
$$471 \text{ INC2UP}_i + 0.01 \text{ REGVOT} + 5462 \text{ PC}_i + 4111 \text{ LIB}_i +$$
$$5068 \text{ REIMB}_i - 0.58 \text{ CEILING}$$

$$n = 285 \qquad R^2 = 0.72$$

Notes:
1. All coefficients are statistically different from zero at the 0.05 level, except those
   of incumbencies, registered voters, and ceiling.
2. Definitions of variables:

EXP_i	= Expenditures of candidate i
MARGIN_i	= Difference between votes received by winner and by candidate i (or, if candidate i was the winner, then between votes received by candidate i and the runner-up), divided by all votes cast in the electoral district (an ex-post measure of expected margin)
CONTRIB_i	= Contributions received by candidate i
INCI_i	= First-time incumbent status: equals 1 when candidate i was a first-time incumbent, 0 otherwise
INC2UP_i	= Other incumbent status: equals 1 when candidate i was a second-time or higher incumbent, 0 otherwise
REGVOT	= Number of registered voters in the electoral district
PC_i	= Progressive Conservative party status: equals 1 when candidate i represented the Progressive Conservative party, 0 otherwise
LIB_i	= Liberal party status: equals 1 when candidate i represented the Liberal party, 0 otherwise
REIMB_i	= Reimbursement status: equals 1 when candidate i was reimbursed, 0 otherwise (an ex-post measure)
CEILING	= Official campaign expenditure ceiling on candidates in this electoral district.

---

observed campaign contributions and expenditures in two somewhat different political systems, the American one and the Canadian variant of the British parliamentary model.

Estimating the Models

The crucial link between voters' decisions and the behavior of the candidates is the closeness of the outcome, which was designated as MARGIN in Table 6–4 and as $(100 - RV)$ or percent of votes going to Democrats (the "other" party) in equation (5).

Clearly, the closeness of outcome is a measure derived from (expected) votes. Thus, candidates and their financial supporters are being influenced in their campaign behavior by the prospective decisions of the voters. Looking over the voting block on one side and over the contribution and expenditure blocks on the other side, we see that they influence each other mutually: money is a causal factor in the distribution of votes, but prospective votes (measured ex-post by actual ones) have an impact on the spending of money, in turn.

In addition, we have seen in equation (3) and Table 6–2 that turnout can have a role to play in electoral success. To have a rigorous estimating procedure, all the four "blocks" of the full-scale electoral market model should be assessed simultaneously:

$$\text{Votes} = f(\text{Expenditures, turnout, other factors})$$
$$\text{Expenditures} = f(\text{Expected margin, other factors})$$
$$\text{Contributions} = f(\text{Expected margin, other factors})$$
$$\text{Turnout} = f(\text{Expected closeness, expenditures, other factors})$$

This calls for advanced econometric estimation techniques that may turn out, in the end, not to be necessary. Such advanced techniques may yield approximately the same results as the simpler ordinary least squares (OLS) regression procedures. Our examples were all taken from OLS estimates, but the reader wishing to see a thorough discussion of simultaneous estimates can peruse the articles by Welch (1981) and Chapman and Palda (1984). Extensive testing of simultaneous and single-equation (OLS) estimation procedures by Chapman and Palda (1984 and 1987) suggest that single-equation procedures yield similar results to the theoretically more appropriate simultaneous equations estimations procedures.

CONCLUDING REMARKS

We hope that the examples presented in this chapter have demonstrated the potential usefulness of econometric analysis in the explanation and prediction of voting and campaigning activities. Economic theory can, we believe, contribute to the analysis of political phenomena. Careful and sophisticated econometric analysis can yield significant findings. In particular, our past empirical research efforts (Chapman and Palda 1983; 1984; 1987) have demonstrated that monetary considerations play a prominent role throughout the voting and campaigning processes. We turn now to a brief discussion of some managerial implications of the results of econometric analyses of campaigning efforts.

In surveying the range of empirical analyses of the determinants of electoral performance, several notable patterns emerge:

1. Campaign spending influences electoral success.

2. Incumbency generally contributes to electoral success.

3. Past electoral success is generally positively associated with current electoral success.

While these are not the only generalizable findings, these particular results have significant implications to the management of political campaign activities.

Since campaign spending pays off (i.e., it influences votes received), candidates must devote considerable effort to raising funds. The candidate's available time is a relevant constraint here, so a careful balancing of fund raising efforts and voter contact activities is required. Little is known about the best way to do this. Little is also known about how best to spend the funds generated. The best mix—if there is one—of campaign spending on personal versus mass media contacts, on the various types of mass media contacts, and on opinion polls is unknown. This "best mix" may also vary for different types of political offices (local, state, and federal). Clearly, more specifically focused research efforts—and experiments—will have to be conducted and publicly documented if we are to build up a comprehensive set of findings that may be codified as "underlying laws of political campaigning." In such an environment, fads and folklore will inevitably arise. Separating folklore from facts will be a special challenge.

Many empirical studies have documented the advantages associated with incumbency status in elections. (See, for example, Chapman and Palda (1984).) The inherent advantage of incumbents (based on personal merit, notoriety, and historical party strength) implies that they do not have to spend as much as challengers. Furthermore, incumbents probably have an easier time raising campaign contributions, since they are more likely to be successful (so the expected returns to contributors will be greater). Thus, incumbents have many substantial advantages over challengers. In marketing parlance, the adroit challenger must find an inept incumbent, a powerful platform position not espoused by the incumbent, or be a much more effective campaigner to be successful. Ultimate electoral success may require active campaigning efforts through successive electoral contests.

There is some evidence that challengers' campaign spending is more effective than the equivalent spending of incumbents. Public arguments for campaign ceilings are often based on equity considerations and avoiding the "deep purse" principle of campaigning. However, such "high road" arguments must be tempered by acknowledging the self-interest issue, as well: campaign ceilings may work to the advantage of incumbents by limiting competition. From this perspective, campaign ceilings act as entry barriers, making it more difficult for a new entrant (the challenger) to unseat the entrenched market leader (the incumbent).

SECTION TWO

Public Policy

CHAPTER 7

The Role of the Mass Media in Limiting the Public Agenda

Terence H. Qualter

INTRODUCTORY NOTE

How do policy questions become matters for public discussion? In this chapter Terence Qualter points out just how important the role of the mass media has become in bringing matters to public attention. In modern mass societies we directly experience very few of the events that could be of public concern. Unless the mass media relate information about a problem or question, it is unlikely that widespread public interest will develop about it.

What gets reported in the mass media and how that information is presented, however, are hardly matters of chance. The mass media in Western democracies are largely profit-making enterprises with interests in presenting news in ways that structure events to comport with a desired "social reality." In covering foreign affairs, for instance, American mass media normally structure their interpretations so that the United States appears as the center of the universe. Events assume importance only to the extent that they affect American citizens or American interests. In covering domestic affairs, the same media generally present news from the perspective of established business interests, as opposed to those of working women, racial minorities, consumer groups, or organized labor.

The media's priorities tend to reinforce elitist views of the proper boundaries of public concerns. Even the soap operas, police dramas, and situation comedies help define the range of topics suitable for public discussion. Qualter sees a danger in the consolidation of media ownership from independent enterprises into chains run by managers of corporate conglomerates. The new managers of the media emphasize the stability and consensus congenial to a good business climate so much that the traditional adversarial relationship between government and the press is giving way to a high level of cooperation. While news reports must have some connection to real events in order for the mass media to retain their credibility, there has been a narrowing in the number of independent channels through which citizens can become informed about matters of public concern.

The Editors

Unless I am to be confronted daily with several hundred pages of newsprint, I cannot be fully informed about everything that happens in the world—nor would I want to be, for not everything is of consequence or relevance. But the decision about what information I receive is largely made by others. People over whom I have no influence, and whom I may know of only by name, if at all, stand as a barrier between the real world and my knowledge of it. I may pay a good deal of attention to some items, although they have little lasting impact on my life, simply because they are prominently reported. On the other hand there may be events having an enormous long-term bearing on my well-being to which I pay no heed because I never hear of them. If, therefore, we accept the rather obvious proposition that information has some impact on the composition of one's attitudes, and hence on one's behavior, it becomes of concern to establish the sources and limits on the type and availability of information. Who are these people who control the flow of information, and how do they do it?

One useful analytical tool for understanding the role of the media in this process of information dissemination and control, especially in the setting of a liberal democratic society, is agenda-setting. The fundamental proposition is that the influence of the media rests largely in the capacity to determine the content of public concerns, to "set the agenda" for public discussion. The crucial point lies, not in the attitudes taken to the specific issues, but the agenda itself. Agenda-setting suggests that there is a tendency for people to accept the mass media version of what are the important issues, without necessarily agreeing with the partisan position taken on those issues in any particular medium. In what is undoubtedly the most frequently quoted statement on the question, Bernard Cohen noted in 1963 that while the press "may not be successful much of the time in telling people what to think, it is stunningly successful in telling its readers what to think about" (Cohen 1963: 13). The same point has been made by several other writers in virtually identical terms (Graber 1984: 268–69; Iyengar and Kinder 1987: 2–3; Dye and Ziegler 1986: 117; Schulte 1983: 133–35). Although agenda-setting has become a fashionable topic in recent years, the basic proposition was put forward in a study of the British press as far back as 1938.

> A useful gauge of the influence of the Press is to consider it as the principal agenda-making body for the everyday conversation of the ordinary man and woman about public affairs, and, therefore, for public opinion in general. . . . The Press . . . wields an immensely powerful weapon in its power to influence the choice of the issue on which public opinion shall make itself felt at any one time (*Political and Economic Planning* 1938: 33).

The implications of the agenda-setting hypothesis are that the media provide signals directing the audience to the most important issues of the day. Events become news, part of the information input of society, not because of their intrinsic importance, but because of their acceptance by the media (see Bosso, Chapter 8 in this volume). Media, not the events themselves, make news. The concept acknowledges that citizens in a liberal democracy, who are expected to have opinions, may need some help in sorting out those topics that they ought to have opinions about. Agenda-setting thus becomes part of the process by which a people adjust to their ideological norms, the acceptable value patterns of their society. In the vast complexity of modern society individuals would be lost, confused, without these cues to their identity in a nation and a people different from other nations and peoples, and without a unifying bond of common interests and common concerns.[1] The agenda-setters contribute to the construction of a social consensus.

Enough has been written in recent years to demonstrate that the media are not as awesomely powerful as was once imagined. An overwhelmingly Republican press could not keep Franklin Roosevelt out of the White House. In England, Richard Hoggart noted that members of the working classes bought "papers by the million," but they appeared to vote with little reference to the propaganda efforts of the largely Tory press. Apparently taking it for granted that the papers were already biased against their interests, they read them largely for entertainment (Hoggart 1971: 198). But the power of the press lies less in its direct influence than in its "power to set the agendas defining the perimeters of social issues" (Glasgow University Media Group 1980: 399–400). Theodore White described this as a "primordial" power, determining "what people will talk and think about—an authority that in other nations is reserved for tyrants, priests, parties and mandarins" (White 1973: 247). Curran and Seaton offered a fascinating glimpse of the power of the press to bring new matters to the forefront of public debate. In 1942 William Beveridge published the Beveridge Plan, which provided the foundation for much of Britain's postwar social change. In the left and liberal press the plan was given enormous publicity and wholehearted support. With this much attention,

---

[1]In this way agenda-setting can be accommodated within Jacques Ellul's concepts of sociological propaganda, although Ellul did not specifically refer to agenda-setting (Ellul, 1965).

even the conservative papers were forced to pay attention to it. "What might have been a relatively obscure official document, which the Tory Minister of Information had wanted to be published quietly, was transformed through the press publicity into a cornerstone of the new consensus" (Curran and Seaton 1981: 101).

Beyond telling the people what to talk about, the media may also indicate how much importance ought to be attached to each item. This distinguishes agenda-setting from the earlier, and more limited, concept of gatekeeping. Research into the role of the media as "gatekeepers" uncovered the selective and arbitrary element in news presentation.[2] Many gatekeeper studies indicated a strong sense of community loyalty among local newspapers, most of which tried to insulate local government from too much public scrutiny (Paletz et al. 1971). Agenda-setting adds a further dimension. It takes into account that not all items passed by the gatekeeper are thereby treated equally. The agenda conveys more than information. It sets priorities among events, establishes saliences, and puts them into a social context which offers further clues as to preferred ways of responding to them (Blumler and Gurevitch 1982: 263). Rather than people or events being displayed on the front pages of the newspapers because of their intrinsic importance, the media make them important by so featuring them. The agenda thus helps the audience construct its own version of "social reality" (see Iyengar and Kinder 1987: chap. 7; Adams 1987).

Foreign observers of the American scene often note with concern the apparent inability of American mass media to accept the independent existence of other nations having their own concerns and priorities. The United States is presented as the center of a universe in which the meaning and significance of external events are found solely in their impact on American interests. Foreign leaders are described, not so much in terms of their status in their own countries, but in terms of their standing as friends or enemies of the United States. A recent news story in the *New York Times* about Jamaican politics, referred to a possible victory by Mr. Michael Manley as "a defeat for the Reagan administration"—an approach which discounts as irrelevant the fact that in an election of Jamaica, Jamaicans will choose a Jamaican government according to Jamaican perceptions of good or bad government. And if Americans are told about the world in these terms, this is how they will think about the world.

The media help provide a link between the interests of the political elites (with access to the media, and whose concerns are regularly reported) and the members of society at large. Agenda-setting thus becomes a major element in the elite control of public opinion, for the elite not only

---

[2]Gatekeeping goes beyond this present paper, but for further information see Buckalew 1974; Donohue et al. 1972; and Gieber 1964.

sets the boundaries within which the public discussion of politics takes place, it also provides the symbols, the language, and stereotypes through which issues are articulated (Golding 1974: 83–84). The elites, with their roots in the class structure of society, operate in an isolated political atmosphere. The masses approach the media largely as receivers, seldom as contributors. The electronic media, far more completely than earlier technology, have democratized the *reception* of communication. At the same time society remains far from democratic in the *dissemination* of communication. The modern age thus combines elite dissemination with mass reception. The mass media do not offer true communication at all. They are all unidirectional—essentially authoritarian, elitist, and manipulative.

This is not an appropriate place to embark on a detailed discussion of media ownership and control. The topic is well covered elsewhere. But there are two modern developments of great consequence to our present interest. The first applies particularly to the press. In recent decades, with the consolidation of ownership, independent owner–editors have been supplanted by media monopolies, combines, and chains. In both the United States and Canada most cities now support only one newspaper, and that, more often than not, is owned by a group. The media world has become one of chain ownership and local monopoly. The second great change has been the absorption of the media into corporate empires with interests and activities extending into other unrelated areas. A new class of managers, accountants, and business-office executives has replaced editors and newscasters as the wielders of media power. This is a fundamental change that has largely gone unnoticed because the new powers have taken care not to draw too much attention to themselves.[3] By their criteria the media exist, above all else, to sell commodities. Stability and consensus are preferred to controversy because they create a better business climate. In this setting the ideological tendency is that of "a vague misty liberalism" and "the triumph of good over evil" (Novak 1975: 15). In this new world the romantic image of the lone crusading journalist seeking to expose and correct wrongdoing in high places is, more than ever, a fiction. The structure of corporate ownership virtually guarantees that the media, while still freely participating in party politics, become integrated with and supportive of the political establishment as a whole. In the modern industrial-capitalist society the traditional adversarial relationship between government and press has given way to a high level of cooperation. The media elites support the established order because it is in their interest to do so, and because they are part of that order (Bagdikian 1983).

---

[3]Recently, concerns over such changes at CBS News have received public airings (see Joyce 1988 and McCabe 1987).

cussion is recognized, the components of that agenda become of vital importance. Why are we talking about this, rather than about that? About the suppression of free trade unions in Poland, but less often about similar oppressions in Chile, or even about union-busting in Canada or the United States? Our attention is drawn regularly to human rights abuses in some parts of the world. Does silence about the rest mean that all is well and happy? Does nothing ever happen in Canada?

In some instances the prominence assigned to specific issues is no more than a consequence of journalistic operating procedures and traditions. The very structure of the news media, with newspapers appearing at clearly specified intervals and broadcasting working with fairly rigidly fixed news times, strengthens an episodic approach. There is little sense of a continuous unfolding of a story, merely an interrupted series of discrete events (Bennett 1988). There is also a preference, especially on television news, for short-term events that have a definite beginning and ending, for the visual rather than the cerebral. Fires, floods and battles make better television news than social commentary. Media operators are poorly equipped to deal with underlying causes, long-term consequences, or with broad social change. Within each medium outlet certain constraints of time and space and certain established formulas require some kinds of news to be featured or presented in a particular way (Epstein 1981; Henry 1981). In addition to the technical problems and production practices, each medium will also be constrained by its own ideological biases and its cultural setting. That is to say, each newspaper, magazine, or television station will be controlled by people with their own world view, directed to a particular kind of audience, in a particular time and space setting. The agenda is at least partly fixed by circumstances of time and place, and by the expectations of the audience. The controllers are not completely free to compose it according to the whim of the moment. No middle-American newspaper, for example, could suddenly decide to accord high priority to flattering pictures and sympathetic reviews of the policies of Fidel Castro, and still hope to survive.

Even more important than the items put on the agenda are those left off. People can have a variety of opinions about items on the agenda. They can hardly discuss matters which are never mentioned. Exclusion from the agenda effectively precludes any discussion or evaluation of a topic. If an issue is not taken up by the media, for large sections of the population it does not exist. "If the mass media ignores the problem of hunger, a good chance exists that a well-fed public and satisfied politicians will neither know nor care that many Americans need food" (Patterson and McClure 1976: 75). A constant frustration among Canadians is the low priority of Canada in the American media. How can Americans ever be expected to understand the differences between Canada and the United States, or Canadian nationalist suspicions about American domination, not only of the Canadian economy but also of its cultural life, when so little about Canada reaches the American media? Because ownership and control of the media are so heavily concentrated, and the agenda so narrowly defined, it is exceedingly difficult for outsiders to bring matters to public attention, to get them on the agenda. The Watergate affair was a classic example of the early reluctance of the media to delve into matters which later became of great public concern (Brown et al. 1978; Weaver et al. 1975). The rhetoric of a free press asserts that it is the responsibility of the press to expose official corruption, that the press is the "watchdog of the nation." Yet the Watergate investigations irritated and even outraged large numbers of American citizens. The public at large condones, and even supports, the limiting of the agenda to "safe," established themes. New ideas may be dangerously unsettling. It is best to let sleeping dogs lie. People who praise a free press as an abstract principle are often deeply upset when matters questioning the established order are made public.

The pressures for conformity, caution, and conservatism in the media work to keep certain types of sensitive issues as quiet as possible, for as long as possible. In North American mass media, commercial considerations, especially the competitive scramble for advertising revenue, ensure what one writer called "the narrowly confined consensus not of opinion but of the agenda for discussion" (Burns 1977: 66). Only a limited number of topics are brought to the foreground of public concern. The agenda generally follows the mainstream, seldom disturbing to powerful elite interests. "The watch-dogs are leashed and the gate-keepers are asleep at their posts. Radical views do not get a good press" (Gilsdorf 1985: 401). By way of example there is Alexander Cockburn's description of several instances of antiadministration political activism on U.S. campuses in the mid-80s which were scarcely mentioned in the national media. One event at Ann Arbor (University of Michigan) apparently involved the arrest of more than 100 students. It was, he commented, an illustration of the capacity of the media to "see a conservative younger generation, but not to see the omens and realities of new insurgency" (Cockburn 1986: 638). If activism is not reported, the image of new conservatism remains unchallenged. In the early 1970s the sheer volume, violence, and novelty of events forced student dissent to the front pages of the newspapers. And because of the publicity the public became concerned about, and had strong views on, student radicalism and youth cultures in general. Protests or demonstrations in the Soviet Union and Eastern Europe are front-page news, perhaps because public dissent there is so rare. We are less likely to hear much about similar outcries closer to home. The North American media, for example, have extensively covered the Solidarity demonstrations in Poland, but how much attention did they give to the long, bitter, and often violent labor disputes at meat-packing plants in

Western Canada in 1985–86? Today it better suits the mood of the age to minimize internal dissent, to preserve as far as possible the image of consensus and system-supporting behavior.

This narrow focus of attention is not only a North American phenomenon. In the United Kingdom the items of concern have been reduced to "the broad centre of British politics from about half-way into the moderate Left to the edges of the extreme Right" (Burns 1977: 66). A similar evaluation would also probably be valid for Canada. It is, everywhere, a limited agenda.

The notion of a public agenda established by the media goes beyond the discrete news items. It is reflected also in the whole structure of the media picture of society. It is, for example, standard practice in most Western newspapers to publish special sections devoted to entertainment, to sports, and to business. But I have yet to see a newspaper which, as a matter of routine, devotes a special section to the affairs of organized labor. The goings-on in corporate board rooms are matters of major news interest, as are projections and analyses of industrial and financial developments. Even internal management changes are often reported. Labor unions, however, become newsworthy only in confrontational situations. Major strikes become part of the agenda for public debate; the peaceful resolution of labor disputes only rarely so. Successful businesspeople are frequently photographed in the press. Labor leaders are likely to receive similar attention only when involved in violence or corruption. The published agenda reinforces the elite world view that business is a "proper" activity for concerned citizens, labor is not. Other conventions establish fairly consistently over time the priorities to be given to local, national, or international affairs, or accept that while certain subject matters belong properly on the news pages, others can safely be relegated to, say, "women's interests."

The media in this way help to define the boundaries of legitimate discussion. At election time independents, or candidates for minor parties and causes, are largely ignored by press and television, except to be patronized as harmful oddities, because "nobody is interested in taking them seriously." And people remain uninterested in them because they are ignored by the media. The media focus on the mainstream of political activity, but their own decisions play a large role in identifying that mainstream and excluding some causes from it (see Parenti, Chapter 12 in this volume). In Canada, for example, a democratic socialist party, the New Democratic Party, is a fully legitimized political force, forming the government of some provinces, and almost everywhere accepted as a permanent part of Canadian political life. The Canadian media recognize and reinforce this role. (This not being a perfectly fair world, the left-leaning NDP receives a less sympathetic press than do the right-wing Liberal and Progressive Conservative parties, but its existence and its activities are still part of the public agenda.) In the United States, however, where socialism is alien and illegitimate, the media largely ignore the socialist voice. A democratic socialist view of the world does not reach the American political agenda. There is no debate because the question is seldom raised.

American writers themselves have acknowledged the broad similarity of the "agenda of concern" within the variety of the media, despite opposing partisan approaches to specific issues. There is considerable reinforcement as the major newspapers and television networks talk mostly about the same things at the same time. The several news media tend to look to each other, in an almost circular process, in deciding what is news. Cohen has asserted that to a large extent foreign affairs reporters determine the important issues of the day by reading other newspapers (Cohen 1963: 58). Throughout both Canada and the United States, the major newspapers, the TV networks, and the wire services, to a large extent control the agenda of the smaller media outlets for everything beyond purely local concerns. In Canada the smaller newspapers reprint from the Canadian Press news service, without alteration or comment, almost their entire nonlocal content.

None of this implies neutrality on the issues which are raised. An agreed agenda can still accept party politics as "fair game," although it might exclude some parties from the game. There can be the bitterest disagreement about detailed positions within a general consensus of what ought to be argued about. Left and right can dispute violently about Nicaragua, while both can agree that Nicaragua is an appropriate topic of debate. In the absence of information from the media they might find it more difficult to argue about Australia or Guatemala or even about the internal self-policing of the legal or medical professions. While the Shaw and McCombs study established that during the 1972 presidential elections the national television news and the local newspapers accorded a different priority to the several issues *within* the election context, they did not seriously consider the status of the election itself in the total agenda of things that might have been of concern to Americans in 1972. It was taken for granted, no doubt correctly, that a presidential election is a matter of importance, one of the topics responsible Americans ought to be thinking about. However, the popular identification of politics with *electoral* politics limits the American world view, making more difficult any popular comprehension of the world outside the United States.

American research has examined agenda-setting largely, although not exclusively, in determining electoral issues.[4] One of the first book-length

---

[4]One could look, for example, at Cobb and Elder (1972) which dealt with the linkage between mass participation and elite decision making. It offered several case studies of how issues came to be placed on the agenda of public concern, and became the subjects of official policy. However, it made only the briefest of references to the role of the mass media in this process.

studies of agenda-setting, that of Shaw and McCombs, was directed entirely to a study of the 1972 presidential elections in the single community of Charlotte, North Carolina (Shaw and McCombs 1977).[5] The object was to establish a correlation between the relative significance of the election issues as interpreted by the city newspaper and by network television news, on the one hand, and as perceived by the voters themselves, on the other hand. The agenda under observation was confined to the partisan issues relevant to an election campaign. This and several other studies have suggested that by stressing some issues, and down-playing or ignoring others, the media play a large part, but only a part, in determining the content of an election campaign. In emphasizing certain issues above others, the media take some of the initiative and control out of the hands of politicians. The candidates are forced to address those points which the media have deemed important. "The power to set the election agenda is the power to establish the context in which presidential candidates are evaluated" (Patterson and McClure 1976: 176; McCombs and Shaw 1972). Public affairs commentators also suggest the same kind of media influence on the selection of election issues is found in Canada. The media do not always talk about what the candidates or parties would prefer them to talk about. In the search for novelty in the coverage of an election campaign they may pay undue attention to the inevitable mishaps, perhaps damning the candidate with an image of awkwardness or drawing attention to mannerisms rather than to the substance of what is said. This self-conferred power of the media to determine the focus of an election has disturbing implications for the future of liberal democracy.

On the other hand it must be remembered that candidates and parties, through their advertising, can publicize their own agendas. Apparently, however, they do not always succeed in persuading the electorate to adopt that agenda. The Shaw and McCombs study indicated little correlation between the candidates' advertisements and the campaign priorities outlined by the press. Both Mr. Nixon and Mr. McGovern in 1972 put personality at the top of their own campaign agenda, although this factor was downplayed, or ignored altogether, in both the media and in the voters' own declarations of what they considered important (Shaw and McCombs 1977: 56–58). Other studies indicate that voters are influenced by their perceptions of the candidates' personal qualities or attributes, but not necessarily in the direction indicated by the candidates (Miller and Levitin 1976; Joslyn 1984: chap. 7; Diamond and Bates 1988: chap. 15).

---

[5]One should also note McLeod 1974. This study, also of the 1972 elections, compared the agendas of two newspapers in Madison, Wisconsin, with the personal agenda of their respective readers. They found a significant, but not absolute, correlation.

British studies do not entirely ignore electoral agenda-setting. As early as 1956 A. H. Birch put it as "a reasonable assumption that the average elector's impressions of what the election was about were shaped largely by what he read in the papers" (Birch et al. 1956: 298). However, compared to American academic concerns, the British tend to focus more on the power of the establishment media to limit social controversy challenging to the existing class structure. Partly this preoccupation with class issues is a consequence of the fact that most of the social scientists involved are themselves ideologically critical of the prevailing social order. Two studies by the Glasgow University Media Group demonstrated that the news bulletins on the supposedly competing BBC and ITA television services reflected the same social values and the same priorities, and often even the same reporting style (Glasgow University Media Group 1976 and 1980). There was a predictability in their ordering of news items, which were heavily skewed against the interests of the working class. Industrial relations were presented almost entirely from a confrontational perspective. The language describing management actions was generally positive, while "the matching vocabulary for workers' actions is negative" (Glasgow University Media Group 1980: 401). The British media agenda affords low priority to items challenging prevailing class stereotypes.

The common practice of limiting agenda-setting research to news programs, while ignoring the other elements of a media society, seriously distorts the full influence of the mass media on the public mind. The agenda of public concerns, the themes and topics, the values appropriate for public discussion are also embodied in the general range of entertainment or feature material. Our soap operas, police dramas, and situation comedies help define the range of topics suitable for public discussion. Their impact may be more telling because it is unrecognized and therefore largely unchallenged. The legitimization of random violence in police dramas—for example, the total disregard for the plight of innocent victims of high-speed car chases—comes to be accepted as a part of life. Those who have been involved in an even moderately serious motor accident, even without physical injury, know how traumatic an experience it can be—a shock to one's nervous system, a disrupted life, and often a serious financial loss. Yet our entertainment media commonly treat a caper in which a dozen or so cars are wrecked, and a fruit stall or two are smashed, as a huge joke. Nobody comforts the victims, ensures they are all right, or offers them psychological or financial assistance. Is it any wonder we are becoming a brutalized society?

On a more positive note we need to be reminded of how such questions as abortion, homosexuality, or conditions in mental hospitals were first drawn to the public's attention by popular films and television shows. It was through prime-time entertainment programs that Americans first saw blacks and whites working together in terms of equality and mutual self-respect. The entertainment programs help establish society's norms by indicating those things which good citizens think and talk about and, by omission, those subjects which are taboo. Questions not introduced by the media are scarcely to be heard outside narrow academic circles. If, therefore, we are concerned with the range of items on the public agenda we must turn our attention to all the sources which add to, or limit, that agenda, and these include the entire content of our mass media.

In Canada and the United States, these media, being capitalist enterprises operating within the context of a capitalist society, are governed by the criteria of capitalism. Within all the liberal democracies the values of a market philosophy inevitably influence media content, even where they do not totally dominate. Corporate interests necessarily play a large part in defining social thinking and feeling. There is no evidence of any sinister conspiracy, overt threats, or prior censorship. Simply by virtue of their role as the principal source of media revenue, advertisers are effective monitors of program content. The president of CBS made the point some years ago: "Since we are advertiser-supported we must take into account the general objectives and general desires of advertisers as a whole. . . . It seems perfectly obvious that advertisers cannot and should not be forced into programs incompatible with their objectives" (Botein and Rice 1980: 193).

The message is seldom openly political. There is little of the blatant, strident, ideological propaganda found in the Soviet Union before Gorbachev. Media policy there seems directed to maintaining a fever pitch of ideological consciousness. In the West we are more subtle. Advertisers generally appear more interested in selling the goods and services produced under capitalism than in directly promoting a capitalist ideology itself. It is implicit that the "good life" as defined in the world of the commercials, and as offered through the mechanism of a capitalist economy, is, of itself, a justification of capitalism. In place of deliberate manipulation of public opinion there tends to be an uncritical acceptance of prevailing middle-class social and ethical norms. Obviously the corporations that either directly own the major mass media, or provide their financial support through advertising, will not encourage radical social change in the system which so richly benefits them. J. A. Barron, for example, offers an account of discriminatory acceptance of "editorial" advertising in American mass media. Labor union or "radical" advertisements are routinely rejected as being too political or controversial, while pro-business or pro-employer advertising is readily accepted (Barron 1973). Divisive ideological positions setting classes, racial or ethnic groups, religions, or regions, against each other, because they are bad for business, must as far as possible be kept off the public agenda. The guiding philosophy is social compromise, consensus politics, and moderation.

Bland is always safer than controversial. The main role of commercial television is to manufacture reassurance. "The object is to disconnect the audience from uncomfortable realities, to lull it on a sea of gentle inconsequence—and then sell it deodorant" (MacNeil 1968: 13).

The general media support for the existing social order does not preclude some sensational exposure of governmental corruption, political knavery, or sexual improprieties in high places, especially if they will increase the advertising audience. Radical, nonconformist, even hostile ideas are not totally banned, but they are kept to a minimum. The occasional piece of critical or antisystem material, set in the context of an overwhelmingly conformist and supportive environment, does little harm. Some critical commentary may even be highly functional in giving credence to the media's own self-image of being open and tolerant. As long as the elite is in control of access to the mass media and sets the agenda for major public debate, it has more to gain from allowing even intemperate assaults from angry or frustrated minorities than from attempting to silence them. There is a valuable social cathartic side effect in the broad acceptance of dissent on lesser issues. To preserve credibility liberal democracies must allow some public dissent from the values of liberal democracy. When the dissent poses no serious threat to the stability of the system, tolerating it is socially functional. Liberal democracy is safe as long as it can mute internal challenges—by controlling the agenda of public discussion so that awkward questions are only occasionally voiced, by diverting dissenting activities to where they will do least harm, or by focusing hostile attitudes on an external enemy.

At first, skimming through the literature on agenda-setting is a depressing exercise. It seems once more that the critics who dismiss democracy as an impractical idea have been vindicated, and the whole process is a fraud, with the few still ruling as they have always ruled. Further reading and further observation moderate this initial pessimism. A more balanced review indicates that while the media are powerful determinants of the salience to be attached to issues, their influence is not unbounded. Because not all people are regularly exposed to the mass media, their impact, while real, is not unlimited. Ownership of the media does not confer absolute power. Other structural and sociopolitical variables, set in the established norms and traditions of society, impose their own constraints. There are also considerable numbers who are immune to the messages, and who set their own agendas. Large numbers do not read newspapers, or pay attention to television news programs. And even those who regularly read and watch do not always fully comprehend what they are reading or hearing. Many are also affected by other influences and other sources of information. Few rely solely on the mass media for guidance. Family, school, church, peer group, and local information networks all add items to the agenda of each individual's concerns, and reorder the priorities of existing items. In this context it is worth noting Stouffer's study undertaken during one of America's periodic fits of anticommunist hysteria. While the national media became absorbed with the antics of Senator Joseph McCarthy, Stouffer's survey indicated that fewer than 1 percent of the respondents mentioned the internal communist threat as a matter which most concerned them (Stouffer 1955). In more recent studies, most analysts seemed to agree that the American public at large did not share President Reagan's obsession with the threat of a Sandinista invasion of Texas. And in Canada in 1986, while members of Parliament furiously and passionately debated the restoration of capital punishment, surveys indicated that for most people it had low priority on the agenda of their immediate concerns. They were far more worried about such issues as unemployment and acid rain.

Nevertheless, the traditional rational democratic idealism is forced back another step. Censors in a dozen guises, the guardians of official secrets, the gatekeepers and the agenda-setters all control, limit, restrict the information available to the public. There can be no informed rational public opinion because the public is seldom given enough information, and the information is focused on an extremely narrow range of concerns.

CHAPTER 8

Setting the Agenda: Mass Media and the Discovery of Famine in Ethiopia

Christopher J. Bosso

INTRODUCTORY NOTE

For the period from late October 1984 through September 1985 the American mass media gave broad and frequent coverage of famine in Ethiopia. As Qualter pointed out in the previous chapter, such thorough coverage of events in a far-off land that affect Americans only indirectly was highly unusual. In this chapter Christopher Bosso explains how the Ethiopian famine became a national concern, and why it subsequently faded from prominence even though millions of Ethiopians still face starvation.

Famine was not new to Ethiopia. The famine of 1973–74 had brought about the overthrow of the old regime of Emporer Haile Selassie, and its replacement by a regime characterized as leftist or Marxist by the Western press. When reports of new famine first emerged in 1982, the media took their cue from the Reagan administration and attributed the famine to government mismanagement and corruption. Famine in Africa was hardly considered important news. Only the serendipitous viewing of unusually shocking footage of thousands of starving men, women, and children by officials in NBC's London news bureau and by New York anchorman Tom Brokaw brought about the alarmed "discovery" of the problem on October 23, 1984.

Using Anthony Downs' (1972) model of the "issue-attention cycle," Bosso shows how Americans responded to this sudden "discovery" with "euphoric enthusiasm." Unfortunately, as Downs predicted, the enthusiasm eventually waned as the true costs of the resolution of the problem became apparent. Eventually, "normal politics" reasserted itself. As predicted by Downs' model, continual exposure eroded the moral force of the problem; it became familiar, less soluble, and more frustrating. It became convenient for the media to draw public attention to "more newsworthy" problems, about which reporters once again sought out issue experts and governmental elites for sources and interpretations.

But what causes public attention to fade? Bosso asks us to consider whether the pattern of coverage of successive "crises" predicted by the "issue-attention cycle" and followed by the news media results from the public's fickleness or from the publics' response to the images or choices presented by government or media elites. The ease with which new communications technologies allow us to bring the world into our homes brings us great opportunities for enlightenment, but it also improves the capacity of governments or media elites to manipulate the information we receive.

The Editors

THE NATION'S AGENDA

The tiny Reuters news service item was tucked in with other international news deep in the *Boston Globe* on October 23, 1986: the Ethiopian government appealed for 1.2 million tons of food for some 7 million people threatened with starvation (p. 10). The irony, for readers with good memories, was that two years earlier, on October 23, 1984, Americans had suddenly "discovered" hunger in Ethiopia. That the situation now seemed no better was another, and tragic, irony.

My purpose here is to examine how the Ethiopian famine forced itself into the American consciousness and temporarily became a dominant national priority. How the famine became a public problem, and why two years later it merited little more than a sideways glance, is the stuff of contemporary issue dynamics. It is the stuff of how those in mass media select and portray what we learn about the world, and about how those in government seek to structure issues both for the media and for us. It is, finally, the stuff of how we respond to tragic images, and how that attention affects public policy.

Contemporary mass media always come under fire for which issues get publicized, why, and how. Be it from the right or the left, such criticism feeds off the reality that, as E. E. Schattschneider stated a generation ago, an "unequal intensity of conflicts" shapes the political system. Politics deals ultimately with the domination and subordination of conflicts, he argued, for "political conflict is not like an intercollegiate debate in which the opponents agree in advance on a definition of the issues. As a matter of fact, *the definition of the alternatives is the supreme instrument of power*" (1960: 69; emphasis in original). No society systematically addresses every possible problem, so how the few get chosen is the guts of politics.

Just deciding whether something *is* a problem in the first place is not preordained. Some "objective condition" can exist, and arguably can be "bad," without being seen to pose undesirable consequences. If so, there is no "problem" to speak of (Jones 1975: 20). Why this is may depend powerfully on our capacity to perceive a link between extant condition and undesirable consequence. After all, as Walter Lippmann once pointed out, "what each man does is based not on direct and certain knowledge, but on pictures made by himself or given to him" (1965: 16). Greater knowledge logically expands our capacity to discern that world, but, even then, awareness does not imply concern, much less action. We may decide to ignore a problem if it challenges core values or ways of life. What is more, those who govern, pursuing their own agendas, may convince us that there is no problem, or one not worth our worry.

That capacity to define what is or is not a problem for a whole society may be the supreme instrument of power, critically influencing elites' ability to set their own paths free of public interference. Every conflict exhibits distinctive political alignments, and displacing one problem with another fundamentally shifts the calculus of political advantage. A problem displaced is now on the political backburner. It also is now judged according to terms set by its successors, held up to standards defined by *other* problems. This dynamic is important, particularly since problems compete for resources, be they budgetary or emotive. It is, very often, a zero-sum game.

Anthony Downs advances this notion of "conflict displacement" with his "issue-attention cycle"—a "systematic cycle of heightening public interest and then increasing boredom with major issues" that is "rooted both in the nature of certain domestic problems and in the way major communications media interact with the public" (1972: 39). Mass attention to some issue, Downs argues, is invariably cyclical, as opposed to more constant concern arguably held by political elites. Thus a grave condition may exist long before public attention gets focused on it through some type of "alarmed discovery." What follows, Downs argues, is "euphoric" public enthusiasm for problem solution, which just as inevitably wanes with time and public recognition of the true costs involved. Public boredom or discouragement about the issue's apparent intractability remands the matter into a "limbo" of low saliency and the reassertion of "normal" politics. The issue may reemerge spasmodically, but it no longer is so "new" (Downs 1972: 39–40).

The type of condition most likely to go through this cycle, Downs argues, is one that does not affect a majority, emerges out of social conditions providing "significant benefits to a majority or a powerful minority of the population," and no longer has any "intrinsically exciting" quality (1972: 41). Thus, most of us are not affected directly by the condition in question; to solve it (and not merely its symptoms) would require changes that may threaten existing distribution of resources or power, and it will almost invariably fade from view with continued exposure. Downs developed this framework to study domestic environmental issues in the early 1970s, but television's role in raising international issues—and their increased interconnectedness with domestic policy questions—merits applying it to a foreign policy area.

Foreign news traditionally comes to us through filters of issue experts and government elites, those whom reporters select to interpret an issue for the audience (Graber 1984: 318; Page et al. 1987: 32). Which elites are sought out, and how they define a problem, strongly influences (if not determines) how media outlets present an issue about which few Americans have direct knowledge. Agreeing that the Nicaraguan rebels are "freedom fighters" or the Japanese are "protectionist" thus may hinge most on how well government elites make their definitions stick. This in turn depends inherently on how well the definitions resonate with extant public biases. Whether Americans are innately anticommunist or believe all Third World governments to be corrupt has less to do with the accumulation of facts than with the sheer repetition of stereotypes by those who control the flow of information and symbols. And, as Graber suggests, geopolitical considerations—the "friend" or "foe" syndrome—dominate how foreign news gets conveyed (1984: 327). If some regime is a "Soviet puppet" it may be because we *believe* it is, just as we all once lumped all "communists" into a single homogeneous mass (McDonald 1985). The current disaggregation of "world communism" into "good" (e.g., China) and "bad" (e.g., Nicaragua) versions may reflect more the shifts in geopolitical dictates than any innate qualities of the regimes in question. And, in their desire to be narrowly "objective," American media almost always pass along the official consensus of reality to us (Bennett 1988; Graber 1984; Parenti 1986).

But what happens when we encounter dramatic foreign news in rawer form as media "retail" it directly into our living rooms? How do our perceptions of a problem align with official versions of truth when the images presented to us actually bypass the filters of government definition? And, in the process of transmitting sensational imagery to the public, what makes media elites go right to their audience without first stopping in the halls of power for official comment? This case seeks to understand some of these questions by examining an issue that Americans first encountered in almost unrefined form.

Some truths about American mass media are worth addressing beforehand. Protestations about their "public service" role aside, those in the press live first and foremost in the world of competition and profit. After all, neither commercial network news shows nor elite newspapers are exempt from the need to "sell" audiences to advertisers, and those who present news know that "entertainment value" is what sells (Downs 1972; Graber 1984). The emphasis is on drama, conflict, and novelty, each news outlet seeking the "hook" to differentiate itself from competitors, because the public absorbs but a fraction of the cascade of information presented nightly. Only a few issues stand out.

But no mainstream media outlet will differentiate itself *too* much, particularly on controversial matters. Doing so invites uncomfortable scrutiny, as those at CBS learned when attacked for an alleged liberal bias. Indeed, there is relatively little heterogeneity in American national news media; the birds of a feather *do* flock together, be it on natural catastrophe or political event (Page et al. 1987; Graber 1984; Parenti 1986). The cumulative effect of the actions by these "rivals in conformity" sets the national agenda for issue attention in generally homogeneous ways (Graber 1984: 80).

Whether mass media "change" public opinion is still debated, but few argue that they do affect what it is Americans pay attention to (Page et al. 1987). And how an issue is presented—both in words and pictures—has everything to do with whether and how well the public responds (Graber 1987). What follows, then, is an examination of how a single condition in a far-off land became a national concern. I use Downs' "issue attention cycle" to guide this essay, so I first examine the conditions in Ethiopia before the famine gained international headlines. Next come the dynamics of "discovery"—how the famine suddenly became a public problem—and the subsequent impacts of public concern on government action. I then follow the politics of famine relief as publicity wanes, concluding with some observations about the power of media to move a society and the power of government to influence how we see the world.

DOG BITES MAN: FAMINE AS NON-NEWS

Issues vault most readily into mass consciousness when they are socially significant, apparently nontechnical, defined broadly, and above all, emotional (Cobb and Elder 1972: 112–24). There is, of course, a law of novelty governing our attention to any condition, no matter how emotive. That famine ravaged sub-Saharan Africa during the early 1980s was a "dog bites man" story as far as many media elites were concerned, not unlike their responses to another overloaded ferry boat sinking on the Ganges or more bombs devastating neighborhoods in Beirut. Bad things happen and people get hurt, but unless the victims are Americans, events in foreign lands merit little space in our news when they occur frequently.

Famine in Ethiopia is a compelling case in point. It was not "new" news, for the roots of the 1984 disaster lay in conditions known years before the disaster hit the headlines. Ethiopia has experienced food shortages almost annually since the famine of 1973–74 caused an estimated 200,000 deaths and led to the overthrow of Emperor Haile Selassie. The regime led by Mengistu Haile Mariam—invariably prefaced by terms like "leftist" or "Marxist" in the Western press—has since then presided over a nation wracked by civil war and characterized by government misman- agement, skyrocketing population growth, drought, and, as a result, by steady declines in food production. And Ethiopia was not alone. Despite billions in Western aid, most sub-Saharan African nations remained de- pendent on annual infusions of foreign food. Drought, soil erosion, pop- ulation growth, misguided development strategies, errant aid programs, war, and, of course, politics—both domestic and global—all played a part in making sub-Saharan Africa the beggar of the world.

More than anything else, politics marks the boundaries of the Ethi- opian disaster. Successive years of severe drought prompted the Ethio- pian government in late 1982 to appeal for Western help in feeding some 2 million people. The Mengistu regime seemed reluctant to broadcast its woes *too* loudly for fear of emulating Selassie's end, but unlike Selassie it did provide ample warning of the impending disaster. That the drought hit hardest in areas where rebel factions dominated complicated matters greatly, and became yet another factor in internal Ethiopian politics.

In geopolitical terms, the Reagan administration certainly hoped that the famine would topple Mengistu, whose Eastern Bloc ties and Marxist rhetoric chilled relations with Washington. Famine-induced unrest in a key Soviet ally would embarrass a Kremlin seeking to enhance its inter- national image, and, at least in the minds of some administration officials, would reaffirm Soviet indifference on humanitarian questions. Said one private relief agency official about some in the White House, "To them it was a chance to make communism look bad, that's all" (*Washington Post,* November 21, 1984: A10). The appeals thus generated minimal American government aid.

The reader should not be shocked by this. Food is used routinely as a lever against regimes not currently in Washington's favor, and the Rea- gan administration from the start clearly saw food as another way to en- force political stability or compliance. "It is naive to assume that food aid has as its major purpose the alleviation of hunger and poverty," said one senior administration official in 1985. *"To give food to countries just be- cause people are starving is a pretty weak reason"* (Shepherd 1985: 5; emphasis supplied). That the electorate rarely finds such a view palatable is not a factor as long as aid issues stay securely out of the public gaze or are seen as somebody else's concern.

Indeed, administration officials through 1984 consistently portrayed the famine purely as the result of the Ethiopians' own policies and prior- ities. "It isn't their ideology that's a problem," argued Jay Morris, deputy administrator of the U.S. Agency for International Development (AID), "it's their behavior toward their own people" (*Washington Post,* August 11, 1984: A14). Such press coverage as existed prior to late 1984 almost uniformly reflected the angle that Mengistu had made his own bed, with materials supplied by the Cubans and Soviets. It is no surprise, therefore, that most Americans responded with indifference to the few stories that emerged. Helping regimes that apparently starve their own people isn't a compelling moral matter.[1]

Two examples illuminate this *realpolitik*. First, as appeals by the Ethiopian government intensified through late 1982, Catholic Relief Services officials there sent urgent messages to AID for emergency supplemental assistance. Such requests, according to a 1985 U.S. General Accounting Office study, normally were approved in three weeks, but this time no response came until the following May (*Washington Report on Africa,* May 15, 1985: 58). The pattern was repeated through 1983, with administration officials arguing that it was "inappropriate" to assist a government that is "spending money fighting its own people" (*Washington Report on Africa,* May 15, 1983: 67). Private relief officials accused AID of stalling because of animosity toward Mengistu, a charge AID director M. Peter McPherson hotly denied. But, according to press accounts, McPherson discovered that the charges bore some truth: many administration officials clearly *did* see food as a weapon in the struggle against communism, and requests for aid made by "friendly" nations like Kenya *were* filled far more quickly than were those made by allies of the Soviet Union. An internal struggle at AID apparently ensued in mid-1983, with at least one key "hardliner" abruptly resigning his African affairs post, and McPherson began to take a more personal role in Ethiopian relief (*Washington Report on Africa,* October 15, 1983: 4). Requests made thereafter by Catholic Relief Services were processed more quickly than before in part because of the changes at AID, but also because administration officials feared adverse publicity as famine stories began to appear in the Western press and attract the interest of many in Congress.

More telling, the administration's fiscal 1984 foreign aid budget completely cut off *all* food for Ethiopia—the only nation so singled out. Only $2.4 million in emergency food aid had been appropriated for Ethiopia during fiscal 1983, despite the severity of conditions there, and private relief officials could not remember another time when emergency food aid had been so excised *during* a famine (*Washington Report on Africa,* May 15, 1983: 67; *Washington Post,* June 26, 1983; A19). Administration officials defended the action, charging the Mengistu regime with diverting aid monies for weapons payments and keeping food from rebel-held areas. These charges, made by a former Ethiopian official now tied to one rebel faction, were subsequently discounted by Western European govern-

---

[1]In Summer 1988 Ethiopian famine was once again in the news. Reports stated that the Mengistu regime was not cooperating with international agencies to assure equitable distribution of supplies for relief.

ments and private relief organizations. Congressional pressure and greater realization of the severity of the famine eventually prompted the administration to reverse its course and appropriate some $5 million for Ethiopian aid for fiscal 1984, though many administration officials, particularly U.N. Ambassador Jeane Kirkpatrick, continued to oppose support (*Washington Report on Africa,* August, 1, 1983: 89).

If politics dictated the shape of U.S. government actions, other factors also figured into a largely tepid international response. Ethiopia was but one of many sub-Saharan nations in trouble, and private donors thus had to divvy up limited resources among more claimants, resources strained further by an actual drop in total U.S. government food aid to Africa between 1981 and 1983 (*Washington Post,* November 1, 1984: A23). Foreign aid, save in select instances (e.g., Israel), is an easy mark for the budget axe precisely because providing regular assistance to countries such as Mozambique or Chad is not rewarding politically. The objective condition of starvation afar is not compelling enough in the world of budgetary politics; where and when it occurs may be more so.

Many also were weary of the repeated Ethiopian appeals, which some in the relief community saw as exaggerated and too often tinged by criticism of the West for not doing more. "The Ethiopians have cried wolf too often in the past," said one official to David Ottoway of the *Washington Post.* "Donor fatigue has become a real problem" (*National Weekly Edition,* October 1, 1984: 16). Many also believed that Ethiopia, torn by war and burdened with the Africa's poorest transportation system, would be hard-pressed to distribute massive new deliveries of food. Questions raised by the Reagan administration as to the Ethiopian government's willingness to feed those in rebel areas always arose, and the Mengistu regime didn't help matters much through its early reluctance to cooperate fully with Western governments. The regime also lent credence to the criticism when it began plans to celebrate its tenth year in power. U.S. government officials claimed that the Ethiopians spent over $100 million on the festivities, funded largely by Eastern Bloc nations, while the Ethiopians claimed that it was closer to $8 million (*Washington Post,* November 3, 1984: 1). Whatever the case, the damage was done: poor nations simply are not supposed to act this way, and Western governments accused the Ethiopians and their patrons of misplaced priorities, if not outright callousness.

Intensified appeals by both the Ethiopian government and international relief agencies through 1983 finally did prompt some media attention and subsequent official concern. A June 1983 series by the *Washington Post* detailing the politics of famine relief led to visits by congressional delegations. These generated calls for more aid and blunted administration efforts to cut off Ethiopia completely. Senator John Danforth (R., Mo.) returned with pictures that he showed to President Reagan, who reportedly was shocked and promised help, despite his administration's earlier actions. Presidential attention and congressional concern would lead to more U.S. aid in late 1983, plus proposals for supplemental appropriations in early 1984.

Elite concern did not, however, translate into widespread media attention, even as the famine worsened. Not that access to Ethiopia was cut off: British and other European news crews managed repeatedly to gain entry, but American networks largely avoided the region. And, insofar as they were concerned, the story had little real "news" value anyway. The three commercial networks had few personnel on the continent to begin with, and yet another famine story would have to compete with "hotter" topics like South African apartheid or Libya's war with Chad. Foreign news makes up the smallest part of the daily network news offering to begin with, and Africa historically gets the least attention of all, so the threshhold for attention was very high indeed (Graber, 1984: 311).

Figure 8–1 shows the level of coverage given to Ethiopian famine stories by the three American television networks in the years 1973–83. From a peak during the last "newsworthy" Ethiopian famine in 1974, network coverage virtually disappeared, and relief agencies seeking to focus national concern about the famine consistently found media elites uninterested. "We would hold press conferences," noted Dick Loudis of

FIGURE 8–1   Cumulative Annual Coverage of Famine Issues, 1973–1983

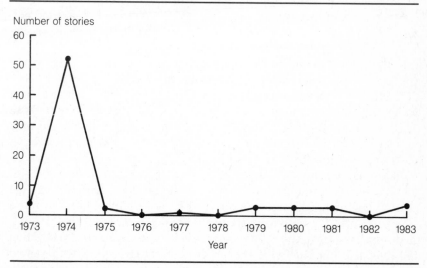

SOURCE: *Television News Index and Abstracts* (Vanderbilt Television News Archive, Vanderbilt University).

CARE, and "we'd have a little bit of turnout, but it wasn't widely reported" (*Washington Post*, November 21, 1984: A10). The Ethiopian Relief and Rehabilitation Commission in March 1984 again warned loudly of disaster and requested some 450,000 tons of food, but these appeals generated only about half of the aid requested. Catholic Relief Services also sent out an appeal for funds, but its mass mailing generated only about $800,000 nationwide (*Washington Post*, November 21, 1984: A10). Few Americans seemed to know or care about the matter.

Emergency appropriations for African relief meanwhile moved quietly through Congress during early 1984, spurred on by sharpened congressional concern about the gravity of the situation. In March the House approved some $150 million in aid, but the package became stalled in the Senate when the administration insisted on linking it with funds to support the Nicaraguan rebels. This action infuriated many on Capitol Hill, and produced great worry in the relief community because of the long lead time needed to ensure that aid reached its targets in time. The administration was charged by Speaker Thomas P. O'Neill with "exploiting the misery in Africa to advance its own political agenda" (*Washington Report on Africa*, March 15, 1984: 41). Senator Danforth managed to pry loose some $90 million in food aid and attach it to a less controversial domestic heating subsidy bill, which the president signed in late March, but the remaining $60 million remained snarled with military assistance to Latin America until July. "Here was the administration saying okay to food if you give us guns," said one private relief agency official. "What shocked me was the press: Clearly that was editorial material, but it wasn't, and that tells you something" (*Washington Post*, November 21, 1984: A10). Both the *Washington Post* and the *New York Times* did editorialize against this linkage, but the debate overall never went beyond "normal" Washington politics.

The Ethiopian famine thus was not a sudden catastrophe, the sort of seismic event that invariably draws media attention. It was instead a condition that developed over several years, predicted well in advance by a wide array of international relief agencies, and fully understood by those in government. But, for a variety of reasons, mostly political, aid only trickled in. Official U.S. aid did increase in late 1983, and it appeared that the administration was willing to do more, but there remained sharp internal disagreements over assisting a communist nation. What is more, these conflicts attracted little public attention. That it would emerge sharply and with an element of shocked surprise proved bitter to those who had worked hard to meet the challenge much earlier. "That was it," said Rep. Harold Wolpe (D., Mich.), who led a congressional delegation to Ethiopia in August 1983. "The facts were there for anyone who wanted to see them two years ago. To say that we were taken by surprise is only to say that we didn't want to see before" (*Washington Post,* November 21, 1984: A10).

"DISCOVERING" FAMINE

"As a result of some dramatic series of events," Downs argues, "or for other reasons, the public suddenly becomes both aware of and alarmed about the evils of a particular problem." What results upsets the "normal" rhythms of politics in America. "This alarmed discovery," he continues, "is invariably accompanied by euphoric enthusiasm about society's ability to 'solve this problem,' or 'do something effective' within a relatively short time. The combination of alarm and confidence results in part from the strong public pressure in America for political leaders to claim that every problem can be 'solved.'" (1972: 39).

Public "discovery" of the Ethiopian famine fit this pattern, particularly because it was the sort of problem that apparently could be attacked without reordering domestic priorities. The problem affected "others," and was presented in such a way that an "easy" solution was in sight. Americans, once they perceived that millions were starving in a faraway land, could mount a national crusade to speed aid to the unfortunate. Results would be immediate: starving people would get food. The Ethiopian famine thus presented a perfect challenge for a society to mobilize on behalf of some apparently unadulterated good. How Americans became mobilized is instructive.

On Tuesday, October 23, 1984, and for three successive nights afterward, NBC News aired stunning footage of starving Ethiopians massed together in immense government feeding stations. NBC anchor Tom Brokaw reported that some 6 million were endangered, while about 500,000 probably would die within a year. The graphic pictures had an immediate impact: UNICEF, the international childrens' relief agency, reported over 5,000 telephone calls during the next four days. The Save the Children Fund received over 12,000 calls in the same period, plus pledges of close to $75,000. Catholic Relief Services, whose earlier appeals produced relatively little, reported over $2 million in a single month. "The switchboards were all lit up here all day long," reported one CRS official, alluding to the day after the first NBC report (*Washington Post,* November 21, 1984: A10). That Americans reacted to the NBC footage with alarm and generosity indicates the power of television to raise awareness of a previously "hidden" issue.

But such film had existed long before NBC brought it to its viewers, and the story had been reported by various media during the previous year. David Kline, an American free-lance journalist, shot film of the famine in October 1983 while on assignment for CBS, but that network rejected the material because, as he later explained, it was not "strong enough." Kline offered the film to both NBC and PBS, but was turned down in both cases. Their reaction, as Kline summed up later was, "You're offering me a story about *kids starving in Africa?* Please. That's not a story—it's like saying the sun rises in the east" (Boot 1985: 47). ABC News Rome correspondent Bill Blakemore likewise sought permission to send a film crew into Ethiopia after hearing about the disaster from European contacts, but his network also rejected the idea. None of the American networks had personnel in the region at this time for a variety of fiscal and political reasons, and the story simply wasn't "strong enough" as yet to compel network executives to reallocate resources. That the networks already were immersed in the presidential campaign, a time when most foreign news takes a back seat in the competition for air time, was of no small consequence.

Britons in fact "discovered" the Ethiopian famine months before most Americans. A film crew from British Central Television was in Ethiopia during May 1984 when it literally bumped into a group of refugees trudging to a government feeding station. The film crew followed and shot dramatic footage, which Central Television rushed into production. BBC correspondent Michael Buerk got into Ethiopia about the same time and shot his own film. Both documentaries were aired on July 17, generating some £9 million in donations.

But American television audiences were not so affected by two network stories on the famine aired before the pivotal October 23 broadcast. An August 2 story by CBS may not have had much impact both because it was tucked in the midst of the nightly broadcast and because CBS treated it as just another "news" item, with heavy emphasis on the civil war, Soviet and Cuban assistance to the government, and the impact of cold war politics. CBS also included an interview with an AID official who blamed the Ethiopian government for the crisis. The "slant" was that this was yet another complex issue in a far-off land, not the sort of matter compelling enough to stir viewers. It thus generated no noticeable impact beyond, perhaps, an August 5 *Washington Post* editorial asking for more aid. NBC, for its part, aired a short excerpt of the Buerk film on August 11, but also with little noticeable impact, probably because it was Saturday (a "graveyard" night in televisionland).

Buerk, meanwhile returned from Ethiopia in late October with even more disturbing material (Boot 1985: 47). NBC personnel in London turned down a BBC offer to view the new film before it was aired. "It was kind of a low priority with us," explained bureau chief Joseph Angotti. But, when London bureau officials watched the footage on television, Angotti continued, "it just knocked us all right through the roof" (*Washington Post,* November 21, 1984: A10). He urged network executives to show it immediately, but they demurred; to do so would cut into election coverage. Angotti sent the film to New York anyway. According to various reports, NBC anchorman Tom Brokaw was equally shocked by the graphic scenes of death and scheduled the story for October 23, in lieu of two campaign pieces. It was the last story of that broadcast, and Brokaw prominently mentioned Save the Children and Catholic Relief Services on the air after the film ended, a rare advocacy for action that prompted the sudden deluge of calls (Boot 1985; *Washington Post,* November 13, 1984: B3).

What also emerged was torrential, if spasmodic, mass media attention to an issue previously ignored. Figure 8–2 shows famine coverage by the three networks during 1984–85, a pattern of virtual inattention to the issue until October 1984, a dramatic surge afterward, and a gradual decline in attention by the spring. The brief peak in July 1985 indicates coverage of the international Live Aid rock concert, an event whose momentary entertainment value outstripped even the famine in cumulative minutes of network coverage for one month.

Even more instructive is the pattern of daily coverage that followed the original NBC broadcast. NBC clearly got the jump on its rivals, and made the best of the situation with successive nights of extensive coverage. The other networks ignored the famine for almost a *week,* undoubtedly because they lacked their own film. The story was there, and public response was measurable, but neither ABC nor CBS went with it until

FIGURE 8–2 · Cumulative Network Coverage, January 1984–October 1985

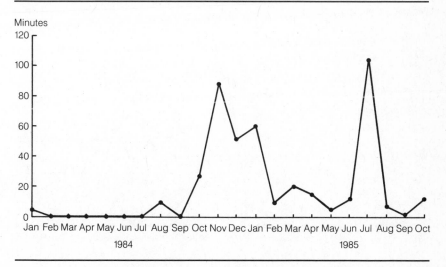

SOURCE: *Television News Index and Abstracts* (Vanderbilt Television News Archive, Vanderbilt University).

October 29. And like NBC, the other two used European sources for their original footage. All three networks, in the meantime, rushed camera crews to a suddenly hospitable Ethiopia. The famine now was newsworthy, and the competitive instincts of the commercial networks—laced with a fear of missing a potentially "hot" issue—overcame any previous ennui with starvation in a foreign land.

The famine as news just as suddenly gave way to the presidential election, and to the October 31 assassination of Indian Prime Minister Ghandi, for almost a solid week. Then came the rush for another major story. Ethiopia was it, and, once the networks got their own film, became *the* story of November 1984. This was true particularly for NBC, which worked especially hard to maintain its "lead" on the story. The network touted its serendipitous triumph in its promotional advertising, just as all three networks lauded their election coverage.

Matters went pretty much the same way in the print media, suggesting how the attention of television to some issue now influences similar decisions by the nation's newspapers. Figure 8–3 contrasts three arguably national dailies. The *New York Times,* traditionally the strongest American newspaper on international news, and the *Washington Post,* known for its thorough coverage of the federal government, both show a modi-

FIGURE 8–3   Newspaper Coverage, January 1984–October 1985

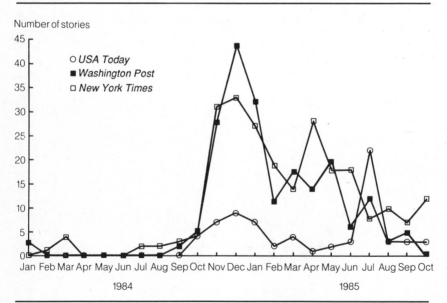

SOURCE: Annual index for each newspaper.

cum of attention throughout the year, but coverage of the famine nevertheless takes off in the wake of the exposure by their electronic cousins. The pattern shown by *USA Today,* a newspaper that unapologetically follows television's lead, is even more telling—no coverage at all until October. That *USA Today*'s peak coincides with the Live Aid Concert only testifies to its focus.

The coverage in selected regional dailies shown in Figure 8–4 reveals a similar pattern. There seems little doubt that newspaper editors used Americans' reaction to pictures of tragedy to set their agendas. And it would be this multiplier effect, the crescendo of coverage by a wide array of media, that proved most critical to making the Ethiopian famine a national concern. The sheer *repetition* of the problem, be it by local television stations or non-elite periodicals, made the famine familiar to most Americans. From *People* to *Newsweek* to *Reader's Digest,* the outlets of mass journalism followed NBC's lead with gusto.

One facet of all this coverage bears some comment. Ethiopia certainly was not the only African nation facing mass starvation—Mozambique and the Sudan, for example, were also in dire straits. Nor were

FIGURE 8–4   Average Monthly Newspaper Coverage, January 1984–October 1985

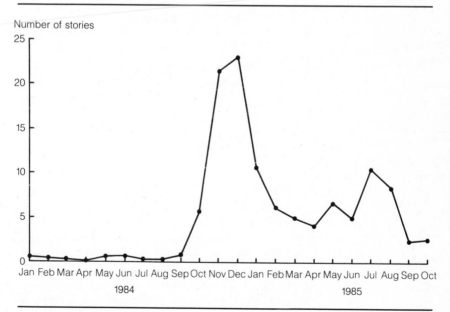

SOURCE: *Boston Globe, Chicago Tribune, Houston Post, Los Angeles Times, New Orleans Times-Picayune, St. Louis Post-Dispatch*

African nations alone in their plight. Oxfam International officials during 1984 warned repeatedly of the peril facing 25 million northeastern Brazilians, yet the situation there went essentially ignored even as reporters traipsed off in droves to Addis Ababa. The reason was partly happenstance, but as the events described above suggest, Ethiopia was better television. Brazil lacked the mass feeding stations, the scenes of dramatic starvation against a parched desert backdrop that seared the souls of viewers (Boot 1985: 47). Said Africare Executive Director C. Payne Lucas, "The starving Ethiopian babies on the evening news have sparked some response, but it's a lot harder to get the Chads and the Malis and the Nigers on television" (*Washington Post,* November 6: A17). A compelling story is not enough—you need good pictures.

THE MORAL CRUSADE AT HOME

Media focus on the famine soon shifted to the efforts to resolve the crisis. Television in particular increasingly emphasized the domestic side of the famine equation, in part because fund-raising efforts themselves constituted news but also because the symbolic "value" of the pictures from Ethiopia (or variations on the same theme) steadily decreased with continued repetition (Downs 1972: 47). It also was difficult to show "progress" by continuing to focus on the victims; fresh infusions of aid were en route, but people were still dying, a fact of both logistics and the nature of starvation perhaps incomprehensible to viewers.

The "crusade at home" thus became the news, be it the British Band-Aid effort or *People* magazine coverage of a visit to Ethiopia by Sen. Edward Kennedy. Later, of course, there would be USA for Africa and Live Aid—not to mention innumerable permutations such as Fashion Aid, or the computer industry's Soft Aid. Famine relief became a movement, something that almost everyone could take part in. "What USA for Africa did, and what Band-Aid did in England, is to make compassion hip," said Bob Geldof, the English singer who sparked the Band-Aid effort. "If all that comes out of this is the perceived attitude that it's fashionable to care, then it's worth it, time and time again" (*Boston Globe,* April 28, 1985: B32). That this involved feeding citizens of a "Marxist" country apparently mattered little to most Americans.

That dimension of moral crusade, as refracted through the gaze of television, fundamentally shifted national priorities and actions—and not only in the United States. The Reagan administration, caught off guard by the sudden deluge of coverage, boosted commitments of aid to Ethiopia in the days between the first NBC story and the presidential election. Total U.S. government food aid to Ethiopia for all of fiscal 1984 amounted to about $23 million, up from about $3 million in fiscal 1983, but jumped to more than *four times* that amount (about $98 million) between October

1 and December 1, 1984. Roughly two-thirds of that money was committed after the NBC broadcast, suggesting the palpable impact of national attention to the issue (*Washington Post,* November 21, 1984: A10).

But if administration officials now were dealing directly with the Ethiopian government on famine relief, they continued to work their own "spin" on the situation. AID director McPherson blasted the Soviet Union for its "callous indifference" to a famine in its "client" state, and traded charges with the Mengistu regime over the extent of aid needed and its delivery to the victims (*Washington Post,* October 31, 1984, A13). These attacks apparently spurred donations of transportation equipment by the increasingly image-conscious Kremlin.

The nation's newspaper editorial writers almost uniformly echoed administration themes. The *Houston Chronicle,* for one, rejected "any notion that the United States should go on a guilt trip over mass starvation in Ethiopia" (November 20, 1984, as reprinted in *Facts on File,* vol. 15, no. 22: 1337), and most other newspapers reviewed likewise hammered the Soviets and Ethiopians for their actions.[2] Almost all, however, also concluded that this was not reason enough for the United States to forgo its moral duty, a duality between the superpowers that is a traditional staple of American politics. Such nuances, however, apparently escaped television viewers, for whom pictures spoke not of politics but human misery, not of Soviet or Ethiopian indifference but of an international effort to aid the suffering. "Pictures," argues Doris Graber, "forge emotional bonds between viewers and viewed. They make audiences care about an issue and the people involved" (Graber 1987: 8). The pictures were far more compelling than any words spoken by government officials or written in editorials.

The moral crusade at home influenced domestic American politics through early 1985. The "normal" politics of foreign aid looks demonstrably manipulative under the public eye, and the debate in Washington quickly turned into recriminations over why aid had not come sooner. Congressional Democrats blasted the White House for its previous legislative actions linking African food aid to support for the Nicaraguan rebels, and responded with a half dozen aid proposals and accompanying committee hearings in January 1985 alone. Their efforts to embarrass

---

[2]Newspapers reviewed: *Arizona Republic; Arkansas Gazette; Augusta Journal* (Georgia); *Birmingham News* (Alabama); *Boston Globe; Buffalo Evening News; Cleveland Plain Dealer; Chicago Tribune; Louisville Courier Journal; Denver Post; Detroit News; Kansas City Tribune; Houston Chronicle; Houston Post; Los Angeles Times; New Orleans Times-Picayune; New York Times; The Oregonian; Pittsburgh Post-Gazette; Rapid City Journal* (South Dakota); *The Register* (Santa Ana, Calif.); *Richmond News Leader; San Fransisco Chronicle; Washington Post.*

Reagan into approving substantial aid and score a few political points in the process predictably turned hearings into partisan battles, with administration officials gamely responding with countercharges of Ethiopian diversion of aid and the dismal support offered by Eastern Bloc countries. These themes were picked up by congressional Republicans, and the whole debate quickly lost whatever nonpartisan luster it may have possessed.

Its reservations about Mengistu notwithstanding, the administration in January requested some $235 million in additional African aid, a proposal quickly outdone by Democrats' move to appropriate about $1 billion (*CQ Weekly Report,* January 25, 1985: 87). Private relief officials tended to see the higher figure as more realistic, but were happy nonetheless to see a turnaround in political conditions after years of unrewarding labor. The relief bill moved swiftly, borne by an urgency not exhibited the year before.

But an issue emerging from the American heartland was to have critical ramifications for African aid. If the famine was the issue of late 1984, media attention shifted in early 1985 to the plight of the American family farm, an issue of more direct relevance to the nation's public and, particularly, its politicians. The problems of surplus on the farm suddenly were juxtaposed with those of famine overseas, and the two issues now were married together in a starkly rational way. Farm-state congressmen demanded swift credit relief for their constituents, and the rapidly moving African relief bill loomed as the most convenient vehicle for such a program. Linkage is the norm in Washington politics, and a crisis once deemed central to the national agenda now was joined to another.

House leaders, fearing that an unprotected African relief bill would become a classic congressional "Christmas Tree," fought back efforts to append the farm credit provisions, but the more entrepreneurial environs of the Senate proved a far different matter. African famine relief stalled through March as the administration and farm-state senators wrangled over the credit issue, with the president forced to use emergency powers to provide more food aid in the interim. Weeks of maneuvering ensued before Congress finally produced an African relief bill worth some $784 million in short- and long-term aid, which the president signed in early April (*CQ Weekly Report,* April 20, 1985: 753). The money had been held up longer than most had wished, but at least it was forthcoming.

AFTER THE DELUGE: THE FAMINE IN LIMBO

The shocking deaths provide the element of novelty. After the novelty has worn off, interest dims and media attention flags, even if the problem remains unsolved.

(Graber 1984: 93)

The problem of famine in Africa thus was "settled" so far as the public, and many of its leaders, were concerned. Mass attention to the famine had subsided by the time the relief bill reached President Reagan's desk, and public gaze would not sharpen again, save for the momentary spasm of interest generated by the media-infused Live Aid Concert.

By mid-1985 the disaster had slipped from the front pages and some of the "normal" politics of famine relief began to reemerge. Ethiopian and American officials sniped at one another publicly on issues of resettling famine victims, supply and use of trucks, and, in essence, about just who would call the shots. Lack of sufficient transport capacity allowed stocks of food to pile up in port, prompting AID director McPherson to charge the Mengistu regime with allocating resources for resettlement and the civil war instead of feeding the hungry. Private relief agency officials rebutted McPherson's charges, but the spats clearly undermined any comity that may have been built up between them during the previous months.

Despite the massive effort, some one million Ethiopians ultimately died during 1984–85, though the number no doubt would have been higher had the disaster not gained international attention (*Washington Report on Africa*, May 1, 1986: 56). African food needs continue to grow, and relief officials fear that public attention to the problem will be difficult to rekindle "so soon" after most Americans thought the matter solved. Their fears probably are justified, if the pattern repeats the legacy of the 1974 famine. The prognosis among relief experts for the long term is not optimistic, for the sustained development assistance necessary to avert future famine hardly is as "newsworthy" or politically safe as emergency relief crusades. The most effective solutions may not be the most likely, particularly given the legacy of foreign aid battles and the added impact of contemporary budgetary politics. The massive relief effort may only have provided temporary balm for the symptoms.

Whether Americans in fact became bored with the famine as soon as media coverage patterns suggest is difficult to divine. One local Boston television reporter, who spent a great deal of time on the issue, suggested that "the media got tired of it before the people did." Those in the media, the reporter added, are notoriously sensitive to "carping" on negative stories for too long, and the fact that food had reached the victims was reason enough to search out fresh stories (personal interview: June 1986).

Whatever the case, the famine receded completely from the national agenda by mid-1986, as Downs might have predicted, to the point that the administration once again was accused of intending to divert African relief funds to finance economic assistance to Central America. Warnings of impending disaster throughout Africa appeared only in short wire-service pieces. Continued drought again threatens Ethiopia as of this writing (Fall 1987), but as far as media attention is concerned, the famine as an issue is in limbo. "There will be no such scenes this time," said David

Morton of the United Nations World Food Program. "If you do get such pictures, it will mean relief has come too late" (*Boston Globe,* November 10, 1987: 10). But without wide media attention, many relief officials fear a repeat of that grim scenario.

CONCLUSION: THE WORLD OUTSIDE AND THE IMAGES IN OUR HEADS

Photographs have the kind of authority over imagination today which the printed word had yesterday, and the spoken word before that. They seem utterly real. They come, we imagine, directly to use without human meddling, and they are the most effortless food for the mind conceivable.

(Lippmann, 1965: 61)

Issues compete for attention, so the choices made by those in mass media as to what constitutes "news" are critical to both policymakers and the mass public. This case essentially examined how a condition that existed for years became a "problem" to Americans, even though the famine did not affect them directly. It also demonstrated the almost serendipitous nature of how we learn about some problems, a reality that may shake any faith we may have about our capacity to address grave conditions systematically.

Only the timing of media exposure was largely random. In a larger sense, this case also demonstrated how an issue can be kept out of the public gaze when its particulars do not constitute novelty or when the victims are not on the "right" side politically. Problems can be defined away through media indifference, or through the capacity of government elites to influence our perceptions. Fortune dictated that most Americans learned about the famine relatively unadulterated by government "spin," but that a Tom Brokaw has the capacity to raise national awareness of an issue certainly raises questions about the role media elites play in our political life. One does not need a conspiracy theory to worry about that sort of power, particularly with respect to foreign news. Current trends in technology that make the "globalization" of news gathering and dissemination more possible and profitable are worth our attention, since the spread of instantaneous and global communication is redefining the relationship between governments and those who bring the news to our television sets. The Ethiopian famine and the worldwide airing of the Live Aid Concert are but precursors of Marshall McLuhan's global village.

There is little doubt that geopolitical considerations fell swiftly before the tornado of public concern for the victims. *Public opinion* may not direct government action, and its substance indeed may be dependent on the actions and words of political and media elites, but concerted *public attention* to an issue certainly narrows the range of options a government can take. To do anything *but* send aid would have appeared immoral so long as the media highlighted the story and so long as the public paid attention. But, as Downs would suggest, the "normal" politics of foreign aid reasserted itself after the camera lights and public gaze both faded, and the public returned to the sidelines.

We indeed create the world about us in our own heads, attaching significance to conditions or events through prior perceptions about that world. Our perceptions are riddled with gaps and stereotypes, which government elites find fertile ground for manipulation. They understand Americans' attitudes about the less fortunate, views that discriminate between the "deserving" and "undeserving." Painting famine victims as the latter because of their government's ideological bent works quite well until rawer images jar the public.

The deliverers of those images may not have their own political agendas to promote, but media elites' attitudes about what constitutes news and how the public should be informed also resonate with our own biases about what problems merit concern. They assume we don't care about foreign affairs, and they certainly know the limits to our compassion. We may care about the less fortunate, but don't want to be reminded constantly that we should. Be it famine in Africa or poverty at home, the moral force of any condition certainly erodes with continued exposure. It is no longer novel, nor perhaps soluble, and thus more frustrating. It is easier to go on to newer problems.

That dynamic—bouncing from one temporarily newsworthy problem to another—also bears further study. Do we really talk of public opinion, or *spasms of public attention?* The former is diffuse and often inconsequential, the latter more focused and powerful, but fleeting. John Dewey, who long ago worried that the industrial age had "so enormously expanded, multiplied, intensified, and complicated the scope of indirect consequences" that the public could not easily identify and act on problems, probably would be astounded by the current age of ephemeral and spasmodic problems, by the cycle of temporarily compelling issues that just as easily fade, as those in media seek out the new (1927: 126).

Downs argues that this pattern of successive "crises" results from public whim, from the audience's fickle fascination or boredom with a particular issue (1972: 48). But I wonder about that. The public in a free society bears a tremendous burden. It must discern and act on problems, or at least compel the government to do so, to fulfill its democratic responsibility. But that public normally *responds* to images and choices presented to it by those in positions of authority or astride the avenues of information. Schattschneider, for one, blames any problems of democracy not on an ill-informed or irresolute public, but on the failure by elites to "define the alternatives of public policy in such a way that the public can participate in the decision-making process" (1960: 141). If those in power define the choices in skewed or ambiguous ways, or decide that there is no problem to speak of, perhaps it is no surprise that the public does not behave as democratic theorists wish it would.

If the public is largely reactive, perhaps it is time we begin to look more closely at the quality of the alternatives presented to it either by governments or those controlling various media. Dewey hinged his hopes on education, while Lippmann thought our capacity for enlightenment would improve "if we do not allow frightfulness and fanaticism to impress us so deeply that we throw up our hands peevishly, and lose interest in the longer run of time because we lost faith in the future of man" (Lippmann 1965: 262). The increasing ease with which we can bring that world into our homes arguably can also bring greater enlightenment, but it can just as easily improve the capacity of governments or media elites to manipulate images. Technology can make the world smaller, but cannot *by itself* promote greater understanding. So long as most conditions are but pictures in our heads, so long as stereotypes and blind spots cripple reason, and so long as those in positions of power pratice various versions of censorship and manipulation in pursuit of narrower ends, any hopes that the age of global communications will create a more enlightened public are to be disappointed.

CHAPTER 9

Revolutionaries of the Status Quo: The Denominational Ministry Strategy, the Unemployed, and the Powers That Be

Michael Margolis
Robert E. Burtt

INTRODUCTORY NOTE

In Section One we have seen how resources—especially money—can be effectively employed to enhance the ability of candidates, parties, and groups to influence public opinion regarding elections and referenda. In the earlier chapters of Section Two, the bias of the media toward established groups has been explained.

In this chapter Michael Margolis and Robert Burtt explore the case of an unsuccessful protest group that tried to place new issues regarding unemployment on the policy agenda in the Pittsburgh area. As the group, called the Denominational Ministry Strategy (DMS), is "resource poor," it is forced to use protests to get coverage by the mass media. The case illustrates some of the difficulties that such reliance typically engenders. For example, although the DMS has succeeded in getting some publicity, the media portrays the group as irresponsible, and consequently most of the publicity it receives is unfavorable.

Margolis and Burtt conclude that in order for such protest groups to affect public opinion favorably, they must be able to present viable policy positions and to stimulate third parties to press such positions upon established decision makers. Lacking an intellectual base with which to

stimulate third-party support, protest groups like the DMS tend to degen-
erate into mere publicity hounds, vainly seeking Andy Warhol's 15 minutes of fame.

The Editors

Politics is . . . that solution to the problem of order which chooses concilia-
tion rather than violence or coercion, and chooses it as an effective way by
which varying interests can discover that level of compromise best suited to
their common interest in survival. Politics allows various types of power
within a community to find some reasonable level of mutual tolerance and
support.

Bernard Crick, *Political Scientist (1982: 30)*

POLITICAL. This is the instinct to be liked or popular, to be stroked for your
nice deed. Those who are political hold in disdain those who do acts that are
not accepted by the culture. They look for support, do things that will get
support, even at the cost of the truth. . . . THE SISTER TO "POLITICAL"
IS ACCOMMODATION. Accommodation avoids the word "root" or "radi-
cal." It covers the sin. It pacifies. It makes things smooth for now only to
erupt later.

Charles Honeywell, *DMS Trainer and Consultant (1985)*

UNEMPLOYMENT AND PROTEST IN THE PITTSBURGH AREA

Suppose Karl Marx is sitting in London with some ideas about the
plight of the unemployed. What should he do? Should he go to the library
of the British Museum, do some research, and write a series of works
explaining his theories about the causes and cures for unemployment?
Should he organize and become active in the International Working Men's
Association? Should he seek to ally himself with revolutionary movements in Germany and France? No. Instead he decides to notify the
Times that tomorrow morning he will chain himself to the front door of
the Bank of England in order to dramatize the bank's role in the oppression of the proletariat.

This fanciful scenario contains several elements that have real-life
counterparts in the Pittsburgh area. Since 1980 a group called the Denominational Ministry Strategy (DMS) has been actively concerned about the
plight of the unemployed. They believe that the causes and cures for this
unemployment lie within the control of the large banks and corporations
that operate in the Pittsburgh region. And instead of seeking to organize
or ally with other groups to effect the policy changes needed to eliminate

unemployment, they have chosen to dramatize the situation by conducting a public campaign against Mellon Bank, the region's largest financial institution, USX Corporation (née United States Steel), formerly the region's largest industrial employer, and the Lutheran Church in America (LCA), whose Pennsylvania–West Virginia Synod they claim has been allied with Mellon Bank.[1]

The problems of the unemployed that worry the DMS are real. In 1982 the official unemployment rate in Pittsburgh and the surrounding suburbs of Allegheny County peaked at 12.3 percent, nearly three points over the national rate of 9.5 percent. Unemployment in mill towns along the Monongahela and Ohio rivers ran as high as 20 percent (Cunningham and Martz 1986: 48). Some 128,000 individuals were out of work and seeking employment, and uncounted thousands were underemployed (Pennsylvania Department of Commerce 1983: 62). The local unemployment figures reflected the decline of heavy industry, particularly the decline in basic steel. Between 1972 and 1983 employment in basic steel fell 41 percent: from 568,000 to 336,000 nationally. In the Pittsburgh region the decline was even steeper. Employment in basic steel fell from 87,000 to 42,000 jobs, 52 percent (University Center of Social and Urban Research 1984: 58).[2] People moved away as job opportunities shrank—over 200,000 in the 1970s. And those who remained needed more help. The suicide rate jumped from 6 per 100,000 in the late 70s to over 11 per 100,000 in 1986 (Allegheny County Coroner 1986: 27–30). Meanwhile, despite the population decline, the county welfare rolls increased from 78,000 to 101,000 between 1969 and 1982 (Pennsylvania Department of Commerce 1983: 124). And even though the situation improved after 1982, local unemployment rates continued to run above both the state and national average through December 1987.

Relief for the unemployed is available from public and private sources in forms as diverse as unemployment compensation, job training, emergency medical services, mortgage and utility subsidies, and counseling, but the procedures for obtaining such services are often complex and burdensome. Moreover, the end results are not very promising: the

---

[1]In summer 1986 the United States Steel Corporation (USS) was reconstituted as USX corporation, and USS became a division of USX. In summer 1987 the LCA merged with two other denominations to form the Evangelical Lutheran Church in America (ELCA). The ELCA was organized into 65 synods, and the Pittsburgh region now belongs to the new Southwestern Pennsylvania Synod. Bishop Kenneth May, head of the Pennsylvania–West Virginia Synod of the LCA, retired when the synod was dissolved in summer 1987, and Reverend Donald McCoid of Trinity Lutheran Church of Latrobe, Pa., was elected bishop at the ELCA synod's first convention in June 1987.

[2]The decline continued after 1983. By 1987 employment had fallen to 180,000 nationally and 30,000 in the Pittsburgh region (see *Pittsburgh Press* 1986: B4; also interview: Haulk).

programs and services offer mostly "band-aid" relief. There is little hope that displaced steelworkers or others from unionized industries will ever find jobs at wages comparable to those that were lost.[3]

Politically, the major problem of the unemployed is that they usually lack the wherewithal either to create jobs for themselves or to organize themselves effectively to force others with sufficient resources to create new jobs.[4] Political scientists suggest that in order to be effective in the American political system, the unemployed, like other relatively "powerless" or "resource-poor" groups, normally must engage in forms of protest that stimulate third parties (reference publics) to bring pressure to bear on those target groups that have the power to respond favorably to the protesters' desires (Schattschneider 1960; Lipsky 1970; Goldenberg 1975). Coverage of protest activity by the news media ordinarily becomes the primary means through which both target and reference groups become aware of the problems and demands of resource-poor groups like the unemployed.

On the surface the DMS's activities seem to comport with this model: DMS activists say their protests are intended to energize the public to pressure the power brokers to provide work for the area's unemployed. But as we shall see, the DMS's reluctance to compromise with their adversaries or to make alliances with third parties has weakened the effect

---

[3]Most people who lose jobs due to circumstances beyond their control are eligible for 26 weeks of unemployment compensation. Application involves a thorough review that requires documentary evidence of employment and salary or wages for the past year. Compensation, which is based principally upon the above factors, can be reduced to account for certain pension or disability incomes or for earning more than 40 percent of the weekly benefit part-time. Those receiving benefits must register for work with the Office of Employment Security, and they are expected to accept any job that is offered for which they are qualified. Low pay or inconvenient working hours are not acceptable reasons for turning down a job offer (Lutheran Church in America et al. 1986: chap. 4).

Since October 1983 programs under the Job Training Partnership Act (JTPA) have been implemented to help retrain and place workers in new jobs. Overseen by a Private Industry Council (PIC), the programs fund efforts by Allegheny County, the City of Pittsburgh, U.S. Steel, the United Steelworkers, and other private agencies. Clients include not only dislocated workers, but also displaced homemakers, unemployed youth, people on welfare, and older workers. Some 12,000 clients residing in Allegheny County (3,800 dislocated workers) enrolled in these programs between January 1984 and December 1986. Overall, about one-third were placed in new jobs, about one-fourth dropped out, and the rest remained in the programs. And even though dislocated workers, and steelworkers in particular, had better placement rates—43 and 55 percent, respectively—the new jobs for dislocated workers averaged hourly wages of $7.60 and those for steelworkers averaged $8.49. The latter wage represented at least a 30 percent reduction from what had been earned in the steel industry (see "Performance Analysis," County of Allegheny; Department of Federal Programs, PRFJUNUP. WK1 and 86DEC,WK1).

[4]Psychologically, the unemployed in the United States have been socialized in a liberal democratic tradition that conditions them to blame themselves for their plight rather than to blame any systemic economic factors (Scholzman and Verba 1979: chap. 5).

of their protest activity within the system. Meanwhile their reluctance to challenge the legitimacy of the political system itself has vitiated the impact of what they call their "prophetic ministry." In short, we shall argue that the DMS has combined the worst aspects of both protest and revolutionary strategies, and in doing so it has, if anything, actually harmed the cause of creating new jobs for the unemployed.

Unemployment has remained high in Western Pennsylvania, not only as reflected by official statistics but as measured by subjective responses to questions about public policy problems facing the region. Indeed, between 1983 and 1985, despite an apparent national recovery, survey data indicate that the proportion of Western Pennsylvanians who named unemployment as the most important regional problem *increased* from 79 percent to 86 percent.[5]

This chapter reviews and evaluates how the DMS has attempted to get across its message to the public at large and to the establishment groups that it has attacked. To this end we have:

1. Reviewed coverage of the DMS in Pittsburgh daily papers and sampled coverage elsewhere.[6]
2. Reviewed materials generated by the DMS, including reports, newsletters, and a video documentary.[7]
3. Interviewed knowledgeable actors in the DMS, the Lutheran, Episcopal, and Roman Catholic churches.[8]
4. Interviewed relevant editors, reporters, and news directors of both of the Pittsburgh dailies and of the three network television affiliates.[9]

---

[5]This increase occurred even though the proportion naming unemployment as the most important national problem fell from 70 percent to 47 percent over the same period. Source: Data tabulated by the authors from the University Center for Social and Urban Research, Southwestern Pennsylvania Surveys, 1983 and 1985. See footnote 12, below.

[6]The daily newspapers are the *Pittsburgh Post-Gazette* (morning Mon.–Sat.) and *Pittsburgh Press* (afternoon Mon.–Sat. and Sunday morning). The newspapers have separate owners and maintain separate reporters and editors, but they share advertising and circulation staffs, and they are printed in the same plant. Weekly newspapers include the church-sponsored *Pittsburgh Catholic*.

[7]The reports and newsletters are produced by the DMS, located at East Liberty Lutheran Church, 5707 Penn Avenue, Pittsburgh 15206 (412–362–1712). The 57-minute documentary, "The Fighting Ministers," is professionally produced by actor David Soul, a brother of DMS minister Daniel Solberg, and is available for purchase or rental from California Newsreel, 630 Natoma Street, San Francisco 94103 (415–621–6196).

[8]Face-to-face interviews of a directed nature, based upon a standard set of questions and lasting 45 to 90 minutes, were conducted by the two authors. Respondents are identified in the list of interviews that follows the bibliography at the back of this book.

[9]Directed interviews, based upon a standard schedule of questions and lasting 30 to 75 minutes, were conducted via telephone or face to face. Respondents are identified in the list of interviews.

5. Interviewed relevant corporate and union officers from Mellon Bank, USX, and the United Steel Workers.[10]

6. Interviewed relevant administrators in governmental and nonprofit agencies involved with programs that serve the unemployed.[11]

7. Analyzed available survey data on the public's views of the causes and cures for problems of unemployment in Western Pennsylvania.[12]

In the next section we present a short history of the DMS's involvement with the problems of the unemployed. This is followed by an evaluation of the success of the DMS's efforts to sway public opinion and to muster support for their avowed goal of helping the unemployed secure jobs with decent pay. Finally, we examine the implications of our evaluation for the successful resolution of the problem of unemployment and for the relevance of political socialization and politics to that resolution.

HISTORY OF THE DMS

As the gradual loss of jobs and population took place throughout the 1970s, many of the churches in Pittsburgh and its industrial suburbs experienced not only shrinking congregations but a distancing of their pastors from those who remained. In 1976 eight inner city pastors headed by Paul Himmelman, then Associate Pastor at St. Michael and All Angels' Lutheran Church on Pittsburgh's northside, formed the "Pittsburgh Coalition" under the auspices of the Lutheran Synod. The pastors met regularly to discuss and share information about how their ministries could reach out beyond traditional priestly duties to help their congregations to deal with social problems brought on by unemployment. The group gradually expanded to an interfaith "Urban Mission" that included pastors of 32 churches in the Pittsburgh area.[13]

The group continued to grow and by 1979 it had acquired sufficient funds to hire a consultant to train pastors in social outreach. The man chosen was Charles Honeywell, a social organizer trained by Saul Alin-

---

[10]Directed interviews were conducted via telephone or face to face. Respondents are identified in the list of interviews.

[11]Directed interviews were conducted face to face. Respondents are identified in the list of interviews.

[12]The principal data sources are two "state of the region" surveys conducted via telephone with randomly selected individuals from the Pittsburgh metropolitan area by the University of Pittsburgh Center for Social and Urban Research in June 1983 ($N = 1767$) and 1985 ($N = 1070$).

[13]All 32 churches were located within the "Yellow Belt," the second of a series of five groups of roads designated as routes around central city traffic. The Yellow Belt encircles the city of Pittsburgh and most of old industrial suburbs of the Monongahela Valley.

sky's Industrial Areas Foundation (IAF), who had been involved with community action groups in Pittsburgh since 1975. With its consultant–trainer on board, the group was rechristened the Denominational Ministry Strategy (DMS).

Charles Honeywell had been brought to Pittsburgh during the mid-1970s to work with the Shadyside Action Coalition (SAC), a neighborhood advocacy group in one of the city's more affluent areas. SAC was best known for its campaign to close down "Fantastic Plastic," a nightclub reputedly financed with underworld money. While Honeywell was credited with strengthening the Coalition's successful effort to scuttle the nightclub and with organizing several neighborhood improvement projects, he was criticized by some for using unnecessarily militant tactics and for seeking his own following. In 1977 the Coalition split, and Honeywell and a number of SAC members, known as the "power action caucus," became associated with the countywide Metropolitan Citizens Organization (Carnahan 1985: A12–A13). In November 1978 the Industrial Areas Foundation severed its connections with Honeywell. The IAF charged that instead of acting merely as organizer and consultant, he "tried to become a leader and refused to be accountable to the people who hired him" (Hodiak and Sheehan 1983, quoting Ed Chambers, President of IAF). The Metropolitan Citizens Organization gradually petered out, but Honeywell remained active as a consultant to local community and church groups. It was Honeywell's successful work with Pastor James Von Dreele in revitalizing St. Matthew's Episcopal Church in the mill town of Homestead in 1979 that brought him to the attention of the DMS.

Honeywell's first major project with the DMS was to send pastors out into their communities to interview broad cross sections of parishioners in their homes. Interviewing some 2,000 parishioners about their problems and concerns in settings outside the church provided many of the middle-class pastors with their first direct encounters with the social and economic problems faced by working-class members of their flocks. Unemployment emerged as the overwhelming problem of concern, and it was selected as the focus for the group's action.

This early work by the DMS pleased church authorities. Pastors were gaining sensitivity to their parishioners' concerns, and the churches were embarking upon programs that promised to minister to material and social as well as spiritual needs. Kenneth R. May, Bishop of the Synod of Western Pennsylvania–West Virginia, was enthusiastic enough to gain a special grant of $10,000 from the Lutheran Center (Strength for Union) to support the DMS. He also pointed to the importance of its work when urging Reverends Kristin Foster and John Gropp to answer calls to churches in Emsworth and Duquesne.

Sometime toward the end of 1981, however, the unity of the group broke down. According to Honeywell and others still active in the DMS, the problem stemmed from a disagreement over fundamental strategy and tactics.

Having identified unemployment as the key issue, Honeywell and his supporters wanted to focus public attention upon those who they felt were responsible, namely the banks and the corporate employers, the largest of which were Mellon Bank and United States Steel. Such focus would be achieved by using tactics that reflected Honeywell's training in Alinsky's style of community organization and social action. Instead of merely providing relief to the unemployed, the DMS would demand that the big banks and corporations use their resources to solve the problem of unemployment. The banks should finance the reindustrialization of the Monongahela Valley, not lend money overseas. The corporations should reinvest in modern steel mills instead of closing down or moving operations out of state or overseas. In the short term the banks and corporations should prevail upon the state and federal governments to declare the Valley a disaster area, making it eligible for emergency aid. If the banks and corporations did not respond satisfactorily, the DMS would employ militant tactics to make life uncomfortable for the affluent corporate officers at work, at home, even in church. The organization would make itself so obnoxious that the corporate leadership would ultimately realize that to invest substantial resources to help the unemployed was not only right, but also in their self-interest.

The overall strategy reflected Alinsky's view of morality:

> We now live in a world where no man can have a loaf of bread while his neighbor has none. If he does not share his bread, he dare not sleep, for his neighbor will kill him. To eat and sleep in safety man must do the right thing, if for seemingly the wrong reasons, and be in practice his brother's keeper.
>
> I believe that man is about to learn that the most practical life is the moral life and that the moral life is the only road to survival. He is beginning to learn that he will either share part of his material wealth or lose all of it; . . . *This is the low road to morality. There is no other* (Alinsky 1972: 23).

The tactics necessary to execute this strategy involve militancy and confrontation. You do not employ quiet diplomacy. You "raise a din and clamor"; you "stink up the place" (Alinsky 1972: 126).

Most pastors, and many in their congregations, were uncomfortable with such tactics. Though aware of their parishioners' needs, they were unprepared to abandon accepted notions of civility in dealing with the banks and corporations. Far from looking upon the business community as the enemy, they saw both business and labor as hurting. Instead of confronting the business community, they preferred to solicit its cooperation to work on immediate relief projects like food banks and job-retraining, and to plan for long-term solutions to regional unemployment. Confrontation would also produce a conflict within the church congregations themselves. Many of the parishioners were pensioners who were less affected by unemployment, and many were white-collar workers who identified with management. Others simply felt that their churches should maintain a spiritual emphasis, not engage in social action.

Honeywell and his DMS supporters claim to have explained to their church sponsors the necessity of direct action. Nothing short of confrontation would induce those in power to commit sufficient resources to relieve the suffering of the unemployed and to revitalize the local economy. But the struggle would have its costs. Honeywell warned that the church establishment must be prepared to resist pressures that the corporate community would bring to bear. Supposedly, the leaders of the sponsoring denominations agreed to support the DMS's militant course on three separate occasions. "They said it—and it was duly entered in the minutes—but they soon backed out when all hell broke loose in 1982" (interview: Honeywell).

Honeywell's critics do not tell the same story. While conceding that militance is at times appropriate, they argue that Honeywell favored militance for its own sake. Following the same pattern that had split SAC, critics charge that Honeywell began to act as leader rather than trainer and consultant, and that after a time he acted more to consolidate his power than to help the unemployed. Within the DMS he would brook no dissent. And his tactics failed to polarize the outside community into the moral "have nots" versus the immoral "haves," as recommended by Alinsky; all they did was polarize the churches (interviews: Bonn, Fleming; Werner; Zundell).

In any case, in the fall of 1982 the DMS began a public campaign that targeted Mellon Bank and secondarily United States Steel and their corporate officers. The DMS joined local unionists of the militant Network to Save the Mon/Ohio Valley in charging that Mellon, the dominant regional bank, had neglected local problems, preferring to take money from Western Pennsylvania and to invest it abroad.[14] The DMS and its Network allies urged customers to protest by withdrawing their savings from Mellon Bank. When Mellon's lending policies hastened the bankruptcy of Mesta Machine in 1983, the United Steelworkers of America briefly

---

[14] The Network to Save the Mon/Ohio Valley consisted largely of members of union locals that had been hard hit by closings and layoffs and whose leaders had criticized their national unions for failing to protect their members. Prominent leaders included Ron Wiesen and Mike Bonn, presidents of United Steelworkers Locals 1397 and 2227, and Darrell Becker, president of Local 61 of the Industrial Union of Marine Shipbuilding Workers. Charles Honeywell, who served as liaison between the DMS and the Network, also acted informally as an adviser to the Network.

joined in the boycott, but union president Lloyd McBride kept the DMS at arm's length.

In the fall of 1983 the DMS and the Network increased the pressure on Mellon Bank through demonstrations and harassment. Local branches were "stuck up" as DMS and Network supporters poured honey and other sticky substances in their doorways; they were "stunk up" as supporters placed dead fish in safety deposit boxes and spread skunk oil in customer areas. Bank offices and the homes of Mellon Bank and U.S. Steel officers were picketed, and on Easter Sunday 1984, services at the Shadyside Presbyterian Church were disrupted. The DMS selected the church because key officers from U.S. Steel and other major Pittsburgh corporations worship there. The church was targeted again in December when the DMS disrupted the annual Advent vespers and Christmas pageant (an event largely for the entertainment of children) using water balloons scented with skunk oil (Paris 1984).

As the DMS expected, these actions often received prominent coverage in the newspapers, radio, and television. But also as expected, the coverage was generally unfavorable, for the demonstrators had disturbed the accepted routines of established institutions. The idea, however, was to embarrass and ridicule the establishment for its neglect of the unemployed (Alinsky 1972: 127–30). If the disruptions and demonstrations caused enough bother or generated enough bad publicity, Mellon Bank would use its resources and its influence within the corporate community to provide substantial relief for the unemployed and, more important, to generate new jobs. "The DMS isn't designed to help people get jobs. It is designed to put pressure on the people that make jobs" (interview: Cochran).

As its militance increased, however, the DMS lost both membership and financial support. It shrank from a core group of nearly 70 pastors of various faiths to a hard core of between 20 and 30 ministers, mostly Lutherans. A major sponsor, the Episcopal diocese, withdrew its financial support in 1982, as did the minor sponsors, the Methodists and Presbyterians. In April 1983, on the recommendation of its executive board, the convention of the Lutheran Synod followed suit (Davis 1983).[15]

Those who remained felt betrayed. When the banks and corporations

---

[15]The Roman Catholic Church, the region's largest denomination, has tended to operate its own programs regarding unemployment or to cooperate with government or quasi-governmental programs like the Tri-State Steel Valley Authority or the Tri-State Conference on Steel (Portz 1987; Rice 1984 and 1985a; interview: Dorsey). Dissatisfied with the Catholic Church's efforts on behalf of the unemployed, the DMS demonstrated outside St. Paul's Cathedral, the diocese's central house of worship, on Sunday, January 13, 1985 (Rice 1985b and 1985c; for further criticism of the Pittsburgh Catholic Diocese by state legislators from the Mon Valley, see Bergholz 1987).

had attacked the DMS, the church leaders had gone back on their word. Instead of affirming the DMS's "prophetic" mission, the bishops had chosen to curry the favor of the worldly. Where the DMS strove to embarrass the power brokers, the church leaders chose to accommodate them. The DMS sought to juxtapose corporate greed—the rises in stock prices and increases in profits—against the suffering of the unemployed—the lack of proper nutrition, housing, clothing, and medical care. They demanded that the corporate powers provide substantial relief. The church leaders, on the other hand, would settle for "band-aids," token programs of planning, retraining, and relief that left the basic contradictions untouched. DMS supporters and spokesmen for the Lutheran Church began to scold each other in public and (each alleges) to threaten one another in private. And relations would worsen.

In 1983 a controversy developed over whether the involvement in the DMS of Pastor D. Douglas Roth of Trinity Lutheran Church, Clairton, was interfering with the proper conduct of his ministry. At the request of some parishioners the Synod sent in an investigatory committee that made a report and recommended some changes. Roth claims that he and the majority of Church Council agreed to the recommendations, but that the dissenting minority would not. According to Synod rules, a settlement must be unanimous, so the problem was returned to the Bishop for resolution. In October 1984 Bishop May resolved the problem by declaring the pulpit vacant. But Roth, backed by the majority of his Church Council, refused to leave.

At this point the Bishop brought secular authorities into what had previously been an internal dispute. The Synod, employing the law firm of Reed, Smith, Shaw & McClay, secured a court order declaring Trinity Lutheran Church defunct.[16] As a consequence of the order, title to the church property itself reverted to the Synod, even though the Church Council held the deed. In November 1984 Roth was arrested and jailed for trespass, and in January 1985 sheriff's deputies enforced the order by evicting his supporters, who had locked themselves inside the church over the Christmas holidays. The eviction and the controversy surrounding it received widespread attention in the mass media, including national and international newspaper coverage and a report on the CBS news magazine "Sixty Minutes."

Conflict within the Lutheran Church continued. In spring of 1985 Reverend Daniel Solberg of Nativity Lutheran Church of Allison Park was dismissed by his own Church Council for his involvement in the activities of the DMS. When Solberg refused to leave, he too was evicted

---

[16]Reed, Smith, Shaw & McClay, one of Pittsburgh's most prestigious law firms, has a long association with Mellon family interests (see Hursh 1978).

and arrested. Denied bail because he would not promise to stay away from the church, he spent four months in the county jail before charges of trespass were dismissed.

In June 1985, on recommendation of a disciplinary committee appointed by Bishop James Crumley of the Lutheran Church in America (LCA) and Bishop May, the convention of the Western Pennsylvania–West Virginia Lutheran Synod voted to defrock Roth for behavior incompatible with the conduct of ministerial office and for his willful disregard and violation of the constitution of the Synod and the Church. One year later the convention voted to defrock Pastor Solberg on similar charges.[17] Despite the defrockings, Roth and Solberg remain active in the DMS. Roth maintains an independent congregation in Clairton, and Solberg, in defiance of the Bishop, acts as an associate pastor at East Liberty Lutheran Church.

The DMS remains active, but its immediate focus has shifted from confronting Mellon Bank and other corporations and to confronting the church hierarchy. In particular, it claims that the regional synod has been corrupted by Mellon and its minions. In 1986 and 1987 its most spectacular actions were against the Church itself.

At a lull in the proceedings of the national convention of the LCA in Milwaukee in late August of 1986, Daniel Solberg managed to seize the podium to denounce the "adulterous merger" of the LCA, the American Lutheran Church (ALC), and the Association of Evangelical Lutheran Churches (AELC), then planned for 1988.[18] In late October DMS supporters turned out to protest AELC Bishop Will Herzfeld's celebration of the upcoming merger at a Reformation Service held at East Liberty Presbyterian Church, an elaborate Gothic structure erected largely with funds donated by the Mellon family (Hursh 1978: 276; Hodiak 1986). DMS protestors were also present earlier in the month when Roth's parish church, now reconstituted as the Lutheran Church of the Holy Spirit, installed its new pastor.[19] In April of 1987 the DMS sent a group of "freedom riders" on a meandering journey through various Lutheran parishes

[17]These are violations of the Lutheran Church in America Constitution, Bylaws, Section II, Item 15a. Defrockings, like impeachments, are extraordinary events. According to Reverend Edward Kappeler, administrative assistant to Bishop May, the Roth and Solberg cases represented only the second and third times in its history that the LCA had occasion to call together such disciplinary committees (see Rathburn 1986: C3).

[18]His speech, broadcast also via telephone to the convention of the ALC in Minneapolis, charged the churches with "whoring after corporate idols," and "accommodating, soothing and ignoring evil." "Defrocked pastor seizes LCA podium, . . ." *The Concord* (Lutheran Northwestern Theological Seminary, St. Paul, Minn.) September 9, 1986, reproduced in DMS Newsletter, October 14, 1986.

[19]The choir that sang for the installation came from Nativity Lutheran of Allison Park, formerly Solberg's parish church, which DMS supporters still picket each Sunday.

to the ECLA convention in Columbus, Ohio, to protest the ratification of the merger and to present a list of resolutions.[20] When DMS delegates were not seated and the resolutions were not considered by the full convention, Pastors Roth and Solberg attempted to lead a group of 30 DMS "delegates" onto the convention floor. Entry was blocked by the Columbus police, who were present to enforce a prior injunction against such disruptions by the DMS, and both Roth and Solberg were arrested.

Since 1985 little has been heard from the Network to Save the Mon/Ohio Valley. In fact, union support for the DMS and its tactics has eroded. Mike Bonn was defeated in a bid for reelection as president of his union local in 1985. According to some union members, his association with the DMS and his participation in its activities were the main reasons for his defeat (interview: McClellan). Darrell Becker maintained the support of his local, but like Roth he found himself barricaded in local headquarters when the national Marine and Shipbuilding Workers Union declared the local in violation of national rules, imposed a trusteeship, and tried to take physical possession of the property. Ron Wiesen also held onto the support of his local, but when his son suffered a paralyzing accident, he turned his attention to family matters and fund-raising to transport his son to the USSR to attempt a rare operation. In May of 1986 the members of his local voted to formally dissociate themselves from the DMS and its activities.

Undeterred, the DMS carries on. "We're like Tuttle the plumber in the movie *Brazil*. We won't play by their rules. We're insignificant, yet the system is so rotten that it feels guilty and tries to destroy us" (interview: Long).

ANALYSIS

Viewed from the perspective of mainstream political science, the DMS story would fall into the category of protest group behavior. Protest is defined as political action directed against existing policies or conditions in a manner characterized by the use of flamboyant behaviors and showmanship. It is most commonly undertaken by the "resource poor" or "powerless," who generally lack sufficient clout to employ conven-

---

[20]The resolutions called for divestment in corporations operating in South Africa; removal of deposits from all financial institutions associated with Mellon Bank; investigation of bank loans to "developers known to be involved with racketeers, such as E. J. DeBartolo in Pittsburgh; advocacy of "major federal relief for the Mon/Ohio Valley of Pennsylvania; and the formation of a nongeographical "free synod" within the church "to conduct our prophetic ministry" (DMS Newsletter, May 1987). In Spring 1988, the DMS leadership unilaterally established the "Confessing Synod" within the ELCA. DMS forms "the collective efforts in confrontational ministry by representatives of congregations" of the new synod (Confessing Synod Newsletter, May 1988: 5).

tional means to gain access to political decision makers. The basic aim is to activate third parties (reference groups) to pressure decision makers (target groups) to act in ways that are favorable to the protestors (Lipsky 1970: chap. 1). The model developed by Lipsky contains four elements: the protest groups, communications media, target groups, and reference publics that are related to the target groups. Protest groups use available communications media to reach their targets indirectly. They appeal to the relevant reference publics with the aim of inducing them, in turn, to apply pressure to the targets. The reference publics must react in favorable ways for the protest to be successful. The chances of getting favorable responses are enhanced by the protest groups' abilities to prioritize their issue agendas, isolate and clarify the important issues, develop possible solutions, and finally, to legitimate their criticisms of existing conditions or programs.

The DMS's target groups are the leaders of the local steel industry and the local financial community. The principal communications media are, of course, the local papers, television, and radio stations. The reference publics would appear to be multifaceted in this instance. Labor leaders and union officials would be obvious members. Government officials at the local, state, and national levels are also good candidates for inclusion. The heads of the local religious denominations could also play a role. Finally, interested voters and citizens would have to be included. In short, the ultimate reference public in the case of the DMS is the general population of the Pittsburgh area. The DMS's campaign for jobs for the unemployed would be greatly strengthened if public opinion held the target groups not only responsible for unemployment but capable of providing long-term relief.

The DMS seems to have made three major mistakes in reference to this model. First, even though they succeeded in highlighting the problems of the unemployed, they failed to appeal to relevant reference groups. Instead, the DMS so expanded their target groups that they treated nearly every other organized interest as though it had been bought off or subverted by Mellon Bank. Second, the DMS failed to prioritize and clarify the issues, and as a result, they dealt a serious blow to the legitimization of their criticisms.[21] Finally, they proposed no coherent program so even those who sympathized had no guidance as to which solutions to work for.

---

[21]Consider the following statement: "Mellon-controlled corporations . . . refuse to leave S. Africa. . . . Our focus against the church is the only organized one in America combining the issues of plant closings, Apartheid, and defrockings, and the rights to prophetic ministry within the institutional church. WATCH FOR THE NEW DMS FREEDOM RIDERS AS THEY EXPOSE THE LUTHERAN CHURCHES AND MOB CONNECTIONS ALONG THE WAY FROM PITTSBURGH TO COLUMBUS" (DMS Newsletter, May 1987).

To what extent did the group's efforts succeed? Did the public become more aware of the problems? How much did the DMS's actions benefit the unemployed? Were the churches, banks, and corporations moved to act more expeditiously to relieve unemployment? Our view is that the DMS succeeded in getting publicity, but not much else.

Attracting the attention of the mass media is a necessary condition for accomplishing the DMS's aims, and by this standard it achieved some notable success. As Figure 9–1 indicates, the DMS's confrontational tactics brought it a considerable measure of notoriety. In fact, for several months during 1984, and for most of 1985, the local press devoted more column inches to stories that focused upon the DMS and its activities than it did to stories that otherwise focused upon problems of unemployment or the unemployed. Much of this coverage was unfavorable, but it nonetheless brought both the DMS and the fate of the unemployed to public attention. None of the people we interviewed professed ignorance of the organization or its avowed aims, and regardless of their opinion of the DMS, they all expressed at least grudging admiration of its initial efforts to highlight the problems of the unemployed.

Even though newspeople and DMS supporters have vastly different views concerning the control exerted by Mellon Bank and the major corporations around Pittsburgh, our interviews affirm that they share a common perception of what constitutes news. News is something new and dramatic, something that tells a story or advances one that is being told. How news gets reported also reflects the standards of the community. The

FIGURE 9–1   Newspaper Coverage—DMS versus Unemployment, Dec. 1982–
                  Dec. 1986

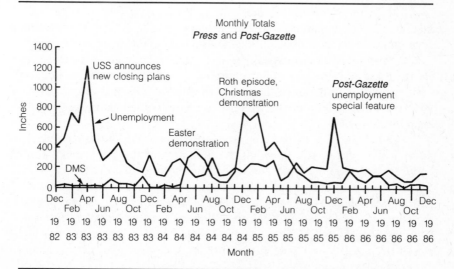

Pittsburgh Post-Gazette, for instance, will not place a picture of a bludgeoned body on page one; most likely it would not print such a picture at all (interviews: Warner; Craig). To gain prominent coverage, therefore, the DMS's activities must be innovative and nonviolent. If the DMS pickets the same church each week, after a while that's not news. And if the DMS becomes violent, it violates community standards.

As the DMS eschews coalition politics, however, these standards present a dilemma. In order to target and then polarize the community against specific groups or specific individuals within those groups, the DMS must continually change tactics, or else the pressure generated by bad publicity will dissipate. Nevertheless, after a while it is bound to run out of innovative tactics, and since it lacks allied organizations to continue to generate the pressure, it must change targets or lose much of the coverage of its activities in the media. As we observed, since 1985 the DMS has shifted its immediate focus from Mellon Bank to the bishops of the Lutheran Church.

The notion of community standards also involves a question of popular interest. Militant actions in service of a moral cause may be newsworthy for a time simply because they signify an unusual level of commitment. But if nothing further develops from the actions, they gradually become less newsworthy. By the time we interviewed newspeople in the summer and fall of 1986, they unanimously expressed the opinion that the DMS had little popular support and was therefore less newsworthy than it had been from 1983 through 1985. Several interviewees doubted that it ever had had substantial popular support, and some regretted having allowed the DMS to orchestrate or manipulate much of the news coverage. One news director pointed to a subjective difference between being "manipulated" and being "used." While it is hard to draw a line between the two, the former—which was acceptable—involved calling out the news media to cover apparently genuine events. The latter, which was unacceptable, involved calling out the news media to cover trivial or pseudo events (crying wolf, so to speak). The DMS evidently got WTAE–TV to show up for certain events that reporters judged to be trivial. "Then the DMS would . . . announce their next event. We felt used after a while. We were their bulletin board" (interview: Rovitto; see also Lipsky 1970: chap. 6).

Their demurrers to the contrary notwithstanding, however, the reporters and editors still find that the activities of the DMS make good copy. In July 1986 the DMS announced that following the lead of United States Steel, which had just changed its initials from USS to USX, the DMS would change its initials to "DMX." The papers dutifully reported the change, and they even went on to dub the organization the "Denominational Ministries Extended" (Lash 1986). This announcement, in fact, was little more than a publicity stunt: the members and official house publications still referred to the organization as the DMS. But for the newspapers the title, "DMX," was something new. Moreover, it lent credence to the story that the dissident ministers were a serious threat to the successful merger of three major branches of American Lutheran Churches into the Evangelical Lutheran Church in America (Hodiak 1986).

The DMS may have succeeded in generating headlines, but if we subscribe to anything like the view of politics expressed in the quotation from Crick at the beginning of this chapter, then it follows that the DMS's campaign has generally been a failure. Far from seeking accommodation or compromise, the DMS has insisted that its adversaries accede to its righteous demands. Indeed, from this point of view, the DMS eschews politics altogether. No coalitions are sought, and no quarter is given. "We have no real organizational allies," Solberg told us. "Twenty of us created a stink and this threatened the other side. We just do what's right. We have the powers that be scared to death" (interview: Solberg).

Instead of acting politically the DMS "importunes" those with power to act. The DMS insists that the banking and corporate elites have sufficient resources to resolve the problems. All they lack is the will. "If you can spend $600 million to dig a ditch in the middle of the city [the "T," Pittsburgh's new one-mile long rapid transit subway], then surely you can come up with sufficient funds to feed and take care of people," Reverend Gropp argued. "We are a thorn in the side of the establishment. We recognize the problem and call it to the attention of others, even if we can't come up with specific solutions" (interview: Gropp).[22]

We need not rely solely upon our own or newspeople's judgments of the DMS's lack of popular support, however. Two public opinion surveys that focused upon regional economic problems suggest that the DMS had little success in getting the public to blame unemployment on big financial institutions like Mellon Bank. Furthermore, it is questionable whether the actions of the DMS served to increase the share of the blame the public laid on the big corporations.

The first survey took place during the summer of 1983, when coverage of the DMS and the Network's actions against Mellon Bank had first become prominent. The Bank was accused of exporting capital instead of reinvesting it in local enterprises like Mesta Machine, upon which Mellon had foreclosed. Smarting from the DMS and the USW's separate campaigns that urged Pittsburghers to withdraw their deposits in retaliation, Mellon launched a public relations effort to emphasize its commitment to the region. The Bank published a "Dear Neighbor" letter from Chairman David Barnes in full page ads in both dailies, and it adopted "Mellon

---

[22]Gropp makes a similar argument in the video, "The Fighting Ministers."

Bank—A neighbor you can count on," as its major radio and television advertising theme.[23] Despite this attention to the accusations, respondents to the survey made no mention of outflow of capital as a major problem, even though 70 percent listed unemployment spontaneously as the most important national problem, and 79 percent called unemployment the most important local problem.

In the second survey, which took place in the summer of 1985, respondents were asked to assess various causes of unemployment in the region. They cited financial institutions as least to blame (36 percent) as compared to big corporations (64 percent), big unions (72 percent), foreign competition (90 percent), or policies of the federal government (68 percent). And even though 64 percent held big corporations to blame, this was less than or equal to the percentages who blamed the unions, foreign competition, or the federal government. Nor did the evidence suggest that the public agreed with the DMS's contention that, with proper reinvestment, steel could come back.[24] Fully 88 percent did not expect the steel industry to remain a major employer; moreover, only 3 and 8 percent, respectively, saw modernization of steel or of other types of heavy industrial plants as useful actions for businesses to take to help create jobs. Finally, when asked about effective actions citizens might take to secure employment, 32 percent recommended job retraining, and 24 percent recommended moving away.

There are even indications that many people consider any association with the DMS as poison. Three of our interviewees, for instance, suggested that the disruption of the Christmas pageant at Shadyside Presbyterian Church in December 1984 moved the DMS beyond the pale. Instead of conducting a demonstration outside the church as planned, the overzealous clergy (perhaps led or goaded by Honeywell) who disrupted the pageant evidently terrified many of the children present, and the incident precipitated a defection of union supporters and a huge loss of public favor (interviews: Werner; McClellan; Bonn). The DMS became so unpopular that, when Reverend Roth and six supporters were arrested in March 1985 for demonstrating outside a Lutheran church in a well-to-do suburb, a jury convicted them all for "disrupting a meeting." The case was so weak that the district attorney's office found itself in the curious position of supporting the defendants' appeal to have the convictions overturned! (The case was finally dismissed upon appeal; Roth has sued the local police chief, pastor, and several church members; see Pitz 1987).

---

[23]See, for instance, the *Pittsburgh Press* and the *Post-Gazette*, June 14, 1983.

[24]Similar findings emerged from a survey of residents of Braddock, North Braddock, and Rankin—three of the boroughs most hurt by plant closings (see Margolis, Burtt, and McLaughlin 1986).

In the winter and early spring of 1987 retired steelworkers—along with activist clergymen like the "labor priest" Monsignor Charles Owen Rice—began protesting the Pension Guaranty Corporation's decision to cut "supplemental" (early retirement) benefits from their underfunded LTV (Jones & Laughlin) pensions. The retirees marched on the LTV plant in Aliquippa almost every day from early February through April (McKay 1987; Rishell and Ireton 1987; Rishell and Moushey 1987). The retirees took the trouble, however, to telephone the local radio station (WMBA, 1460 AM, Ambridge) to repudiate the support offered by clergy of the DMS.

Still, lack of popularity has never been a prime concern of the DMS. Not only does the group shun politics in the broad sense of seeking coalition and conciliation, its members have little to do with politics in its formal institutional sense. Only one of the currently active DMS members or supporters we interviewed even considered bringing the group's concerns to the attention of public officials, let alone making an effort to promote legislation or administrative policies that might better the lot of the unemployed. Indeed, their self-definition as a prophetic ministry, responsible only for pointing out problems and importuning authorities to find solutions, relieves them from the difficult task of developing policy alternatives that are practical and popular enough to be implemented. At bottom, the DMS does not want or need allies. Being outside of politics, it does not want or need to work with any institution, official, or group. It never needs to adapt or change in order to promote any positive program. In practice, except for "making the papers," it doesn't need to accomplish anything.

We expect that at this point most readers will find themselves inclined to agree with the above analysis. As political scientists in a pluralist society, we tend to view the failure of the DMS to garner allies and win popular support for its cause as "punishment" for the "crime" of refusing to engage in politics. We tend to dismiss those whose principles are too pure to compromise as political naïfs at best, or political extremists at worst. This comfortable view, however, has its own dangers, for it limits our analysis by focusing our attention only on elements that fit the pluralistic "pictures in our heads" (Lippmann 1965: chap. 1; see also Wildavsky 1965).

Let us adopt for a moment the viewpoint of the DMS. What if the city of Pittsburgh were organized as the DMS charges? What then? Would the actions of the DMS in fact seem so politically naive?

We might stress at this point that even though the DMS is a marginal group politically, its clergy hardly resemble stereotypical radicals. To begin with, the ministers look like conventional middle-class Americans. All whom we interviewed were married and had children. All but one had graduated from seminaries associated with colleges or universities as op-

posed to church-oriented schools of divinity, and most had advanced degrees. Their training, while admittedly religious in orientation, was not
exclusively so: several held degrees in subjects other than religious studies or theology.[25] None claimed to be Marxists; most professed faith in
what we commonly call the "American way of life." Moreover, the conduct of a successful ministry would seem to require attitudes of conciliation and proclivities for peaceful resolution of conflict. Although two
members of the DMS have been defrocked, only one—Solberg—actually
lost the support of his congregation. Throughout the period of our study
the rest of the DMS clergy managed to maintain their positions as leaders
of their congregations. Indeed, on the surface, there is little to distinguish
them from the "Lutheran Ministers" of Garrison Keillor's "Lake Wobe-
gon" stories. "I used to think that only bad people get arrested. . . ,"
says Colleen Gropp, mother and minister's wife. "Do I look like the 'ar-
restable' type?"[26]

The DMS charges that Pittsburgh is a "company town" dominated
by Mellon Bank. It claims that the Bank uses its enormous assets to determine the important economic and political decisions in the Pittsburgh
region. The DMS points out that the Mellon family holds major shares in
corporations headquartered in Pittsburgh, and that its members have exerted considerable influence over Pittsburgh's cultural, social, and political institutions. So great is this influence, the DMS contends, that no
major social, political, or economic plan could succeed if the Bank chose
to oppose it. Conversely, the DMS contends that Mellon Bank could muster sufficient resources to put right the region's economy, if it so desired.

The DMS charges that instead of investing in the region, Mellon
Bank has sought greater profits in the world market. It has lent money
abroad for investment in steel plants instead of lending it to modernize
the region's industrial base or to attract new industries to the region. To
the extent that it has lent money for investment locally, it has favored
office buildings and shopping malls, projects that tend to create low-pay-
ing nonunion jobs and that allegedly provide a means to launder "drug"
and "racket" money (interviews: Honeywell; Gropp; see also DMS
Newsletters, January 1986 and May 1987). The latter charges, of course,
have not been proven, but they are not on the surface preposterous. The
DMS names names and indicates dates (Long 1985). The charges are in-

---

[25]Foster, Gropp, and Solberg, for instance, took their theological training at Yale, and
Long holds an M.A. in classics from the University of Pennsylvania and a Ph.D. from
the University of Pittsburgh.

[26]Colleen Gropp addressing a group in the video, "The Fighting Ministers."

vestigable, but neither the mass media nor we in the academic community have scrutinized them.[27]

If DMS's view of the local power structure were true, would their actions not seem more sensible? If the real decisions are made in the board rooms, then politics is merely a form of mass entertainment. It becomes understandable then for the DMS to eschew or contemn ordinary politics, for politics is irrelevant for resolving the problems of the unemployed. What can one say, for instance, about electoral contests like the 1986 senatorial and gubernatorial races in Pennsylvania? In those races both major party candidates professed great concern for jobs and unemployment, but none said anything of substance about an ongoing lockout at USX that had idled 2,900 workers in the Pittsburgh area for the previous 10 weeks. Does it not make sense to "raise a din and clamor" or "to stink up the place" in an effort to use the media to unmask the actors and expose the show?

This view of politics may be nothing more than a fantasy that the DMS uses to justify its failures. Yet the DMS consists largely of otherwise conventional middle-class ministers whose original involvement with the problems of the unemployed was encouraged by their bishops. And their view does comport with the analysis of the power structure in the United States that has been advanced over the years by critics in the academic community (Hunter 1953; Mills 1956; Domhoff 1967 and 1979; Kotz 1978).

As we see it, the problems of the DMS stem from the fact that upon closer inspection their actions are inconsistent with the above expressed viewpoint. If the DMS really believes that the system is as corrupt as they allege, it would seem that they ought to direct their efforts not toward reform, but toward some form of fundamental change. At the very least the organization's demonstrations should be part of a program of education directed toward radical solutions that inhibit the power of capital to determine the community's social and political policies.

As we have noted, however, DMS activists have proposed neither innovative nor viable remedies. Instead of suggesting any new courses of action, the DMS has importuned the corporate elite to use their resources

---

[27]The DMS points out that the mass media and the major academic institutions rely upon the Mellon Bank and the corporate community for major proportions of their revenues. While editors and news directors we interviewed spoke of norms of "fairness" and "objectivity" and "going after the 'round' story," they also admitted that the pressure of turning out a daily paper or nightly newscast precluded much investigative reporting (interview: Ross). As one editor observed, fairness in practice usually amounts to quoting the positions of various actors involved. The positions quoted may or may not be true, and the reporters seldom check (interview: McGough).

to restore and revitalize the region's manufacturing base. Unlike many protests of the 1960s, the DMS's actions have not been directed against the "system" or the "establishment" per se. Rather, they have been designed to educate the public about the plight of the unemployed and thereby to stimulate public pressure for the corporate elite to accede to the DMS's importunities. Supposedly, such pressure will threaten, cajole, or shame those with capital to do the right thing, namely, to create jobs through reinvestment in local industries. The implicit premise here is that access to the latest technology and protection from unfair practices (like subsidized foreign competitors dumping products at less than cost) would allow the well-trained workforce of the region to make heavy manufacturing profitable once again. The shame is that the drive to maximize profit directs corporations like USX and Mellon Bank to seek higher returns by investing elsewhere.

The difficulty, however, is that regardless of whether or not the corporate elite has as much control over public policymaking as alleged, the DMS's criticisms lose their force if, demonstrably, there are no profits to be made. Those who defend the status quo need only respond to the effect that (1) some groups are always hurt during times of economic transition; (2) the injury is not deliberate and eventually even those who are hurt will benefit from the transition; (3) trying to save dying industries in the face of economic realities will only slow the attrition and prolong the misery; (4) the faster we get on with the transition, the quicker the regional economy can recover; (5) the efforts of groups like the DMS serve only to delay the transition; therefore, they do more harm than good.

The officers of USX and Mellon Bank whom we interviewed freely acknowledged (as have other corporate spokespersons) that their corporations had directed capital out of the region, not only to invest in traditional manufacturing enterprises, but often to invest in new lines of business. One can argue that the corporate elites should have done more in the postwar decades to maintain the long-term viability of the regional industrial base, but by the mid-1970s they had little choice: most manufacturing plants in the Pittsburgh region could no longer compete in the world market; either the corporations had to rationalize their local interests and diversify their investments, or else they would go under (interviews: Hoffman; Fletcher; Fritz; Haulk; see also Nader and Taylor 1986: chap. 1; Wade 1987).

As might be expected, the corporate officials we interviewed considered the villainous role into which the DMS tried to cast them as preposterous. Far from seeing their company as destroying the industrial belt of the Monongahela-Ohio Valley, United States Steel officials pointed to their efforts to maintain and modernize plants like the Edgar Thomson and Irvin works. But despite these efforts, the sad fact remains that the world-wide market for steel has shrunk: even some of the most modern foreign plants are failing, despite the ridiculously low cost of labor compared to the United States. USS (now a division of USX) has also shown its concern for displaced workers not only in supporting and administering JTPA programs, but also with a commmitment to devote at least $600,000 annually during the life of the current labor contract (1987–1990) for operating job training and placement centers for laid-off steelworkers. The company has also made efforts to lure new industry to the area, first by offering to lease its land at favorable terms and, later, by conveying land and structures from recently closed plants to the County of Allegheny for development as regional industrial parks, accepting no payment until the parks are actually developed (interviews: Hoffman; Broderick. See also Gaynor 1987; Wilson 1987).

Mellon Bank officials whom we interviewed were even more emphatic in rejecting their company's role as chief villain. Mellon officials really do consider the Bank to be a good neighbor. Whereas in Andrew W. Mellon's time, or even as late as Richard King Mellon's postwar alliance with Mayor David Lawrence, the Mellon family might exert decisive control over both industrial and public policy, Bank officials contend that the Mellon family interests no longer exert significant direct control in either the Bank or the local corporations in which the family holds stock. The Bank itself doesn't "invest" directly. It loans money to corporate customers for projects in which those customers decide to invest. "USS would be the customer to borrow such money for investment in the Valley. If they were to come for such a loan, we would be eager to lend them money. But the fact of the matter is that there is no marketplace to absorb steel" (interview: Fletcher).

Mellon's traditional corporate customers have entered the world market, and Mellon has attempted to follow them. Yet, although Mellon ranked as the 11th largest bank holding company in the United States (15th largest in deposits) in 1985, both the proportions and magnitudes of its foreign operations are miniscule compared to those of the big banks in New York and California (Moody's 1984: al–a5; 991–95; 2100–105; Moody's 1985: a2–a6; 144–45). Moreover, the Bank now faces new sorts of competition: its corporate customers have discovered that they can raise capital more cheaply in new ways, such as through Eurobonds, junk bonds, or new types of commercial paper. Far from making an inordinate profit, Mellon's foreign operations have been losing money. Indeed, the Bank has closed down a number of foreign offices, cut its domestic payroll, and, following the announcement of huge losses projected for the first two quarters of 1987, it fired David Barnes, the CEO under whom the Bank had embarked on its programs of expansion in 1980 (Oravecz 1987a, 1987b; Wade 1987).

Despite its expanded operations in new domestic and foreign markets, Mellon views itself as largely a major regional bank. Mellon's main offices remain in western Pennsylvania, and it maintains a policy of encouraging its employees to become involved in their local communities. Its contributions to the community operations of nonprofit agencies exceed $12 million annually (interviews: Haulk; Clark. See also Mellon *1985 Community Report*). And notwithstanding cutbacks in other operations, it plans to continue expansion of its small business loan division in western Pennsylvania (interview: Fritz). Mellon Bank officials expressed the unanimous judgment that the Bank's prosperity remains intimately tied to the prosperity of the region. And the most immediate path to that prosperity is not reinvestment in heavy manufacturing, but in newer "high tech" manufacturing and in various related small businesses. This will take time. Even though the worst of the contractions in the local job market was over by 1987, Mellon's economists judged that it would take another five to seven years for the more successful of the new business ventures to generate a great expansion in employment in the region (interview: Haulk).[28]

Even the officials of labor unions and nonprofit groups—who generally take a far less benign view of the investment strategies and community goodwill of the corporate and banking communities—do not accept the DMS's contention that USS and Mellon Bank could turn the economy around. Several whom we interviewed suggested there was no way to make most of the idled plants viable without government protection from cheaply made foreign manufactures (interviews: Bonn; Peterson; Werner). Indeed, in the midst of a bitter labor dispute in September 1986, pickets allowed demolition crews to begin dismantling the "Dorothy Six" facility of the Duquesne Works when the USW's own study concluded that, as USS had contended, the plant could not be run profitably even as an employee-owned operation (McKay 1986). Union people are not optimistic about the future, but they were willing to make concessions to support USS's present program to save and upgrade its remaining facilities in the region (Piechowiak 1987).

The bottom line is that neither the majority of activists nor the public at large accepts the DMS's argument that both the blame and the remedy for the economic decline of the region lie solely or even principally in the hands of USS and Mellon Bank. And aside from this one argument, the DMS has proposed no well-developed programs or policies to resolve the problems of unemployment.

---

[28]A recent study by *Inc.* ranked the Pittsburgh Metropolitan Area as 141st of 154 areas on composite index of job growth, business start-ups, and high-growth companies (see Pearlstein 1987: 51).

CONCLUSIONS

We believe that the story of the DMS and its struggle to resolve the problems of unemployment in the Pittsburgh area provide important examples of the difficulties that are inherent in the activity of protest itself, especially from the perspective of leadership. In addition, this episode illuminates important aspects of the political landscape of the American mind, and says something very telling about how political socialization shapes this geography.

According to the protest model, the demands placed upon the leadership of protest groups may limit the effectiveness of their political activity. Leaders must deal with four different constituencies: the group itself, the media, the target group, and the reference groups. Each of these constituencies makes different, and often conflicting, demands. As protest groups usually lack traditional political resources, the passion and commitment of their members normally become their greatest assets. But in order to maintain the enthusiasm and support of the rank and file the leaders must usually employ radical rhetoric and make stronger demands than they can reasonably expect to be satisfied. Moderation will inevitably erode the emotional fervor of the group, and this could undermine the leaders' support.

The media set limits on what is acceptable protest activity and behavior, and these limits usually reflect community standards. This demand for civility by the media can conflict with what the group demands from its leadership. In addition, the media will only accept newsworthy activity as legitimate "news." Thus the protest leaders are forced to think of ever new and different methods of (nonviolent) protest to meet these criteria. In this search for the exotic, it becomes easy for the protest leader to lose sight of the purpose of the protest activity itself. Also, in order to maintain group morale, leaders sometimes find it necessary to embellish the facts, exaggerating their groups' strengths or successes. But such embellishment tends to destroy their legitimacy in the eyes of the media, who cannot afford to waste their limited resources gathering information from unreliable sources.

Due to the inflammatory rhetoric needed to maintain the protest group's morale, the leader may be viewed as too militant to deserve serious consideration by third parties or reference groups. Potential allies may be unwilling to become associated with the protest group. In addition, it becomes easier for target groups to discredit the demands made upon them, portraying the protest group's agenda as unrealistic or impossible to meet.

As we have seen, all of these things seem to have happened to the DMS. It has managed to alienate the local media through perceived dishonesty, and it has lost sight of its original purpose: to illuminate its targets, not simply to garner publicity. Its leadership, while using inflammatory actions and language to maintain group cohesion, has alienated potential allies and made it easy for its demands to be discredited. Through its lack of concern with reference groups, the DMS has isolated itself almost totally. Finally, by playing exclusively to the media, the DMS has managed to obscure a complicated economic problem that potentially affects everyone in the Pittsburgh area.

Lipsky suggests that one solution to the problem of divided constituencies is the division of leadership within the protest group itself (Lipsky 1970: 172–75). One set of leaders could concentrate upon group maintenance while another could deal with mobilizing potential allies and reference groups. A casual observer might note that either Charles Honeywell, or some number of the Lutheran clergymen, could have filled either role.

The DMS episode also says something about the consequences of political socialization in American society. At first glance this conclusion might seem puzzling. The group we have been describing ostensibly embraces a conspiratorial view of American society. They claim to see sinister, hidden powers at work in the community. They disdain coalition building and almost any form of what would be recognized as conventional politics. Even their protest activity sometimes seems strange or bizarre. We have come to the conclusion, however, that the DMS and its basic ideas are well within the American political tradition and that the failure to achieve its goals might also be explained within this context.

This realization arose gradually as we reviewed comments during interviews that could only be described as examples of cognitive dissonance (Festinger 1965; chap. 1). In the midst of their critique of the Pittsburgh community power structure, the conventional upbringing of the DMS ministers would occasionally surface through incongruous comments. Perhaps the best illustration occurred during the course of one interview, when, after reciting a long list of complaints about unemployment and hidden elites in the Pittsburgh area, a DMS pastor concluded: "Still the system we have is the best one there is" (interview: Gropp).

Statements like this—fiery rhetoric aside—tell us that the DMS basically subscribes to the capitalist system of values that American society embraces. In the postwar era, the role of government in our society has been that of referee and provider of social services to mitigate the "unacceptable face of capitalism."[29] It falls to the private sector to provide jobs, goods, and services. What is striking about the DMS's ideology is that it contains no major role for government in the economy, despite its demands that "something be done" about the problem of unemployment

---

[29]The phrase is attributed to former British Prime Minister Edward Heath.

and its consequences. When things go wrong in the economy, the DMS feels compelled to importune the private sector to ameliorate the situation: expand private production to create jobs for the unemployed. The possibilities of New Deal–type programs by the state or federal government or community control of planning and investment are given short shrift by the members of the DMS. Socialist alternatives are not even considered.

The subscription of the members of the DMS to the dominant capitalist values of American society has had a decisive effect on their level of success. Charles Lindblom has summarized these values as belief in private enterprise, private property, corporate autonomy, and opportunities for great wealth (Lindblom 1977: 226). The DMS believes it is immoral that we have poverty and unemployment in the midst of great wealth. There is no reason for such suffering. But as one activist explained, "Don't get me wrong. I'm not saying redistribute the wealth. I'm not for that" (interview: Bonn). The engine of capitalism, the profit motive, is accepted—not challenged—by the DMS members. Their argument is that Mellon Bank and the USX Corporation should reinvest in the steel industry not only because reinvestment is the right thing to do, but also because it is a profitable course of action.

The tactics of the DMS are designed to embarrass the corporate community to do the "right thing," which is also the profitable thing. What they neglect is that capitalism's imperatives do not arise from the fear of embarrassment. The corporate representatives that we interviewed generally seemed sympathetic to the plight of the local unemployed. They pointed with pride to their own charitable work, and to their job retraining and placement programs. They refuse, however, to be intimidated into investing in losing propositions. They can show that the demand for steel has simply declined in recent years, and the present world production capacity is more than adequate for current and forseeable demands. It makes no economic sense to attempt to revive a large-scale steel industry in western Pennsylvania.

Having been socialized to accept the tenets of capitalism, members of the DMS have no way to address this aspect of the problem. As much as they rant, protest, importune, and criticize, they cannot break out of the logic of their position. Deep down, they are a part of the system they are fighting; they can envision no other. They might be termed "revolutionaries of the status quo." The outcome of the economic system outrages them, yet they support the system itself.

The activity of protest is open only to members of a system. The truly alienated in any society work to undermine or overthrow the existing order. Protestors implicitly accept the basic tenets of their world and are only concerned about marginal adjustments. But in order for protest to be effective, the "rules of the game" must be followed. Yet the members of the DMS have neither followed these rules nor worked to undermine or alter them radically. They are caught in a maelstrom of protest, revolutionary rhetoric, and appeals for fundamental change whose implications they fail to acknowledge.

The relevance of the opening scenario of this paper should now be clear. The members of the DMS have chosen to chain themselves symbolically to the front door of the Bank of Mellon rather than delineate an alternative to the economic system. The DMS has helped to focus public attention upon the plight of the unemployed, but it has no practical political, social, or economic plan to alleviate unemployment. What made Marx such an original and powerful thinker was his willigness to look outside his world in order to critique it. Instead of decrying the results of capitalism and pouting about its outcomes, he strove to invent an alternative.

CHAPTER 10

The Christian Right and the Powers of Television

Michael Johnston

INTRODUCTORY NOTE

Few doubt the importance of the mass media. Television can reach a wide audience and can enflame strong passions. Nevertheless, the power of the media to mobilize or manipulate the public is limited. As the political primaries leading up to the 1988 presidential election demonstrated, even televangelists, who claim to have millions of intensely loyal viewers, have great difficulties in mobilizing their supporters to carry out their political goals.

Michael Johnston's analysis of the political opinions and behavior of the people who watch video ministers demonstrates some of the important limits upon the mass media. He argues that televangelism is best regarded as a dialogue between communicators and audience, not as a tool by which the few manipulate the many. Religious broadcasters, if they wish to keep their audiences, must cast their arguments within the familiar and relatively fixed images that those audiences find comfortable. Johnston asserts that the video preachers have succeeded at what the mass media can do best: to engage, through the skillful use of language and symbols, the inner feelings of large numbers of people, and then to skillfully read, and adapt their messages to, the responses which the audiences send back. Like other forms of ritualistic behavior, these activities are circular and self-contained. Johnston points out that people generally use media for their own purposes: mostly, to devise meanings for themselves.

Even though several televangelists have used political appeals to help them build large and loyal followings, their ability to mobilize such followings for political purposes is questionable. Because of the high cost of television productions, the ministers find that fund raising must come first. Political issues may serve more as means to that end than as a real agenda in their own right. The gap between political messages and overt response is a wide one. Indeed, many of the symbols used by the preachers—the nuclear family, the Bible, and Jesus—tend to induce quiescence. For many people, watching religious broadcasts may simply be a way of reaffirming their standards and beliefs in a confusing world; a substitute for actually doing something about the social problems that upset them (Edelman 1985).

Johnston's essay illustrates the difficulties of mobilizing any interest group. As Schnattschneider (1960) observed, even the largest interest groups "deliver" far less support than their leaders claim or their critics fear. Despite the growing sophistication of media techniques, evidence of decisive impacts upon mass behavior is mixed. Critics fearful of "mass manipulation" by the media have yet to show how people can be politically inert and uninformed, yet ready to jump into politics at the drop of a subtle cue. Most people, after all, view politics from a distance, and as only one of life's concerns. Their time, resources, and interest in politics are limited. Personalities and elections come and go, but both personal and social problems remain, and the results of participating in politics are often unclear. Televangelists, no less than traditional party leaders, can expect only limited political support, even from those who profess loyalty to their cause.

The Editors

We have enough votes to run the country. . . And when the people say, "We've had enough," we are going to take over.

Rev. Pat Robertson, *Washington Post*, March 30, 1980, p. C1

TELEVANGELISM AND MASS POLITICS

Pat Robertson's quest for the presidency in 1988 raised the hopes of some, and the fears of many others, about the political power of America's Christian Right. In particular, his career as founder of the Christian Broadcasting Network and host of television's "700 Club" symbolized the rapid growth of "televangelism" or the "electronic church": sophisticated religious broadcasting on a national scale, often with a strong political message. Robertson's media visibility, together with relatively strong early showings in the first rounds of the Michigan caucuses, led some to expect that he would be a significant force in the 1988 Republican race. Better-than-predicted strength in the Iowa caucuses added to these expectations. But Iowa was to be Robertson's high-water mark. Even what amounted to a southern regional primary on March 8 failed to reverse his campaign's subsequent decline. By early April, Robertson and his handful of delegates had ceased to be a factor in the 1988 presidential campaign.

Robertson's campaign revealed both the strengths and limitations of the political power of televangelism. Its strength lay in the strong commitment of hard-core viewers, and was manifested in caucus states such as Michigan and Iowa, where low turnouts and a field split among many candidates helped committed minorities achieve a significant impact. But in primary *election* states, where turnouts were somewhat larger, and the list of candidates shorter, Robertson met with much less success. As the campaign wore on, and the losers retired to the sidelines, support flowed to mainstream candidates, not to Robertson. Instead of assuming the mantle of leader of the party's right wing, he retained essentially the same small committed following with which he had begun the campaign.

No election year is "typical," and Robertson's failure can hardly be regarded as a final verdict on the political power of the Christian Right. The presence of George Bush, heir apparent to Ronald Reagan's still-considerable popularity and an experienced campaigner in his own right, proved to be more than such prominent Republicans as Robert Dole and Jack Kemp could handle. Robertson himself was a first-time political candidate, and his inexperience was revealed on a number of occasions. His resignation from the ministry and from Christian broadcasting on the eve of the race, and his subsequent claims that he was a political candidate and not a preacher, presented an ambivalent image even to his own following.

Moreover, his campaign was shadowed by a number of scandals which tarnished the image of televangelism. Early in 1987, Oral Roberts claimed that if viewers failed to contribute $8 million to one of his medical education projects within three months, God would "call me home." Jim and Tammy Bakker lost control of their PTL (for "Praise the Lord," or "People That Love") ministry, and their Bible-oriented theme park, after revelations of her past drug use and his sexual misadventures and payments of "hush money." The Bakkers in turn contended that Rev. Jimmy Swaggart was leading a "hostile takeover." Rev. Jerry Falwell assumed control of PTL for a time, but resigned in the fall of 1987 after unfavorable court decisions regarding PTL's debts and assets. Early in 1988 Swaggart was embroiled in a prostitution scandal through evidence revealed by another evangelist whom he had earlier accused of sexual misconduct. Nor was Robertson himself immune from scandal: for some time critics had charged that his father, a U.S. senator from Virginia, had used his influence during the Korean War to prevent the younger Robertson from having to face active combat duty. Robertson filed a libel suit over these allegations, but later dropped the case and assumed all costs himself. And early in 1988, it was revealed that Robertson had lied about the date of

his wedding; his oldest son had in fact been born only ten weeks after the
actual wedding date.

These unusual events make it impossible to say with any certainty
that the Christian Right, or even a more experienced Robertson himself,
will not be back as a stronger force in some future presidential campaign.
Moreover, the movement is active in nonelectoral politics as well, mounting strong efforts in some communities to change school curricula, ban
books from libraries, and stop the sale of pornography. But the 1988 campaign still raises intriguing questions about the apparent weakness of the
Christian Right, and of religious broadcasters in general, in the electoral
arena.

This chapter is an analysis of the relationships between religious
broadcasting and the political opinions and behavior of its audience. I will
argue that while the appeals of the "video church" and the views of its
audience are closely intertwined, in general, people are not easily mobilized or manipulated. Indeed, people's responses (or lack of them) can
powerfully constrain the users of mass media. The major effects of the
broadcasts are to be found, not in massive shifts of opinion or tides of
support at the polls, but rather within individuals themselves, at the level
of their own emotions, values, and perceptions of the world. People selectively retain and reinterpret media messages to the extent that they
serve to reassure, to help identify enemies and threats, or to confirm prior
beliefs. For these reasons, many of the political effects of the media are
best studied "from the inside out." These notions will help us understand
both the limited political impact of the "electronic church," and its more
enduring appeal for many people on more personal grounds. They also
suggest that for all their technical, rhetorical, and symbolic sophistication, when it comes to political mobilization the video ministers are subject to much the same challenges and difficulties as any other group.

The Video Church

Religious programs have been a feature of American broadcasting
since regularly scheduled radio began in the 1920s. Father Coughlin's
broadcasts were a focus of much controversy during the 1930s; some television preachers such as Rev. Oral Roberts have been on the air for decades. But the emergence during the 1970s of a new generation of aggressive "video ministers" such as the Revs. Jerry Falwell, Pat Robertson,
Jimmy Swaggart, and Jim Bakker made broadcast religion more pervasive
than ever. Nearly a quarter of the nation's radio stations are religious
stations, and most of these are evangelical in character. And even though
higher costs mean that only about 5 percent of all television stations
broadcast religious programs full-time, individual broadcasts are available
virtually everywhere (Fowler 1985: 218).

As this electronic church became increasingly visible, it also became the focus of debate over its role in politics (see, for early discussions, Hadden 1981; Martin 1981; Fitzgerald 1981; Rosenberg 1982). The uncertain separation of church and state in American politics and culture, and the optimistic political claims of the preachers themselves, gave rise to dire predictions about armies of activists controlled from the video pulpit. *Time* magazine, for example, warned in 1986 that "Preachers like Robertson command audiences that form, if not a true Moral Majority, at least several potent and readily mobilized minorities" (*Time*, 17 February 1986: 62). But neither the most optimistic claims of the ministers nor the worst fears of their critics seem likely to be borne out. Reliable estimates place Rev. Falwell's weekly audience at only about 1.5 million (Fowler 1985: 221), of which the committed are just a part. Many ministers have encountered money troubles. Surveys in "Middletown" (Muncie, Indiana) concluded that Christian Right efforts had little or no effect during the 1980 presidential election, and may actually have *backfired* in 1984 (Johnson 1986: 7; see also Johnson and Tamney 1982, 1985). In March 1988, the Christian Right lobbied hard against the Senate override of President Reagan's veto of the Civil Rights Restoration Act, producing a wave of letters and telephone calls. But senators of both parties took to the floor to criticize what they saw as false and inflammatory claims made by the Christian lobby groups; in the end, the campaign was generally regarded as helping the override forces.

Few doubt that the television evangelists have aroused strong emotions and a sense of distrust. But translating this into coordinated political action and policy change is no easy task. Even among regular viewers there is considerable skepticism. The *New York Times* and CBS News surveyed 1,394 adults in March 1987—shortly after the Roberts fund raising controversy, and while the Bakker/Swaggart battle was still making news—and found that 505, or 36 percent, said they "made a point of watching" at least one major religious program. Of that group, 26 percent had sent money to a television ministry. But 50 percent of the regular viewers held a generally unfavorable opinion of television evangelists, and 75 percent thought they were "too concerned about money." Even among contributors, 64 percent held this view. Fifty-six percent of the viewers said Pat Robertson should not run for president. On the Oral Roberts affair, 81 percent of the viewers said they did not believe God would "call him home," whereas only 6 percent said they did believe it. Even among Rev. Roberts's own viewers, only 10 percent said they believed the claim, while 73 percent did not. Finally, "about three-fourths [of the viewers] also expect more accusations against other ministers to follow the adultery scandal that arose over the Rev. Jim Bakker" (*New York Times*, 31 March 1987: A1, B8).

Mobilizing the Constituency

A generation ago, E. E. Schattschneider (1960) pointed out the difficulties of mobilization politics. Even the largest interest groups are small when compared to political parties, "delivering," far less support than their leaders claim, and their critics fear. Parties remain the only organizations that can win elections. As a result, interest groups need the parties more than the parties need them (see Xandra Kayden's essay, Chapter 4 in this volume). Schattschneider's argument remains instructive even in the modern era of weakened party organizations. It points to real problems for any group, religious or otherwise, which deliberately distances itself from the political mainstream, or which tries to capture a party from without.

Most people, after all, view politics from a distance, and as only one of life's concerns. Their time, resources, and interest in politics are limited. Personalities and elections come and go, but life's problems remain, and the results of participating in politics are often unclear. Moreover, we are bombarded with dozens of conflicting appeals, most of which are of doubtful relevance to our lives. Despite the growing sophistication of media techniques, evidence of decisive impacts upon mass behavior is mixed. (For an early work alleging such impacts but lacking evidence, see McGinniss 1969; a contemporary survey of research appears in Graber 1984: chap. 5.) Observers making claims about the "mass manipulation" of the public by the media have yet to show how people can be politically inert and uninformed, yet ready to jump into politics in response to the media's cue. Declining turnouts, disillusionment, and a reduced ability to govern American society are probably the most enduring legacies of politics in the media age (Ranney 1983).

Predictions of a Christian mass movement mobilized over the airwaves encounter more specific problems as well. The movement and its leadership are deeply divided, as the scandals and squabbles of 1987–88 make clear. Moreover, by no means do all video evangelists project a strong political message. Rev. Jerry Falwell's appeals are overtly political, but Jimmy Swaggart devotes relatively little time to politics. Even those who do emphasize politics, such as Pat Robertson, also cover other topics in their broadcasts. And the audience is even more varied than the message; the terms "Christian" and "born-again" embrace great social and religious diversity (Johnston 1982: 181–99). Whereas the linkage between religion and politics is clear and compelling for some fundamentalist Christians, others hold to a belief of even longer standing that worldly affairs matter little compared to salvation.

Still, it would seem that if anyone can mobilize the masses through television, the video ministers should be able to. Their broadcasts are technically sophisticated and backed by substantial fund raising and follow-up organizations. They not only enjoy First Amendment protections, but also are largely exempt from "fairness" and "equal-time" rules, and thus from the reluctance of broadcasters to accept political programs for fear of having to provide time to opponents (Graber 1984: chap. 4). Indeed, when in the early 1970s the FCC agreed to count "paid" as well as "unpaid" religious broadcasts as "public service" time (Fitzgerald 1981: 54), it created a positive incentive for broadcasters to fulfill their license requirements while making money in the process. (The FCC dropped its public-service requirements altogether in 1984; see Graber 1984: 51.) Video ministers employ powerful symbols and appeals, drawn not only from the Bible and formal religion, but also from our history, culture, and "civil religion" (Bellah 1974), which can engage a lifetime of political and religious socialization. Televangelists have their critics, such as Norman Lear's "People for the American Way." But whereas political candidates and interest groups know that their media messages will often evoke a response from the opposition, televangelists have no opponents who can compete in terms of media coverage. Hadden contends they "have greater unrestricted access to media than any other interest group in America" (*Time*, 17 February 1986: 63).

Thus it remains intriguing as to why video ministers have not mobilized more of a political following. To find tentative answers, we must consider the ways media users interact with their audiences.

POLITICS AND THE MEDIA

For most Americans, politics is a spectator sport—one of many competing for their attention and resources. Most Americans delve no further into politics than casting a vote—and usually, half do not even do that, despite the expensive and carefully crafted media campaigns directed their way. Still, politics is important (Edelman 1985: 5–6). Through politics we can be taxed or subsidized, coerced or left free; we may enjoy peace, or be conscripted and even blown into oblivion. Moreover, most of us have been socialized since childhood to feel loyalty to a country, its flag and institutions, and to identify our own well-being with that of the nation. Thus politics engages emotions that help shape our reactions to distant appeals and events. Indeed, politics and religion have much in common: both utilize symbols and language to simplify and clarify complex ideas, and both evoke distant but powerful threats and reassurances with which we must somehow come to terms.

If "coming to terms" meant merely the ability to adapt our ideas and emotions to an objective outside world, then mass mobilization would be more effective, if not necessarily easy. But the "uses and gratifications" school of research suggests that often the reverse is true: through selective perception and interpretation, we use media messages for our own purposes (Becker 1976; Mulder 1980; Palmgreen, Wenner, and Rayburn 1980; Bogart 1981; McLeod and Becker 1981). Berger and Luckmann (1966) write of the "social construction of reality," through which we devise meanings for ourselves within the context of language, culture, and experience. So too with media: Graber argues that "the early models that depicted a straight stimulus-response relationship were incorrect. There is no "hypodermic effect": information presented by the media is not transferred unaltered into the minds of the audience. Rather, media and audience interact: the images conveyed by the media stimulate perceptions in audience members that reflect each individual's perceptual state at the time the message was received" (Graber 1984: 151). Schwartz adds that most television is not intended "to get stimuli across, or even to package . . . stimuli so they can be understood and absorbed." Instead, the goal is "to evoke stored information . . . in a patterned way" (Schwartz 1974: 25). We construct the "messages" for ourselves.

Not surprisingly, Nimmo and Savage (1976: chaps. 3, 4, 6) find that voters form images of candidates primarily in terms of personalities, not policy. But they also find that the most important aspects of personalities are not shining teeth and smiling faces, but "personal intangibles" such as strength, honesty, and compassion. Thus, not only do voters interpret politics by relating it to their own emotions; they do so *in the almost total absence of evidence*. Virtually *all* candidates emphasize personal intangibles, and few voters have any real knowledge of how trustworthy or compassionate a candidate really is. Even when a long-standing reputation is the basis of such an assessment—Richard Nixon is "devious," Ronald Reagan is a "nice guy"—these impressions are formed at a distance and represent a convenient simplification of complex political events.

By its responses to political symbols and appeals, the "audience" gives important cues as to what works and what does not. In this way ordinary citizens, far from being "manipulated," can influence political communicators. Willie Stark, in *All the King's Men*, learned this the hard way. After a long, hot stump campaign in favor of a "balanced tax plan," he found he was losing badly—indeed, that he had been the dupe of political operators who knew such a campaign would fail. A reporter gave Stark some advice:

> Hell, make 'em laugh. Make 'em cry. Stir 'em up. They aren't alive, most of them and haven't been in twenty years. . . . Hell, their wives have lost their shape, likker won't set on their stomach, and they've lost their religion, so it's up to you to stir 'em up. Make 'em feel alive again. For half an hour. They'll love you for it. Hell, heat 'em up (Warren 1960: 40).

Stark took her advice and won the next election by a landslide. Michael Dukakis evidently didn't learn this lesson very well. Granted, it would have been difficult for any Democrat to win the 1988 presidential election, given George Bush's efforts to wrap himself in President Reagan's popularity (not to mention the American flag). But Dukakis decided not to use emotional advertising until quite late in the campaign, preferring to believe the American people already knew his record. Future candidates will note that if the choice is between seriously discussing a candidate's record and frightening people with pictures of "furloughed" murderers, they should choose the latter. So too with broadcast news: "Officials, reporters, and interested groups depict news events in ways that will appeal to audiences. In that basic sense the audiences create news stories rather than being created by them" (Edelman 1985: 205). For better or worse, we are given the kinds of media we have shown we will respond to.

Edelman points out that political discourse mainly consists of the repetitious invocation of ambiguous symbols—what he terms "myth and ritual," or simply "banality" (Edelman 1985: 16–19, 209–11). If we use those symbols to avoid social conflicts and resolve inner tensions (Smith, Bruner and White 1956), we might then expect media messages to pacify people rather than arouse them. Indeed, Edelman argues that most political symbols produce quiescence, not an aroused response (Edelman 1985: 14–15). Thus the Reagan "nice guy" image, for example, was less the driving force behind a massive right-wing movement than the cause of the "Teflon factor"—the fact that negative events did not stick to the president's image (Bennett 1988; Parenti 1986).

I do not suggest that users of the media failed to affect their audiences, or that they are imprisoned by the lowest common denominator of mass response. We know, for example, that media use is linked to learning, and plays an important role in political socialization (Graber 1984: chap. 5). News broadcasts also perform an agenda-setting function, influencing our impressions of the day's important problems (Iyengar, Peters, and Kinder 1982; Cohen 1963: 16). But these effects are limited: Graber points out that for topics that are new to us, images are typically "stimulus-determined," but when we have preexisting knowledge and opinions, images are more likely to be "perceiver-determined." The more one "preaches to the converted," the more difficult mobilization can become.

Video Ministers and Their Followings

Televangelists discuss distant but emotional concerns and make skillful use of symbols; their programs showcase conventional religious symbols, eye-catching graphics, and scenes from everyday life interpreted in religious terms. Many of these are what Edelman, drawing upon the work of Edward Sapir (1934: 492–95) calls "condensation symbols":

> Condensation symbols evoke the emotions associated with the situation. They condense into one symbolic event, sign or act, patriotic pride, anxieties, remembrances of past glories or humiliations, promises of future greatness: some one of these or all of them (Edelman 1985: 6).[1]

The cross and the flag, pictures of families at prayer, and images of crime and drug use are examples of condensation symbols used by video preachers. Many of these symbols are ambiguous, and political problems are often discussed in sweeping, general terms. Shadowy enemies abound, such as "pornographers" or (in a different vein) "secular humanists." As Edelman (1985: 9) said of news stories, they are "dramatic in outline and empty of realistic detail."

Thus, unlike the "mainstream" churches that dominated religious broadcasting for years, televangelists make frequent and skillful appeals to emotions. They learned well the "make 'em laugh, make 'em cry" lessons taught Willie Stark; indeed, an outsider's status and persistent money problems made this tactic a matter of survival. When technological developments and changes in FCC policy gave evangelical preachers wider access to television, their audience swelled—as did their church attendance and membership as well (Fowler 1985: 3–6, 20–22).

But the televangelists, like any other users of the media, are constrained by their audiences—indeed, powerfully so. The reason is money: most religious broadcasts are paid programs, and each broadcast in each market must eventually "pay for itself." Preachers building networks and other enterprises have an even greater need for money: many ministries are economically marginal or financially overextended and must appeal for a continuing flow of contributions. In this respect, the stakes for televangelists are higher, and audience feedback is more immediate and direct, than they are for advertisers who seek long-term product loyalty or marginal market shifts within a larger and more diverse audience.

Viewers will choose to respond (or not) based on their own situations, emotions, and perceptions. While experienced ministers know which fund-raising techniques have worked best, there is still a strong incentive to "play it safe"—to make sure that broadcasts have a little something for almost everybody. Some of the most successful broadcasts, such as "The 700 Club," are a potpourri of music, pictures, and diverse appeals—none very demanding, all engaging emotions, and all presented

---

[1] Like Sapir, Edelman originally distinguished between condensation and referential symbols—the latter serving simply to identify political objects. But he has since argued (1985: 198) that there are no purely referential symbols.

in a comfortable talk-show format which allows easy movement from one item to the next. Even Jimmy Swaggart, whose mainstay is straightforward, dynamic preaching, also produces "softer" programs of music, scenes from the Holy Land, and the like. The programs are less a set of political marching orders than a careful attempt to fit a message to as large an audience as possible.

There is no doubt that several ministers have built a large and loyal following, and that for some, political appeals have played a major role in that process. But the uses to which such followings can be put are another question. Fund raising must come first; and political issues may serve more as means to that end than as a real agenda in their own right. The gap between political messages and overt mass response is a wide one, especially if symbols induce quiescence—for they would then be a substitute for the activities and goals they represent (Edelman 1985: 9). People upset by social problems may not really be able to do much about them, but sending a contribution to a preacher who brings a vivid message about these problems may be the next best thing, and may temporarily ease their apprehensions. For many people, watching religious broadcasts may simply be a way of reaffirming their standards and beliefs in a confusing world.

THE VIDEO CONGREGATION

The growth and recent problems of televangelism, and the failure of the 1988 Robertson campaign, provide only indirect evidence about the political influence of the video preachers. Such trends and events are only the aggregate consequences of millions of individual choices as to whether or not to view, to contribute, and to vote. If televangelists have any "power," it lies in an ability to mobilize individual viewers by influencing those choices. But the foregoing discussion has suggested that while religious and political appeals receive a pervasive and sophisticated airing via mass media, people choose to view (or not view) the broadcasts for their own reasons, and to make their own uses of the symbols and appeals which these programs contain. Thus we must study the audience itself in order to understand its responses, or lack of them, to the symbols and appeals of the video church. How large an audience (and thus potential political constituency) do the televangelists attract? The composition of this audience, and the other mass media it uses, will affect the ease or difficulty with which it can be mobilized. What sorts of attitudes toward politics and society do the viewers hold, and what do these attitudes suggest about why they view religious broadcasts—literally, the "uses and gratifications" involved? And what linkages, if any, are to be found between use of religious media and patterns of political participation? To answer these sorts of questions, sample survey data are essential.

To study the video ministers' audience, a student research group under my direction conducted a telephone survey of the Pittsburgh metropolitan area between February 10 and 17, 1983. Using computer-generated random telephone numbers for each exchange in the greater Pittsburgh calling area, we obtained two interviews for each exchange, plus an extra interview for each 1,500 telephones over 3,000 in an exchange. The result was a sample of 241 persons. The only exchanges excluded were in the Pittsburgh central business district, and those of universities and hospitals. Refusals totaled fewer than 10 percent of all completed calls, and were not concentrated in particular areas. The survey took 10 minutes to administer, and included, among other questions, items on general political opinions, a group of political information items, and questions on respondents' backgrounds, political participation, and frequency of using various mass media.

This approach yielded a small sample,[2] but it allows us to compare media use to a wider range of attitudinal variables and levels of political participation than are typically found in national surveys. The goal here is not only breadth of focus, but also depth. Many surveys gather data on religious media use which are then compared directly to some political outcome—voting, for example, or approval of government or religious leaders. But I have argued that media use is interactive, and that its major results are to be found not in the form of overt mass responses, but in

---

[2]A total of 241 respondents completed the interview. Some 56 percent were females, compared to 52.6 percent of the population of Allegheny County as a whole. The age distribution of the sample, and of the county's population aged 15 or over, can be directly compared as well:

Allegheny County		Survey Sample
Age	Percent	Percent
15–24	22.0	21
25–34	18.9	24
35–44	12.7	15
45–54	14.2	15
55–64	15.4	10
65 and over	16.8	15

Data for occupation and education were gathered in categories not directly comparable to census data, though it is worth noting that in terms of educational attainment, the data significantly overrepresent college graduates (26 percent of the sample had graduated from college, compared to 16.5 percent of Allegheny County's population in 1980) and underrepresent those who had not graduated from High School (10 percent of the sample, compared to 30.9 percent of the population). These last results may be reasons for interpreting the survey results with caution, even though education as such did not figure significantly into the statistical results.

terms of more subtle effects upon "intermediate" attitudes such as hopes, apprehensions, and the standards by which people judge the world. In those terms, this survey is quite useful: it relates media use not only to overt political behavior, but also to a range of those "intermediate" attitudes.

The setting and the timing of the study were opportune as well. Greater Pittsburgh, located where the Northeast and Midwest meet (and not far from Appalachia) is a socially diverse metropolitan area. Its full-time religious television station and several religious radio stations expose residents to the full range of broadcast evangelism. The data were gathered in 1983, after several years of vigorous activity by, and controversy over, televangelism, but before the more recent scandals which have damaged the image of specific preachers. The students who worked on the project participated in training sessions in administering the interviews; the fact that they could introduce themselves as students working on a research project may have helped reduce refusals. These data will hardly give us a final verdict on the political effects of televangelism, but they are well suited to a discussion of some of its more subtle effects.

Table 10–1 shows that, in Pittsburgh, about one person in seven (14 percent) watches or listens to religious broadcasts "often," or "almost always":

TABLE 10–1 Frequency of Watching or Listening to Religious Broadcasts

Listen to or Watch	Frequency	Valid Percent
Never	132	55
Seldom	74	31
Often	20	8
Almost always	14	6
NA	1	Missing
Total	241	100

Just how these results compare to the *New York Times*/CBS survey finding, noted above—that 36 percent of the public "make a point of watching" one or more evangelists—is unclear; perhaps the *Times* question prompted a stronger response by naming prominent preachers. Fowler (1985: 221) points to an even smaller audience than Table 10–1 would suggest, concluding that "no more than 5 percent of the American population look at even one of the major TV preachers in a week." What these results have in common, however, is the implication that only a portion of the viewers can be regarded as "hard-core," and that claims of very large *and* devoted audiences must be treated skeptically. These contrasting results may mean that Pittsburgh is an atypical locale. But the data might also discriminate more effectively than the *Times* survey among those who are committed viewers, those who only occasionally tune in, and those who do not watch or listen at all.

Frequency of viewing religious broadcasting is related to one's age, level of political information, and self-labeled liberalism or conservatism, as Table 10–2 shows:

TABLE 10–2   Regression of Religious Media Use on Respondents' Background Characteristics

Dependent Variable: Frequency of Use, Religious TV and Radio

(Never = 0   Seldom = 1   Often = 2   Almost all the time = 3)

Multiple R	.346	$F = 10.27$
Adjusted R Square	.108	Significance $F = .0000$
Standard Error	.813	

Independent Variables

Variable	Beta	T	Significance
POLINFO	−.276	−4.35	.0000
AGE	.220	3.44	.0007
LIB ID	−.122	−1.93	.0551

Notes: "POLINFO" represents the number of correct responses to six basic questions on state and national government. The "LIB ID" question was, "Would you consider yourself very liberal (coded 3), somewhat liberal (2), somewhat conservative (1), or very conservative (0)?"

The "congregation" thus tends to be made up of older people possessing relatively low levels of political information—not the likeliest candidates for activism—who are more likely to label themselves "conservatives" than "liberals." It is also worth noting that although gender was not related to frequency of use across the board, 12 of the 14 respondents who said they tuned in religious broadcasts "almost all the time" were women.

Religious broadcasts, of course, represent only a part of the media environment. The survey suggests that frequent viewers of religious broadcasts read news magazines somewhat less than do others: only 29 percent of the respondents who "often" or "almost always" watch religious broadcasts read a news magazine "often" or "almost always," compared to 41 percent of those who seldom or never watch. But they are exposed to national newspapers such as the *Washington Post* or the *New York Times:* 36 percent of the most frequent viewers said they read a national newspaper "often" or "almost always," compared to 18 percent of those who "never" use religious media. And the most faithful viewers also watch other forms of television—if anything, *more* often than do others. Of the 34 respondents who use religious media "often" or "almost always," 27 (79 percent) "almost always" watch local broadcast news (as against 58 percent of the rest of the sample), and 19 (56 percent) "almost always" watch network television news (as compared to 38 percent of the other respondents). Frequent viewers thus receive many other sorts of broadcast messages besides the religious. Some people may watch religious television less because they are committed to its message than because they simply enjoy watching television.

While the equation above accounts for only 10.8 percent of the variance in use of religious media, it is still striking that two of the three independent variables—political information [POLINFO] and liberalism/conservatism [LIB ID]—are relevant to politics. We might thus expect religious media use to affect levels of political participation, or opinions about political matters. But such patterns were nowhere to be found. Extensive efforts to demonstrate a linkage between religious media use and five types of political participation—voting, displaying political signs, campaign work, donations to candidates, and running for office—produced little, whether types of participation were considered individually or in groups. Weak zero-order relationships vanished when respondents' background characteristics were taken into account. The strongest association between religious media use and political participation was a weak *negative* partial correlation (partial $r = -.116$, p $= .087$) with donations to candidates—after education, age, frequency of reading national newspapers, and gender were taken into account. If anything can be inferred from such a result, it might be that televangelists' financial demands leave their followers less able (or inclined) to put their money to political use. Even weaker relationships were found with a variety of opinion items, including questions on government intervention in the economy, attitudes toward inequality, and scales intended to tap feelings of political efficacy. Indeed, the most striking result was the apparent weakness of religious media. Use of news magazines and local newspapers was strongly associated with higher levels of participation, but reliance on network television (itself linked to more frequent viewing of video preachers, as noted) was associated with lower levels of involvement.

Data from one metropolitan area offer only a tentative description of opinions and behavior. But we may still ask why these broadcasts—despite their technical sophistication, themes of discontent, and demonstrated effectiveness at fund raising—have so little apparent effect upon political attitudes and participation. We should recall, first, the sheer diversity of political messages to which everyone is subjected. Televangelists, like any political group, must compete with the appeals of many others. Even the faithful will receive only a fraction of the whole range of evangelical appeals. And as noted, the fraction they do watch will differ in religious and political content.

Conventional political factors may be at work too: relatively low levels of political information would not seem conducive to extensive participation, and might even mean that the evangelists' political messages and expected responses are not fully understood. Viewers of religious broadcasts presumably care about many of the same nonreligious issues—jobs, taxes, and the quality of public services—as do most other voters. Self-labeled conservatism also means different things to different people, perhaps pertaining to personal habits or cultural values as well as (or instead of) explicitly political concerns. And to the extent that these viewers are conservative, the political climate (of 1983) should be considered as well. A popular president, effectively employing conservative rhetoric and symbols through the same medium used by the video ministers, may be a reassuring part of the political picture—all the more so for viewers whose levels of political information are low.

These data, however, should not be taken as indicating that the religious broadcasts have no political effects. Some effects might be intermediate, influencing our view of the political world but not what we do about it. And if we interpret media messages in our own ways, these effects might not take the form of mass effects, but could instead vary from person to person. A full assessment of this view must await in-depth study of people who tune in the broadcasts. But the Pittsburgh survey does provide tentative evidence in support of the view that the video church, with its strong themes of political distrust, helps viewers reaffirm their moral standards and beliefs without necessarily turning discontent into political action.

The Nature of Distrust

Vivien Hart argues that political distrust is a complex thing—involving not only a given state of the political world, but also the standards by which we judge it for ourselves:

> Political distrust—the unfavourable evaluation of politics by citizens who see a discrepancy between the ideal and the reality—is not alienation or anomie. It differs from the classic terms of Marx and Durkheim in being a subjective condition. It differs from the recent uses of these terms by involving the subject's norms, as well as his perceptions of politics, as an integral part of the condition. . . . The essential point is that it is subjective *and* evaluative; by definition the condition combines both normative and cognitive elements—it is the discrepancy between these two which measures the depth or intensity of distrust (Hart 1978: 28).

Hart reminds us of the complex linkages among political perceptions, opinions, and behavior. Our moral standards and our political responses are separate things; as Hart adds, "the norms themselves become an important variable" (Hart 1978: 28). Moreover, if distrust is not the same thing as alienation, then distrust will not necessarily be expressed in politically alienated ways. Indeed, one could be quite distrustful of people, institutions, and leaders without doing very much about it.

To examine these possibilities, I used opinion items from the Pittsburgh survey to construct a three-item "standards" scale, tapping the normative aspects of distrust. It measures support for strict rules and standards of fairness, in terms of agreement with the following statements:

> Wrongdoing is wrongdoing, no matter what, and must always be punished.
>
> The only thing a person is entitled to in this world is a fair start in life.
>
> If people are taking advantage of others, it may be necessary for government to step in.

A second, "evaluation" scale is directed at cognitive judgments of the current situation:

> Sometimes politics and government seem so complicated that a person like me can't really understand what's going on.
>
> Parties are only interested in people's votes, not in their opinions.
>
> People who accept large gifts from business or political associates are really being "bought."[3]

These scales were regressed on the religious media variable and a number of demographic characteristics of respondents. And here, the results were intriguing. As was the case with political behavior, use of religious media was statistically unrelated to variations on the "evaluation"

---

[3]For each item, responses and scoring were: Disagree strongly (-2), Disagree somewhat (-1), Agree somewhat ($+1$), Agree strongly ($+2$). For each respondent, responses to the three questions were summed, and then divided by three, to yield a score. Correlations for each item with the remainder of its own scale were as follows:

STANDARDS scale:

"Wrongdoing is wrongdoing . . ."	$r = .295$	$p = .000$
"The only thing a person is entitled to . . ."	$r = .216$	$p = .000$
"If people are taking advantage . . ."	$r = .124$	$p = .028$

EVALUATION scale:

"Sometimes politics and government seem so complicated. . ."	$r = .182$	$p = .002$
"Parties are only interested in votes . . ."	$r = .363$	$p = .000$
"People who accept large gifts . . ."	$r = .254$	$p = .000$

scale, once social characteristics were taken into account. But it was linked to respondents' *standards,* as Table 10–3 shows:

TABLE 10–3   Regression Analysis of "Standards" Scale

Dependent Variable: "Standards" Scale			
Multiple R	.360		$F = 11.39$
Adjusted R Square	.118		Significance $F = .0000$
Standard Error	.597		

Independent Variables			
Variable	Beta	T	Significance
RELIG MEDIA	.169	2.63	.0090
AGE	.235	3.67	.0003
POLINFO	−.186	−2.90	.0041

Other things being equal, more frequent users of religious broadcasts tend to judge the world by stricter standards. But apparently this does not translate into a more negative opinion of the current state of politics, or an overt political response. This result is consistent with the notion that the frequent viewers use religious media and interpret its appeals primarily for their own purposes—not to take on the ministers' views of the world, but to reaffirm their own—and do not necessarily translate this experience into political action. Televangelists go to great lengths to provide such symbolic reaffirmations, for financial as well as religious reasons. But in so doing, they may not so much mobilize a political following as produce quiescence. This is an interactive process: those with strict moral standards would also seem more likely to watch, and to contribute to, the video ministers. Indeed, another regression analysis of religious media use on personal characteristics (not shown) found not only that the "standards scale" was significantly linked to more frequent viewing (as we would expect), but also that in a stepwise procedure it supplanted the liberalism/conservatism variable included in Table 10–2.

This process of reaffirming standards involves a self-selected audience, evangelists who carefully tailor their appeals to that audience, and continuing feedback in the form of letters and contributions. It is a process which can be of significant symbolic and emotional importance to all participants. But if Edelman is right about quiescence, and if Hart is correct in distinguishing among the independent components of political distrust, this process would not necessarily spill over into mass politics; and indeed the survey data support this view.

CONCLUSION

Televangelism is best regarded as a dialogue between communicators and audience, not as a tool by which the few manipulate the many. In this sense, the religious media do not have "minimal effects." Instead, their effects are subtle, intermediate, and idiosyncratic: complex interactions between evangelists and viewers evoke, and largely reaffirm, the ideas and symbols which people use to come to terms with their own particular experiences. This view reconciles the televangelists' obvious success at attracting viewers and money, on the one hand, with their modest political impact on the other. This is not an assertion that the video preachers have failed. Indeed, they are succeeding—perhaps more than most others—at what the mass media can do best: to engage, through the skillful use of language and symbols, the feelings and values of large numbers of people, and then to skillfully read, and adapt the message to, the responses which the audience sends back. If this activity sounds circular and self-contained, it is; but it must be said, so are many of the other ritualistic activities which make up the visible face of politics.

Whether or not the televangelists constitute some sort of "threat" cannot be decided here. But if the data above on the small size of the video congregation, and on the evangelists' weak effects upon political participation are correct, some of the more dire predictions are unlikely to come true. When video evangelists venture into politics, the rules of the game are not suspended; for all their media visibility, Pat Robertson, the Liberty Federation, and others on the Christian Right confront the same opportunities and limitations faced by more conventional political groups.

The preachers' apparent lack of influence upon political participation, as indicated by the survey data, and the relative strength of personal standards as an influence upon religious media use, also suggest that mechanistic notions of cause and effect may not only lead us to false findings of "minimal effects," but also distract us from some of the more intriguing political processes going on within individuals. People are not like billiard balls, rolling in the directions they are pushed. The intentions of media practitioners may have little or nothing to do with the results (if any) which are obtained. And the audience, acting upon individual needs and motives not even necessarily understood by themselves, constantly affect the communicators. As democracy goes, this is an imperfect variety, one in which it is very difficult to engage "the people" in political life, whatever the agenda. But it is also a kind of democracy which is more resistant than we might have thought to manipulation by the users of the mass media.

CHAPTER 11

Presidential Leadership and Public Followership[1]

Jon Hurwitz

INTRODUCTORY NOTE

Teddy Roosevelt called the presidency of the United States a "bully pulpit," and most occupants have not been shy about using their powers to influence the public agenda and to mobilize public support. Nevertheless, even the powers of the presidency are limited.

Jon Hurwitz sets out in this chapter to evaluate the conditions under which the public is willing to support the president. Does the president have the capacity to mold public opinion on any important issue? Presidents are increasingly being judged by their abilities to maintain public support. Under what circumstances is the public most susceptible to influence? Which individuals are most susceptible? Which types of issues does the president have the most latitude to manipulate the public? Answers to these questions provide clues about the ability of the mass public to control elite policymaking. The president would have much greater powers if people followed him out of a sense of obedience or civic obligation than if they supported him because of partisanship or preferences on a limited number of issues.

To investigate the determinants of "followership," Hurwitz presents a sample of American adults with various hypothetical—yet plausible—presidential positions in order to discover how many people will switch their own positions to match those of the president. For example, after ascertaining a person's opinion about sending U.S. troops to Central America, respondents who favored sending troops were confronted with

[1]The author is grateful to the editors of this volume, as well as to Lee Sigelman, for their helpful comments. Special thanks are due to Mark Peffley, who not only took part in collecting the data but, as well, carefully read and offered suggestions to improve the quality of the manuscript.

the questions, "What if President Reagan opposed the use of U.S. troops there? Would you favor or oppose sending troops to Central America?" Using similar sets of questions, Hurwitz looks at the public's susceptibility to persuasion in three issue areas: military foreign policy, nonmilitary foreign policy, and domestic policy.

His evidence is consistent with previous findings that presidents have greater influence on public opinion in international than in domestic affairs, particularly regarding the military. But his results also suggest that presidents face severe limitations in attempting to mobilize support, even among those who are favorably disposed to them personally or to their policies. Importantly, Hurwitz finds little evidence that the willingness to yield to the president's position is rooted in civic obligation.

More disturbingly, his results suggest that followership is more common among those lacking in political information. However, because such individuals tend to pay little attention to politics, they are less susceptible to attempts to mobilize them. Hurwitz concludes that it is difficult to speak of presidents "manipulating" public opinion, since they seem limited to winning new support from those who are least involved. Despite the significant numbers of people willing to follow, in no sense do presidents have "an almost free hand" (Lipset 1966) to pursue initiatives without restraint, even in foreign affairs.

The Editors

While the power of the presidency has been disputed (Rossiter 1960; Cronin 1980), it is not a matter of controversy that presidents who exercise power are dependent on the tool of persuasion. Richard Neustadt (1980: 10) is most notable for placing the concept of persuasion at the heart of the exercise of power: "Presidential power is the power to persuade."

Of the various actors whom the president must persuade, arguably none is more crucial to executive success than the public. This assertion is based on the premise that public support for presidents has both a direct bearing on success (i.e., executives are judged, in large part, on their ability to sustain adequate levels of public approval) and an indirect link to success. This indirect impact exists because, as Neustadt has argued, an executive's "professional reputation," and hence his success in dealing with elites in Washington, is largely dependent on his ability to maintain the public trust and support. This speculation has received support from the empirical work of Edwards (1980) and others. Indeed, Kernell (1986) argues that this indirect approach of presidential leadership, which he terms "going public," is increasingly used by modern executives.

In this chapter I investigate two related questions of presidential leadership (or public followership). First, and most basically, does the president have the capacity to mold public opinion on important issues? Prominent theories of the presidency, of course, assume an affirmative answer to this question. I address this assumption by asking respondents from Lexington, Kentucky, if they would change their support for various policies if President Ronald Reagan advocated a position different from their own.

More important, I investigate the *determinants* of presidential persuasion. Under what circumstances are respondents most susceptible to influence? When is influence most likely, and why? Which individuals are most susceptible, and for which types of issues are they most manipulable?

Answers to these questions are important, first, because they provide clues to executive strategy. Presidents would have to fashion very different types of appeals to the public if followership is tied to a sense of civic duty or patriotism, on the one hand, or to partisanship, on the other hand. While a highly partisan approach would be successful in the latter case, it would likely fail in the former instance.

Second, it is important to investigate the antecedents to followership because of the implications for the ability of the mass public to control elite policymaking. Especially in the foreign policy domain, it has been argued that presidents can manipulate the public to a dangerous degree. For instance, Lipset (1966) has written that the commander-in-chief has a "free hand," and Ippolito et al. (1976) that he has "carte blanche," to launch virtually any policy initiative without worrying about a lack of public support. This disturbing possibility is likely if, in fact, it is found that citizens follow the president out of a sense of obedience and civic obligation to support the nation's leader.

Yet, the president's success at manipulation will be more limited and conditional if it is found that followership is tied, instead, to partisanship or there is ambivalence regarding the issue on the agenda. In short, we must understand the determinants of followership if we are to understand the limitations of presidential manipulation—a topic to which I will return below.

BACKGROUND

As noted, Kernell (1986) has argued that modern presidents turn increasingly to going public in order to bolster their clout with Congress. They are correspondingly less likely to utilize the traditional approach of forging majority coalitions in the legislature. According to that author, this modern strategy requires the president to have a particular skill: the "recognized ability to rally national public opinion is the keystone of this new style of presidential leadership" (p. 145).

Kernell's conclusion regarding the increasing usage of going public suggests that presidents must have at least two capabilities. The desired outcome of going public, from the executive's perspective, is that individuals can be mobilized to contact their representatives and encourage them to support the administration's position. But this outcome is possible only given the prerequisite that the president can create a near-consensus of opinion (or at least the perception of a strong majority position) among the electorate. For unless legislators believe that the president is backed by a consensual constituency, they are unlikely to be affected by the contacts from the home district.

It is important to note that presidents do not necessarily need to be able to effect attitude change; the strategy of going public can work nicely even if presidents do not change a single opinion. But presidents must be capable of convincing citizens to *support* the administration's position, even if the individual does not fully believe the position to be the appropriate one.

What does the literature say about the ability of presidents to engender support for their policies? Sigel (1966) found that by a three-to-one ratio, her respondents supported the propriety of a president sending troops to a foreign country if he thought it was necessary, even if the American people opposed the idea. Rosen (1973) also found evidence of deference toward the president, but to a lesser degree. Using a split-ballot technique, he found fewer respondents would oppose a "family assistance plan" if they were told it was President Richard Nixon's plan than if they were not told it was Nixon's policy. The differences in support, however, were modest. Rosen speculates that Sigel found greater deference toward the president because the earlier study examined a foreign policy matter, while the later work focused on a domestic issue.[2]

Sigelman and Sigelman (1981) also used a split-ballot technique but came to very different conclusions. Specifically, they found that subjects were *less* likely to support policy options if they were told the proposals belonged to President Jimmy Carter than if the initiatives were unattributed. The authors, labeling this the "kiss of death phenomenon," demonstrated that Carter supporters were likely to support the policy regardless of whether it was attributed or unattributed, while anti-Carter subjects rejected the proposal if they knew it to be Carter-related. Thus, the president's ability to influence the public is clearly related to support levels. In addition, no differences were found in support for foreign vis-à-vis domestic policies, although the authors acknowledged that subjects'

---

[2]The notion that presidents should receive greater public support on international than on domestic issues is an extension of the "two presidencies" argument first made by Wildavsky (1966).

reactions to a foreign-aid bill may not typify support levels for other types of foreign (especially military) policies.

Several have examined the relationship between the support for a president and aggregate changes in public opinion on an issue (see, for example, Mueller 1973 and Page and Shapiro 1984). Not surprisingly, it was determined that presidential popularity can, in fact, lead to aggregate opinion shifts in the direction advocated by the president. Page and Shapiro, for example, found that while popular presidents have a substantial effect on public opinion, "unpopular presidents . . . have no effect at all or maybe even a negative impact" (1984:658).

Although the findings are not conclusive, several themes are suggested. First, there is a reason to suspect at least a modest difference between presidential persuasiveness over the public in foreign versus domestic policies. Despite criticisms leveled at the "two presidencies" argument in recent years (see, for example, Edwards 1986), it seems likely that the president is given somewhat greater latitude in the international domain—at least from the electorate and particularly regarding matters of military or national security. I would anticipate, therefore, more willingness by individuals to support the president on foreign versus domestic policy issues, and on military versus nonmilitary foreign policy issues.

In addition to this inter-issue difference, I would expect to find individual differences in willingness to support the president *within* an issue area. In the first place, it is likely that some individuals will defer to the president simply because of the president's position—i.e., some citizens are simply more deferential toward authority, especially legitimate authority figures, than are others. This deference was demonstrated in the Rosen and Sigel studies, especially when the issue is a military initiative. Without going into the question of whether this tendency toward deference is a part of one's personality (see, for instance, Adorno et al. 1950) or simply a political attitude based on a belief in the importance of supporting one's country and its leaders, this *deference hypothesis* implies that certain individuals are predisposed to support the president—not because they lack an ability to make their own independent judgment about the wisdom of a policy but, rather, because they feel it is the appropriate (and patriotic) response.

A second expected type of individual difference in presidential support is predicted from the Mueller (1973) and Page and Shapiro (1984) studies which argue, implicitly or explicitly, from a balance theory perspective (Kernell 1976). Balance theory (Heider 1958) contends that individuals like to preserve consistency in their beliefs. Simply put, the theory holds that in order to maintain or restore consistency, we will be predisposed to agree with an individual with whom we have a "positive" relationship.

Theoretically, a positive relationship with others depends on one or both of two conditions. We have such a relationship with another if we have "positive sentiments" toward the person—that is, if we like him or her. Additionally, positivity comes about if we develop "unit formation"—that is, we perceive something in common with the individual.

This *balance hypothesis* thus suggests that individuals should be more likely to support the president's policy position, first, if they support the president's performance (positivity from liking) and, second, if they share the president's party identification (positivity from unit formation).

A third, and quite obvious, source of individual differences in followership is predicted from what is labeled an *intensity hypothesis*. It is expected that some individuals may be willing to support a president-advocated issue position even though they initially disapprove of the position, but also this willingness should be *minimal* among those who disapprove most strongly. Presidents should have an easier time soliciting support from those who initially mildly disagree with the administration than from those who strongly disagree—because individuals holding more extreme or intense preferences tend to be more resistant to persuasive appeals (Tesser 1978). And presidents should be more successful with individuals who, regardless of the intensity of their disagreement with the administration, share the president's ideological stance (but who, for whatever reason, oppose the president on the particular measure).

I expect individuals to differ in their willingness to support a presidential initiative for a fourth reason: cognitive differences render citizens more or less susceptible to executive influence. More specifically, some individuals are likely to comply with the president because of the ease of doing so. Presidents can greatly simplify decision making for those who are neither aware of, nor opinionated about, an issue by essentially providing them with an issue position and thereby simplifying their information and decision costs. Such uninformed persons should be more likely to yield to the influence of another (the president, in this case) both because they lack the information to stick to an independent judgment and because they will be unable to generate counterarguments to the persuasive message from the president. Conversely, those with more information about an issue who devote more thought to the topic have been found to generate more counterarguments which, consequently, make them relatively resistant to influence attempts.[3]

This *cognitive hypothesis,* therefore, motivates the expectation that those least willing or able to pay information costs should be most willing to comply with the president. Most obviously, individuals with relatively

---

[3]This line of reasoning is borrowed from the "cognitive response" approach to persuasion. See Petty and Cacioppo (1981: 225–52) and Petty, Ostrom, and Brock (1981) for discussions.

lower levels of education and/or political information should have the greatest difficulties with such costs.

I similarly expect support for presidential policy positions to vary with levels of political interest. Those who are more interested in the political world should devote relatively more thought to issues and, consequently, be more likely to form opinions on issues which are resistant to persuasive attempts. By the same token, those for whom an issue is salient would also be expected to form opinions on such matters and would therefore, as well, be less susceptible to presidential persuasion.

Finally, the cognitive hypothesis suggests the possibility that followership is also related to the structure of one's beliefs. The information processing literature (e.g., Hastie 1986) maintains that individuals require heuristics, or simplifying devices, to help them understand issues, particularly those which are complex. In politics, it has been argued that individuals often process issues within a belief system—or a consistently organized set of attitudes (Converse 1964). When one is faced with a new policy, for instance, he or she may process it, and ultimately come to take a position on the issue, based on whether or not the policy is consistent with the other components of the belief system. Thus, those with consistent belief systems germane to the policy (which can assist the individual in processing the issue) should be relatively less susceptible to presidential appeals. Put differently, administrations may well have an easier time soliciting support from citizens who lack other guidelines which could enable them to make decisions independently of the president.

In sum, the cognitive hypothesis leads to the expectation that presidential success in persuading the public should be highest among individuals who are (a) least educated; (b) least informed about the issue; (c) least interested in the issue; (d) least concerned about the issue (i.e., to whom the issue is not salient); and (e) who do not possess consistent belief structures, or heuristics, relevant to the issue.

In forming these expectations, the traditional "other things equal" clause is assumed. But "other things," of course, are seldom equal. Most important, while the least educated, informed, interested, concerned, and consistent individuals should be most easily persuaded by the president, they should also be least likely to expose themselves to presidential persuasive attempts (Patterson 1980). Thus, the prediction is more accurately stated as: those with cognitive "limitations" should be most likely to yield to persuasion *if* they hear and understand the message.

METHODS

In order to investigate the determinants of followership, a probability sample ($N = 501$) of adults in the Lexington, Kentucky, area was interviewed by the professional staff of the Survey Research Center at the

University of Kentucky.[4] Interviews, which ranged from 15 to 20 minutes each, were conducted from February 6 to 18, 1986—a period when President Reagan's Gallup popularity rating stood at 64 percent.

Dependent Measures

The willingness of respondents to support the president—followership—was assessed in three issue areas: military foreign policy, nonmilitary foreign policy, and domestic policy. In the military domain, respondents were asked if they strongly favored, favored, were uncertain about, opposed, or strongly opposed "sending U.S. troops to stop the spread of Communism in Central America." Those who *favored* (strongly or not) using U.S. troops were asked the follow-up question: "What if President Reagan opposed the use of U.S. troops there? Would you favor or oppose sending troops to Central America?" Those who initially favored using troops but who changed their stance to opposition after hearing that President Reagan opposed the policy are classified as "followers" (coded as "2" on the dependent variable), while those who consistently favored troop use (both before and after the mention of Reagan's position) are classified as "nonfollowers" and assigned a score of "0." Those moving from support for the policy to a position of uncertainty (in response to the Reagan prompt) are placed between the followers and nonfollowers (and given a score of "1" on the dependent measure).

Those initially *opposed* to (strongly or not) or *uncertain*[5] about troop use were asked: "What if President Reagan felt it was necessary to send U.S. troops there? Would you favor or oppose sending troops to Central America?" Once again, those changing their responses (from opposition

---

[4]Approximately 73 percent of individuals contacted by the Survey Research Center completed interviews. The demographic characteristics of these respondents come reasonably close to approximating those found in the Lexington population. While the 1980 U.S. Census indicates that 52 and 13 percent of residents of the area are female and black, respectively, the sample includes 50 and 13 percent from these groups. I do slightly oversample more affluent and better-educated individuals. While the median income in Lexington is $15,915 according to the Census, the median-income category in our sample is $20,000 to $30,000. Respective population and sample percentages for education are: less than high school: 29 and 14; completed high school: 28 and 26; some college: 18 and 26; and graduated college: 25 and 34.

[5]The decision to categorize the initially uncertain respondents with those who are initially opposed to a policy is, to some extent, arbitrary. These individuals could just have easily been grouped with the initially supportive group. The decision is also, however, largely inconsequential to the analysis. If the initially uncertain respondents later support a policy after told that President Reagan advocates the measure, they are, in fact, yielding to presidential influence. In any event, the percentage of respondents selecting the middle scale position is quite small for each of the three policy areas.

to support for the policy) are labeled "followers," those consistent in opposing troop use are classified as "nonfollowers," and those moving from opposition to uncertainty are placed in the middle category.

Comparable questions were asked dealing with nonmilitary foreign policy ("What about restricting foreign imports to protect American jobs?") and domestic policy ("What about cutting government services in such areas as health and education to reduce government spending?"). As with the Central America question, respondents were then asked about their support for these policies if President Reagan advocated a position opposite to their own. "Followers" and "nonfollowers" are defined as above—i.e., the former including those changing their responses so that the revised positions are similar to the president's, and the latter including those who remain consistent despite the realization that they do not share Reagan's view.

Note that switching in response to a survey prompt is *not* claimed as evidence of bona fide attitude change. In fact, it is likely that the tendency to follow the president's wishes in this context indicates a willingness to conform to the president's preferred position rather than an abandonment of the respondent's initial position on the issue. I do believe that the measures effectively assess a respondent's *susceptibility to persuasion*—a willingness to support the president's position simply because the individual feels support is appropriate. Kellman (1958) distinguishes among three types of yielding to another's position: compliance (yielding to an influence attempt without a private acceptance of the position); identification (yielding in an attempt to emulate the other individual); and internalization (internally accepting the other's position). Clearly, the measure used in this analysis is more likely to pick up incidents of compliance and, to a lesser extent, identification than to assess internalization. But it should be emphasized that presidents are not dependent upon *changing* opinions to be successful at going public. Rather, presidents need only count on a public which is willing to support their position, regardless of whether the public actually embraces that position in all its particulars.

Independent Variables

Deference Hypothesis.   The measure used to estimate levels of deference, or belief that presidential support is appropriate and necessary in our society, has been formed by summing responses to three items:

> In a time of crisis abroad, the press should not ask a lot of questions or demand a lot of answers from our presidents.
>
> When it comes to foreign affairs, we should not criticize a president or openly disagree with him, because it only weakens our country's position.

Some people feel when it comes to foreign affairs we should stand behind our government even if we disagree with its policies. Others feel in foreign affairs we should support our government *only* if we agree with its policies.

The first and second items were coded on a five-point ("strongly agree" to "strongly disagree") scale; respondents were asked in the third item if the position to which they adhered was "very close" or "somewhat close" to their own belief (also forming a five-point scale). On all three items, the middle scale position was assigned to those with uncertain opinions. Lower scale values correspond to maximum levels of deference (scale range: 3–15). Reliability analysis indicates that the items do a reasonably good job of measuring the underlying construct—unifying behind our nation and its leader (Cronbach's alpha = .55).[6]

Balance Hypothesis.   The balance hypothesis emphasizes the relationship between willingness to follow the president, on the one hand, and affect toward the president, on the other hand. Specifically, it is expected that maximal support will come from those who approve of presidential performance and those who share the president's party affiliation (i.e., Republicans).

Partisanship has been measured with the conventional seven-point scale (with lowest scale values corresponding to "Strong Democrats"). To assess presidential support, respondents were asked "How would you rate Ronald Reagan on his handling of his job as President—excellent, pretty good, only fair, or poor?"

Intensity Hypothesis.   To determine the initial issue-related attitudes of respondents, two different types of measures have been used. First, it should be recalled that, to form the dependent measures, respondents were asked about their initial positions on three issue scales before being asked if they would support President Reagan if he advocated the opposite position. Truncated versions of these initial scales have been used as

---

[6]While it would be preferable to use scales with larger alpha values, two factors must be taken into consideration when evaluating the reliability of scales employed in this analysis. First, because Cronbach's alpha is based on correlation coefficients between the component variables, alpha tends to be an underestimate of reliability when variables are measured using varying formats. The Deference Scale, for instance, is composed of two Likert items and one two-sided item; the average correlation among the items, consequently, is suppressed by nonrandom measurement error, which necessarily reduces the level of alpha. This condition also applies to the first scale in the Appendix. Second, because Cronbach's alpha is sensitive to the number of items in the scale, it is generally not possible to construct a scale with a large alpha value if only two or three items are used, unless the items are highly correlated (and therefore redundant) with one another.

measures of respondents' attitudinal position. For example, among those asked about sending U.S. troops to Central America "if President Reagan opposed the move," those strongly favoring troop use (coded "2") are assumed to be more initially antagonistic to Reagan's position than those who merely favor (i.e., not strongly) using troops ("1"). By the same token, among those asked about troop use "if President Reagan felt it was necessary," those initially strongly opposed to the policy ("2") are assumed to be more difficult to persuade than those who are initially only opposed (coded "1"), and these in turn should be more difficult to persuade than those initially uncertain ("0").

Second, I would expect followership to depend not only on one's intensity of opposition to the *specific* advocated position, but also on one's predisposition to agree or disagree with the *general philosophy* behind the advocated position. For example, an individual may oppose the specific use of American troops south of the border, but generally support, in the abstract, the widespread use of the U.S. military throughout the world. Such a respondent should be more likely to yield to Reagan's position encouraging troop use than would an individual who opposed both military engagement in Central America and, more abstractly, Pentagon involvement under virtually any condition. In other words, those who are ideologically sympathetic to the advocated position (even though they initially oppose the president on the specific issue) should be most likely to yield.

For the purpose of this analysis, three of these abstract predispositions, or "postures," are of particular importance. First, one's position on the *Militarism Posture* is indicative of his or her general preferences for military solutions as opposed to nonmilitary, diplomatic solutions to international problems. Items used to measure individuals' positions on this posture can be found in Section 1 of the chapter appendix. It can be seen that these items tap only a generalized belief in the soundness of military strength (or "toughness"), rather than preferences for specific uses of military force. This generic quality is characteristic of all postures. I would expect, consistent with findings by Hurwitz and Peffley (forthcoming), that one's position on the Militarism Posture should be an important predictor of willingness to support President Reagan's advocated position regarding troop use in Central America—i.e., those who are most militaristic should be more willing to support the president's recommendations to use American troops, and should be least supportive of Reagan's position against American troop deployment.

Second, the *Isolationism Posture* is a dimension anchored, on one end, by those favoring U.S. involvement in world affairs, and, on the other end, by those wishing to avoid any type of international involvement (see the Appendix, Section 2, for scale items). Positions on this posture are expected to predict willingness to support the president in two policy areas. First, isolationists should be relatively more likely to oppose U.S. involvement in Central America. Consequently, they should be more likely to support the president if he opposed sending American troops, and less likely to support Reagan if he favored sending troops. In the second place, I also expect isolationism to predict individuals' attitudes on the international trade issue. Because interventionists support international involvement, they should be more likely to support a president who opposes trade restrictions, and more likely to oppose a president who supports trade restrictions. Hurwitz and Peffley (1987) found positions on the Isolationism Posture to be related to attitudes on specific questions of both military involvement and trade.

The third posture, *Governmental Assistance,* is a dimension which is defined, at one pole, by the belief that the government ought to provide assistance for the disadvantaged; those at the opposite pole feel that the government does not have the responsibility for doing so (see the Appendix, Section 3). This posture, which has been found to be related to attitudes of individuals on specific domestic issues (Peffley and Hurwitz 1985), is expected to be a predictor of susceptibility to presidential influence on the issue of whether governmental services in the areas of education and health should be cut. Specifically, those who are most supportive of governmental assistance for individuals should be least likely to support a president who favors budget cuts to health and education, and most likely to support a president who opposes such reductions.

Cognitive Hypothesis.   According to the cognitive hypothesis, presidential support is expected to be most likely among those with lowest levels of education, and of issue-related information, interest, salience, and consistency. Information was estimated on an interval scale (0 to 4), based on the number of political fact questions which respondents could answer correctly.[7] Respondents were assigned political interest scores (1 to 4) depending on whether they "follow what's going on in government and public affairs most of the time, some of the time, only now and then, or hardly at all."

Different salience measures were used, depending on the issue area. Regarding foreign policy, respondents were asked whether they considered nuclear arms control to be "extremely," "very," "somewhat," or "not" serious. And in the domestic domain, respondents were asked to

---

[7]Respondents were asked to identify (a) the Premier of the U.S.S.R.; (b) the U.S. Secretary of State; (c) the head of the Palestinian Liberation Organization; and (d)the side which the U.S. government is supporting in Nicaragua (i.e., the "guerrillas"/"contras" or the Nicaraguan government). (Cronbach's alpha = .82.)

indicate the seriousness of the "jobs and unemployment" problem, using the same classification.

It should be noted that the information, interest, and salience measures are not truly issue specific, as the hypothesis demands. Rather than employing three different sets of measures in the three different issue areas, I use only one generic measure of information and interest, and only two (domestic and foreign) measures of salience. While not ideal, these measures should provide adequate estimates of the appropriate constructs.

Finally, estimates of issue consistency were calculated using a method proposed by Barton and Parsons (1977). These measures are weighted standard deviations of individuals' responses to the battery of posture items (described above and listed in the Appendix); the smaller one's standard deviation across the postural questions, the greater one's level of attitude consistency. Three such measures of consistency are employed: Militarism Consistency, Isolationism Consistency, and Governmental Assistance Consistency. For reasons explained above, the Militarism and Isolationism Consistency measures were used in the troop-use equations, the Isolationism Consistency measure was used in the trade equations, and the Governmental Assistance Consistency measure was used in the service cuts equations.

TABLE 11–1   The Frequency of Followership

A. Troop Use in Central America

	Respondents Initially Favoring Troop Use		Respondents Initially Opposing Troop Use			All Responses	
	N	(%)	N	(%)		N	(%)
Favor	108	53	86	34	Change	176	40
Uncertain	7	3	11	4			
Oppose	90	44	157	62	Stable	265	62
Total	205	100	254	100		441	100

TABLE 11–1   (continued)

B. Import Restrictions

	Respondents Initially Favoring Restrictions		Respondents Initially Opposing Restrictions			All Responses	
	N	(%)	N	(%)		N	(%)
Favor	176	64	55	28	Change	149	32
Uncertain	7	2	8	4			
Oppose	94	34	133	68	Stable	309	68
Total	277	100	196	100		458	100

C. Domestic Service Cuts

	Respondents Initially Favoring Service Cuts		Respondents Initially Opposing Service Cuts			All Responses	
	N	(%)	N	(%)		N	(%)
Favor	47	69	37	9	Change	57	12
Uncertain	1	2	6	1			
Oppose	20	29	377	90	Stable	424	88
Total	68	100	420	100		481	100

Note: Boxes designate followers (those changing responses).

FINDINGS

Inter-Issue Difference in Persuasion

Table 11–1 shows that followership is more common in some issue areas than others. For each of the three issues (troop use in Central America, import restrictions, and domestic budget cuts), respondents who initially favored (first column) or opposed (second column) the policy are categorized according to whether they favor, are uncertain about, or oppose the policy when asked to offer their opinion should the president take a position opposite to their initial view. The number (and percentage) of respondents willing to change their preference can be found in the bottom row of the first column and the top row of the second column for each issue. These "followers" have been boxed in the table. The third column documents position change regardless of initial position.

It is impressive, first, that so many individuals are willing to admit to an interviewer that they would alter their responses solely because of the president's influence. On average, approximately 3 out of 10 change their answers in response to the follow-up inquiry. As noted, though I do not claim to be measuring attitude change, it is still impressive that so many respondents seem susceptible to persuasion.

In comparing the percentages of those willing to change, there are reasonably large differences between those initially supporting and initially opposing a policy in two of the three issue areas (troop use and domestic service cuts). And in both areas, interestingly, more respondents changed positions if they initially shared President Reagan's *actual* advocated view than if they took the opposing position. The president, for example, had occasionally suggested that U.S. military involvement in Central American politics might become necessary. Among respondents sharing this view, 44 percent yielded to presidential influence, while only 34 percent changed responses among those initially opposed to sending troops to the region. By the same token, the president had consistently demonstrated, through speech and behavior, his belief that domestic services should be funded at a lower level. And while 29 percent of those supporting such domestic cuts were willing to change positions, only 9 percent yielded if they initially opposed the health and education spending reductions.

This finding[8] is fully consistent with work by Goodin (1983), who finds that "out-of-character" presidential actions (e.g., President Reagan opposing U.S. involvement in Central America or resisting cuts in domestic service budgets) can often be extremely appealing to supporters of the executive. Those who generally side with Reagan, therefore, may continue to side with him if they learn that he advocates an out-of-character position. Because Reagan has such "firmly established credentials in the opposition camp" (Goodin 1983: 432), they may believe that there is a very good reason why the president is taking a position different from that which he usually takes. This argument may explain why such a large number of respondents are willing to follow Reagan, especially if they share his initial beliefs.

More important, there is clear support for the hypothesized relationship between followership and the issue area. Specifically, my expecta-

---

[8]For a similar conclusion based on rational choice principles, see Calvert (1985).

tion was that the president should be able to attract more support in foreign than domestic affairs, and more support in military and security foreign affairs than nonmilitary/security foreign policy. In fact, the data fit this pattern remarkably well. While 4 out of 10 individuals change positions on the troop-use question, about a third do so with import restrictions, and only an eighth of the respondents vacillate on the domestic issue. Put differently, individuals are three times more likely to change international as domestic positions, and the differences are even more impressive on the troop-use question than on the import-restriction item.

Because only one issue in each of the three domains is examined, it is possible that results are attributable to unique properties of the specific policies selected, rather than to more general properties of the policy domains. In other words, it is not certain that troop employment in Central America is representative of the military/security domain, or that domestic budget cuts are representative of the domestic domain.[9]

It nonetheless seems likely that, at least for the mass public, a distinction is made between supporting domestic and international initiatives of the president. While political elites have sufficient information about, and interest in, foreign relations to develop crystallized opinions on matters of foreign policy, many in the mass public, doubtless, do not. Thus, citizens are probably more dependent on presidential guidance, and more likely to be impressionable. It is also possible that the belief that "politics stops at the water's edge" is more often endorsed by mass than elite groups. In any case, it appears that presidents have a better potential for going public successfully on international issues than on issues in the domestic domain.

Individual Differences in Followership

In the remainder of this chapter, I present and discuss an analysis of the determinants of followership in the three issues areas. Specifically, the following equations have been estimated:

---

[9]Fortunately, however, another data set is available which permits a replication of this finding. In another survey (a nonprobability sample [$N = 196$] administered in Lexington, Kentucky, in December 1986), respondents were asked five questions analogous to the three dependent variables used for this analysis. Specifically, they were asked about their support for funding for the "Star Wars" initiative, sending troops to the Mideast if the "Arabs threatened to cut off our supply of oil," bombing nations supporting terrorism, cutting off ties to South Africa, and increasing taxes to reduce the budget deficit. They were also asked about their position if President Reagan advocated a contrary position. The pattern of switching on these issues largely conforms to the findings of the present analysis. While only 13 percent of respondents indicated a willingness to yield to the president's position on the sole domestic issue (tax increases), almost twice as many (24), on average, would change positions on the four foreign policy questions.

1. Military Troops:

Followership = β_0 + β_1 [Deference] + β_2 [Party ID] + β_3 [Pres. approval] + β_4 [Extremity of initial support for/opposition to troops] + β_5 [Militarism Posture] + β_6 [Isolationism Posture] + β_7 [Education] + β_8 [Information] + β_9 [Political Interest] + β_{10} [Foreign policy salience] + β_{11} [Militarism consistency] + β_{12} [Isolationism consistency].

2. Trade Restriction:

Followership = β_0 + β_1 [Deference] + β_2 [Party ID] + β_3 [Pres. approval] + β_4 [Extremity of initial support for/opposition to restrictions] + β_5 [Isolationism Posture] + β_6 [Education] + β_7 [Information] + β_8 [Political Interest] + β_9 [Foreign policy salience] + β_{10} [Isolationism consistency].

3. Budget Cuts:

Followership = β_0 + β_1 [Deference] + β_2 [Party ID] + β_3 [Pres. approval] + β_4 [Extremity of initial support for/opposi-

TABLE 11–2   The Determinants of Followership

A. *Troop Use in Central America*

	Respondents Initially Favoring Troop Use		Respondents Initially Opposing Troop Use	
	β	t	β	t
Deference	−.014	.178	.150	2.358**
Party ID	.046	.591	.054	.886
Reagan support	.031	.375	.182	2.784**
Extremity	.131	1.804*	.108	1.893*
Militarism	−.181	2.223*	.196	3.072**
Isolationism	.256	3.209**	−.050	.806
Education	.110	1.362	.075	1.189
Information	.160	2.184*	.090	1.560
Interest	.058	.804	−.036	.632
Salience	.051	.701	.098	1.742*
Military consistency	.041	.542	.131	2.206*
Isolation consistency	.038	.515	.146	2.541**
Adjusted R^2	.067		.267	
N	199		255	

B. Import Restrictions

	Respondents Initially Favoring Restrictions		Respondents Initially Opposing Restrictions	
	β	t	β	t
Deference	.060	.838	.113	1.432
Party ID	−.006	.080	.214	2.791**
Reagan support	.026	.360	.042	.508
Extremity	−.007	.107	.143	2.007*
Isolationism	.009	.127	.052	.661
Education	.031	.426	.041	.519
Information	.114	1.735*	.107	1.472
Interest	.022	.345	.159	2.233**
Salience	−.061	.960	−.003	.041
Isolation consistency	.001	.009	.000	.999
Adjusted R^2	.000		.094	
N	268		196	

C. Domestic Service Cuts

	Respondents Initially Favoring Service Cuts		Respondents Initially Opposing Service Cuts	
	β	t	β	t
Deference	−.014	.107	.032	.589
Party ID	.118	.876	.124	2.280*
Reagan support	−.013	.092	.021	.360
Extremity	.197	1.571	.137	2.666**
Governmental assistance	.092	.611	.018	.300
Education	.036	.264	.038	.700
Information	.108	.854	.001	.982
Interest	.172	1.384	.021	.412
Salience	.314	2.477**	.103	1.996*
Gov. service consistency	.107	.754	.084	1.462
Adjusted R^2	.093		.044	
N	65		412	

Note: Coefficients are standardized beta coefficients.
*$.01 < p < .05$
** $p < .01$

tion to cuts] $+ \beta_5$ [Governmental Assistance Posture] $+ \beta_6$ [Education] $+ \beta_7$ [Information] $+ \beta_8$ [Political Interest] $+ \beta_9$ [Domestic policy salience] $+ \beta_{10}$ [Governmental Assistance consistency].

For each policy area, two separate equations are estimated—one for those initially supporting the policy, and one for those initially opposing it. Regression estimates are presented in Table 11–2 for the six equations. Entries are standardized beta coefficients[10] derived from Ordinary Least Squares (OLS) procedures.[11]

Far more striking than commonalities between the equations are the obvious differences. Put simply, not only does followership have different determinants across issue areas, but, more puzzling, even within an issue area the responses of those *opposing* a policy are generally explained by a different set of antecedents than the responses of those *supporting* the initial policy.

Troop-Use Equations.   The data show, for example, that switching to a position of opposition to the use of U.S. troops is quite different from switching to a position of support. Among "hawks," or those who initially favor sending American troops to Central America, the strongest predictor of willingness to yield to executive influence is the respondent's Iso-

---

[10]An analysis of the correlations between the independent variables in each of the six equations offers very little evidence of multicollinearity. With only two exceptions, none of the bivariate correlations between independent variables is greater than $r = .36$. Partisanship and Reagan support variables (used in each of the six equations) are correlated at $r = .43$. To investigate the possibility of inefficient estimators (multicollinearity presents a problem because the estimates of the regression affected coefficients of variables have wide confidence intervals and, consequently, will tend to be imprecise), the equations were twice reestimated with, first, the partisanship variable omitted and, second, the support variable left out. The results were essentially similar to the models contained in Table 11–2—that is, both coefficients and their accompanying t values were quite similar across the three equations.

The second set of suspect variables includes the governmental assistance scale and the government services consistency measure ($r = .53$), variables which were included in the domestic service cut equations. The only notable difference in the reestimated equations is that the consistency measure becomes significant ($b = .113$; $t = 2.002$) when the governmental assistance scale is omitted from the equation which includes individuals initially opposing service cuts. Followership is significantly less likely, in other words, among those with consistent attitudes pertaining to domestic policy.

[11]Some methodologists would contend that, with a trichotomous dependent variable, OLS estimates are less appropriate than LOGIT estimates. The six equations were reestimated using a LOGIT model with results virtually identical to those presented in Table 11–2. Only OLS models are presented, however, for two reasons: First, OLS coefficients are more widely understood, and second, LOGIT models do not yield a widely accepted goodness-of-fit measure equivalent to R^2 in the OLS model.

lationism belief. Specifically, those most strongly advocating the avoid-
ance of international entanglement—the classic isolationists—are most
likely to follow the president's lead in deciding to subsequently oppose
the use of American troops.[12] The extremity of the individuals' initial positions also proved to be important. As predicted, persons initially
strongly supporting troop use are significantly less likely to follow than
respondents whose initial position was less extreme. Further, as expected, those with lower levels of political information are more likely to
follow the president.

As noted, switching among "doves," or those initially in opposition
to troop use in Central America, was very different from switching among
hawks. Notably, support can be found for all four hypotheses in this
(dove) equation. First, followership is more likely among those originally
moderately opposed to troop use than among those originally strongly
opposed (intensity hypothesis). In addition, those highest on the deference scale are more likely to change positions in this troop-use equation
(deference hypothesis), and, as well, yielding to the president's influence
depends substantially on ratings of Ronald Reagan (balance hypothesis).

And finally, there is support for the cognitive hypothesis: those most
willing to change positions on the issue tend to regard arms control as
relatively nonsalient. It is likely, consequently, that such individuals
would lack incentive to pay the costs necessary to reach an independent
judgment about the issue and so should be more likely to defer to another
authority on the matter. Moreover, the two measures of issue consistency
("militarism constraint" and "isolationism constraint") are found to be
significantly related to followership. Those who have the most consistent
positions (i.e., the smallest standard deviations across the postural scale
items) on the two postures, and who are consequently assumed to rely on
belief systems to help them make decisions on specific political issues,
are least likely to abandon their initial position because of the president's
advocacy. This is an intriguing finding, for it suggests that, at least for
some individuals, followership may be a way of compensating for a lack
of other decisional strategies.

The most surprising finding in the troop-use equations concerns the
Militarism Posture variable. Among the doves (i.e., those initially opposing troop use), Militarism is related to followership in the expected direction: the most militaristic respondents are most willing to abandon their
initial "oppose troop use" response to support the president's hypothetical hawkish position. Among hawks, however, the direction of the rela-

---

[12]All variables have been recoded so that positive coefficients are consistent with hypotheses detailed in the prior section, while negative coefficients contradict these hypotheses.

tionship runs counter to the expectation that those who favor military options in a general sense would stand pat when told that the president opposed the use of U.S. troops. Instead, the opposite is found—that is, the more militaristic respondents are *more* likely to follow the dovish presidential lead.

Why should the president have an easier time persuading the most militaristic respondents to oppose troop commitment? The answer is not obvious. One possibility is that militarists are more chauvinistic and are therefore more likely to believe that they should support their nation (and its leaders) *regardless* of its actions. Yet this interpretation has problems. Specifically, chauvinism should be closely related to deference, and, consequently, deference should be strongly related to militarism. But the bivariate correlation between deference and the Militarism Posture is only .33. Further, the deference variable is included in the multivariate model, essentially controlling for chauvinism. In short, this possibility is not well supported.

Another possibility is suggested by an experimental study by Sigelman and Sigelman (1986), who asked both hawk and dove subjects to read about either hawkish or dovish actions taken by a fictitious president. Interestingly, the dove subjects judged the president according to his actions—that is, they liked both a dove president and his policies better than they liked a hawk president and his policies. The hawks responded differently, however. They were supportive of a hawk president taking dovish actions, but antagonistic to the same actions undertaken by a president described as a dove. According to Sigelman and Sigelman,

> Hawks reasoned . . . that a president who shared their own hard-line foreign policy beliefs was obviously compelled to act like a dove by something other than his own policy preferences; that being the case, hawks did not hold a president's dovish actions against him (p. 283).

Thus, just as hawks in their study were willing to lend support to a dovish action advocated by a militaristic president, so too were hawkish respondents willing to stand behind the actions of a Pentagon-oriented president, whether actions are in character (i.e., using troops) or out of character (opposing troops).

The least militaristic individuals may be driven by an ideological pacifism and consequently may oppose military intervention regardless of its advocates. The most militaristic are perhaps more pragmatic; they will base decisions on the perceived *need* for a military response (which, in turn, may be established by a trusted and military-minded leader). Thus, the most militaristic are most willing to follow or yield to the president in both equations, but for different reasons. Those initially *opposing* troop use are most likely to change responses because the president is advocating a policy (troop commitment) that is consistent with their postural view. But those initially *supporting* troop use are perhaps more likely to follow because they believe that the hawkish president must have good reasons for recommending against troop use.

Import Restriction Equations.   The most obvious feature of the import restriction equations, relative to the troop-use equations, is the inability to explain variance in followership in the former. Among those initially supportive of restrictions, the only variable even marginally important is political information—that is, those with higher levels of information are slightly more likely to remain stable in their responses.

While the information variable is not significant in the equation which includes those originally in opposition to restrictions, another cognitive variable, political interest, is important in this equation. Put simply, those less interested in politics are more likely to yield to presidential influence than those who claim a higher level of interest, presumably because the latter "group" is motivated to form opinions on the issue independent of the claims of a political authority figure.

Also significant are the extremity and party identification variables. Those who initially oppose import restrictions are somewhat more likely to alter their responses if President Reagan favors such restrictions if, first, they are not initially *strongly* opposed to the policy and, second, they are Republicans (and therefore more closely associated with the president).

Domestic Budget Cuts.   The determinants of followership in the budget-cut equations are quite similar to those which were found to be important in the import restrictions domain. Only one indicator significantly predicts followership for those initially supportive of domestic cuts, and again it is a cognitive variable—issue salience. Those most likely to regard the issue of jobs and unemployment as serious, and who, theoretically, should devote the most thought to cutting government domestic services, tend to be most resistant to a president who attempts to persuade them to abandon their initial opposition to domestic cutbacks.

Also similar to the import-restriction equations are the determinants of followership among those who initially favored domestic cuts. Once again, the president seems to have more success lessening initial opposition to the policy among Republicans (those most likely to follow a GOP president) and those who initially are moderately—not strongly—antagonistic to the policy. And although followership in the domestic spending area is not significantly predicted by interest, it *is* found to be related to another cognitive variable—salience. As with those initially supportive of domestic cuts, those initially opposed to such a change are more likely to yield to presidential influence if they do not regard jobs and unemployment as a serious problem.

General Discussion

Despite differences among equations, several tendencies are evident. However, it is important to bear in mind that, with only one exception, the ability to explain followership is not impressive. Better than a quarter of the variance is explained by the second troop-use equation, but no other equation explains more than a tenth of the variance. The point is not that this analysis is unproductive, for I have identified several theoretically predictable determinants of followership, but rather that willingness to yield to the president is best explained by considerations which have not yet been isolated.

With this caveat in mind, some important consistencies can be identified. First, with the single exception of the troop-use equation which includes those initially opposed to the policy (doves), the deference hypothesis receives little empirical support. In the other five equations, there is virtually no evidence that willingness to yield to the president's position is rooted in a general belief that presidential support is obligatory or necessary, regardless of the policy in question.

This conclusion—that there does not seem to be a "type" of individual who habitually defers to presidential authority—is substantiated by looking at the number of times each respondent changed positions on an issue. It is theoretically possible for an individual to change responses from zero times (i.e., those who are consistent on all three issues) to a maximum of three times (i.e., those who are inconsistent on all three issues). In fact, 52.7 percent of respondents were perfectly consistent (yielded zero times), while 31.7, 13.2, and 2.4 percent followed the president one, two and three times, respectively. Thus, approximately 85 percent of the sample switched positions only once or not at all. Put differently, of those respondents who yielded at all, more than two out of three did so only on one of the issues. Thus, several types of evidence suggest that followership does not result from a generalized belief in the appropriateness of deference regardless of the issue area.

Second, the partisanship variable, which significantly affects followership for at least some respondents in the import and the domestic spending equations, does not even approach statistical significance in the two troop-use equations. As noted, the "two-presidencies" thesis (which holds that presidents can almost always count on bipartisan support for foreign, especially military/security, policy initiatives) has come under attack in recent years. Edwards (1986), for example, has argued that this virtually guaranteed bipartisanship disappeared subsequent to the Eisenhower administration. Perhaps the sentiment that partisanship should not affect international relations no longer exists among the elites; the equations suggest, however, that bipartisanship regarding international relations remains an important standard for many in the mass public.

Third, while the partisanship variable is significant in two of the issue areas, there is curiously little impact from the presidential support variable. Despite the studies cited which find support for the balance hypothesis, followership was found to be predicted by presidential support only for those initially opposing troop use in Central America. Otherwise, those approving of President Reagan are not significantly more likely to yield to his influence than are those who do not support the president.

This finding can be explained in several ways. Perhaps I have unintentionally controlled for presidential support by segregating those initially supporting a policy, in one equation, from those initially opposing it, in other equations. But this possibility exists only if approval of the president is highly correlated with one's initial position on the three issues. And analysis[13] indicates that this is not the case. Another explanation is statistical: presidential support may be unrelated to followership because the former variable had little variance due to the uniformity of support for Reagan. Consequently, if this analysis were replicated when presidential popularity is more variable, approval of the president should turn out to be a more important predictor of followership. Yet another possibility is that other studies (which have found significant relationships between approval and willingness to yield to presidential influence) differ from this analysis because they do not examine presidential support using multivariate equations and, consequently, are susceptible to specification problems.

Fourth, I have found consistent support for the cognitive hypothesis, which holds that respondents will be most likely to yield to presidential influence if they are unable, or unwilling, to pay the costs required come to an independent judgment about a policy. I had predicted that several "groups" would be less likely to form stable opinions on issues (and consequently be more susceptible to presidential influence): those who have little interest in politics or to whom an issue is nonsalient (who lack incentives to judge issues), those with little education or political information (who lack resources to form such judgments), and those without consistent belief systems pertaining to the policy (who find it difficult to process relevant information efficiently). With the exception of education, each of the cognitive variables figured prominently in at least one equation. There is particular support for the role of political information—in three of the equations, the least-informed respondents yielded disproportionately to presidential influence. And in a sense, information is the most direct measure of the cognitive hypothesis.

---

[13]The highest bivariate correlation between presidential support and an initial issue position is only .172 (troop use in Central America).

And fifth, there is also considerable support for the intensity hypothesis. The issue-extremity measures, in particular, perform as significant predictors of followership in four of the six equations.[14] It may, at first blush, appear to be a trivial finding that followership is inversely related to the extremity of one's position on the issue. In a sense, it would be surprising to learn that those strongly supportive of, or opposed to, a policy do *not* resist presidential influence more than those who are relatively more moderate in their views. Yet, the finding leads to an important implication: followership is characteristic mainly of those who do not have strong opinions about an issue. This suggests, of course, that presidential leadership may be limited by the inability of the executive to convert those who have strong feelings, and restricted in its effectiveness to citizens who are relatively neutral, indifferent, or ambivalent.

IMPLICATIONS

Caution must be exercised in drawing implications from the conclusions of this study. Questions can be raised about the sample employed: Would a national sample produce the same results as the local sample from Lexington, Kentucky? More important, was this sample exceptionally susceptible to presidential persuasion because it was responding to an unusually popular and trusted president? It should be noted, further, that followership is examined in the context of only three issues, which may or may not be representative of military/nonmilitary foreign policy, and domestic policy domains.

More generally, the mundane realism of the dependent measures requires greater attention: it is not certain that individuals yield to presidential influence on the hypothetical scenario measures the same way they would in the "real world." Two biases of the measure are especially likely. First, the followership measure may overestimate the proportion of individuals who support the president's position simply because it ensures that all respondents—or at least all who pay attention to the question— are *aware* of his position. Real-world presidents, in contrast, must at-

---

[14]Note that the two equations in which the extremity coefficients are *not* significant both include respondents who were initially supportive of the policy. In large part, this result is doubtless an artifact of the way the policy-extremity measure has been constructed. It should be recalled that if a respondent "strongly favors" or "favors" a policy, he or she is then asked about his/her support if Reagan opposed the same policy. The extremity variable, therefore, only incorporates the *two* values or degrees of support for the policy, while it incorporates *three* degrees of opposition ("strongly oppose," "oppose," and "uncertain"). Conceivably, then, the extremity coefficients could have been significant in all six equations if we had been able to use extremity measures with a larger range for all respondents.

tempt to mold public opinion in an environment in which many persons remain apathetic to, and uninformed about, their leader's urgings.[15]

A second possible source of measurement error operates more selectively. Specifically, it is likely that individuals who are most susceptible to persuasion—that is, those who are least informed or interested—would also be most likely not to hear presidential persuasive attempts, or to somehow distort what they do hear (Kessel 1984). Thus, it is possible that, in addition to overestimating the total number of individuals who yield to the president's position, I more seriously overestimate the tendency of political novices to follow the executive. Novices may be changing their answers to align with the position of the president simply because the questions explain Reagan's position clearly and unambiguously. In other words, the survey questions artificially overcome a low degree of political awareness.

Even though these potential biases suggest the need for replications using different methods under different administrations, I maintain that the measures are extremely useful for studying tendencies to support the policy positions of the president of the United States. Those individuals willing to admit that they would change their answer simply because the president has advocated a particular position, after all, can *only* be responding to executive influence.

In another sense, the measures may *underestimate* the "follower mentality" (as labeled by Mueller 1973) because of the likelihood that many respondents would not want to admit changing positions. Still, 3 out of 10 respondents have been found (on average) to acknowledge that they would follow the president's lead, and many more on the military issue. Although much of this followership may be attributed to President Reagan's unusual appeal, the large number of individuals yielding stands as an example of the ability of executives to use the strategy of going public successfully.

It would therefore appear that at least some presidents would have great latitude in forging public support for their programs. This finding, clearly, raises the normative concern whether this type of follower mentality is functional or dysfunctional in our polity. In general, of course, the follower mentality becomes more attractive as the qualities of the president and his policy pursuits become more attractive. We worry more about a president molding public opinion when the executive's agenda is dangerous or otherwise suspect.

More generally, the notion that presidents can manipulate public opinion is, in many ways, an anathema in a republic. If followership becomes extreme, there are serious problems of elite accountability, disre-

---

[15]See Hovland (1959).

gard for constitutional restraints, and public control of the political process.

But it is important to specify the antecedents of followership because
it is more disturbing under some circumstances than others. Most troublesome are the implications of the deference hypothesis. If a substantial
number of citizens felt obligated to support the president, almost without
regard to the wisdom of his actions, executives could act arrogantly, unilaterally, and virtually without restraint in many areas of international
relations, justifying their initiatives as publicly popular. Further, they
would likely gain an upper hand vis-à-vis the legislature because of their
electoral backing. In short, followership would be particularly disturbing
if presidents could count on support for their decisions almost automatically.

Fortunately, however, there is little evidence to support the deference hypothesis. Not only does the deference variable fail to predict in
five of the six equations but, further, very few respondents systematically
altered their responses for each of the three issues. Instead, susceptibility
to presidential influence seems to be a function of cognitive and issue
factors. Specifically, I found that presidents can count on more support
from those who are least informed (or who otherwise lack incentives or
resources to pay information costs) and those without strong opinions on
the issues.

It is somewhat disturbing that followership is more common among
those lacking in political information, particularly given the consistently
low levels of public information about foreign policy matters in general.
Nevertheless, it is probably also true that while less-informed individuals
are more susceptible to influence, they are also less susceptible to presidential attempts to mobilize them to contact or lobby legislators to support the White House (Verba and Nie 1972).

It is more encouraging to find that followership is closely linked to
moderation, uncertainty, ambivalence, or whatever else keeps an individual away from the extremes of an issue dimension. The ability of presidents to nurture followership, in short, is largely restricted to those who
do not have strong opinions about the particular issue. Put differently,
presidents should have little success at winning over those who have
taken an opposing position. It is difficult, consequently, to speak of presidents "manipulating" public opinion. They seem to be limited to winning
new support from those who are least opinionated. Despite the large number of individuals who yield, in no sense do presidents have "an almost
free hand" (Lipset 1966) to pursue initiatives without restraint, even in
foreign affairs.

Appendix

POSTURAL MEASURES

1. Militarism Posture (Cronbach's alpha = .50):
   A. *Some people feel that in dealing with other nations our government should be strong and tough. Others feel that our government should be understanding and flexible.
   B. *Some people feel that the best way to ensure peace is through military strength. Others feel that the best way to peace is to sit down with other nations and work out our disagreements.
   C. **The United States should maintain its dominant position as the world's most powerful nation at all costs, even going to the brink of war if necessary.

2. Isolationism Posture (Cronbach's alpha = .64):
   A. **We shouldn't risk our happiness and well-being by getting involved with other nations.
   B. **The United States shouldn't worry about world affairs, but just concentrate on taking care of problems here at home.

3. Governmental Assistance (Cronbach's alpha = .43):
   A. **The government has a responsibility to help the poor in this country in their efforts to achieve a better life.
   B. **The government should see to it that every person who wants to work has a job and a decent standard of living.

*Respondents were asked which viewpoint came closer to their own opinion and whether it was somewhat close or very close to their own view, producing a 5-point scale with "depends" at the midpoint of the scale.

**Respondents were asked whether they agreed or disagreed with the statement and whether they agreed or disagreed strongly or not so strongly, producing a 5-point scale with "uncertain" responses at the midpoint of the scale.

SECTION THREE
Long-Term Influences

CHAPTER 12

News Media Bias and Class Control

Michael Parenti

INTRODUCTORY NOTE

The mass media play a vital role in liberal democracy. In modern societies, television, radio, and popular magazines constitute the primary source of information about public affairs that most citizens receive. According to democratic theory, the news media are supposed to monitor and criticize the actions of government and elite groups. But do they? Are the media independent? While the media are criticized from both the right and the left, the media themselves operate under the pretension that they have no established ideology and no biases—in short, that the news media are independent.

Michael Parenti argues that the ostensibly neutral news media in the United States consistently demonstrate ideological and class biases. Despite the well-publicized attacks by the Far Right, the bulk of the news media presents a picture of reality that supports powerful groups and established causes. In Western democracies, the mass media are profit-making businesses whose long-term survival is intimately intertwined with the success of established institutions. Thus, whites tend to be favored in news reports over nonwhites, males over females, management over labor, and officialdom over protestors. Moreover, news reports demonstrate ideological biases in that the media systematically support private enterprise over socialism, capitalism over communism, nationalism over internationalism, and militarism over disarmament. He argues further that these biases stem more from media elites consciously pursuing their self-interest than from a shared American political culture.

While convinced of the awesome powers of the media, Parenti observes that there are limits to the media's domination by conservative interests. The most important among those he cites is that: Ideological control over the media is only informal and covert so that dissenting information can sometimes slip through. The myth of the "free press" forces publishers to give a modicum of autonomy to working journalists so that news reports sympathetic to dissenting groups occasionally emerge. Finally, and most important, the media reflect serious differences that sometimes emerge among elite groups. Readers are asked to decide whether we should see ourselves as the victims of impersonal technology and culture or as alert citizens who are skeptical enough to maintain our independence.

The Editors

The news media operate under a well-established ideology that claims they have no established ideology, no racial, gender, or class biases. Supposedly the media just report things as they see them. But more than ever we hear complaints to the contrary. It is these complaints I would like to investigate critically herein, and by way of doing so, I will offer a critique of my own regarding the class biases of the print and broadcast news media for press.[1]

ATTACKS FROM THE RIGHT

Criticisms of the media emanating from the political Right are given much attention and exposure within the press itself. This alone points to the media's willingness to entertain attacks from conservative sources while generally ignoring or downplaying the existence of a Left critique. There are the well-publicized salvos from rightwingers such as Richard Vigurie, Reed Irvine, Jerry Falwell, and Jimmy Swaggart, from whose ideological perspective the media do appear as atheistic, liberal, and soft on communism. If the Far Right had its way, the mainstream media would be dedicated exclusively to a glowing portrayal of American business complete with upbeat reports on the economy, the blessings of the American Way of Life, and the superiority of private-profit capital investment over public-spending programs. And of course the press would be heavily larded with anticommunist tales about the horrors of life in collectivist societies. As a matter of fact, the mainstream media do provide ample amounts of those very things, but if the Far Right has its way that would be *all* we would be fed.

At the same time, with no sense of how it contradicts its own professed opposition to "government meddling," the Far Right would want

---

[1]"Press" and "media" are used interchangeably herein. Portions of this article are adapted from my book (Parenti 1986).

the media to come down hard on the side of more authoritarian controls over private and public life, including elimination of the Freedom of Information Act, greater secrecy and unaccountability for the "national security state," and repression of offensive forms and expressions found in popular culture, including certain song lyrics and situation comedies, and pornography (much of which the rest of us might also want outlawed were it not that we find the "cure" of censorship even more disturbing).

There are many newspapers in the United States and many radio and television stations that pretty much fit the above description. Do not for a moment think that the Right is shut out of the "liberal media." Many parts of the country are literally awash with rightwing radio commentators and conservative-oriented television stations. And there are hundreds of conservative newspapers—ones that hew closely to the Right's ideal delineated above: they are cluttered with puffery and novelty items, offer almost no hard news to speak of, are monopolized by conservative columnists, opinion features, and editorials, and inject a conservative slant into whatever news stories do appear. These broadcast and print news organizations greatly outnumber any that might be described as liberal (Bagdikian 1983, 1974; Aronson 1970; Schiller 1978; Paletz and Entman 1981).

Even in the "more liberal" mainstream media—the ones most regularly targeted by the Right, including the *Washington Post,* the *New York Times, Newsweek, Time,* and the major networks—one finds few if any owners, publishers, news producers, or network bosses who qualify as leftist or even liberal, and a good number who are conservative. However, many members of the working press identify themselves as of liberal persuasion, a fact which fuels the Right's conviction that the media are a liberal tool.

Aside from the ideologically Far Right, the somewhat more mainstream conservative business community also attacks the media for "failing to show business's side of things" and for running occasional reports about corporate wrongdoings. The occasionally negative story that appears in the news, along with TV dramas like "Dynasty" and "Dallas," which have portrayed individual tycoons as ruthless cutthroats, convince business people that the media are a liberal tool bent on portraying business in the worst possible light.

These rightist attacks help the media maintain an appearance of neutrality and objectivity. Being criticized by "extremists both on the Left and the Right," the broadcast and print news media see this as proof that they must be free of ideology and political bias. The truth is that while the press may not be totally uncritical nor totally adulatory toward the big business community, it is not an autonomous adversary, independent of the corporate class. As we know, the big media are themselves a part of the business class, owned and controlled by the same individuals, conglomerates, and banks that own most of America (and much of the rest of the world) (Drier and Weinberg 1979; Compaine 1979; Sterling and Haight 1978). If anything, the print and broadcast media underplay most of the more damaging information and commentary about corporate doings. What is reported is but the tip of the iceberg, but even this is more than business cares to endure and is seen as an attack on the entire business system.

BLAMING JOURNALISTS, TECHNOLOGY, AND THE PUBLIC

Not all the criticism is from conservatives. "Moderates" and liberals, including some journalists, have criticized the press for failing to inform the public about the crucial issues. Criticism from the political center focuses less on content than on the lack of it. The critics complain that the news is superficial and trivial, focusing on personalities rather than issues, on surface happenings rather than substantive matters. I agree with such observations, but I want to point out that this mainstream criticism of the media remains more of a complaint than an analysis. When these critics get around to explaining why stories are so poorly reported, they are likely to blame the journalists (as do the rightwingers). Again and again, we are told that reporters are misled by their sources, inept, poorly informed, too reliant on officialdom, and riddled with personal prejudices.

These kinds of criticisms are often true, but they place too much blame on the weakest, lowliest link in the news manufacturing chain: the reporters. The critics say nothing about the editors who cut and rewrite their copy and control their jobs, and nothing about the executive heads who hire, fire, pay, and promote the editors, and who exercise ultimate control over them. The centrist-liberal critique fails to note that while the journalist's product may be gravely wanting in depth and accuracy, it remains acceptable copy to the reporter's superiors. Journalists who produce more penetrating stories, ones that reveal too much about the exploitative, undemocratic nature of corporate capitalism at home and abroad, will run into difficulties with superiors. By fingering the working journalists as the main or only culprit, critics are implicitly treating reporters as free agents when in fact they are not. The working press works for someone other than itself (Aronson 1970; Gans 1979; Parenti 1986).[2]

Sometimes media critics will fault not the journalists or anyone else

---

[2]Many members of the press may actually feel they are "independent" and not under the ideological suzerainty of their employers; they experience no restraints because their opinions and perceptions do not deviate from the mainstream interpretations of American politics. See the discussion on pages 262–264.

involved in manufacturing the news but the technology of the media themselves. In this day and age, it's all the rage to blame technology. By its nature, we are told, television emphasizes the visual over the ideational. Action events, national leaders, and political candidates have visual appeal; issues and policy analysis do not. Hence there is bound to be more surface than substance. This problem is also said to exist, to a lesser extent, with the print media, which have limited space and time to frame vastly complex events on a daily basis. So, it is said, news organizations latch on to simple images in order to reduce their subject matter to easily manageable components.

There is no denying that stereotyping and reductionism are the common tools of shallow thinking, but why must such shallowness be treated as inevitable? That the media so frequently resort to slick surface treatment does not mean such treatment is the only way news organizations can function. Rather than being a criticism, this "blaming the technological nature of the media" is a disguised defense. It gets everyone off the hook and treats television, or whatever medium, like a disembodied technological force all on its own. However, it is not television as such that chooses to cling to surface events but the people who run it. With the right script and right intentions visual media can offer engrossingly penetrating presentations on vital subjects, as demonstrated by the many fine independently produced documentaries which the major networks deign not to carry.[3]

The basic distortions in the press are not innocent errors, for they are not random; rather they move in the same overall direction again and again, favoring management over labor, corporatism over anticorporatism, the affluent over the poor, private enterprise over socialism, whites over blacks, and other minorities, males over females, officialdom over protestors, conventional politics over dissidence, anticommunism and military build-ups over disarmament, national chauvinism over internationalism, and U.S. dominance of the Third World over revolutionary change. The press does many things and serves many functions, but its major role and irreducible responsibility are continually to recreate a view of reality supportive of existing social and economic class power (Parenti 1986).

---

[3]See for instance such fine documentaries as *Controlling Interests* and *The Global Assembly Line*, dealing with U.S. economic imperialism in the Third World; *Harlan County, USA*, on the class struggles of U.S. coal miners; *The Battle of Chile* and *El Salvador—Another Vietnam*, critiques of U.S. support of autocracies in Latin America; *Fidel*, a portrait of the Cuban revolution and its leader that would not be allowed on network television; *Paul Jacobs and the Nuclear Gang*, a criticism of the deadly domestic effects of the nuclear industry. However, a few of the above have been on the Public Broadcasting System, much to the anger of the Reagan administration.

Money, or the lack of it, is another excuse given by those who prefer innocent explanations that avoid questions of power and interest. All sorts of vital issues go unmentioned in the broadcast and print media, they argue, because it would be too expensive to try to cover all that is happening in the world. But the truth is, the major news organizations compose a vast newsgathering structure with correspondents and stringers throughout much of the world. There are more than 1,000 correspondents in Washington, D.C., tripping all over themselves trying to "develop sources" in the White House, and every four years some 12,000 newspeople descend upon each of the major-party national conventions to report on nominations that are known in advance. As Adam Hochschild (1981) pointed out, "The press competes all right, but over ridiculous things."

With television evening news limited to 22 minutes (8 minutes for breaks and commercials) and with prime time being so expensive, there simply is not enough opportunity for more than "snapshot and headline service," media apologists have argued. And newspaper production costing what it does, there supposedly is not enough affordable print space. In truth, if one were to count the political daytime talk shows, late night news shows, local and national evening news, and hourly news programs on commercial and public radio and television, there is something close to round-the-clock news programming—but almost all of it is thin and repetitious in content. Although the network evening news has only a scant 22 minutes, it finds time for plenty of frivolous subjects. If the evening news were expanded to one hour, this would not guarantee coverage in depth. If anything, the surface quality of broadcast news would become even more evident, and an hour of it more unsatisfying—as has been the case with the local TV news programs that have gone to an hour format. Time is not an ironclad factor in determining how deep one might go. In five minutes one could make some devastating revelations and connections on any number of issues. But how often would a network news team attempt to do so?[4]

---

[4] I can think of one occasion when a network news team *did* do so. In 1983 CBS evening television news ran a special on Guatemala by Bill Moyers which noted that the first democratically elected government in Guatemala's history was overthrown by rightist militarists, armed and assisted by the CIA, and that the subsequent government abolished labor unions and environmental protections and lowered wages. Moyers also noted that a tiny portion of Guatemala's population owned most of the wealth, in collaboration with U.S. corporations, while the bulk of the population lived in poverty and under police state oppression. What was significant about the Moyer's special was: (*a*) the entire footage time was not more than five minutes; (*b*) it was an anti-imperialist statement with a class perspective; (*c*) to my knowledge, it was the first and last time such revelations appeared on CBS.

Similarly it is not true that our leading newspapers lack the space or staff for more comprehensive coverage. Radical publications with only a fraction of the material resources and staff available to the major press organizations probe into controversial issues with far more depth and persistence. The startling news that the CIA was funding cultural, academic, and student organizations was first publicized by the now-defunct *Ramparts* magazine. Ralph Nader's widely received work on automobile safety was ignored by the mainstream press and first began appearing in the *Nation,* a low-budget publication. Journalist Seymour Hersh sent his account of the My Lai massacre to an outfit almost nobody had heard of, Dispatch News Service, after none of the major wire services would pick it up (Cirino 1972).

Stories about hunger in America, the chemical poisoning of our environment and our people, the illegal activities of the CIA at home and abroad, U.S.-sponsored torture and assassinations in Latin America and Iran (under the Shah), the dangers of nuclear power plants, revelations about the real nature of the KAL 007 flight, and other such shockers were uncovered by radical and progressive publications long before they were finally picked up—if ever—by the mainstream press.

There are some liberal critics who agree that the public is being manipulated and misinformed by the news media, but they contend, as does Arthur S. Miller, that "there is no groundswell among the people to have it otherwise." The American public, it seems, has not the interest in being fully informed, and probably not the capacity, given the "immensely complicated" nature of "public policy problems" (Miller 1986: 42). This image of a public lacking the capacity to fathom the complexities of public policy has been propagated by conservative elites all the way from Plato down to Spiro Agnew. It may sound surprising coming from a liberal like Miller, but it is a widespread notion, another form of blaming the victim, which overlooks the fact that the public's level of information can only be as good as the information accessible to it.

In any case, the public does not have to master all the technical complexities of public policy. As Aristotle said: a person need not be a carpenter to know if the roof is falling in. We did not have to grasp the complicated operations of U.S. Vietnam policy to know that we did not want it. So today, policies may not be as simple or simpleminded as the media would have us think, but neither are they as complicated as our rulers (and some critics) would want us to suppose. Those of us who actually make detailed studies of public policies are often struck by how *uncomplicated* are the underlying plans, interests, and goals. Whether it be selling arms to Iran, or supplying guns to mercenaries to attack Nicaragua, or providing multibillion dollar tax cuts to the rich, or cutting human services, or giving aid to rightwing dictators, or refusing to negotiate arms reductions, one is struck by the lack of any real technical complexity in the *political* dimensions of these policies—which is all the public needs to judge. Conflict, contradictions, lies, misrepresentations, and cover-ups abound, creating complexities all their own, but the policies are fairly clear—or could be made so without too much effort—when it comes to knowing which interests they serve and which they harm and in what ways.

As to whether the public really *wants* to know more, the evidence is mixed. There are opinion surveys showing that many people feel they are exposed to more news than they desire and other surveys showing that people would like longer news programs with more content. People also complain about not knowing what's going on and express a distrust for opinion-making elites in government, business, the media, and other institutions.

Perhaps the confusion is in treating "the public" as one undifferentiated mass. There are in fact many different publics; some are turned off while others are turned on to political affairs or to particular issues. Thus in 1987 there were people who complained of too much coverage of the Iran-contra scandal, especially persons friendly to President Reagan, and others who complained that the truth was not coming out and they were not getting enough information. If anything, those who want more or better information about events of the day are growing in numbers, given the dramatic increase in educational levels since the 1950s (which was when the "public-doesn't-want-to-know" school came upon its discoveries). Even among many who have turned off, apathy is sometimes little more than a psychological defense against powerlessness and against being misled.

Aside from the question of news quantity, we must keep in mind the more important question of news *quality,* a topic already addressed above. It does not take that much time and space to tell the forbidden truths about capitalism, imperialism, and the realities of class power and interest. What it takes is a different arrangement of social and economic power and more open access to an alternative communication universe.

CONSPIRACY, CULTURE, AND CLASS INTEREST

News production is not a purely autonomous process, responsive only to its own internal conditions. Many distortions are more political than productional. What is it about the interior dynamics of news gathering and the foibles of reporters that obliges the press to treat capitalism as a benign system and socialism as a pernicious one? Not much. But there is plenty in the pattern of ownership and control, the vested class interests, the financial muscle of big advertisers, and in the entire capitalist social and cultural order which explains that bias. News producers—from owners to reporters—are so immersed in the dominant political culture that they may not be fully aware of how they misrepresent, evade, and suppress the news. From this some people have concluded that distortions in the news are due to cultural factors rather than to deliberate manipulation, and that to argue otherwise is to lapse into conspiracy theory.

Several comments are in order. First it should be noted that while much of the "mobilization of bias" is indeed built into the political culture, we cannot treat every communicational evasion and distortion simply as the product of a tainted culture. Nor can we assume there is no such thing as conspiracy. Just because some people have fantasies about conspiracies does not mean every conspiracy is a fantasy—as Watergate, the Pentagon Papers, the FBI's COINTELPRO campaign, the Iran-contra scandal, and the CIA's daily doings have demonstrated. Like most other cultural institutions, the media exercise their influence through overt means. Given the nature of the institution, it would be hard to imagine *secret* mass media. But there may be something secret and conspiratorial, something deliberately slanted and politically motivated, about news production as found in the unpublicized owner and advertiser dominance over news personnel and editorial content, and in the instances of government interference and manipulation.

The existence of a common pool of culturally determined (systemic nonconspiratorial) political values cannot be denied, but where did this common pool come from? Who or what determines the determining elements in the culture itself? And can we reduce an entire culture, including its actively struggling political components, to a set of accumulated habituations and practices that simply build up over time?

In any case, the values and dominant opinions of our political culture are not all that ingrained and ubiquitous. Major portions of the public, often majorities, do not support present levels of taxation, military spending, military interventionism, the cold war, the arms race, nuclear power, and various domestic policies that are harmful to the environment, to the poor, and to working people. In other words, it may be true that most media elites (and political elites) share common views on these subjects, but much, and sometimes most, of the public—and much of the working press—do not. The "dominant shared values and beliefs," which are supposedly the natural accretions and expressions of our common political culture, are not shared by all or most—certainly not at the issue level—although they surely are dominant in that they tend to preempt the field of opinion visibility because their proponents own and control so much of the communication universe.[5]

---

[5]For evidence that mass opinion is significantly less conservative than the views propagated in the established media and advocated by U.S. policymakers and other elites, see the discussions and opinion poll citations in Paletz and Entman 1981: 162–212, Ferguson and Rogers 1986: 12–28, and Parenti 1986: 90–108 and *passim*.

Like any other social group, media elites consciously pursue their self-interest and try to influence others in ways that are advantageous to themselves. They treat information and culture as vital instruments of class power. Even if they never put it in those words, they keep control of the command posts of communication systems. Regardless of what their academic and journalistic apologists say on their behalf, they have no thought of leaving political discourse and mass communication openly accessible to an unrestricted popular development. Why recognition of these unexceptional facts should brand one a "conspiracy theorist" is not clear.

Can it really be argued (as it often is in the academic literature) that elites have no power over the news organizations they own and finance? Or that if they do have power, they never use it? Or that they use it only in the belief they are fostering the common interest? Certainly all modern ruling classes justify their role in universalist terms—and have a way of believing their own propaganda. But whether they think of themselves as patriots or plotters is not the point. No doubt they like to see themselves as the defenders of American democracy even as they bolster their class privileges. Like everyone else, they believe in the virtue of their cause and equate the pursuit of their class interests with the pursuit of the general interest. Indeed much of their propaganda is designed to treat these two things as coterminous.

The question is not how they see themselves, but how we see them. That a particular class has achieved cultural hegemony over the entire society does not mean it has created a democratic culture. Nor need we struggle with the question of whether the causal factor is "class" or "culture," as if these terms were mutually exclusive; for class dominance both helps to create and is fortified by cultural hegemony. News distortion is a product *both* of shared cultural values *and* deliberate acts of disinformation. Political beliefs do not automatically reproduce and sustain themselves. They must be (at least partly) consciously propagated. And with time and repetition yesterday's propaganda becomes today's "shared cultural values and beliefs."

Consider a specific example: the untruth repeated in the press about the Soviet Union being unable to feed its people. Stories about the starving Russians are as old as the Bolshevik Revolution itself (and indeed, during the years of foreign invasion and civil war immediately after the Revolution, there was some truth to them). Uttered today the assertion is false. The USSR is the world's leading producer of milk and other dairy products. It produces more than enough grain to feed its people but it imports grain for fodder in order to increase its meat supply. Western Europe imports more grain from the United States than does the Soviet Union, yet no one accuses West Germany or the Benelux nations of being unable to feed their people. But through unchallenged and ubiquitous repetition, be it Flora Lewis in the *New York Times,* Dan Rather on CBS, Tom Brokaw on NBC, or *Time* magazine, the falsehood about the starving Russians becomes part of the conventional wisdom—especially in the absence of contrary information of equal currency.[6]

Whether or not newspeople are deliberately lying when they circulate such misinformation is less significant than that they feel free to make such statements without checking the facts. Often they do believe what they say, in large part because such beliefs are not a personal invention but are shared by almost all the opinion manufacturers of the capitalist press, and also because there are rewards for orthodox belief and penalties for ideological deviation. We do know there are variations among members of the working press; some are consciously aware of the coercive controls exercised over them in the news hierarchy—even if the ideologists of pluralism deny the existence of such things. And other journalists maintain that they are never censored and never feel they have to watch what they say. To which we can respond: they are free to say what they like because their employers like what they say. Since they pretty much share the same perspective as their bosses, they never stray beyond it, and rarely if ever feel any restraint on their freedom (Miliband 1969; Gans 1979).

Much of the information universe to which the press responds is of its own making. So the media find confirmation for their images in the very images they have previously created. In such situations, misinformation can be so widespread that the line between intentional and unintentional distortion is not always easy to discern, neither for those who transmit the untruths nor for those of us who try to detect them. An American sovietologist relates the following incident:

> Two years ago, an American newspaper correspondent in Moscow wrote an account of the May Day parade in which he describes people singing and dancing in the streets and enjoying themselves thoroughly. His newspaper published the account, but at the same time it ran an editorial in which it portrayed an embittered Russian people forced by their hated government to demonstrate in favor of a revolution which they did not want.
>
> The correspondent, in recounting this to me, said that he thereupon wrote a letter to his editor in which he said, "I was there—I saw it—they were not bitter, they were happy, they were having a good time." The editorial writer wrote back, in effect that they may have appeared happy, but that actually they could not have been happy in view of the evils of the system under which they live (Berman 1958: 148).

---

[6]See the data provided by the American economist Harry Schaffer in the *Christian Science Monitor,* December 13, 1982. On the advances in living standards among the Soviets, see the American sovietologist Samuel Hendel, "The Role of Theory," in Hendel 1980. For a further discussion of this see Parenti 1986: 137–140, 142–143.

It is hard to say whether the editorial writer was deliberately bending things to present a picture more in keeping with the orthodox view (the view of his publisher) or was "correcting" the reporter's perceptions in order to bring them more in line with what he honestly believed to be the truth. Like everyone else, reporters and editors either sincerely share in the political ideology that makes it so easy for them to believe the news they produce, or they go along with things because they know on which side their bread is buttered. It is difficult to know at what exact psychological point an individual's self-serving rationalization turns into sincere belief.

OWNERSHIP AND CLASS BIAS

At bottom, freedom of the press belongs to those who own the press—and that means freedom to lie and to suppress information. On rare occasions even conservatives will admit as much. Consider what nationally syndicated conservative columnist James Kilpatrick says. It is an unusual event when a journalist of Kilpatrick's stripe stops pretending he is an independent agent and admits that a property-power relationship exists in the media. In a *Washington Post* column Kilpatrick did just that in regard to a controversy at Howard University. It seems that after giving prominent coverage to a sex discrimination case involving the university, the editor of the Howard student newspaper, Janice McKnight, was expelled, supposedly because of discrepancies in her admission application of four years before. McKnight charged that the action constituted a violation of freedom of the press. Entering the fray in one of his columns, Kilpatrick allowed that McKnight "was fired because of her editorial insistence" and then asserted that "Howard's president clearly had the power to remove her as editor" since he did not like what she printed. Warming to his subject, Kilpatrick continued:

> Where did McKnight get the right and power to publish whatever she damn well pleases? The answer is, nowhere. The Hilltop is not her paper; she has invested not a dime in its costs of publication. Like every other student editor, she is here today and gone tomorrow. . . . I was for 17 years editor of a major newspaper, but I never had the slightest misapprehension of any "free press rights." If my publisher, in his gentle way, said that we ought to think a while before running one of my fire-eating editorials, that was it; the piece didn't run. It was his paper, not mine. . . . If student journalists want unabridged freedom of the press, their course of action is clear; let them buy their press and move off campus. Until that happens, let them grow up to what life in the real world is all about (Kilpatrick 1983).

Kilpatrick is wrong when he says that McKnight "invested not a dime" in the student newspaper. In fact, student publications, including Mc-

Knight's, are funded out of student activity funds. And the student editor is elected by the newspaper's staff—all students. In contrast, the president of Howard University, who is elected by nobody, is the one who has "invested not a dime" in the paper. Yet he has the power to censor its contents.

That issue aside, what is interesting about Kilpatrick's comments is the way he admits, indeed, proudly proclaims, that he was never editor of a free and independent press. His publisher, "in his gentle way," exercised prior censorship over his editorials. All of which is just fine because freedom of the press for Kilpatrick is not a political right but a prerogative of property and wealth. He is correct when he concluded that's "what life in the real world is all about." It is just not often that mainstream newspeople so forthrightly announce such truths about the real world.

The evidence of ideological and class bias is overwhelming. There are liberal columnists and commentators and conservative ones, but very few socialist ones in the mainstream press. (Alexander Cockburn's column in the *Wall Street Journal* comes to mind as one of the few, and he is his more subdued self when writing for that publication.) Within the mainstream media themselves, as noted earlier, it is the conservatives who predominate over the liberals, being more widely syndicated in the print media and presiding over most of the radio talk shows that have a political orientation. How could it be otherwise when the print and electronic media—both the local stations and newspapers and the networks and large chains—are owned overwhelmingly by rich conservative Republicans and get most of their revenues from big corporate advertisers? Judging from their editorial policies, news content, and electoral endorsements, about 80 percent of the nation's newspapers lean to the right, varying from moderately to extremely conservative (Bagdikian 1974; Brown 1971).

That's "what life in the real world is all about." You don't need a conspiracy theory to conjure up such evidence, although a conspiracy theory helps to deny the evidence. For instance, Reed Irvine and his Accuracy in Media organization never mention the ownership pattern of the press. He would have us believe that the media are riddled with liberals and radicals who control news content and that conservative opinion is shut out. But to agree with him, we would have to deny the evidence before us. We would have to overlook what Irvine overlooks about himself: that he is repeatedly invited to appear on national television; that his media-policing organization has an annual budget of $15 million, which includes generous corporate backing; that his weekly column circulates in some 100 newspapers and his daily radio commentary reaches listeners of 70 stations; and that he meets annually with the publisher of the *New York Times* and occasionally with other media tycoons (*The Utne Reader*

1987). Many spokespeople on the Left would love to be shut out of the mainstream media the way Irvine is.

In contrast, Ralph Nader, the well-known public-interest advocate, who has been on the scene at least twice as long as Irvine, has no regular radio show and his column appears in only about 20 or so small-circulation publications. The difference is that while Nader is a better writer and a far more intelligent investigator than Irvine, he criticizes the status quo and the abuses of corporate America while Irvine propagates that brand of repressive anticommunist conservatism which is one of corporate America's mainstays.

THE LIMITS OF CONTROL

If economic and political elites control the press, why are they often distrustful of, and irritated by, what appears in it? And why do they find it necessary to exert repressive measures against their own media? The ruling class rules but not exactly in the way it may want to. No ruling elite can be sure of perfect compliance. There are a number of troublesome things that make the press less than absolutely compliant, introducing an element of indeterminacy and even resistance.

The media's general class function is to help make the world safe for those who own and control news organizations and who exercise their power by direct control over the careers of organizational personnel. But the media also have a specialized institutional function, which is to produce a marketable daily product called "the news." The news must be packaged so as to be (*a*) pleasing to press moguls, advertisers, and other politicoeconomic elites; and (*b*) informative or at least believable to the public. But these two functions are not always automatically reconcilable. The goal of the owning class, as Marx and Engels put it, is to present "a particular interest as general or the 'general interest' ruling" (Marx and Engels 1947: 41). This indeed is what the press does, presenting the elite perspective as the objective, general one, as representative of things as they really are. But the press also must give the appearance of performing a public information service. To sustain such an appearance it must make substantive concessions now and then to real public concerns, even revealing negative things about certain outputs of the system so as to protect its own credibility.

Despite its best efforts, then, there are limits to how much the press can finesse reality. These are the limits of propaganda itself, as Dr. Goebbels discovered when trying to explain to the German public how invincible Nazi armies could win victory after victory while retreating on both fronts during the latter part of the war. Coverage of troublesome realities, even if essentially sympathetic to economic elites and top policymakers, as it almost always is, can itself prove annoying. Thus for years the press transmitted the official view of the Vietnam war but the actual persistence of this costly conflict outweighed the upbeat predictions and anticommunist rationales manufactured by both the government and the media. The press could suppress and distort what happened in Indochina but it could not ignore the awful *actuality* of the event itself.

Of course, this is no iron rule; the press is also capable of ignoring whole wars as with the horrible air wars conducted in Cambodia and Laos during the Vietnam era and in El Salvador today. The latter, an air war of terrible attrition that is financed, equipped, and supervised by the United States, has not been brought up by the press at a presidential news conference in over two years (as of 1987) and has not received any coverage to speak of in the major media in that time, despite its accelerated pace of destructiveness.[7]

Efforts by the media to make some minimal response to reality, even while attempting to invent another reality, sometimes educate the public in unintended ways. Rather than responding only to the manifest content, filled with images and arguments about how the United States is fighting communism and saving democracy, the public eventually picks up on the latent message: war, U.S. involvement, death, destruction, more taxes, and the draft.

Now if the public does not support an interventionist or probusiness or militaristic policy, the conservative Right and often the centrists (if they are in power) will conclude that it cannot be because of anything wanting in the policy but in the way the media packaged it. Leaders are often tempted to blame the press when things go wrong with their plans or when policies fall into public disfavor. If the press had not said this or that, had held its tongue or cast things in a more favorable light, then the leader presumably would have had less trouble managing the world, and certainly less trouble managing U.S. public opinion. One might recall an interview with Henry Kissinger on the ABC television show "Nightline" in 1986, during which he denounced the media for having undermined U.S. policy in Vietnam. Or again, the attacks against the press delivered by almost every leader of the Reagan camp, including Ronald Reagan himself, for "causing" the Iran-contra scandal and seeking to undermine the presidency. Expecting the press corps to be a press chorus, the lead-

---

[7]The accelerated massive and secret aerial war in El Salvador was voted the top story of "The Ten Best Censored Stories of 1985" by Project Censored, a national panel of media experts who each year locate significant stories that have been suppressed by the mainstream news media (see Dr. Carl Jensen, Project Censored, Sonoma State University in California). For evidence on the aerial war see *Alert,* publication of the Committee in Solidarity With the People of El Salvador (CISPIS), Washington, D.C., Spring and Fall 1985, and Spring 1986; also Alexander Cockburn, "Remember El Salvador?" *Nation,* June 1, 1985.

ers of government and industry, like any imperious maestro, react sharply to an occasionally discordant note.

There are other reasons why troublesome things will sometimes make it into print or onto the airwaves. These might be listed briefly:

1. Sometimes editors run stories because they are unable to foresee their embarrassing implications and unintended spin-offs. While the "blame-the-journalist" critics argue that distortions are caused by inadequate information and hasty preparation, I am suggesting there are times when haste and low information levels lead to greater revelations than would normally be allowed were reporters and editors better apprised of a story's potentially discordant ideological effects. Early news reports (1980–81) about the growing effectiveness of guerrilla forces in El Salvador, while intending to alert the public to the emergency of a new communist menace (and having been planted by the government itself in many instances) had the unintended effect of activating an anti-interventionist peace movement in the United States, causing officials in the Reagan administration to request that the press not give so much attention to El Salvador. And the press indeed obliged.

2. Ideological control over the U.S. news media is not formal, overt, and explicit, but informal, covert, and implicit. Therefore it will work with more subtle effect but sometimes imperfectly, sometimes allowing dissenting information to slip through. Thus the print media might carry revealing items, buried in otherwise standard stories, exceptional things that are likely to go unnoticed—except to the closely critical reader—because of their poor placement and lack of projective framing. The presence of such nuggets scattered here and there in the mountains of dross is what enables critics of capitalism occasionally to draw damaging information from the capitalist media themselves.

3. The idea of a free press is more a myth than a reality, but myths can have an effect on things and can serve as a resource of power. Journalists who believe they are autonomous professionals expect to be able to report events as they see them (although not all of them live with this expectation). Publishers and network bosses regularly oversee the news production process and frequently intervene with suggestions and direct commands, but to avoid being criticized as censors and autocrats, some of them grant their news organizations a modicum of independence when specific differences arise, relying on hiring, firing, and promotional policies and more indirect controls over the long haul.

4. Serious differences sometimes arise among politicoeconomic elites on how best to advance their common class interests. These differences will be reflected in the news media. Thus, while remaining generally supportive of President Reagan's adversarial approach to the Soviets, the press gave space and time to such elite critics as Cyrus Vance and Robert McNamara, who called for a return to a policy of mutual deterrence and detente. To the extent such differences among elites are played out in the media, they add to the appearance—and substance—of diversity, if not on fundamental questions then on tactical ones.

5. The press is not totally immune to the pressures of those democratic forces that struggle for a more egalitarian and peaceable world. The emergence of the civil rights movement in the United States, which won the sympathy and support of large sectors of the public, brought dramatic shifts in the media's coverage of the struggle for racial equality and of black people in general—although it hardly ended racist reporting and stereotyping. As opposition mounts against a leader or a policy, the press becomes emboldened in its treatment. As opinion turned against President Nixon during the Watergate scandal, the press delivered negative judgments upon him, "but only then—with his prestige and power in dramatic decline and his attempts at media manipulation more transparent than ever"; for it was then safe to do (Paletz and Entman 1981: 69).

In sum, the press's systemic class function is to purge popular consciousness of any awareness of the disturbingly inequitable, exploitative, repressive, and violent consequences of capitalist rule at home and abroad. While it cannot perform that task thoroughly enough to satisfy all elites all the time and maintain its own credibility, it does—as I have tried to show in more detail elsewhere—a far better, more skillful job of it than many elites appreciate (Parenti 1986). Were it to follow the government or corporate line always in perfect lockstep, the press would cast doubt on its own credibility as a neutral objective social institution. So the media go along on most stories, but not all the time and sometimes not all the way. This "relative autonomy" is what irritates and sometimes infuriates those who complain of "liberal biases" whenever the media hint at realities that do not fit their picture of the world.

Defenders of the existing capitalist system are forever looking for causalities that disguise its class nature. We are told that the problems we face are caused by technology, or the lack of time and money, or by an apathetic public (as indeed some of our problems are). Or, it turns out, we are supposedly trapped by cultural forces about which we can do little. And to suggest otherwise, to suggest that conscious class interest and power are part of present social arrangements, is to be branded a "conspiracy theorist"—a charge which is supposed to drive us to instant denial out of fear that we are being "reductionist" and "simplistic" in our thinking. But what is more simplistic and reductionist than to reduce the actualities of class struggle and class-dominated cultural formations to a problem of an abstracted "technology" or "culture"?

If the dominant culture were a mystically self-sustaining *deus ex machina,* there would be nothing left for us to do but throw up our hands and wait for the natural, gradual process of change to unfold across the centuries. But neither history nor society work that way. In fact, there is an element of struggle and indeterminancy in all our social life and political culture. Along with institutional stability we have popular agitation; along with elite manipulation we have widespread skepticism; along with ruling-class coercion we have mass resistance (at times). Things are not as innocent and inevitable as the apologists of this system (including some of the critics of the media) would have us believe.

Those who rule this country and control most of its communication universe are not somnabulists. It used to be said that the British empire grew in a state of absentmindedness. But no class order was ever so sustained, and the claim is no truer today than it was during the time of the British empire. By becoming aware of the conscious and deliberate elements of class control, we are less awed by its seemingly ubiquitous and omnipotent quality, and can better appreciate how conscious struggle leads to betterment. The rulers of this society, who try to keep history from happening, have a keen sense of the potentials of popular powers at home and abroad. So too can we—when we see ourselves not only as the victims of a supposedly impersonal technology and culture but as the makers of our own history.

CHAPTER 13

How Polling Transforms Public Opinion[1]

Benjamin Ginsberg

INTRODUCTORY NOTE

Benjamin Ginsberg asks: Does public opinion polling contribute more to government by the "will of the people" or to government by the management of popular attitudes? He argues that polling transforms public opinion from a powerful group behavior into a manageable individual phenomenon. Polling acts to "domesticate" public opinion by shifting the responsibility for raising issues from the mass public themselves to the elites who formulate the questions, and by so doing, public opinion is transformed from a spontaneous expression to a constrained response to a set of alternatives preselected by the elite.

Ginsberg argues that polls not only enhance the power of those who formulate the questions, but that their primary effect is to undermine mass-based pressure groups, such as labor unions, Common Cause, or the NAACP. While polling has come to be seen as the most accurate and reliable means of gauging public sentiments, it is not the only source of knowledge about public attitudes. Some of the more obvious means would include statements from interest-group representatives as well as letters to the press and to public officials. If poll results differ from the interpretation given by some other source, almost invariably the polls are presumed to be correct. For example, the bona fides of labor leaders as spokespersons can be challenged by polling the rank-and-file union members.

---

[1]An earlier version of this paper was presented to the 1984 annual meeting of the American Political Science Association. Portions of this material draft appeared in Benjamin Ginsberg, *The Captive Public* (New York: Basic Books, 1986). The author wishes to thank the American Political Science Association and Basic Books for permission to reprint these materials.

Polling is especially useful when voluntary expressions of public opinion indicate strong opposition to a government or its programs. Polling allows a government faced with demonstrations, protests, or other manifestations of public hostility, to claim that its policies are compatible with true public opinion and opposed by only an unrepresentative group of malcontents. Which is the more valid indicator of public attitudes? The relatively passive majority, whose only opinion consisted of responding to polling questions, or the activist opposition angrily opposed to the government policy?

Ginsberg argues that polling contributes to the transformation of public opinion from an unpredictable, extreme, and often dangerous force into a more docile expression of public sentiment. Opinions stated through polls impose less pressure and make fewer demands upon government than would spontaneous or natural assertions of popular sentiment. While survey research has undoubtedly enhanced governmental responsiveness to popular opinion on some occasions, polling has also contributed to government efforts to manage or manipulate public sentiment more effectively.

The Editors

The "will of the people" has become the ultimate standard against which the conduct of contemporary governments is measured. In the democracies, especially in the United States, both the value of governmental programs and the virtue of public officials are typically judged by the extent of their popularity (Nisbett 1975). Twentieth-century dictatorships, for their part, are careful at least to give lip service to the idea of popular sovereignty, if only to bolster public support at home and to maintain a favorable image abroad. Some despots manage to convince even themselves that they truly speak for or, in fact, actually embody the popular will (Langer 1972; Kirkpatrick 1964).

Much of the prominence of opinion polling as a civic institution derives from the significance that present-day political ideologies ascribe to the will of the people. Polls purport to provide reliable, scientifically derived information about the public's desires, fears and beliefs, and so to give concrete expression to the conception of a popular will. The availability of accurate information certainly is no guarantee that governments will actually pay heed to popular opinions. Yet, it has always been the belief of many students and practitioners of survey research that an accurate picture of the public's views might at least increase the chance that governments' actions would be informed by and responsive to popular sentiment (Childs 1965; Gallup 1940).

Unfortunately, however, polls do more than simply measure and record the natural or spontaneous manifestation of popular belief. The data reported by opinion polls are actually the product of an interplay between opinion and the survey instrument (Landau and Lifshitz 1958). As they measure, the polls interact with opinion, producing changes in the character and identity of the views receiving public expression. The changes induced by polling, in turn, have the most profound implications for the relationship between public opinion and government. In essence, polling has contributed to the domestication of opinion by helping to transform opinion from a politically potent, often disruptive, force into a more docile, plebiscitary phenomenon.

PUBLICIZING OPINION

Over the past several decades, polling has generally come to be seen as the most accurate and reliable means of gauging the public's sentiments. Indeed, poll results and public opinion are terms that are used almost synonymously. But, despite this general tendency to equate public opinion with survey results, polling is obviously not the only possible source of knowledge about the public's attitudes.

Means of ascertaining public opinion certainly existed prior to the development of modern survey techniques. Statements from local notables and interest-group spokespersons, letters to the press and to public officials, and sometimes demonstrations, protests and riots provided indications of the populace's views long before the invention of the sample survey. Governments certainly took note of all these symptoms of the public's mood. As Chester Barnard once noted, prior to the availability of polling, legislators "read the local newspapers, toured their districts and talked with voters, received letters from the home state, and entertained delegations which claimed to speak for large and important blocks of voters" (Barnard 1939).

Obviously, these alternative modes of assessing public sentiment continue to be available. Polling has not become the only possible source of information about popular opinion. But it is significant that whenever poll results differ from the interpretation of public opinion offered by some other source, it is almost invariably the polls that are presumed to be correct. The labor leader whose account of the views of the rank and file differs from the findings of a poll is automatically assumed to have misrepresented or misperceived membership opinion. Politicians who dare to quarrel with the polls' negative assessments of the popularity of their programs are immediately derided by the press.

This presumption in favor of the polls stems from both the scientific and representative character of opinion polling. Survey research is modeled after the methodology of the natural sciences and at least conveys an impression of technical sophistication and scientific objectivity. Occasional press accounts of deliberate bias and distortion of survey findings only partially undermine this impression.

At the same time, the polls can claim to offer a more representative view of popular sentiment than any alternative source of information is likely to provide. Group spokespersons sometimes speak only for themselves. The distribution of opinion reflected by letters to newspapers and public officials is notoriously biased. Demonstrators and rioters, however sincere, are seldom more than a tiny and unrepresentative segment of the populace. The polls, by contrast, at least attempt to take equal account of all relevant individuals. And, indeed, by offering a representative view of public opinion the polls have often served as antidotes for false spokespersons, correctives for mistaken politicians, and guides to popular concerns that might never have been mentioned by the individuals writing letters to legislators and newspaper editors.

Nevertheless, polling does more than offer a scientifically derived and representative account of popular sentiment. The substitution of polling for other means of gauging the public's views also has the effect of changing several of the key characteristics of public opinion. Critics of survey research have often noted that polling can affect both the beliefs of individuals asked to respond to survey questions and the attitudes of those who subsequently read a survey's results (Weissberg 1976). However, the most important effect of the polls is not a result of their capacity to change individuals' beliefs. The major impact of polling is, rather, on the cumulation and translation of individuals' private beliefs into collective public opinion. Four fundamental changes in the character of public opinion can be traced to the introduction of survey research.

Changing the Character of Public Opinion

First, polling alters both what is expressed and what is perceived as the opinion of the mass public by transforming public opinion from a voluntary to an externally subsidized matter. Second, polling modifies the manner in which opinion is publicly presented by transforming public opinion from a behavioral to an attitudinal phenomenon. Third, polling changes the origin of information about public beliefs by transforming public opinion from a property of groups to an attribute of individuals. Finally, polling partially removes individuals' control over the subject matter of their own public expressions of opinion by transforming public opinion from a spontaneous assertion to a constrained response.

Individually and collectively, these transformations have profound consequences for the character of public opinion and, more important, for the relationship of opinion to government and policy. To the extent that polling displaces alternative modes of gauging popular sentiment, these four transformations contribute markedly to the domestication or pacification of public opinion. Polling renders public opinion less dangerous, less disruptive, more permissive and, in some instances, more amenable to governmental control.

Polling does not make public opinion politically impotent. Nor, as the recent failure of the Reagan administration's efforts to "disinform" the American public on the government's policies toward Iran and Central America indicate, does the availability of polling guarantee that governments will be able to successfully manipulate public beliefs for an indefinite length of time. Nevertheless, polling helps to diminish the danger that public opinion poses to those in power and helps to increase the potential for government management of mass beliefs.

FROM VOLUNTARISM TO SUBSIDY

In the absence of polling, the cost and effort required to organize and publicly communicate an opinion are normally borne by one or more of the individuals holding the opinion. Someone wishing to express a view about civil rights, for example, might write a letter, deliver a speech, contribute to an organization or join a protest march. A wealthy individual might employ a public relations expert; a politically astute individual might assert that he or she represented the views of many others. But, whatever the means, the organization and public communication of opinion would entail a voluntary expenditure of funds, effort, or time on the part of an opinion-holder. The polls, by contrast, organize and publicize opinion without necessitating any initiative or action on the part of individuals. With the exception of the small sample asked to submit to an interview, the individuals whose opinions are expressed through the polls need take no action whatever. The polls underwrite or subsidize the costs of eliciting, organizing, and publicly expressing opinion.

This displacement of costs from the opinion-holder to the polling agency has important consequences for the character of the opinions likely to receive public expression. In general, the willingness of individuals to bear the costs of publicly asserting their views is closely tied to the intensity with which they hold those views. Other things being equal, individuals with strong feelings about any given matter are more likely to invest whatever time and effort are needed to make their feelings known, than are persons with less intense views. One seldom hears, for example, of a "march on Washington" by groups professing not to care much about abortion. As the example of abortion might suggest, moreover, individuals with intense points of view are also more likely than their less zealous fellow-citizens to be found at the extremes of opinion on any given question (Lane and Sears 1964; Cantril 1946). Thus, so long as the costs of asserting opinions are borne by opinion-holders themselves, those with relatively extreme viewpoints are also disproportionately likely to bring their views to the public forum.

The polls weaken this relationship between the public expression of opinion and the intensity or extremity of opinion. The assertion of an opinion through a poll requires little effort on the part of the opinion-holder. As a result, the beliefs of those who care relatively little or even hardly at all, are as likely to be publicized as the opinions of those who care a great deal about the matter in question. Similarly, individuals with moderate viewpoints are as likely as those taking extreme positions to publicly communicate their opinions through a survey. The upshot is that the distribution of public opinion reported by the polls generally differs considerably from the distribution that emerges from forms of public communication initiated by citizens. Clausen et al. have shown that the public opinion reported by surveys is, on the aggregate, both less intense and less extreme than the public opinion which would be defined by voluntary modes of popular expression (Clausen et al. 1965). Similarly, poll respondents typically include a much larger proportion of individuals who "don't know," "don't care," or exhibit some other form of relative detachment from the debate on major public issues than is found in the population of activists willing to express their views through voluntary or spontaneous means.

This difference between polled and voluntarily expressed opinion can have important implications for the degree of influence or constraint that public opinion is likely to impose upon administrators and policymakers. The polls, in effect, submerge individuals with strongly held views in a more apathetic mass public. The data reported by the polls are likely to suggest to public officials that they are working in a more permissive climate of opinion than might have been thought on the basis of alternative indicators of the popular mood. A government wishing to maintain some semblance of responsiveness to public opinion would typically find it less difficult to comply with the preferences reported by the polls than to obey the opinion that might be inferred from letters, strikes, or protests. Indeed, relative to these other modes of public expression, polled opinion could be characterized as a collective statement of permission.

Certainly, even in the era of polling, voluntary expressions of public opinion can still count heavily. In recent years, for example, members of Congress were impressed by calls, letters, and telegrams from constituents—and threats from contributors—regarding President Reagan's various tax reform proposals. Of course, groups like the National Rifle Association are masters of the use of this type of opinion campaign. Nevertheless, contradiction by the polls tends to reduce the weight and credibility of other sources of public opinion. This effect of polling can actually help governments to resist the pressure of constituent opinion. Constituency polls, for example, are often used by legislators as a basis for resisting the demands of political activists and pressure groups in their districts (Wilcox 1966).

Polling is especially useful when voluntary expressions of public opinion indicate severe opposition to a government and its programs. The relatively permissive character of polled opinion can allow a government faced with demonstrations, protests, and other manifestations of public hostility a basis for the claim that its policies are compatible with true public opinion and opposed only by an unrepresentative group of activist malcontents. A notable contemporary illustration of this role of the polls is the case of the "silent majority" on whose behalf Richard Nixon claimed to govern. The notion of a silent majority was the Nixon administration's answer to the protestors, who demanded major changes in American foreign and domestic policies. Administration spokespersons frequently cited poll data, often drawing upon Scammon and Wattenberg's influential treatise, *The Real Majority* (1970) to question the popular standing of the activist opposition. According to the administration's interpretation, its activist opponents did not represent the views of the vast majority of "silent" Americans who could not be found in the polls but not on picket lines, marches, or in civil disturbances.

Undoubtedly, a majority of Americans were less than sympathetic to the protestors. But from the administration's perspective, the real virtue of the silent majority was precisely its silence. Many of those Americans who remained silent did so because they lacked strong opinions on the political issues of the day. Thus, the silent majority imposed few restrictions on the administration while allowing it to claim that it, rather than the protestors, truly represented the public's views. The use of the polls to identify a "silent majority" was a means of diluting the political weight and undermining the credibility of those members of the public with the strongest views while constructing a permissive majority of "silent" Americans (Wheeler 1976). In a sense, the polls came to be used against those persons who truly had opinions.

Even more illustrative, however, of the permissive character of polled opinion is Lyndon Johnson's reaction to surveys of public opinion about the Vietnam war. Johnson was apparently somewhat more concerned with the public's feelings than his successor. Johnson constantly referred to the polls to attempt to convince friends, visitors, colleagues, and most of all himself that the public supported his war policies. Indeed, Johnson's eventual realization that public opinion had turned against his administration weighed heavily in his decision not to seek another term in office (Wheeler 1976; Harris 1973). The significance of the Johnson case is that the polls permitted a president who was apparently actually concerned with his administration's responsiveness to public opinion to believe that he was doing what the people wanted. The polls appeared to indicate that, despite the contrary assertions of protestors, demonstrators, and rioters, public opinion did not really demand an end to the war. After all, until late in Johnson's term a majority of those polled did not disapprove of his policies (Mueller 1971).

FROM BEHAVIOR TO ATTITUDE

Prior to the advent of polling, public opinion could often only be inferred from political behavior. Before the availability of voter survey data, for example, analysts typically sought to deduce electoral opinion from voting patterns, attributing candidates' electoral fortunes to whatever characteristics of the public mood could be derived from election returns. Often, population movements served as the bases for conclusions about public preferences. Even in recent years, the movement of white urbanites to the metropolitan fringe, dubbed "white flight," has been seen as a key indicator of white attitudes toward racial integration. Particularly, however, where the least articulate segments of the populace were concerned, governments often had little or no knowledge of the public's mood until opinion manifested itself in some form of behavior. Generally, this meant violent or disruptive activity.

In the modern era public opinion is synonymous with the polls. But, certainly through the 19th century, public opinion was usually equated with riots, strikes, demonstrations, and boycotts. Indeed, 19th-century public sentiment could sometimes reveal itself through the most curious forms of behavior. In London during the 1830s, for example, a favorite mechanism for the expression of popular opinion was the "illumination." In an "illumination" those espousing a particular point of view placed lanterns or candles in their windows. Often mobs went from house to house demanding that the occupants "illuminate." Householders who declined might have their windows smashed and dwelling sacked. On April 27, 1831, for example, a large mob formed to demand electoral reform. According to a contemporary account:

> On that evening, the illumination was pretty general. . . . The mobs did a great deal of mischief. A numerous rabble proceeded along the Strand, destroying all windows that were not lighted. . . . In St. James' Square they broke the windows in the houses of the Bishop of London, the Marquis of Cleveland, and Lord Grantham. The Bishop of Winchester and Mr. W. W. Wynn, seeing the mob approach, placed candles in their windows, which thus escaped (Silver 1967).

Obviously, this sort of behavior shed a good deal of light on the state of popular sentiment long before the development of survey research.

The advent of polling transformed public opinion from a behavioral to an attitudinal phenomenon. The polls elicit, organize, and publicize opinion without requiring any action on the part of the opinion-holder. Public presentation of an opinion via the polls by no means precludes its subsequent expression through behavior. Nevertheless, polling does permit any interested party an opportunity to assess the state of the public's mood without having to wait for some behavioral manifestation. From the perspective of political elites, the obvious virtue of the polls is that they enhance the possibility of recognizing and dealing with popular attitudes—even the attitudes of the most inarticulate segments of the populace—before they materialize in some unpleasant, disruptive, or threatening form of political action. In the democracies, of course, the most routine behavioral threat posed by public opinion is hostile action in the voting booth. Polling has certainly become one of the chief means employed by democratic political elites to attempt to anticipate and avert the electorate's displeasure. But, in both the democratic and dictatorial contexts, governments have also employed polling extensively to help forestall the possibility of popular disobedience and unrest.

In recent years, for example, many Eastern European regimes have instituted survey programs. Polling has been used, in part, to forewarn the leadership of potential sources of popular disaffection, hostility, or antigovernment activities. As Bodgan Osolnik has observed, in Eastern Europe opinion research provides, "a warning that some attitudes which political actors consider to be generally accepted . . . have not yet been adopted by public opinion." Such "misunderstandings" says Osolnik (1955), "can be extremely harmful—and dangerous." Polling allows the regime an opportunity to resolve these potential "misunderstandings" before they pose a serious threat.

As early as the 1950s, to cite one concrete case, the Polish government obtained extensive survey data indicating that strong religious sentiment was widespread among the young. The regime became quite concerned with the implications of the continuing hold of "unorthodox ritualistic attitudes" on the generation that was expected to possess the strongest commitment to socialism. In response to its survey findings, the government embarked on a major program of antireligious and ideological indoctrination aimed at young people (Conner and Gitelman 1977). Over the past several years, the government of Poland has commissioned a number of studies of public opinion on political issues, designed to avert the sort of popular unrest that has frequently shaken the Polish state (Smith 1977). Obviously, however, recent events in Poland suggest that opinion polling is not precisely a guarantee of political stability.

The Polish government's response to surveys indicating potential trouble has been to seek to modify the attitudes deemed to be threatening. Attitude change campaigns, though, are not the only possible governmental responses to dissent in the authoritarian context. Gestapo chief, Heinrich Himmler, is reputed to have carefully studied polls of German attitudes toward the Nazi regime and its policies. Apparently, whenever he noted that some of those surveyed failed to respond with the appropriate opinions, Himmler demanded to know their names (Smith 1972).

In the United States, polling has typically been used as an adjunct to policy implementation. The execution of governmental programs and initiatives is obviously facilitated to the extent that administrators are able to secure popular compliance. Polling can provide administrators with some idea of what citizens are and are not likely to tolerate and, thus, help them to avoid popular disobedience and resistance. As early as the 1930s, federal agencies began to poll extensively. For example, during the 30s the United States Department of Agriculture established a Division of Program Surveys to undertake studies of attitudes toward federal farm programs (Hennessey 1975). At the same time, extensive use was made of surveys by the Works Progress Administration, the Social Security Administration, and the Public Health Service (McCamy 1939; Wallace and McCamy 1940).

In recent years, polling of one sort or another has become a routine aspect of the process of policy implementation. In their well-known study of policy implementation, for example, Pressman and Wildavsky note the matter-of-fact manner in which Floyd Hunter's Social Science Research and Development Corporation was awarded a $400,000 contract for an "economic power structure survey" as part of the Oakland redevelopment project. Project officials were not certain what role this survey was to play. Surveys had simply become an expected part of any major project (Pressman and Wildavsky 1979).

Polling by United States governmental agencies is not confined to the domestic policy arena. Various units of the State Department and other foreign policy agencies have engaged in extensive polling abroad to assess the likely response of the citizens of other nations to American foreign policy initiatives aimed at them. For example, during the era of American involvement, both the Defense Department and the Agency for International Development sponsored extensive polling in Vietnam to examine the effects of existing and proposed American programs (Wheeler 1976; Schiller 1973). Similarly, polling was conducted in Cuba and the Dominican Republic to assess likely popular reaction to contemplated American intervention (Cantril and Free 1967). A good deal of polling has also been sponsored in Europe by American governmental agencies concerned with European reactions to American propaganda appeals (Cantril and Free 1967). Of course, American administrative agencies are hardly the only ones to make use of opinion surveys. During the 1960s, for example, Soviet administrators began to employ polls of their programs' target populations, in attempts to avoid a repetition of the sort of massive and costly popular resistance that hampered Soviet agricultural collectivization (Conner and Gitelman 1977).

Again, even the most extensive and skillful use of polling does not ensure that public opinion will only manifest itself attitudinally. Behavioral expressions of opinion in the form of protests, riots, strikes, and so on are common enough even in the era of survey research. The most accurate information about public attitudes is no guarantee that governments can or will act effectively to forestall their expression through some form of behavior. Yet, polling can offer governments a measure of knowledge about public opinion while it remains purely attitudinal in form. In an attitudinal form, opinion poses less of an immediate threat and remains amenable to modification or accommodation prior to the onset of trouble.

In some instances, of course, the knowledge of popular attitudes gleaned from the polls may convince those in power simply to bow to the popular will before it is too late. Such a response would certainly be consistent with the hopes expressed by the advocates of polling. Yet, often enough, the effect of polling is to lessen the threat or pressure that public opinion is likely to impose on administrators and policymakers. By converting opinion from a behavioral to an attitudinal phenomenon, polling is, in effect, also transforming public opinion into a less immediately threatening and dangerous phenomenon. The polls can give a government a better opportunity to manipulate and modify public opinion and thus to avoid accommodation to citizens' preferences. One interesting recent example of this process is the activity of the 1965 American "Riot Commission." Charged with the task of preventing repetitions of the riots that rocked American cities during the 1960s, the National Advisory Commission on Civil Disorders sponsored and reviewed a large number of surveys of black attitudes on a variety of political, social, and economic questions. These surveys allowed the Commission to identify a number of attitudes held by blacks that were said to have contributed to their disruptive behavior. As a result of its surveys, the Commission was able to suggest several programs that might modify blacks' disagreeable attitudes and, thus, prevent further disorder. Significantly enough, the Riot Commission's report did not call for changes in the institutions and policies about which blacks had been violently expressing their views (National Advisory Commission 1968; Fogelson 1971). The effect of polling was, in essence, to help the government find a way to *not* accommodate the opinions blacks had expressed in the streets of America's urban ghettos.

FROM GROUP TO INDIVIDUAL

Mass behavior was not the sole source of information about popular opinion prior to the advent of polling. Reports on the public's mood could usually also be obtained from the activists, leaders, or notables of the nation's organized and communal groups. Public officials or others interested in the views of working people, for example, would typically consult trade union officers. Similarly, anyone concerned with the attitudes of, say, farmers would turn to the heads of farm organizations. Of course, interest-group leaders, party leaders, and social notables seldom waited to be asked. These worthies would—and still do—voluntarily step forward to offer their impressions of membership opinion. Such impressions might not always have been fully accurate. But certainly group, party, and communal leaders often do have better opportunities to meet with and listen to their adherents than would be available to outsiders. Before the invention of polling these leaders quite probably possessed the most reliable data available on their followers' views. In the absence of contradictory evidence, at least, the claims of these leaders to have special knowledge of some portion of public opinion were strong enough to help give them a good deal of influence in national affairs. In essence, public opinion was a valuable property belonging to partisan, interest, or communal groups and their heads.

The advent of polling transformed public opinion from a property of groups to an attribute of individuals. Opinion surveys can elicit the views of individual citizens directly, allowing governments or other interested observers to bypass group leaders, social notables, party bosses, or any other putative spokespersons for public opinion. The polls have never fully supplanted communal and interest-group leaders as sources of information about popular attitudes. Yet, the polls do lessen the need for such intermediaries by permitting whatever agencies or organizations are interested in learning the public's views to establish their own links with opinion-holders. At the same time, polling often has the effect of undermining the claims of group leaders and activists to speak for membership opinion. Frequently enough, the polls seem to uncover discrepancies between the claims of leaders or self-appointed spokespersons, on the one hand, and the opinions of the mass publics whose views these activists claim to reflect, on the other. For example, during the 1960s and 1970s opponents of the American antiwar movement often took heart from poll data apparently indicating that youthful antiwar protestors who claimed to speak for "young people" really did not. Some poll data, at least, suggested that on the average individuals under 30 years of age were even more "hawkish" than respondents over the age of 50 (Scammon and Wattenberg 1970).

This conversion of public opinion from a property of groups and their leaders to a more direct presentation of popular preferences has several consequences. On the one hand, the polls undoubtedly provide a somewhat more representative picture of the public's views than would usually be obtained from group leaders and notables. Leaders and group representatives sometimes carelessly or deliberately misrepresent their adherents' opinions. But, even with the best of intentions, the leaders of a group may be insufficiently sensitive to the inevitable disparity of viewpoints between activists and ordinary citizens. Polling can be a useful antidote to inaccuracy as well as to mendacity.

At the same time, however, by undermining the capacity of groups, interests, parties, and the like to speak for public opinion, polling can also diminish the effectiveness of public opinion as a force in political affairs. In essence, polling intervenes between opinion and its organized or collective expression. Though they may sometimes distort member opinion, organized groups, interests and parties remain the most effective mechanisms through which opinion can be made to have an impact on government and politics. The polls' transformation of public opinion into an attribute of individuals increases the accuracy but very likely reduces the general efficacy with which mass opinion is publicly asserted.

One recent example of this phenomenon concerns the role of labor unions during the Nixon era. Many of the Nixon administration's policies (wage and price controls in particular) were strongly opposed by organized labor. Yet, the capacity of labor leaders to oppose the administration's program or to threaten electoral reprisals against legislators who supported it were constantly undercut by the polls. Poll data seemed generally to suggest that Nixon was personally popular with union members, and that the majority of rank and filers had no strong views on the programs that particularly troubled the unions' leadership. As a result, the administration came to feel that it was reasonably safe to ignore the importunities of organized labor on a host of public issues (Harris 1973). By enhancing the visibility of the opinions of ordinary workers, the polls surely drew a more representative picture of working-class opinion than had been offered by union officials. Yet the real cost of this more fully representative account of workers' views was, in a sense, a diminution of organized labor's influence over policy.

A similar example relates to the controversy over the 1947 Taft-Hartley Act. The capacity of organized labor to oppose this piece of legislation, which it regarded as virulently anti-union, was constantly undermined by poll results. The polls indicated that labor union members were far less concerned than the unions' leaders with the Act's provisions. Moreover, union members did not appear to regard legislators' positions on Taft-Hartley as the major factors that should determine their choice at the polls. As a direct result of these poll data, a number of United States senators and representatives with large trade union constituencies were emboldened to vote for the Act and, subsequently, to vote to override Truman's veto. Apparently, Senator Taft, himself, only decided to stand for reelection after polls in Ohio indicated that union members—a key voting bloc in the state—did not oppose him despite his sponsorship of a piece of legislation that union leaders dubbed a "slave labor act" (Roll and Cantril 1972).

It is not entirely a matter of coincidence that both these examples of the adverse effects of polling on the political influence of organized groups were drawn from the experience of the labor movement. Historically, the introduction of polling was, in fact, most damaging to the political fortunes of the social formations that represented the interests and aspirations of the working classes. Polling erodes one of the major competitive advantages that has traditionally been available to lower-class groups and parties—a knowledge of mass public opinion superior to that of their middle- and upper-class opponents. The inability of bourgeois politicians to understand or sympathize with the needs of ordinary people is, of course, the point of one of the favorite morality tales of American political folklore, the misadventures of the "silk-stocking" candidate. And, indeed, office-seekers from Easy Street often find it difficult to communicate with voters on Cannery Row. To cite just one example, during the New York City mayoral race of 1894, the Committee of Seventy, a group that included the city's socially most prominent citizens, argued vehemently for improvements in the city's baths and lavatories, "to promote cleanliness and increased public comfort." The Committee's members seemed undisturbed by the fact that the city and nation in 1894 were in the grip of a severe economic downturn accompanied by unusually high unemployment and considerable distress and misery among the working classes. The Committee of Seventy did not receive the thanks of many working-class New Yorkers for its firm stand on the lavatory issue (McFarland 1975).

Simply as a matter of social proximity, working-class parties or associations may have better access to mass opinion than is readily available to their rivals from the upper end of the social spectrum. As one Chicago precinct captain told Harold Gosnell during the 1930s,

. . . you think you can come in here and help the poor. You can't even talk to them on their own level, because you're better, you're from the University. I never graduated from high school, and I'm one of them (Gosnell 1968).

Even more important than social proximity, however, is the matter of organization. In general, groups and parties which appeal mainly to working-class constituencies rely more heavily than their middle- and upper-class rivals on organizational strength and coherence. Organization has typically been the strategy of groups that must cumulate the collective energies of large numbers of individuals to counter their opponents' superior material means or institutional standing. In the course of both American and European political history, for example, disciplined and coherent party organizations were generally developed first by groups representing the working classes. "Parties," Duverger noted, "are always more developed on the Left than on the Right because they are always more necessary on the Left than on the Right" (Duverger 1954).

What is important in the present context is that their relatively coherent and disciplined mass organizations gave parties of the "Left" a more accurate and extensive view of the public's mood than could normally be acquired by their less-well-organized opponents. In western Europe, the "branch" style of organization evolved by working-class parties in the 19th century gave them direct access to the views of a nationwide sample of ordinary citizens. In the United States, the urban political machines that mobilized working-class constituencies employed armies of precinct workers and canvassers. Among their other duties, these functionaries were responsible for learning the preferences, wants, and needs of each and every voter living within an assigned precinct or election district. A Chicago machine precinct captain interviewed by Gosnell, for example, "thought that the main thing was to meet and talk to the voters on a man-to-man basis. . . . It did not matter where the voters were met— in the ball park, on the rinks, at dances, or at the bar. The main thing was to meet them" (Gosnell 1968). Through its extensive precinct organization, the urban machine developed a capacity to understand the moods, and thus to anticipate and influence the actions, of hundreds of thousands of voters.

The advent of polling eroded the advantage that social proximity and organization had given working-class parties in the competition for mass electoral support. Of course, any sort of political group can use an opinion survey. Polls are especially useful to carpetbaggers of all political stripes as means of scouting what may be new and foreign territory (Javits 1947).

But, historically, polling has been particularly valuable to parties and candidates who lacked disciplined organizations and whose own social roots might not offer many clues to the desires of ordinary voters. Part of the historical significance of polling is that it represented a major element in the response of the Right to the Left's twin political advantages— greater organizational coherence and social consanguinity with ordinary citizens. In the United States, systematic political polling was initiated during the second half of the 19th century. Most of the early polls were sponsored by newspapers and magazines affiliated with conservative causes and middle- and upper-class political factions. A conservative paper, the *Chicago Tribune,* was a major promoter of the polls during this period. Prior to the critical election of 1896, the *Tribune* polled some 14,000 factory workers and purported to show that 80 percent favored McKinley over William Jennings Bryan (Jensen 1969). Many of the newspapers and periodicals that made extensive use of political polling in the 19th century were linked with either the Mugwumps or the Prohibitionists—precisely the two political groupings whose members might be least expected to have much firsthand knowledge of the preferences of common folk. During the 1896 campaign the Mugwump *Chicago Record* spent more than $60,000 in 12 midwestern states to mail postcard ballots to a random sample of one voter in 8. 328,000 additional ballots went to all registered voters in Chicago. The Democrats feared that the *Record* poll was a Republican trick and urged their supporters not to participate (Jensen 1969). Other prominent members of the Mugwump press that frequently sponsored polls before the turn of the century included the *New*

York Herald, the *Columbus Dispatch,* the *Cincinnati Enquirer,* the *Springfield* (Mass.) *Republican,* and the *Philadelphia Times* (Robinson 1932).

In the early years of the 20th century, many of the major polls were affiliated with groups on the political Right. The Hearst newspapers, for example, polled extensively. *Fortune* magazine published widely read polls. The *Literary Digest* which, of course, sponsored a famous presidential poll, was affiliated with the Prohibitionists (Jensen 1969). The clientele of most of the major pre–World War II pollsters, Gallup, Roper, and Robinson, for example, was heavily Republican, reflecting both the personal predilections of the pollsters and relative capacities of Democrats and Republicans of the period to understand public opinion without the aid of complex statistical analysis (Wheeler 1976). In recent years, the use of political polling has become virtually universal. Nevertheless, the polling efforts and uses of other forms of modern political technology by groups on the political Right have been far more elaborate and extensive than those of other political factions (Ginsberg 1986). Indeed, liberal Democrats are presently bemoaning the technological lead of their conservative Republican rivals.

Until the past several decades, polling was employed with much greater frequency in America than in Europe. It is worth noting, moreover, that the first extensive use of political polls in western Europe occurred after World War II under the aegis of several agencies of the United States government. These polls were designed, in large measure, to help centrist and right-wing political forces against their socialist and communist foes (Schiller 1973).

At the present time, in America and all the European democracies polling is used by parties and candidates of every political stripe. Opinion surveys are hardly a monopoly of the political Right. Yet, the fact remains that in the absence of polling, parties and groups representing the working classes would normally reap the political advantage of a superior knowledge of public opinion. Indeed, such groups traditionally depended heavily on their capacity to understand the mass public's mood as a counter to their opponents' generally superior material and institutional resources. The irony of polling is that the development of scientific means of measuring public opinion had its most negative effect upon precisely those groups whose political fortunes were historically most closely linked with mass public opinion.

FROM ASSERTION TO RESPONSE

In the absence of polling, individuals typically choose for themselves the subjects of any public assertions they might care to make. Those persons or groups willing to expend the funds, effort, or time needed to acquire a public platform, normally also select the agenda or topics on which their views will be aired. The individual writing an angry letter to a newspaper or legislator generally singles out the object of his or her scorn. The organizers of a protest march typically define the aim of their own wrath. Presumably, 19th-century mobs of "illuminators" determined of their own accord the matters on which the larger public would be enlightened.

The introduction of opinion surveys certainly did not foreclose individuals' opportunities to proffer opinions on topics of their own choosing. Indeed, in the United States, a multitude of organizations, groups, and individuals are continually stepping forward to present the most extraordinary notions. Nevertheless, the polls elicit subjects' views on questions which have been selected by an external agency—the survey's sponsors—rather than by the respondents themselves. Polling thus erodes individuals' control over the agenda of their own expressions of opinion. With the use of surveys, publicly expressed opinion becomes less clearly an assertion of individuals' own concerns and more nearly a response to the interests of others.

The most obvious problem stemming from this change is that polling can create a misleading picture of the agenda of public concerns. The matters which appear significant to the agencies sponsoring polls may be quite different from the concerns of the general public. Discrepancies between the polls' agenda and the general public's interests were especially acute during the political and social turmoil of the late 1960s and early 1970s. Though, as we saw, polling was used by the government during this period to help curb disorder, the major commercial polls took little interest in the issues which aroused so much public concern. The year 1970, for example, was marked by racial strife and antiwar protest in the United States. Yet, the 1970 national Gallup Poll devoted only 5 percent of its questions to American policy in Vietnam and only 2 of 162 questions to domestic race relations. Similarly, in 1971, despite the occurrence of a number of major episodes of racial unrest and student violence or protest, the national Gallup Poll that year still devoted only 2 of its 194 questions to race relations, and asked no questions at all about student protest. By contrast, Gallup in 1971 asked 42 political "horse race" questions, concerning citizens' candidate preferences and electoral expectations as well as 11 questions relating to presidential popularity. An observer attempting to gauge the public's interests from poll data might have concluded that Americans cared only about election forecasts and official popularity, and were blithely unconcerned with the matters that were actually rending the social fabric during that era. In fact, the commercial polls' almost total disregard for questions pertaining to civil rights, race relations, and poverty in the 1960s led former American Association for Public Opinion Research (AAPOR) President, W. Phillips Davison, to call the polls' failure to anticipate the development of violent racial conflict, "a blot on the escutcheon of survey research" (Davison 1972).

Especially, perhaps, given the commercial character of the polling industry, differences between the polls' concerns and those of the general public are probably inevitable. Questions are generally raised by the polls because they are of interest to clients and purchasers of poll data—newspapers, political candidates, governmental agencies, business corporations, and so on. Questions of no immediate relevance to government, business, or politicians can have some difficulty finding their way into the surveys. This difficulty may be particularly manifest in the case of issues such as the validity of the capitalist economic system or the legitimacy of governmental authority, issues which business and government usually prefer not to see raised at all, much less at their own expense. Because they seldom pose questions about the foundations of the existing order, while constantly asking respondents to choose from among the alternatives defined by that order—candidates and consumer products, for example—the polls may help to narrow the focus of public discussion and to reinforce the limits on what the public perceives to be realistic political and social possibilities.

But, whatever the particular changes polling may help to produce in the focus of public discourse, the broader problem is that polling fundamentally alters the character of the public agenda of opinion. So long as groups and individuals typically present their opinions on topics of their own choosing, the agenda of opinion is likely to consist of citizens' own needs, hopes, and aspirations. A large fraction of the opinion which is publicly expressed will involve demands and concerns that groups and individuals wish to bring to the attention of the government. Opinions elicited by the polls, on the other hand, mainly concern matters of interest to government, business, or other poll sponsors. Typically, poll questions have as their ultimate purpose some form of exhortation. Businesses poll to help persuade customers to purchase their wares. Candidates poll as part of the process of convincing voters to support them. Governments poll as part of the process of inducing citizens to obey. Sometimes several of these purposes are combined. In 1971, for example, the White House Domestic Council sponsored a poll dealing with a host of social issues designed both to assist the administration with policy planning and to boost the president's reelection efforts (Wheeler 1976).

In essence, rather than offer governments the opinions that citizens want them to learn, the polls tell governments—or other sponsors—what they would like to learn about citizens' opinions. The end result is to change the public expression of opinion from an assertion of demand to a step in the process of persuasion.

MAKING OPINION SAFER FOR GOVERNMENT

Taken together, the changes produced by polling contribute to the transformation of public opinion from an unpredictable, extreme, and often dangerous force into a more docile expression of public sentiment. Opinion stated through the polls imposes less pressure and makes fewer demands upon government than would more spontaneous or natural assertions of popular sentiment. Though opinion may be expressed more democratically via the polls than through alternative means, polling can give public opinion a plebiscitary character—robbing opinion of precisely those features that might maximize its impact upon government and policy.

Many of those involved with survey research have long believed, or hoped, that the collection of accurate information about the public's wishes would enhance governmental responsiveness to popular opinion. No doubt, there are occasions when the polls help to increase the degree of correspondence between official policy and citizens' needs. But, obviously, accurate information is no guarantee of governmental responsiveness to popular desires. Indeed, reliable knowledge of public opinion can permit governments to manage, manipulate, and use public sentiment more effectively (see the essay by Page and Shapiro, Chapter 14 in this volume). At the same time that some early students of survey research purported to see only the polls' implications for enhanced governmental sensitivity to opinion, others clearly recognized the value of polling as an instrument of governmental administration and policy implementation.

One academic representative of this latter group was David Truman. While a young World War II naval officer attached to the Joint Production Committee of the Joint Chiefs of Staff, Truman published a paper with the telling title, "Public Opinion Research as a Tool of Public Administration" (Truman 1945). Surveys, Truman indicated, can help administrators to identify and correct popular attitudes that might interfere with the successful operation of governmental programs. An example was the experience of "one of the oldest and best-managed federal conservation agencies":

Active operations had been started a short time before in several major conservation projects in the South. The methods employed were those which had been successfully used in the less sparsely populated sections of the West, where the population affected was comparatively close to national markets and nationwide trends. Activation of the program in the southern area was accompanied by resistance, hostility, and, in a seriously large number of cases, acts of criminal destructiveness which threatened the entire project. The findings of the government opinion researchers who were asked

to study the program revealed that the agency had, while acting in a completely legal manner, ruptured the established habits of living in the communities and to some extent had even violated certain parts of what might
be called the local code of public morality. Community standards thus con-
doned and even encouraged individual and group acts of violence aimed at
retaliation and at destroying the project (Truman 1945).

The agency's reaction to these findings was not to terminate the program
that had provoked such violent popular opposition. Rather, the poll data
allowed administrators to develop more effective means of convincing the
populace of the program's value. In due course, the project was able to
proceed without further local resistance.

The role of polling in this case was to transmute public opinion into
a form in which it could more easily be managed. Rather than promote
governmental responsiveness to popular sentiment, the polls served to
pacify or domesticate opinion, in effect helping to make public opinion
safer for government. In a sense, of course, the polls did contribute to
the realization of a measure of consistency between public opinion and
public policy. Polling helped administrators change public opinion to
match existing policy.

GOVERNMENT: FROM ADVERSARY TO MANAGER
OF OPINION

Because it domesticates public opinion, polling has contributed to
one of the 20th century's major political transformations—the shift from
an adversarial to a managerial relationship between government and popular opinion (see Bennett, Chapter 15 in this volume). Prior to the 20th
century, governments mainly perceived mass opinion as a potentially dangerous adversary. As Davison observes, "rulers looked upon public opinion with something akin to terror." Eighteenth- and 19th-century political
elites often would have only the vaguest understanding of popular attitudes before "the government, the church hierarchy, and the aristocracy
suddenly saw the roof blown off" (Davison 1972). As a result of governments' fear of popular sentiment, before the 20th century the two basic
policies of most regimes toward public opinion were secrecy and censorship. Incumbent elites might occasionally attempt to sway popular feelings. But, on a routine basis, the central thrust of official action was to
block access to information about governmental plans and operations and
to seek, through secrecy, to inhibit the development of potentially hostile
opinion on as many matters as possible.

In the United States, secrecy became part of the official policy of the
executive branch as early as 1792 when President Washington sought to
prevent a congressional inquiry into a military expedition conducted by

General Arthur St. Clair. Later, citing the importance of secrecy, Washington declined to provide the House with information concerning a proposed treaty with Great Britain. Subsequent administrations also asserted the need for secrecy in the activities of the executive branch. Various congressional requests for information were refused by Jefferson, Monroe, Jackson, Tyler, Polk, Fillmore, Buchanan, Lincoln, Grant, Hayes, Cleveland, Theodore Roosevelt, Coolidge, Hoover, Franklin D. Roosevelt, Truman, Eisenhower, Kennedy, Nixon and Reagan. Attempts by private individuals to obtain information about governmental activities are often fruitless. Even the enactment of "freedom of information" legislation in recent years has by no means opened the process of government to full public scrutiny (Breckinridge 1974).

All contemporary governments, of course, continue to employ some measure of censorship and secrecy to guard against real or imagined popular antagonism. But, during the 19th and 20th centuries, national policies toward public opinion underwent a profound change as rulers began to discover the value of popular support. The unprecedented size, ardor, and military success of the citizen armies of post-revolutionary France provided what was perhaps the first concrete demonstration of the power that could be tapped by enlisting the active cooperation of a populace. But, the importance of popular cooperation became even more evident through the late 19th century as the scope and complexity of national governments increased. On a day-to-day basis, the 20th-century state depends upon considerable support, cooperation, and sacrifice from its citizens in forms ranging from military service and large tax payments, through popular adherence to a multitude of rules and regulations. The scope and technical complexity of the modern state's activities, moreover, render governmental administration extremely sensitive to popular opposition. In the short term, opposition can often be forcibly quelled and a populace forcibly compelled to obey its rulers' edicts, pay taxes, and serve in the military. But, over long periods, even many of those governments commanding both the requisite armed might and appropriate lack of scruples have come to appreciate the wisdom of the Napoleonic dictum that one "may do anything with a bayonet but sit on it." By cultivating favorable public opinion, present-day rulers hope to persuade their citizens to voluntarily obey, support, and make whatever sacrifices are needed to further the state's goals (Ginsberg 1982, 1986). In the 20th century, management of public opinion has become a routine public function in the democracies as well as in the dictatorships. Typically, the censor has been supplanted, or at least joined, by the public relations officer as the governmental functionary most responsible for dealing with public opinion.

In the United States, of course, efforts have been made by every administration since the nation's founding to influence public sentiment, but, the management of opinion did not become routine and formal until World War I. In some respects, the First World War is the point of transition from government-as-censor to goverment-as-manager of popular opinion in the United States. On one hand, the Wilson administration created a censorship board, enacted sedition and espionage legislation and attempted to suppress groups like the International Workers of the World (IWW) and the Socialist party that opposed the war. Eugene Debs, it might be recalled, was arrested and convicted for having violated the Espionage Law, and sentenced to 10 years in prison, for delivering a speech which defended the IWW (Karson 1965).

At the same time, however, World War I was the first modern industrial war requiring a total mobilization of popular effort on the homefront for military production. The war effort required the government to convince the civilian population to bear the costs and make the sacrifices needed to achieve industrial and agricultural, as well as battlefield success. The chief mechanism for eliciting the support of public opinion was the Committee on Public Information (CPI), chaired by journalist and publicist George Creel. The CPI organized a massive public relations and news management program aimed at promoting popular enthusiasm for the war effort. This program included the dissemination of favorable news, the publication of patriotic pamphlets, films, photos, cartoons, bulletins, and periodicals, and the organization of "war expositions" and speakers' tours. Special labor programs were aimed at maintaining the loyalty and productivity of the work force. Much of the CPI's staff was drawn from the major advertising agencies. According to Creel, the work of the Committee "was distinctly in the nature of an advertising campaign . . . our object was to sell the war" (Creel 1920).

The CPI's program was a temporary wartime effort. Within several months of the armistice, much of the government's opinion management apparatus was disbanded. The work of the CPI, however, was a harbinger of the permanent expansion of government opinion management that began in earnest with the New Deal. The enlargement of the scope of governmental activity during the Roosevelt administration, was accomplished by an explosion of official public relations efforts. Each new department, agency, bureau, office, or committee quickly established a public relations arm to persuade the citizenry to cooperate with its programs and support its objectives. The link between the expansion of governmental activity and the increased role of opinion management during the New Deal was put into very clear focus by Chester Bowles. Early in his long career of public service, Bowles served as Director of the Office of Price Administration (OPA). Under Bowles' leadership, the OPA developed an extensive public information program whose large budget eventually drew congressional criticism. Bowles' defense of the program is recalled in his memoirs.

> At one point Congress threatened to cut our information budget. I testified that if they deprived us of the means of explaining our program to the people, our requirements for investigators and inspectors to enforce our regulations would be greatly increased. With a $5 million annual budget for information, I said I could keep the American people reasonably informed about our regulations and their own obligations and rights as citizens. But if Congress cut this $5 million, I would have no alternative but to make a public request for $15 million to hire law enforcement inspectors to prosecute the many people who, often through their own ignorance and lack of information, had acted illegally. If Congress preferred this, it was their prerogative. I myself preferred persuasion to police-state tactics (Bowles 1971).

The government's interest in "explaining programs to the people" has, of course, increased substantially since the New Deal. Many departments and agencies engage in opinion-management efforts that dwarf the OPA's $5 million program. One recent estimate suggests that the annual salaries of federal public information and public relations personnel totaled almost $100 million. In 1976, the federal government spent over $30 million on television and motion picture products. In 1975, federal agencies paid almost $150 million to private agencies for advertising campaigns. In recent years, the Defense Department's Defense Information School has graduated more than 2,000 "public information specialists" each year. Every American citizen is routinely exposed to some aspect of the federal government's information—and disinformation—program the news releases, films, public service spots, travelling exhibits, tours, open houses, commercial television programs and motion pictures produced with the cooperation of a federal agency, or to one of the many other public relations efforts that have become such a routine part of the process of government in the 20th century (Steinberg 1980; Weissberg 1976; Wise 1973).

Polling is the spearhead of this vast opinion-management apparatus. Opinion surveys provide governments with more or less reliable information about current popular sentiment, offer a guide to the character of the public relations efforts that might usefully be made, and serve as means of measuring the effect of "information programs" upon a target population. Though it cannot guarantee success, polling allows governments a better opportunity to anticipate, regulate, and manipulate popular attitudes. Ironically, some of its early students believed that polling would open the way for "government by opinion" (Gallup 1940). Instead, polling has mainly helped to promote the governance of opinion.

CHAPTER 14

Educating and Manipulating the Public[1]

Benjamin I. Page
Robert Y. Shapiro

INTRODUCTORY NOTE

Clearly, the opinions of ordinary American citizens often influence what their governments do, but this does not necessarily imply that populistic democracy is at work. Government responsiveness to the public would be a hollow exercise, if public opinion were itself manipulated by elites or interest groups in such a way that policymakers simply followed a deceived public. Accordingly, some of the most important questions to ask about public opinion are: Who or what influences public opinion? And how is it done—with correct information or by lying or misleading? And concomitantly, are there systematic biases in the provision of political information that may distort the public's policy preferences?

In this chapter, Benjamin Page and Robert Shapiro report on some results from a long-term research project in which they analyzed several thousand survey questions about public policy, asked of nationwide U.S. samples taken over the past 50 years. They demonstrate that public policy often responds to genuine public preferences, and that these preferences arise from objective circumstances or are informed about political realities. The American public is not merely a passive receptacle into which the media pour information about public affairs. Indeed, far from being

[1]An earlier version of this paper was presented at the 1987 annual meeting of the Midwest Political Science Association, Chicago, April 8–11. We are grateful to Lance Bennett, Tom Ferguson, Ben Ginsberg, Sam Kernell, Michael Margolis, Richard Sobel, and Aaron Wildavsky for comments and suggestions.

influenced by information supplied by elites, many of the changes in public opinion are better understood as responses to historical economic and
social trends, such as rising levels of income and education, changes in
workforce participation, or alterations in the global balance of power.

Page and Shapiro caution that the congruence between public opinion and policy is neither complete nor fully indicative of public control
over policymakers. They estimate that about one-third of the time policy
actually moves in an opposing direction, and sometimes government simply ignores or "marginalizes" the views of the public. The authors note
the many instances in which political leaders or organized interests have
provided misleading information. They also observe that the long-term
impact of the major American agencies of socialization, such as market
forces, government influence over the media, and the resources of corporations and established interests, act to reinforce the legitimacy of nationalistic, anticommunist, and procapitalistic values.

The Editors

We are convinced, on the basis of our own and others' research, that the
opinions of ordinary American citizens often influence what their governments do. When the public's policy preferences change, government policies tend to move in the same direction. This is true at the federal and
state levels; it holds for policy measures taken by legislatures, executives,
and even the judiciary; and for policies concerning foreign and domestic
affairs, taxes, regulation, social and economic welfare, and many other
matters (Page and Shapiro 1983; see also Weissberg 1976; Monroe 1979).

The fact that public opinion has a strong proximate effect upon policymaking, however, does not necessarily imply that populistic democracy
is at work. The question of democracy is more complicated. Government
responsiveness to the public would constitute a hollow victory, for example, if public opinion were itself manipulated by elites or interest
groups in such a way that policy followed the mistaken wishes of a deceived public. On the other hand, leadership of public opinion would not
(in our view) be inconsistent with democratic ideals if it involved educating citizens, informing them correctly about what kinds of public policy
could satisfy their needs and values.

Our concern with democratic theory has therefore directed our attention toward two questions: What sorts of people and institutions and
events bring about changes in collective public opinion? And what quality
of information is involved in those effects? That is: Who or what influences public opinion? And how do they do it—with correct information,
or by lying or misleading? Are there systematic biases in the provision of
political information that may distort the policy preferences of the public?

THE CAUSES OF COLLECTIVE OPINION CHANGE

In the course of a long-term research project we have gathered data from several thousand survey questions about public policy that were asked of U.S. national samples (by many different survey organizations) at various times from 1935 to the mid-1980s. Among those questions we find about one thousand that were asked more than once, with identical wording, so that they provide information about the direction and magnitude of changes—if any—in collective public opinion.

Using the repeated survey questions, we have identified all cases of significant opinion change (556 of them, from 473 questions with one or more changes) and put them in historical context, examining what relevant political events or social changes may have occurred between the different times that a given survey question was asked. Such post facto efforts at explanation cannot provide conclusive evidence about causation, but they can be very helpful, particularly to the extent that they reveal patterns across many instances of opinion change. We will report some generalizations from this historical analysis and then discuss our more systematic study of mass media impacts upon short-term opinion changes. Next we turn our attention to the quality of information conveyed. A fuller discussion of these matters is given in Page and Shapiro (1987).

Social and Technological Change

Some important long-term trends in public opinion are best understood in terms of gradual political, economic, or social changes that alter citizens' life circumstances or their understandings of the world. Such changes include the enormous economic growth and rises in average income levels since the 1930s; the decline in agricultural and rural population, increased industrialization and urbanization, and movement toward service industries and the suburbs; increases in leisure time, formal education, and the enjoyment of consumer goods; and improved transportation and communication.

Since several of these changes have occurred in a more or less linear fashion and are collinear with other trends, it is difficult to be certain of their impact. The up-and-down variation that gives bite to time series analyses is not present. But there is good reason to believe that long-term social and economic changes have had profound effects on public opinion. Rising incomes, to take one example, have undoubtedly led to desires for shorter workweeks and higher minimum wages as well as increased willingness to spend money on workplace safety, environmental protection, and other things once viewed as luxuries. Urbanization has brought more support for action to deal with problems of the cities.

Similarly, the great increase in the number of women working outside the home has undoubtedly spurred demands for women's rights, for equal treatment in the workplace and in politics, and for the legalization of abortions. Rising crime rates, in the 1960s and later, increased desires for strict courts and harsh punishment, including capital punishment.

In the realm of foreign affairs, the emergence of the United States as a world power during and after World War II, facing challenges from the Axis and then from the Soviet Union and from Third World nationalism, surely contributed to increased numbers of Americans that favored taking an active role in the world, supporting the United Nations, forming alliances, stationing troops abroad, providing foreign aid, and so forth. The rise of new nations, which reduced U.S. domination of the UN, cut into public support for that body. Declines in the relative strength and economic competitiveness of the United States that became evident in the 1970s led to more of the public favoring a military buildup and certain kinds of protectionism and retrenchment.

Public opinion concerning various social issues seems to have been strongly influenced by rising levels of formal education. Education exposes people to diversity, to information about many kinds of people and ideas and lifestyles, and to norms of tolerance and rational discourse—given elite support for such ideals. As larger proportions of Americans completed high school and college in the 1960s and 1970s, more expressed tolerance for allowing dissenters—communists, socialists, atheists—to give speeches, have their books in public libraries, and teach in schools. (Of course the decline of the Cold War and of religious commitments made such tolerance easier, and new cohorts supported civil liberties even beyond what their educational levels could account for.)

The massive increase in Americans' support for civil rights for blacks—the greatly increased acceptance of integration in public accommodations, neighborhoods, schools, jobs, and marriages that occurred over several decades from at least the 1940s on—undoubtedly partly reflected rising levels of education. But also important were a decrease in beliefs that blacks were genetically inferior, as blacks' achievements in wartime and in northern urban settings offered evidence to refute racist thinking (Young 1979), and greater awareness of the pernicious nature of segregation, brought to public attention by the Supreme Court and by the civil rights movement.

The strong trend of public opinion in favor of women's rights and of abortion, too, may have been related to education levels but also rested on some other trends: not only the increasing role of women (especially middle- and upper-class women) in the workplace, but also the improvement of birth control technology and of safer abortion procedures, and the rise of the women's movement. Gradual social changes seem to have affected public opinion about marijuana and other drugs, immigration restrictions, and various other issues as well.

Many of these social and economic trends can be seen as involving objective processes that altered people's circumstances and interests in ways that led naturally to changed policy preferences. Insofar as they can be considered exogenous influences upon public opinion, purely based on social reality, they are presumably not subject to manipulation. But that is not always the case. The nature and policy implications of "objective" changes are not always obvious. An assessment of their significance (indeed even awareness of their existence—for people not directly affected) often depends upon *information* provided by social movements or the mass media or in other ways. Such information may be true or false, helpful or misleading. Thus there exists a possibility of manipulation of opinion, even in reaction to objective changes in circumstances. And sometimes, of course, objective circumstances may themselves be manipulated.

Events

In many cases public opinion moves in connection with discrete events rather than gradual trends. In these cases causal inference is a bit easier, though still far from ironclad. If opinions change between two surveys that are conducted close together in time, and if a major, highly visible event of obvious relevance occurs in between, it is not unreasonable to infer that the event has affected opinion. A pattern of association between particular kinds of events and particular kinds of opinion change strengthens the causal inference.

War.   By far the most important kind of event affecting public opinion has involved war or armed conflict. Imminent threat of war, the outbreak of hostilities, battlefield events, and the coming of peace have altered Americans' views about many matters: the draft, defense spending, alliances, foreign aid, and the like; domestic sacrifices and economic controls; the appropriate terms for peace; postwar international involvement, world organization, alliances, the use of military force abroad; and indeed the whole range of foreign policy issues.

During the half century of American history for which we have survey data, the strongest and most pervasive influence on public opinion has undoubtedly been World War II. The details are discussed elsewhere (Shapiro and Page 1988; Page and Shapiro 1987); here we will simply mention some general patterns. The coming of war in Europe led more Americans to favor a larger army and navy, aid for Britain and France, and a military draft. The Japanese attack on Pearl Harbor inflamed the public, propelling U.S. entry into the war. As the fighting progressed, more Americans were willing to accept wage and price controls, long working days, high taxes, and prohibitions on strikes. When Germany invaded the USSR, more Americans came to favor aiding and cooperating with the Soviets. As the Axis powers proved hard to defeat, more Americans approved of aid and forgiveness of debts to the Soviets, the Chinese, and other allies, and began to insist upon harsher peace terms, pacification of Germany after the war, and the taking of new U.S. military bases abroad. Wartime cooperation among the allies helped build support for a postwar United Nations.

The end of World War II brought desires for relaxing wage and price controls, permitting strikes, reducing work hours and increasing pay, and cutting taxes. It also brought support for the UN, and for international control of atomic energy, free trade, and assistance to European war victims. These trends were counteracted only by the growth of the Cold War.

The war in Korea brought about analogous, though more limited, changes in public opinion: more support for a military buildup and armed resistance in Korea, military and economic aid for Asia, and strengthening the NATO alliance in Europe. During the fighting in Korea the public again expressed more willingness to make sacrifices in terms of wage and price controls, taxes, forbidding strikes, and the like; support fluctuated with the fortunes of war. The Chinese intervention led to larger majorities rejecting U.S. diplomatic recognition or admission of the People's Republic to the UN, and many advocated bombing Chinese territory. The end of the Korean war led more people to favor ending controls and lowering taxes, negotiating and trading with the Soviet Union, recognizing China and admitting it to the UN, and aiding developing countries.

The Vietnam war, too, caused a variety of changes in public opinion. The Tonkin Gulf incident and other preliminary skirmishes, as they were reported at the time, increased public willingness to fight. The events of the war, including battles and "peace feelers" and South Vietnamese government crises, led to increased or decreased public support for military measures, peace talks, and withdrawal. The apparent lack of progress, despite increasing U.S. troop levels and increasing numbers of casualties, eroded support for domestic sacrifices and increased opposition to the war, especially after the 1968 Tet offensive. Later, opinions about the desirable pace of troop withdrawals varied with the actual rates of withdrawal: more people wanted faster withdrawal whenever the pace slowed. Antiwar demonstrations led to increased desire for "law and order," more opposition to the vote for 18-year-olds, and some loss of support for civil liberties. The financial demands of the war increased opposition to domestic spending. The Vietnam experience, taken as a whole, raised public skepticism about the use of military force abroad; it led to reluctance to spend money on defense, resistance to foreign aid and foreign involvement generally, and to suspicion of presidential power.

Crises and International Events.   Short of war, major international events and crises have also had substantial (and often abrupt) effects on public opinion.

The actions of the Soviet Union (as reported and interpreted in the U.S. news media) after World War II—especially Soviet backing of the 1948 coup in Czechoslovakia and the blockade of West Berlin—decreased the number of Americans favoring trade or negotiations or cooperation with the USSR and cut support for the United Nations and for international control of atomic energy.

With regard to the Middle East, a number of events have affected opinions. The 1948 establishment of the state of Israel and its quick recognition by the U.S.; the 1956 Suez invasion; the 1967 war and Israeli occupation of the West Bank and Gaza; the 1973 war and subsequent OPEC oil boycott and price rise; the Camp David agreements; and the 1982 Israeli invasion of Lebanon, all led to ups and downs in support for and sympathy with the Israelis and the Arabs.

Similarly, the imminent collapse of the French in Indochina in 1954 provoked some backing for U.S. assistance or intervention. The Quemoy and Matsu crises affected opinions about China policy, as did China's testing of a nuclear device and such internal changes as the Cultural Revolution. The gradual increase in support for a U.S. military buildup during the 1970s was much accelerated by reports of the 1979 Soviet intervention in Afghanistan and by the highly publicized captivity of U.S. hostages in Iran—which also aroused desires for economic and/or military action against Iran. (In many of these foreign policy cases, as we will discuss below, news reports and interpretations—not just objective events per se—played a key part in opinion changes.)

Domestic Events.   Dramatic events are less common in the domestic realm, but when they occur they, too, can affect public opinion. The accidental release of radioactive material at the Three Mile Island nuclear power plant in 1979 did so: opposition to nuclear power, already growing, took a sudden jump. Similarly, the revelations of Watergate-related wrongdoings by the Nixon administration led to increased backing for the resignation or impeachment of the president. The urban riots of the middle and late 1960s apparently affected support for aiding minorities and spending money on urban problems. The assassinations of John Kennedy,

Robert Kennedy, and Martin Luther King each brought temporary increases in support for gun control.

The Economy.   Many important domestic events involve the economy. Depressions, recessions, periods of growth, and episodes of inflation have had broad impact on opinions about many domestic and foreign policies. The Great Depression presumably led to increasing support for relief programs, job assistance, social insurance, and stricter government regulation of business, though we lack predepression surveys to document the extent of change. Within the period for which we have opinion data it is clear that the business cycle has strongly affected attitudes about taxes, spending, and foreign trade. The recessions of 1974–75 and 1979–80, for example, led to substantial declines in support for spending on medical care, welfare, income redistribution, the cities, foreign aid, and space exploration; more people considererd taxes too high, and more backed tariffs and other trade restrictions. Attitudes bounced back as the economy improved.

High inflation rates (e.g., in the mid-1970s) have led more Americans to want wage and price controls and balanced government budgets. The huge budget deficits of the early 1980s greatly expanded public support for deficit reduction, even at the cost of higher taxes. The oil boycott and price rises of 1973–74 and 1979 led more Americans to favor measures for energy conservation, price controls, rationing, and the breakup of big oil companies. There was also greater favor for aid to, and friendly relations with, Arab oil-producing countries.

The Mass Media and News Sources

Certain kinds of events and objective conditions are felt directly by many people at once; for example, rising and falling prices, taxes, or incomes; increased formal education; or greater abundance of consumer goods. But others, such as unemployment, criminal victimization, or combat abroad, are experienced directly by relatively few. Still other events are quite remote from the personal experience of nearly everyone and are perceived only indirectly—usually through news reports in the mass media. This is particularly true of foreign affairs, though it applies to many domestic events as well. A coup in Latin America, a conflict in the Middle East, or a nuclear power accident, comes to the attention of most Americans only by means of TV news or a newspaper headline.

Even events that are experienced personally are seldom known in their full magnitude or their political significance except through the mass media. Someone who is laid off from his or her job may think it a purely personal mishap, unless there is news of rising unemployment in the nation as a whole. A combat death of a family member or friend brings personal grief, but its political meaning becomes apparent only when TV news reports the deaths of many others as well. Rising prices may be noticed at the gasoline pump or the grocery store, but their nationwide significance is felt only when the media focus on inflation as a national problem. Thus public opinion seldom responds to events themselves: it responds to *reported events*. The reports may or may not faithfully reflect reality.

Furthermore, when citizens do become aware of an event, whether through personal experience or from the media, it is rare that its policy implications are unambiguous. True, a Japanese attack on Pearl Harbor will be taken by almost every American as a strong argument for declaring war on Japan. But need it also entail war against Germany? Does a sharp rise in oil prices dictate imposition of price controls, or windfall-profits taxes, or the breakup of big oil companies? After an OPEC boycott should the United States court Arab oil producers or use military force against them? Should a civil rights demonstration be met with antidiscrimination laws or with political repression?

Understanding events' implications for the costs and benefits of alternative public policies requires complex reasoning—that proceeds from general goals and objectives, through assumptions about facts and causal connections, to concrete conclusions about policies. It requires *interpretation*. We believe that ordinary citizens are capable of such reasoning to a greater extent than they are usually given credit for. Still, the high costs of obtaining and processing detailed political information, together with the generally low benefits of doing so and the existence of more attractive (or more pressing) uses for time and energy, mean that most people delegate much interpretation of the news to trusted and like-minded agents.

Many chosen agents of interpretation and analysis are respected figures or groups whose words and behavior are reported in the media. That is, particular *sources* of news and commentary who speak to the public through the media serve as important influences upon public opinion. The reported statements and actions of these sources provide much of the interpretation and information about facts and causal connections that mediates the effects of objective events upon opinion.

We have been able to learn something about the impact of such news sources through a series of studies relating the content of news reports to the magnitude and direction of changes in public opinion. For one such study of the 1969–83 period (described more fully in Page, Shapiro, and Dempsey 1987), we selected 80 survey questions about public policy that were asked, in identical form, twice (at times "*t1*" and "*t2*") within a short period of time—mostly within three to six months. We then analyzed how changes in the marginal frequencies of survey responses were related to the content of network TV news from 10 different sources.

Some regression results are reproduced in Table 14-1. (For the sake of clarity the table omits coefficients for pre-$t1$ news from each source, which was controlled for in estimating the impacts of news broadcast between $t1$ and $t2$.)

Obviously we have had a great deal of success in predicting changes

TABLE 14–1   Opinion Change and Television News from Various Sources
(Relevant Stories)

News Source	(Impact of news between t_1 and t_2)
President	0.30
	(1.34)
Party of president	−0.09
	(−0.73)
Opposition party	0.44
	(2.00)
Interest groups	−0.38
	(−1.93)
Events	0.54
	(1.27)
Commentary	4.34*
	(4.25)
Experts	3.37*
	(2.32)
Foreign—friendly, neutral	0.08
	(0.14)
Foreign—unfriendly	0.48
	(0.99)
Courts	−2.02*
	(−2.22)
Intercept	−1.34
	(−0.56)

$$R^2 = .94$$
$$\text{Adjusted } R^2 = .91$$
$$N = 80$$

Note: Entries are unstandardized coefficients from a regression of opinion at t_2 on opinion at t_1 and on 20 different sums of relevant pro versus con news story scores, 10 pre-t_1 and 10 between t_1 and t_2. The t_1 opinion and pre-$t1$ news variables are treated as controls and their coefficients omitted here.
*Significant at the .05 level or better by a two-tailed test (t values in parentheses).
SOURCE: Page, Shapiro, and Dempsey 1987: 30.

in public opinion. When our 20 variables (10 for pre-t_1 and 10 for t_1-t_2 news), plus the level of opinion at t_1, were used to predict the level of opinion at t_2, they accounted for more than 90 percent of the variance across issues. Even when opinion at t_1 was dropped and the news variables alone were used to predict *opinion change* from t_1 to t_2, they accounted for nearly half the variance (R^2 = .57; adj. R^2 = .41). That is to say, what appears on TV news really does account for changes in public opinion.

There are big differences in the effects of news from different sources. News commentary (from the anchorperson, reporters in the field, or special commentators) has the most dramatic positive impact. A single "probably pro" commentary is associated with more than four percentage points of aggregate opinion change! Stories about experts or research studies, too, have a strong positive impact on public opinion: after a single story indicating that experts probably favor a particular policy, public support tends to rise by about three percentage points.

Presidents are estimated to have a modest impact of about three-tenths of a percentage point per "probably pro" story. (Although this estimate does not meet the usual criterion for statistical significance, it is confirmed by analysis of split samples and by a study of *New York Times* stories; see Page and Shapiro 1984.) Such small effects add up, because presidential stories appear much more frequently than do stories about experts or news commentary (see Kernell 1986). Stories about opposition-party statements and actions may also have a positive effect.

Interest groups and the courts, on the other hand, seem actually to have had negative effects in recent years. That is, when their statements and actions push in one direction (e.g., when a corporation demands subsidies or a federal court orders school integration through busing) public opinion tends to move in the opposite direction. We are not certain about the negative effect of courts, however, because of the instability of these coefficients across two other independent data sets.

The president's administration and fellow partisans, when acting independently of the president himself, do not appreciably affect public opinion. It is also striking that events, which we have emphasized as fundamentally important in bringing about opinion changes, do not generally have very strong direct effects. Events do not usually speak for themselves. They have most of their impact through the interpretations and reactions of other news sources. Much the same applies to statements and actions from foreign countries, whether friends or foes. Americans do not usually react to events or to foreigners directly, but only through interpretations by U.S. opinion leaders. This confirms our view of the importance of the media and indicates that there are substantial possibilities for educating or manipulating public opinion.

One factor accounting for the markedly different effects of different types of news is undoubtedly source *credibility*. The public apparently tends to place great trust in the positions taken by network commentators and by (ostensibly) nonpartisan experts. By contrast, interest groups that are presumed to pursue narrowly selfish aims may serve as negative reference points. But there are also some further complications in understanding exactly how various news sources influence public opinion.

News Commentary. The remarkably strong estimated impact of news commentary, controlling for all other sources, has held up in the analysis of three independent sets of data, and it does not appear to be an artifact of reciprocal impacts of anticipated public opinion upon commentary. But we are somewhat reluctant to believe that commentators' remarks in and of themselves have such great potency. We suspect that they may stand for other influences as well.

The commentary coded from TV news may serve partly as an indicator of collinear factors that influenced public opinion at the same time. These could include the positions of many journalists or other elites who communicate similar messages through various channels. Or commentators' positions might be indicators of network biases, including subtle influences by reporters and editors and owners upon the selection of news sources and the ways in which stories are filmed and reported (e.g., the choice of visual footage, questions asked in interviews, camera angles and so forth). Or, indeed, commentators and other sources with whom they agree might reflect a national "climate of opinion" or an elite consensus on an issue, which could weigh heavily with citizens as they form their own opinions. (The estimated commentator effect, however, is controlled for the other elite news sources we measured.)

We cannot easily distinguish among these possibilities, several of which could play a part in opinion manipulation. News commentators either constitute, or stand for, major influences upon public opinion— most or all of which are presumably communicated through the media.

Experts. The large estimated impact of those we have categorized as "experts" is somewhat less ambiguous, at least in terms of direct effects. The credibility of experts is presumably high because of their actual or portrayed experience and expertise and nonpartisan status. It is not surprising that members of the public give great weight to expertise, since complex technical questions often bear on the merits of policy alternatives. Some reciprocal influence by anticipated public opinion upon reported expert statements cannot be ruled out (audience-seeking media may decide which experts to feature, based on the popularity of their policy views) but it is probably limited in the short run.

Our estimate of experts' impact is not, however, completely free of causal ambiguity; to a substantial extent, the direct effects of experts may reflect indirect influence by others in society. Experts may be selected by the media in such a way as to promote the media's own biases. Or the emergence of expert testimony at a particular moment may tend to reflect a consensus among elites; reported expertise certainly seems to vary with the political tides of the day (e.g., the party in power in Washington). Moreover, corporations and organized interest groups are important in funding and publishing favorable expert studies, so that the fundamental force behind experts' influence on public opinion may sometimes be the efforts of such actors. Any such indirect effects apparently act through media reports of experts' views.

Presidents.   Our finding of only a relatively small impact by presidents requires qualification. It resulted from lumping all presidents together during a period when most presidents, most of the time, were rather unpopular and (presumably) not very credible. When we separated our cases into two groups, those in which the president had a Gallup approval rating of 50 percent or more at $t1$ and those in which he was less popular, we found that *popular* presidents have an estimated effect nearly twice as great as that indicated in Table 14–1: .58 percentage points per speech, compared to .30. Unpopular presidents have essentially no effect at all, .05 percentage points per speech.

Part of the estimated effect of popular presidents probably reflects a reciprocal relationship, in which presidents take a stand in response to public opinion or in anticipation of how it will change. It is also true that talkative presidents cannot hope to multiply the impact of a single speech indefinitely, because of saturation and overexposure. Still (controlling for other sources), on an issue of great concern a popular president who hammers away with repeated speeches and statements can reasonably expect to achieve a 5 to 10 percentage point change in public opinion over the course of several months (see Page and Shapiro 1984; Page, Shapiro, and Dempsey 1987).

Interest Groups.   The finding that interest groups tend to have a negative effect on public opinion holds only on the average, and only for direct effects. Our closer examination of specific cases has suggested that the public tends to be uninfluenced—or negatively influenced—by the statements of groups whose interests are perceived to be selfish or narrow or antisocial, while it responds more favorably to groups and individuals thought to be concerned with broadly defined public interests. Negative effects seem to have come from protestors and demonstrators, corporations and business associations, and some relatively broad groups representing blacks, women, the poor, and organized labor. On the other hand, environmental groups and perhaps also general "public interest" groups such as Common Cause appear to have had positive effects on public opinion.

Even organized interests that do not have a direct positive effect on opinion when they speak out in public may have important indirect effects, however. The messages of protests and demonstrations may sink in over time. Organized groups and corporations with a lot of money may be able to encourage and publicize the work of chosen "experts," and may influence news commentary as well, in turn affecting the general public. By these and other means, including institutional advertising and influence upon school textbooks and curriculum (Miliband 1969; Bowles and Gintis 1976), interest groups probably have very important impacts on public opinion.

EDUCATION AND MANIPULATION OF PUBLIC OPINION

The central role of media-reported statements and actions in influencing public opinion casts a particular light on our earlier finding (Page and Shapiro 1983) that public opinion has substantial proximate effects on policymaking. It means that public opinion cannot be taken as an entirely autonomous force, welling up from objective needs and circumstances and determining what governments do. Instead, public opinion may in part simply serve as a transmission belt for groups and institutions and interests that influence the public.

If this is so, the populistic democratic ideal—that governments should do what their citizens want—is not necessarily realized in any meaningful sense by a congruence between policies and the public's expressed desires. In particular, if the public is systematically manipulated or deceived or misled, one should draw little normative satisfaction from the translation of its mistaken wishes into policy. Lindblom (1977) discusses this problem in terms of the "circularity of preferences."

As we see it, the crucial question concerns what *quality of information* is conveyed to the citizenry. To the extent that the public receives correct and helpful information—information that helps it arrive at the policy choices it would make when fully informed—policy preferences can be considered "authentic," well adapted to achieve people's basic values and goals. Individuals or institutions that influence public opinion by providing correct, helpful political information can be said to *educate* the public.

On the other hand, to the extent that the public is given false or incorrect or biased information, or is deprived of important relevant information, people may make mistaken evaluations of policy alternatives and may express support for policies harmful to their own or society's interests, or in conflict with values they cherish.

Those who influence public opinion by providing false, incorrect, biased, or selective information may be said to *mislead* the public. If they do so consciously and deliberately, by means of lies, falsehoods, deception, or concealment, they may be said to *manipulate* public opinion. This term implies conscious, intentional human action. More loosely, however, we will sometimes speak of institutions or processes or patterns of behavior as manipulating opinion if they systematically provide the public with false or misleading information.

It is difficult to be certain in identifying instances or patterns of education or manipulation. The crucial distinction between correct and incorrect information is not easy to work with. Reasonable people differ about truth and falsehood; scientists and scholars and others who are supposed to seek the truth often disagree, and indeed their very livelihoods are based on the premise that much of the truth is not yet known or agreed upon. Few judgments about the truth or falsehood of political claims (let alone judgments about the awareness and motivations of political actors) are likely to pass without controversy.

We are aware of the minefields of subjectivity and controversy into which one can wander when trying to study manipulation of opinion. But when the objective is sufficiently important, one should be willing to brave minefields. This topic is so central to any serious discussion of public opinion and democracy that we believe the attempt should be made. Accordingly, we have done our best to identify cases in which the public appears to have been educated and misled or manipulated, and to uncover systematic ways in which misleading information may be conveyed.

Educating the Public

In many cases experts and research studies have provided new information (information which, as best we can tell, is accurate) that has helped the public better to understand problems facing the country and better to calculate the costs and benefits of policy alternatives. Thus scholars, researchers, and experts, and those publicizing their work, have helped educate public opinion.

The anthropologists and sociologists who first studied the cultural bases of human characteristics, for example, laid the basis for a new public understanding of racial differences as environmental rather than genetic, and undermined much of the rationale of racism (Myrdal 1944; Young 1979). Together with later studies of the detrimental effects of segregation upon minorities, they helped lead the public to adopt civil rights policies aimed against discrimination and segregation.

Similarly, research in the late 1950s and early 1960s, and publications such as Michael Harrington's *The Other America,* revealed how widespread poverty was in America and introduced many Americans to information about the formerly invisible poor. This knowledge helped increase public backing for various antipoverty programs.

Again, the writings of Rachel Carson (1962) and others revealed the environmental effects of heavy pesticide use and led the public to perceive problems that might be solved through environmental legislation. Ralph Nader and his associates (1965, 1980) did much the same for automobile safety and various consumer issues. George Stigler and other economists pointed out the inefficiency (and the pro-producer bias) of many regulatory policies, and thus gave impetus to sentiment for deregulation (Cohen and Stigler 1971; Stigler 1975).

A similar role could be claimed for studies, at various times, of such matters as effects of tax loopholes and incentives; the workings of Head Start and other social welfare programs; negative effects of wage and price controls; safety and environmental problems with nuclear power; counterproductive effects of protectionism; the consequences of nuclear war; the workings or nonworkings of strategic missile defenses; and many other subjects. Often scientific or scholarly studies have led to expert consensus and widespread agreement among elites, eventually entering the public's consciousness through the media.

The rhetoric of presidents and other politicians sometimes draws attention to the existence of problems and the merits of possible solutions. It rarely, however, rises to the level of education, because it usually emphasizes values or goals rather than facts or analysis, and it frequently encapsulates arguments in symbols or slogans that are misleading or, at best, incomplete. Oversimplification or misrepresentation should not necessarily be forgiven merely because it is used in what the observer may consider a good cause.

Thus Franklin Roosevelt's warnings about the threat from Hitler and the need to aid Britain and France were marred by his crafty maneuverings with Japan, his misrepresentations of incidents in the Atlantic, and his denial that American troops would be needed when he knew they would (Beard 1948). Similarly, Harry Truman's warnings of Soviet expansionism and his plea for a Marshall Plan to help rebuild Europe suffered from too strident an indictment of the Soviets, neglecting historical context. John Kennedy's urging of an activist foreign policy and aid to developing countries also relied on excessive portrayals of Soviet threat (and an illusory "missile gap") to constitute an unequivocal case of education. One might find more evidence of education in Dwight Eisenhower's embrace of peaceful coexistence or Jimmy Carter's discussions of human rights in other countries.

In the domestic realm, one could find many claimants to education of public opinion, among them Roosevelt's espousal of New Deal programs; Eisenhower's advocacy of sound and efficient management; Kennedy's urging that the country "get moving again"; Johnson's arguments for civil rights and antipoverty programs; Reagan's advocacy of small, efficient government. But here, too, the quality of information conveyed is suspect. (See Tulis 1987.) To the extent that presidents lead public opinion, it is more often by articulating widely held values and pointing out their application to some policy area, than by educating the public about specific facts of causal connections related to policy.

Below the presidential level, examples of educational efforts by politicians can be found, but less often do they gain enough audience to have important direct effects on public opinion. Exceptions might include the unusually thoughtful campaign rhetoric of Adlai Stevenson; Senator William Fulbright's critiques of American foreign policy; and many congressional investigations (Kefauver on pharmaceuticals and on organized crime; McClellan on labor corruption; McGovern on hunger; Erwin on Watergate; Church on intelligence activities) which brought together expert testimony and provoked commentary quite influential with the public.

Social movements, like politicians, lead opinion mainly by drawing attention to problems and articulating goals, whether they be equal treatment for blacks, women, and Hispanics; peace in Vietnam; disarmament; a nuclear freeze; or help for the poor. But social movements also stimulate research and encourage books and articles and commentary that may educate public opinion. Much the same is true of corporations and other organized interests which fund research and generate commentary that (on occasion, at least) may help the public better understand public policy.

Misleading and Manipulating the Public

Some conspicuous cases of misleading or manipulating public opinion have occurred in foreign affairs. On foreign policy matters government officials often control access to information and can conceal or misrepresent the truth with little immediate danger of being challenged.

One of the most important cases is the 1957–61 myth of a "missile gap," which originated with intelligence estimates that the Soviet Union might be capable of producing some 500 ICBMs by 1960—and perhaps as many as 3,000 by 1963—against only 30 or so for the United States. Although such speculative figures were disputed within the intelligence community and were repeatedly revised downward, the Air Force, whose "bomber gap" had recently evaporated, leaked its alarming estimates to Senator Stuart Symington, columnist Joseph Alsop, and others, who publicized them. Candidate (and later President) John Kennedy took up the cry, implying that the United States was in grave danger. In fact, however, the USSR fielded no operational ICBMs at all until 1961, when it had 4.

The United States enjoyed a 6:1 ICBM advantage in 1961 and an 8:1 advantage in 1963, in addition to the enormous lead it had in nuclear-armed bombers and submarines. By early 1961, if not before, Kennedy and Secretary of Defense McNamara knew that the "gap" did not exist, but instead of correcting the false impression they proceeded with a huge buildup of Minuteman and Polaris missiles (Kaplan 1983; Bottome 1971; Ball 1980).

Another important instance of opinion manipulation concerns the Tonkin Gulf incident off North Vietnam in August 1964. President Johnson's condemnation of "unprovoked" aggression against two U.S. destroyers was double deceptive. The first North Vietnamese PT boat attack (which caused no damage) was provoked by the destroyer *Maddox*'s electronic stimulation of North Vietnamese coastal radar, which created the impression of U.S. armed attacks not far from where South Vietnamese commandos were actually raiding the north (in a long-standing U.S.-organized operation). And the second alleged attack, on the *Turner Joy,* apparently never occurred: an inexperienced sonar man got confused in stormy seas. President Johnson and his staff knew of doubts about the second attack and were fully aware of U.S. and South Vietnamese provocations from the first. Indeed the very purpose of the destroyers' mission may have been to create an incident to justify U.S. retaliation and convince the public and Congress (for whom a draft of the Tonkin Resolution had been prepared in advance) that the United States should escalate its military involvement in Vietnam (Windchy 1971; Goulden 1969; Gravel 1971). Wise (1973) gives a popular account.

A third case of special importance is the Soviet arms scare of the 1970s and early 1980s, in which the Committee on the Present Danger and various politicians and experts portrayed the USSR as engaged in a massive buildup of strategic nuclear weapons that threatened to open a "window of vulnerability" to a first-strike attack on the United States (Sanders 1983). Much like the missile gap, the window of vulnerability never materialized. It did not take long before U.S. intelligence quietly acknowledged that the Soviet buildup had been vastly exaggerated. But the Reagan administration continued to repeat its rhetoric of vulnerability long after the revised estimates were widely known (Gervasi 1986; Halloran and Gelb 1983).

These cases are unsually clear and well documented, but they do not by any means stand alone. As we have noted, Truman's and others' early Cold War rhetoric portrayed the Soviets as less reasonable and more militant than they were. Truman and Acheson glossed over the civil war aspect of the Korean conflict. Mainland China was depicted as far more a tool of the Soviet Union than was the case. During the 1950s the U.S. government overstated the communist threat in Iran, Guatemala, Indonesia, and many other places, and denied the existence of the CIA operations that overturned the nationalist Mussadiq and the leftist Arbenz governments in 1953 and 1954 and that attempted to overthrow neutralist Sukarno in 1958. The government concealed the U.S. organization of the Bay of Pigs invasion of Cuba in 1961. It hid multiple attempts to assassinate Fidel Castro; efforts to overthrow or assassinate Patrice Lumumba in the Congo; U.S. support for the military coup in the Dominican Republic in 1965; and many other covert operations (Wise and Ross 1964; Marchetti and Marks 1980: chap. 4; U.S. Senate 1975).

Of course it is impossible to be sure whether or not the public would have opposed these covert operations if it had been fully informed about them, but in at least some cases public opinion seems to have been manipulated by secrecy and/or falsehood (e.g., President Johnson's talk of headless bodies on the streets of the Dominican Republic and of bullets whizzing through the American embassy: Wise 1973).

The Tonkin incident was not the only occasion on which the public was misled about Vietnam. From start to finish, misinformation was provided about such matters as the revolt against the French, the origins and character of the Diem regime, the nature of the insurgency, the role of U.S. "advisers," the bombing of North Vietnam, the U.S. troop buildup, battle outcomes and "body counts," "peace feelers," the destruction of Laos and Cambodia, troop withdrawals, and even the nature of the final "peace with honor." Only belatedly did critical reporting and disturbing TV news footage lead to distrust of official sources and disillusionment with the war, demonstrating both the possibilities of, and certain limits to, manipulation of opinion (Hallin 1984, 1986; Gravel 1971; Chomsky 1978).

Nixon and Secretary of State Kissinger and others continued to propagate deceptive information about Indochina as the war wound down (e.g., Shawcross 1979). In addition, the program to "destabilize" the Allende government of Chile was concealed (Hersh 1983: chaps. 21–22), as was the covert operation in Angola (Stockwell 1978). To some extent, however, the post-Vietnam retrenchment of the 1970s brought a respite from covert operations and from official opinion manipulation, until the allegations of a Soviet arms buildup gathered steam. Massive media attention (magnified by President Carter) turned the Iranian hostage incident from a minor diplomatic irritant to a major international crisis (Dorman and Farhang 1987), and portrayal of the Soviet intervention in Afghanistan as an "invasion" aimed ultimately at the Persian Gulf (ignoring internal Afghan politics and Soviet security interests) fed public enthusiasm for increased military spending.

The Reagan administration seems to have engaged in widespread manipulation of opinions on foreign policy: interpreting the behavior of the Soviet "evil empire" in the darkest fashion, as in alleged SALT treaty violations (Talbott 1984; Gelb 1985), the downing of the KAL 007 airliner

(Hersh 1986), and the Chernobyl nuclear accident; concealing renewed CIA military operations in Afghanistan, Ethiopia, Cambodia, and Angola, as well as in Nicaragua; misleadingly explaining the invasion of Grenada and the bombing of Libya (Hersh 1987); falsely characterizing the nature of the Nicaraguan Sandinistas and Contra "freedom fighters"; and of course concealing and then misrepresenting the nature of arms transactions with Iran and the Nicaraguan Contras (U.S. 1987).

Recital of such incidents reminds us again that facts are often subject to dispute and motives, uncertain. But in many foreign policy cases, during many administrations, there is evidence of deliberate efforts to deceive the citizenry. The official line is often transmitted to the public, more or less intact, by mass media commentary and reports from experts and other sources, as well as by government officials themselves.

With regard to domestic policy, sources of information are usually more diverse and competitive, so that outright government manipulation of opinion is less common than in foreign policy. Nonetheless, certain kinds of misleading information sometimes dominate public discourse for long periods of time.

Murray Edelman (1964) has pointed out how merely setting up and publicizing a regulatory agency can mislead the public into thinking that a particular problem has been "solved." The Interstate Commerce Commission was widely assumed to take care of abuses by railroads and truckers, and the Federal Communications Commission to do likewise with broadcasters, even though these agencies actually tended to further the anticompetitive interests of the regulated industries. Agencies also sometimes suppress information critical of their clients, as the Atomic Energy Commission repeatedly did when it withheld reports questioning the safety of commercial nuclear reactors (Ford 1984).

Government agencies have also concealed the domestic equivalents of foreign covert operations, and thereby manipulated the public into unawareness of and/or acquiescence in actions against dissident groups, such as the FBI's harassment of Martin Luther King and other civil rights leaders, or the "COINTELPRO" operations of the Nixon years in which antiwar groups were infiltrated and harassed and their files and offices destroyed (Goldstein 1978; Donner 1981).

Presidents have sometimes misled the public about domestic policy—although probably less often, or at least less blatantly, than with foreign policy. Lyndon Johnson, for example, oversold his "war on poverty," building support for policies that were useful but limited by implying that poverty could be ended at low cost while fighting a war in Southeast Asia (Tulis 1987). Richard Nixon did just the opposite, overstating the problems with Great Society programs and suggesting that poverty and racism could be overcome through benign neglect. Ronald Reagan's talk of massive government waste, and his colorful anecdotes of welfare queens driving Cadillacs and of cheaters spending their food stamps on gin, misled the public about the functioning of social welfare programs (Green and McColl 1983).

More broadly, the 1970s were a time of misleading rhetoric from many sources about many domestic programs. Politicians and economists characterized the price rises that followed the OPEC oil boycott as a major problem of "inflation," to be cured with monetarist medicine of tight money and budget cuts—which led to sharp recessions and might well have been opposed by a fully informed public. A strong public relations offensive against social and regulatory programs was conducted by politicians and experts financed by conservative interests (Saloma 1984; Blumenthal 1986; Ferguson and Rogers 1986; Edsall 1984). Studies purported to show that Great Society programs such as Head Start and the Job Corps had "failed" (Aaron 1978), that Social Security was going bankrupt, and that vast amounts of tax money were being wasted on domestic programs (see Schwarz 1983). Even as elite politics turned rightward, however, the propaganda barrage largely failed to convince the public, which remained firmly committed to social welfare programs (Ferguson and Rogers 1986: chap. 2).

Businesspeople's complaints about the difficulty of complying with health and safety and antipollution regulations helped energize economists' studies and public support for "deregulation." The consumer movement to abolish anticompetitive regulations of transportation and communication was deflected into opposition to any government regulation at all, including that of the environment or health or civil rights—though again public opinion did not change as much as elite politics did.

At the end of the 1970s a miraculous vision of "supply side" economics was used to befuddle the public. The idea, proposed by certain economists and political scientists on the fringes of academia, and taken up by businesspeople and others who wanted to reduce their taxes, was that federal income taxes could be cut sharply without hurting government programs because, with productive forces unshackled, government revenues might actually rise (Blustein 1981). This alluring (but wholly speculative and implausible) notion captured the popular imagination and won support for the deep tax cuts of 1981, which proved to be a bonanza for corporations and the wealthy and a source of huge budget deficits and pressure on spending. Government officials seem to have been aware of the likelihood of these effects from the start (Greider 1981; Stockman 1986).

Over a number of years the fight of organized labor for "minimum wage" laws has no doubt persuaded the public that such laws actually help those with low incomes, whereas the main effects are probably to increase unemployment at the lowest skill levels and to facilitate unionization by reducing non-union wage competition. Similarly, attractive-sounding "right to work" laws have been promoted by business groups as helping workers, whereas they mainly lower wages (and employers' labor costs) by weakening unions—preventing union shops and thereby burdening unions with free riders.

Again, the campaign against the Equal Rights Amendment for women was characterized by half-truths or deceptions about combat service and unisex bathrooms and the like (Mansbridge 1986). Supporters of ERA shared some responsibility for the distortions.

Patterns of Misleading and Biased Information

Many of the instances of misleading information we have discussed (together with many we have not) seem to fit into persistent patterns. That is, they appear to represent not just isolated incidents of manipulation by particular groups or individuals, but general tendencies in the kind of political information that is provided to the public by American society as a whole.

It is very difficult to be sure about such patterns. To do so would require not only judgments of truth and falsehood but also quantitative assessments: that particular kinds of misleading information are (1) very common (more common, for example, than errors in the opposite direction) or (2) that the information reaching the public represents some sort of biased sample from the universe of potentially relevant information. It is not easy to make such assessments in a rigorous fashion. Therefore our suggestions of possible patterns, based on our own readings of the mass media and the historical record and supported in some measure by others' research, cannot at this point be considered definitive.

We believe that the American public is regularly exposed to certain kinds of misinformation or biased information that affects opinions concerning a wide range of foreign and domestic policies. These patterns appear to result from normal market forces (together with government control of certain types of information); from the nation-state system and the loyalties and interests it generates; from our predominantly capitalist economy; and from the enormous resources of business and other organized interests for producing, disseminating, and consuming political information in the United States.

The most pronounced pattern in information about foreign affairs is a *nationalistic* and *ethnocentric* bias. This means, for one thing, disproportionate attention to U.S. policies and activities and to those nations closest to the U.S. in culture and language and geography—or most tied to U.S. interests. The death of one American abroad often gets more media coverage than the deaths of hundreds or thousands of foreigners, especially Asians or Africans. (See the essay by Christopher Bosso, Chapter 8 in this volume.) Such an allocation of attention follows from the economics of the media and the preferences of American audiences: people care most about matters close to home. But ignorance of the world encourages stinginess with foreign aid, support for aiding repressive dictatorships and subverting popular regimes, concern with alliances rather than the well-being of other peoples, and a number of other opinions that a well-informed public might not hold.

The content as well as the coverage of news about foreign affairs is slanted in a nationalist direction. Since much relevant information is controlled by U.S. government sources, the media must rely heavily on them (Sigal 1973; Bennett 1988). The government can therefore focus attention on particular events or alleged events (a Soviet arms shipment to Nicaragua; Soviet "combat troops" in Cuba) and offer an official, U.S.-centered interpretation (a Soviet beachhead in the Western hemisphere; a threat to U.S. security) that often goes uncontradicted. Regimes and movements defined as "enemies" of the United States at a given moment are generally portrayed in the most negative light, and "friends" in a favorable light, even if they are hated by their own people—as Batista, Somoza, Shah Pahlevi, and Marcos were (Dorman and Farhang 1987; Bonner 1987).

The flow of misleading information about foreign affairs is probably furthered by multinational corporations that invest abroad and want stable friendly governments that will guarantee docile workers and good profits. But this is more important to the particular definition of U.S. interests than to the fact that such interests dominate foreign information. A nationalistic bias undoubtedly pervades the news in most countries of the world, because of the selfishness of individuals organized into competing nation states.

A closely related pattern in information about foreign affairs has been an *anticommunist* bias. Especially since World War II, because of ideological anticommunism as well as a nationalistic focus on American security interests and markets and investments abroad, officials (and corporations and other actors) have set out to convince the public of the evils of the Soviet Union and its allies and kindred spirits in the world. The Russian people have been said to be oppressed by a monolithic dictatorship that starved them and crushed dissent. National liberation movements and revolutionaries, even those with little or no Russian connection, have been portrayed as tools in a Soviet scheme to dominate the world (Parenti 1986).

One need not reject the elements of truth in such characterizations (a colleague has likened the anticommunist bias to a bias against earthquakes) in order to conclude that the public's anticommunist sentiments have been inflamed, and its support for military spending and alliances and sending troops abroad inflated, by systematic misinformation. The very rapidity with which détente was accepted in the early 1970s and then switched off again shortly thereafter suggests the extent of official control over relevant information. (By the same token, however, the persistence of popular desires for cooperative relations with the Soviets indicates that there are limits to manipulation.)

In the information Americans receive about both foreign and domestic issues we believe there is a pervasive *procapitalist* slant. American schools teach the virtues of free enterprise, and corporate advertising trumpets them; government officials and news organizations take capitalism for granted, even while investigating or publicizing malfeasance by particular firms. The average American is bombarded by messages about the productive power and efficiency of "free enterprise," the high standard of living it has provided, and the personal liberties it promotes (Miliband 1969; Parenti 1986). Rare is the voice that seriously questions the fairness of the system or explores economic and social alternatives.

Of course one might argue that this reflects reality: facts and experience, not propaganda, have convinced a once-skeptical U.S. working class that capitalism is acceptable or even ideal. Quite possibly so. But our evidence, without insisting on any particular vision of the counterfactual consequences should the American public have complete information, simply shows that the information it does receive is one-sided. Americans are exposed to a virtually hegemonic world view, in which corporations and experts and commentators and officials all take for granted that a capitalist system is best. Corporate ownership of the major media (Bagdikian 1983) reinforces this tendency.

One facet of the anticommunist and procapitalist biases is a tendency to ignore, or to malign and degrade, movements and individuals on the political "extremes," especially the left. Their messages are seldom heard except for sensational strikes or demonstrations, which are often portrayed as bizarre, violent, and deviant (Gitlin 1980). Together with official repression (as in the Palmer raids, McCarthyism, and the "security" investigations of the late 1940s and the early 1950s, and the infiltration and harassment of the civil rights and antiwar movements of the 1960s and 1970s—not to mention the Socialist Workers Party), this has limited the scope of political discourse in the United States (Goldstein 1978; Donner 1981; see the essay by Michael Parenti, Chapter 12 in this volume).

The slant toward capitalism also reinforces a *minimal government* view with roots that go back to Jefferson and beyond. If the free market promotes productivity and efficiency and personal freedom, the argument goes, what need is there for government, beyond essentials like national defense, enforcement of contracts, and maintenance of a monetary system? Anything more tends to be viewed with suspicion as potentially wasteful and interfering.

This tendency is not all-pervading, of course; it coexists with an ambivalent but firmly rooted acceptance of the welfare state, and it seems to pass through cycles of ascendancy and descendancy—in which the 1970s and early 1980s saw the most recent revolt against government. Year in and year out, however, Americans, compared to citizens in other countries, are exposed to a remarkable barrage of misinformation about government waste and inefficiency. Those who have the most to lose from taxes and redistribution—especially wealthy individuals and corporations—have abundant resources to subsidize and publicize research, affect school curricula, place advertisements, and otherwise influence the media and politicians and other communicators to promote the minimal government line (Miliband 1969; Ferguson and Rogers 1986; Blumenthal 1986).

A pattern of biased information that partly, but only partly, counteracts the minimal government slant is a *pro-incumbent* and *pro-status quo* bias. True (as many candidates for office have discovered), scandals and exposés make good press. If a prominent congressman is caught frolicking drunk in a Washington pond or is arrested snorting cocaine, he is likely to make the news, and more serious derelictions are sometimes pursued as well. But over the long haul, incumbent officials and the order they represent tend to be treated well. Officials are the prime sources of news and can control much of what is made public.

Reporters have to cultivate friendly ties with officials. Moreover, the corporations that own most major communications media depend upon the government for TV licenses and for help with labor relations and taxes and the like; it would not be wise for them to seem too hostile. The result is a flow of information that tends to reflect official points of view, to emphasize the merits and accomplishments of incumbent officials, and to neglect the opposition.

A strong *partisan* bias results from the deference paid to incumbents. The party that holds power in Washington (especially the party of the president) can shape much of the debate over public policy, both directly through officials' speeches and remarks and testimony, and indirectly through the reporters and commentators who gain access and share the administration's views. Research money, too, tends to flow to the visible and "effective" scholars and think tanks that generally agree with the administration, so that eventually the tide of expert opinion seems to support the line of those with power.

This partisan bias means that at different times the public is exposed to quite different views of the political world, even when underlying realities remain much the same. Information conveyed about the nature and causes of poverty in America, for example, seemed to differ radically between the Johnson and Reagan (or even Nixon) administrations (see Aaron 1978), as epitomized by the relative prominence of the Institute for Research on Poverty and the Hoover Institution. Given the somewhat different positions of Republicans and Democrats on the desirable scope of government activity, alternations of the parties in power have contributed to cycles, or at least ebbs and flows, in the informational bias toward minimal government.

Our account of information biases should be considered suggestive rather than conclusive. Taken together, however, the evidence of media influence upon public opinion and the indications of patterns of biased and misleading information conveyed through the media have troubling implications for the working of democracy.

We see the public as substantially capable of rational calculations about the merits and deficiencies of alternative public policies, based on the information made available to it. To the extent that the available information is false, misleading, or biased, however, the public may be led astray, so that the outcome of public influence on policy should not really be characterized as democratic. To this extent, the true underlying influences upon policymaking are not the wishes (or the needs and values) of the public, but those of the individuals and groups that provide misleading information. Insofar as misinformation is widespread and systematic, neither populistic democracy nor what Bessette (1980) calls "deliberative democracy" works properly.

CONCLUSION

Our research suggests a mixture of relationships between public opinion and policymaking in the United States. Three distinct processes occur: (1) democratic responsiveness to public opinion; (2) an ignoring or thwarting of the public's views; and (3) manipulation of public opinion so that it is congruent with policies that are pursued for other reasons.

Policy sometimes responds to genuine public preferences—preferences that arise from objective needs and circumstances or are informed and educated about political realities. Our exploration of events and historical contexts indicates that such factors as rising levels of income and education, changes in workforce participation, alterations in the global balance of power and the like underlie many changes in public opinion. Collective public education about policy also occurs, through such mechanisms as research studies, congressional hearings, speeches, and publications.

At the same time we must not forget that congruence between public opinion and policy is not complete. By our estimate (Page and Shapiro 1983), policy actually moves in the opposite direction from opinion about one-third of the time. Sometimes government simply ignores or "marginalizes" the views of the public (see Lance Bennett's essay, Chapter 15 in this volume).

In this paper we have been particularly concerned with the third process named, in which policy may be congruent with public opinion but

that opinion is itself misled or manipulated through false or biased information. We have noted many cases in which political leaders or organized
interests or others have provided misleading information. We have also
suggested that some pervasive patterns of information bias seem to exist
(nationalistic, anticommunist, procapitalist, minimal government, pro-
incumbent, and partisan). These biases are brought about by such factors
as market forces, government control of information, the resources of
corporations and organized interests, the capitalist economy, and the nation-state system. At the same time, opinion manipulation has its limits;
the public can be remarkably resistant to persuasion, at least in the short
run.

　　If we want to know how well democracy works in America it is important to assess more fully how often each of these processes occurs,
and under what circumstances: to what extent policy responds to genuine
public opinion, to what extent opinion is ignored, and to what extent it is
misled or manipulated.

CHAPTER 15

Marginalizing the Majority: Conditioning Public Opinion to Accept Managerial Democracy[1]

W. Lance Bennett

INTRODUCTORY NOTE

To what extent do government elites, intellectuals, or the mass media anticipate shifts in public policy and "prepare" or "manage" public opinion in advance of those shifts? While it is clear that some portion of American public opinion is translated into government policy, it is equally clear that some other opinion-policy linkages are managed. Given the popular perception among elites that mass opinion is uninformed and unstable, it is hard to imagine that policymakers acquire a standing disposition to follow grass-roots sentiment.

Lance Bennett's chapter outlines a theory of public opinion in a managerial democracy. He points out that in many instances where active public support for policy is hard to obtain, the needs of policy managers for stable climates of public tolerance can be satisfied equally well by public acceptance, or "quiescence" in Edelman's words (1964). He argues that passive popular acceptance of unrepresentative policies is most likely to occur when people use voices in the news rather than public opinion polls to evaluate the legitimacy of their own opinions. On most policy questions, polls are seldom given the same weight as the voices of experts, officials, and decision makers, and it is only on certain amorphous concerns such as presidential approval and candidate popularity that people hear their opinions expressed forcefully as a regular, legiti-

---

[1]The author would like to thank Cheryl Mehaffey for heroic assistance in manuscript preparation. Steve De Tray gathered most of the data and served as one of the coders. Peter May provided helpful suggestions for displaying the data.

mate voice. Bennett calls this the "marginalization" of public opinion.

Three basic assumptions underlie Bennett's marginalization thesis: *popular inferiority,* a prevailing distrust of the quality and legitimacy of popular opinion; *institutional superiority,* institutional voices (e.g., political parties and organized lobby groups) are presumed to speak for the public; and *media passivity,* the media ignores discrepancies between institutionally voiced opinion and indicators of mass opinion such as opinion polls.

Bennett analyzes the struggle between the White House and Congress over funding the Nicaraguan "Contras" from 1983 to 1986 to test his hypotheses about marginalization. His chapter demonstrates how the Reagan administration's marginalization of public opposition to military support for the Contras succeeded not only because of adroit manipulation of mass media but also because of the media's own assumptions about "popular inferiority" and "institutional superiority." He shows how the media fell silent when institutional voices ceased to disagree in public in the final stages of the congressional battle over support for the Contras. This case study illustrates the process through which a "public opinion" can be constructed by an institutional voice with little or no reference to popular opinion as measured by polls. Bennett argues that his case epitomizes a set of general conditions under which stable, longstanding popular majorities can be ignored in the policy process with little immediate risk.

The Editors

It is clear that some portion of American public opinion is translated into government policy. The potential for electoral reprisal (Fiorina 1981) undoubtedly creates some opinion representation in salient issues. Reliable estimates suggest that shifts in national policy follow significant shifts in public opinion around two-thirds of the time (Monroe 1979; Page and Shapiro 1983). The Page and Shapiro findings (1983: 182) even extend to foreign policy issues, which are often regarded as dark areas of public ignorance and apathy and, consequently, as areas of greater elite policy discretion. Impressive as these relationships seem, they do not answer (as the authors, themselves, acknowledge) key questions for democratic theory, such as: to what extent do government elites, intellectuals, or the mass media anticipate forthcoming state policy shifts and "prepare" public opinion in advance of those shifts?

It would be naive to think that some opinion-policy linkages are not prepared or otherwise "managed" by elites in anticipation of future policy requirements. Given the popular perception among elites and academics that mass opinion is uninformed and unstable, it is hard to imagine that policymakers acquire a standing disposition to follow the grass roots. This is not to deny the potential for effective grass-roots opinion formation of the sort evident in the civil rights movement of the 1950s, the antiwar movement of the 1960s, the environmental movement of the 1970s, and the nuclear freeze movement of the 1980s. We can also expect effective grass-roots sentiment to arise from "pocketbook" economic issues such as inflation, and in response to moral concerns such as prayer in schools. However, it would be dangerous to overestimate the routine policy impact of grass-roots formations in a mass society presided over by increasingly concentrated, imitative and system-supportive media that devote disproportionate coverage to a nation with clearly defined interests and impressive "public information" capabilities.

Evidence, both anecdotal and systematic, suggests that various opinion-management strategies operate in the process of defining and pursuing the interests of the modern democratic state—a state managed by professional political elites who seek to minimize electoral and social disruption from below. Works that presage the ideas of opinion management and managerial democracy include: Lippmann (1965), Schattschneider (1960), Ellul (1965), Edelman (1964), Gamson (1968), and Lipsky and Olson (1977), among others. The memoirs of presidents, diplomats, and prominent civil servants suggest that the managerial attitude has become something of a conscious elite ethos in the years since World War II during which the United States' world power reached its zenith (see, among others, Acheson 1969; Barnet 1972; Kearns 1976; Kennan 1969; and Stockman 1986).

ELEMENTS OF A THEORY OF PUBLIC OPINION IN MANAGERIAL DEMOCRACY

Managerial democracy may have become a self-conscious political philosophy in the golden age of American empire following World War II, but its roots run deep in the American political culture. Among the cultural themes underwriting opinion management is the enduring concern expressed originally by Madison in *Federalist,* no. 10, and elsewhere, that public opinion is ill-considered, unstable, tyrannical, and therefore, dangerous to liberal democracy. These themes of the irresponsible public, supplemented in recent times by concerns about apathy, continue to rationalize elite governance to the present day (e.g., Dye and Zeigler 1975).

The belief in public ignorance, apathy, and irresponsibility gives elites cultural license to "prepare" opinion at least some of the time on grounds that disorganized mass opinion must be "led" from above. Equally important, elite disregard for mass opinion on issues of low salience can be justified on grounds that popular opinion, no matter what its direction, generally lacks the information, intensity, and coherent social organization to serve as a policy guide. Whether elites propagandize popular opinion or ignore it, they reinforce the underlying ignorance, apathy, and disarray that justify departure from traditional "representative" democracy in the first place. We have here the sort of vicious cycle that is characteristic of a cultural system in operation (i.e., social processes creating the material conditions that sustain the beliefs that drive the social processes, etc.). Dynamics of change in this cultural system include things like secrecy laws that further diminish public information and accountability, and new communication technologies that could be used either for enriching or impoverishing the quality of public debate.

Another important aspect of the political culture that informs our developing theory of opinion management is the problem of the isolated, vulnerable individual described initially by Tocqueville (1948) and elaborated more recently by Noelle-Neumann (1984). In this view, vulnerability to social pressure is a by-product of a deep cultural strain between social equality and individualism—a strain found in liberal democracies in general and in the United States in the extreme. The absence of strong social group formation (e.g., class, region, subculture) leaves individuals unprotected from shifting climates of opinion. Vulnerable individuals are liable to go along with, or (equally important for our theory) to be silenced by opinion voiced by vocal minorities and elites with media access. As Noelle-Neumann suggests, "Those whose point of view is not represented by the media are effectively mute" (1984: 170). Hence, it is not the number of people holding an opinion that matters; it is the strength of social expression or "voice" (i.e., the communications signal) that makes opinion public.

In a political system in which public voices are filtered both through institutions and the mass media, the mass public becomes dependent on at least these two powerful "gatekeepers" for gaining any public voice on most issues. Moreover, in a double-gated system of the sort described here, it is easy to imagine that institutional elites will be granted the right to speak for the public much of the time. It is, after all, defensible culturally (if not empirically) for institutional and media gatekeepers to assume that elites in the system somehow represent public interest and popular reason.

The cultural themes outlined above enable our emerging theory of opinion management to go beyond simple, Orwellian visions of conspiratorial elites manipulating a hapless people. There are, of course, occasions when the manipulation model makes sense, as in the case of political campaigns where the goal is to shift the perceptions of some segment of the voting public in line with a particular ballot proposition or candidate choice (Mauser 1983). However, beyond elections and the few sustained public information campaigns that can be run at any given time on "big" agenda items (e.g., war, economic austerity, public health and safety, patriotic mobilization), the assumption that opinion management usually equals opinion manipulation begins to break down. Not only is public attention hard to get and even harder to keep (Downs 1972), but opinions are hard to change, and there are simply too many issues to contemplate manipulating opinion on them all. In many instances where active public support for policy is hard to obtain, the needs of policy managers for stable climates of public tolerance can be satisfied equally well by passive public acceptance or "quiescence," as Edelman (1964) calls it.

Passive popular acceptance of unrepresentative policies is most likely to occur when people use voices in the news rather than opinion polls to evaluate the legitimacy of their own opinions. People are more likely to use public voices rather than opinion polls as means of interpreting their own opinions if for no other reason than the fact that polls are reported sporadically, if at all, on most policy questions. Even when reported, polls are seldom given the same weight as the voices of officials, experts, leaders and decision makers. Only on amorphous concerns such as presidential approval and candidate popularity do people hear their opinions voiced forcefully and regularly in the context of a general public opinion (usually expressed in poll data) that can be heard as a loud, persistent and legitimate voice.

The failure to report, much less take issue with, discrepancies between popular opinion and policy outcomes reflects a passive stance on the part of the mass media. This passivity does not require active collusion between the media and some power elite. Like the above elements of "inferior popular voice" and "superior institutional voice," media passivity is also a cultural phenomenon. The mass media receive considerable pressure from above, below, and within to be passive transmitters of events rather than active critics of the political system and its policies. Perhaps the most dramatic change in the American political culture in the past 200 years has been the transformation of a competitive, local, and ideologically critical press into a national, standardized mass media constrained by cultural expectations of fairness and ideological neutrality (see Tuchman 1978; and Bennett 1988: chap. 4, for discussions of the evolution and consequences of media neutrality). These expectations of neutrality make it difficult for the media to take critical stands in the absence of strong supporting voices from within political institutions. The cultural assumptions of popular inferiority and institutional superiority that make marginalization possible would be hard to sustain without a passive media loathe to publicize and criticize discrepancies between public policy and popular opinion in the polls.

The important theoretical implication of this discussion is that if institutional and media gatekeepers ignore or "silence" popular opinion some substantial portion of the time, there may be, as a result, a long-term conditioning effect—leading people not to expect their personal opinions to count much of the time. In this view, marginalization of opinion may be as important a factor as manipulation in a general theory of public opinion. To the extent that marginalization and manipulation enter the political picture, the policy process becomes, to that degree, less a bottom–up representation process and more a top–down management operation. Opinion becomes more a dependent than an independent variable in the political equation (Margolis 1985).

SPECIFYING THE ASSUMPTIONS OF THE THEORY

The existing theoretical mix of grass roots and manipulation hypotheses must be enriched by a better grasp of the marginalization process if we are to understand how the American variant of liberal democracy works. It is important to know, for example, the circumstances under which the public can be ignored without risk to specific policies or general state legitimacy. Also, in light of the difficulties of engineering genuine attitude change in large numbers of people, it is reasonable to suspect that much of the propaganda that initially seems manipulative in nature might be understood better in the context of marginalization. That is, vigorous propaganda campaigns may fail to create popular support for pending policies, yet succeed in drowning out opposition voices—including the voices of majorities who may forfeit viable claims to representation on grounds of intimidation, frustration, or sheer misperception of opinion distributions in society.

The general proposition here is that marginalization and manipulation work together, along with grass-roots formations, to constitute the dynamics of elections and policymaking in the American democracy. The ultimate question is what is the "mix" of these three opinion processes across different issue areas and at different points in history? A related question is whether or not the mix is changing in any enduring way, and if so, what is the emerging pattern? These are empirical questions. Before they can be answered, it is necessary to show that the basic cultural assumptions about the inferiority of "popular voice," the superiority of "institutional voice," and the desirability of a passive media are all reasonable ones that can be observed to operate in the world. I propose to devote the rest of this discussion to evaluating the "marginalization thesis" since it is already fairly well established that both grass-roots opinion and elite manipulation operate in the system to some degree.

The Marginalization Thesis

The marginalization thesis can be boiled down to three basic assumptions:

First, there is a prevailing cultural distrust of the quality and overall legitimacy of popular opinion (i.e., socially and institutionally unmediated mass opinion). This cultural bias results in a standing disposition on the part of "gatekeepers" (including public officials and media representatives) against granting sheer numerical majorities automatic, sustained voice in policy debates. Public opinion is coterminous with opinion polls only in special cases such as elections and presidential popularity. Call this the *popular inferiority assumption*.

Second, representatives of public institutions, parties, and organized lobby groups are presumed, again by gatekeepers, to speak for "the people." Institutional voices thus become the standing voices of public opinion for most issues. Call this the *institutional superiority assumption*.

Third, in order for marginalization to occur, gatekeepers for the popular voice (particularly representatives of the mass media) must passively ignore discrepancies between institutionally voiced opinion and indicators of mass opinion such as opinion polls. In short, popular opinion is marginalized when popular voice is not amplified to the levels of discrepant institutional voice. Call this the *passive media assumption*.

A conditioning process leading to passive popular acceptance of nonrepresentation would result if these three conditions converged frequently in the policy process. That is, conditioning would occur if discrepancies between institutional and popular voice frequently are not amplified by the media or by dissenting institutional elites via the media, on culturally accepted grounds that there is no automatic justification for direct popular representation. This sort of cultural conditioning environment could give elites considerable discretion over important areas of policy. The absence of popular and media scrutiny of (some range of) elite decisions might invite policymakers to relax their search for the broadest possible (i.e., the most "responsible") expression of public interest. The resulting dynamic for change would be a cultural conditioning environment in which popular opinion becomes more ignorant and passively tolerant of issues beyond street-level morality and pocketbook economics, while elites become more autonomous and therefore less responsible. The worst empirical case would be a system, still labeled "free" and "democratic," drifting toward increasing levels of concentrated power and institutional autonomy—at odds with practical assumptions of pluralistic democracy. The full empirical assessment of the opinion theory appropriate to the American case is beyond the scope of this introductory discussion. However, we can assess empirically the reasonableness of the three assumptions on which the conditioning model and, more immediately, the marginalization thesis rests. The following discussion formulates testable hypotheses for each of the three assumptions underlying the marginalization thesis.

The *popular inferiority assumption* may at first glance seem at odds with the proliferation of polling and opinion polls in everyday political life. Although expressions of popular voice may seem to be everywhere present, a closer inspection suggests that polls play a considerably more restricted role in the policy arena than in other areas of public, mass-mediated life.

True, in matters of lifestyle and taste, the media keep the public in touch with its own pulse. In the electoral arena and on matters of presidential popularity the voice of the people is raised loud and often. From these expressions of popular sentiment one might receive the diffuse impression that popular democracy is alive and well. However, this impression of democracy is burdened by the nagging suspicion that when it comes to many areas of serious state policy considerations, the polls, while equally available, are barely whispered around the edges of the policy process, and are seldom drawn on centrally by the media in coverage of emerging policies.

Face validity for the above suspicion is gained by looking at critical cases where areas traditionally open to popular voice become transformed into serious matters for state decision. For example, when Richard Nixon's presidential popularity became entangled with momentous questions of impeachment during the Watergate crisis, the media gates began to close on expressions of popular voice in the evolving coverage of Watergate-related issues and decision outcomes. Gladys and Kurt Lang note that, although Watergate was one of the fiercest battles for public opinion in modern times (from the standpoint of a White House propaganda campaign), only 10 of 38 available Gallup press releases on Nixon's popularity made it into at least one TV evening newscast during the critical period from September 2, 1973 to July 18, 1974 (Lang and Lang 1983: 131). Even more impressive is the observation that the polls received less than one percent of Watergate news time on the networks (Lang and Lang 1983: 131).

What do we make of such puzzling findings, particularly in an area such as presidential popularity where we might expect the media gates to swing wide open to expressions of popular voice in times of misconduct and error? In one of the most ironically revealing moments of the Watergate episode, Richard Nixon offered a self-serving account of the standing cultural bias against granting legitimacy to popular voice on important political matters. In a public address on March 15, 1974, the embattled president asked a fateful question and provided the standard, culturally salient answer:

Why doesn't the President resign because his popularity is low? . . . Because if the time comes in this country when a President makes decisions based on where he stands in the polls rather than what is right or wrong, we have a very weak President. . . . Resignation simply because he happened to be low in the polls would forever change our form of government (quoted in Lang and Lang 1983: 95).

Madison could not have put it better: if institutions yield directly to popular opinion on important matters, it would "forever change our form of government." But why, we must ask, did Nixon continue to wage his vigorous propaganda campaign in the Watergate "battle for public opinion"? Not only did he show every sign of truly believing his claim that institutional managers are not obliged by the American form of government to follow public opinion, but from a purely practical standpoint, his manipulations had failed: the Nixon message was not "playing in Peoria." As he noted in his diary, "it seems almost impossible to break through in the polls" (Lang and Lang 1983: 95). Perhaps Nixon persisted in the battle for opinion for reasons having more to do with marginalizing the hostile majority than manipulating it. The voice from the White House added considerable noise to a context in which the popular voice threatened to emerge clearly against Nixon. Moreover, the drone of self-serving claims and threats of a constitutional crisis from the White House might have dampened the chance that Congress, searching for guidance from anywhere, would find irresistible support for impeachment from the polls.

The task before us is to assess the empirical reasonableness of the *popular inferiority assumption*. En route to a testable hypothesis, this assumption might be restated as follows: for some substantial range of policy issues over time, the polls will not be given the same weight as other voices (e.g., institutional officials) in the policy process. Formulated as a null hypothesis, the proposition goes like this: popular voices (*PV*) as expressed, for example, in the polls will be given the same weight as institutional voices (*IV*) in policy deliberations:

$$H_0: PV = IV$$

A number of measures can be generated to test this null hypothesis. For example, we could determine whether or not members of institutions (most likely the losers of policy battles) routinely speak to the misrepresentation of popular majorities in cases where policies are at odds with majority opinion. Another useful test would be to determine if the news regularly reports emerging (elite) opinion formations in institutions alongside opinion polls on the issues involved. A third test of the hypothesis is whether or not news stories take note of, or editorials regularly object to, discrepancies between popular opinion and institutional opinion expressed in policies. The last test could be simplified by determining the degree to which policy outcomes are reported regularly in the news along with opinion polls.

In a political culture biased toward popular representation in the policy process, we would expect to accept the null hypothesis by finding that some or all of these linkages between popular voice and institutional voice do, in fact, exist. The prediction in the case of the United States is that the null hypothesis will be rejected in some policy areas, particularly those pertaining to fiscal policy and state security. In these policy areas, mentions of polls in news accounts should not come close to equaling even the most conservative measures of institutional voice.

The belief in popular inferiority that buffers institutional elites from popular voice constitutes a cultural context in which marginalization can occur relatively often. In the context of good cultural reasons, being conditioned to be ignored may be accompanied by various coping strategies on the part of individuals, ranging from frustration, anger, and helplessness among the unacculturated, to meaningful self-denial on the part of the loyal and well acculturated "silent majority."

The *institutional superiority assumption* claims that the voice of the people is, for the most part, spoken adequately by institutional elites. There is considerable anecdotal evidence to provide face validity for the institutional superiority assumption. For example, media coverage of El Salvador dropped off noticeably following the election of Jose Napoleon Duarte in 1984. The White House declared the election a major victory for democracy, and the media played up the democratic victory angle. Congress, too, found the electoral developments salutary and approved massive aid packages with relatively little debate. Despite the premature consensus that a happy ending was in store for the Salvador story, conditions in the war-torn country continued to deteriorate: the war escalated, the civilian population came increasingly under attack, land reform once again stalled out, human rights violations continued, the economy all but collapsed, and Duarte lost support from virtually all political factions on the scene save the U.S. Congress and the White House. These and other indicators pointed to a "big story," yet none emerged.

A panel of media critics and journalism school faculty put El Salvador at the top of the list of the "Ten best-censored stories of 1985" (Jensen 1986). Why the media self-censorship? I had the opportunity to ask this question of NBC anchor Tom Brokaw who had personally covered the 1982 constituent assembly elections and had issued several critical reports on the political scene in El Salvador prior to 1984. Brokaw seemed frustrated and a bit wounded by the question of what happened to his coverage after 1984. He finally dismissed the question with one of his own: "What do you expect us to do? Congress is *supposed* to represent the people, and where there is no opposition in Congress, there isn't much that we can report" (Brokaw 1986).

If key gatekeepers in the political culture, such as the media, implicitly filter political reality through the lenses provided by institutional policymakers, important (and unintended) consequences may follow for opinion and representation. For example, if factions within institutions approach consensus (however ill-conceived) on an issue, the cornerstone of public opinion is set, and the media lack culturally safe grounds to go on reporting a big story. Put differently, only when some substantial bloc of institutional actors provide a major part of the script can the media safely develop a big political story (compare: Vietnam, Watergate, the Iran-Contra affair). El Salvador was a telling case of this institutional superiority principle. When voices were raised in Congress between 1981 and 1984 in opposition to U.S. policy, the media ran extensive coverage on all aspects of the political scene in El Salvador: land reform, death squads, state corruption, military unpreparedness, the weakness of political institutions, and so on. Yet, when Congress fell relatively silent and overwhelmingly supported administration policy, coverage of the issue fell off precipitously.

The safe assumption for political gatekeepers to make is that the distribution of voices in institutions *is* public opinion for most practical, that is, policy-related, purposes. A simple test of this proposition is to see if opinion on policy questions in the news emanates disproportionately from institutional voices. This goes beyond the popular inferiority prediction that just addresses the polls. The institutional superiority proposition is that the sum of institutionally voiced opinion (IV) will be greater than the sum of *all* other opinion voices (OV) such as the polls, lobby groups, recognized authorities, academic experts, and community leaders. The null hypothesis here is:

$$H_0: IV = OV$$

We would expect to reject this null hypothesis for a substantial number of policy issues if marginalization is an important element of the opinion process.

An important counter intuitive test of the institutional superiority assumption would involve looking at the patterns of editorial and "op-ed" opinions expressed in the nation's prestige newspapers such as the *New York Times,* the *Washington Post, The Wall Street Journal,* and, perhaps, a few others. What does newspaper editorial policy have to do with variance in institutionally voiced opinion? Ordinarily, we would think that there is no connection, since papers are expected to establish an editorial position and hold the line on it as a means of influencing institutional elites looking for some responsible expression of community sentiment. This model of editorial independence may hold for some issues and for some local newspapers. However, the few national prestige papers are operating in a different league, with a different agenda. The prestige papers are "responsible" to at least three audiences beyond the day-to-day reading public. First, the prestige papers are read by other editors and correspondents in the print and broadcast mass media (Gans 1979: 91,

126). The responsibility for giving cues to the rest of the media about what to cover and how to weight it may affect the editorial policy of the prestige papers. Second, these papers are read by the institutional elite every morning. Members of Congress, the executive branch and the judiciary receive their overall impressions of political issues and events from the prestige papers. This special readership also may temper editorial policies. Third, the prestige papers, especially the *New York Times*, have an historical audience to keep in mind. The *Times* is overwhelmingly the paper of record for scholars and future generations to use in studying past history (Chomsky 1986). These three audiences may make the prestige papers more attentive to national political currents and climates of opinion than to any "in-house" policy agenda or idiosyncratic ideological bent. In short, editors and publishers of the prestige papers may see their mission as keeping the political record of the times more than promoting particular policy agendas or ideological points of view.

The implication that the prestige papers may be documenting the historical record is important for our theory of opinion and democracy. For one thing, this view of the prestige press suggests that when its editorial policy swings to the left (or at least turns to criticism of state policies or regimes) as in cases like Vietnam and Watergate, we should understand this less as an expression of standing ideological bias in the media (e.g., Lichter, Rothman, and Lichter 1986) than as a standing disposition to register and, perhaps, amplify national ideological divisions, institutional struggles, and turning points in policy agendas. The key question for our theory is what do these record-keeping papers use as indicators of national pulse, ideological division, and public opinion? My guess is, they use the distribution of voices in institutions as their indicators of public opinion, and, only minimally, do they use measures of popular sentiment such as the opinion polls.

This leads to a bold, or at least counterintuitive, prediction: editorial policy, including expressions of editorial opinion, will be constrained by the range of voices within institutions, and only rarely by popular sentiment. This does not mean that majority views in institutions will dictate editorial content; this would be too simplistic a formulation. What it means is that strong institutional opposition to emerging or existing state policies can be expected to attract editorial attention. Editorial voice may give amplification to dissenting minorities and trend-setting majorities in institutions on "responsible" grounds that changing ideological divisions within institutions are historically significant and probably reflect even larger political divisions within the nation, and therefore, should be voiced and explored by a press responsible for keeping the historical record. The counterintuitive prediction, then, is that the prestige press, most notably the *New York Times*, will display patterns of editorial opinion that vary with the rise and fall of institutional opposition to existing state policies. There may be a tendency for these *Times* editorials to sound liberal, but the key question is whether this reflects a standing liberal bias or a commitment to amplify opposition institutional voices that just happen to be liberal more often than not on the issues in question.

If *Times* editorials only reflect a standing ideological bias, they should not vary with changes in institutional opinion formations (e.g., shifts in legislative outcomes in Congress). This null hypothesis is consistent with commonsense understandings that newspapers, particularly prestige newspapers, use their editorial voice systematically as a disciplining instrument vis-à-vis policy elites. A simple formulation of this null hypothesis is that measures of editorial voice on a specific policy issue at the time of a particular institutional opinion formation (EV_{t1}) should be equal in direction or intensity across subsequent time periods in which institutional opinion formations change in directions or intensity ($EV_{t2...tn}$):

$$H_0: EV_{t1} = EV_{t2...tn}$$

This hypothesis may well hold for lesser papers, but for the national paper of record on consequential state policy initiatives, I expect this hypothesis to be rejected. The predicted finding is that for some range of marginalizing issues (probably located in the macroeconomic and foreign policy domains), both the frequency and direction of editorial opinions will vary with the frequency and direction of institutional blocs voicing similar opinions about policy. Phrased as a continuous function, the prediction is that editorial voice is a function of institutional voice: $EV = f(IV)$.

The *passive media assumption* provides the acid test of the marginalization thesis. It could be argued up to this point that institutions tend to reach more enlightened consensus in the absence of popular pressure and that any tempering of editorial opinions on the part of the "paper of record" merely reflects sound editorial judgment that successive formations of institutional opinion are more reasonable and, hence, more supportable editorially. The response to this response is that the degree of institutional enlightenment on policies must be phrased as an empirical question. Surely not all institutional opinion formations are equally informed and enlightened, and surely not all marginalizing policy debates are automatically more reasonable due to the exclusion of popular sentiment.

A critical test of whether the American democratic system is "intelligent" in its inclusion or exclusion of popular opinion in the policy process would be to look at the response of gatekeepers—particularly the media—in cases where institutional opinion formations change due to factors that seem at odds with rational policymaking. For example, if the press knew that bad or incomplete information had been used by policymakers we would expect the sanctity of institutional voice to be suspended and the legitimacy of resulting policies to be challenged. We would also expect media challenges to be raised in cases where winning institutional majorities are forged through political intimidation (e.g., red-baiting) that silences institutional opponents of policies.

The critical test is to see what the prestige press does when institutional policy opposition declines due to known use of faulty information or political intimidation, and the resulting policies run counter to popular opinion. Do the prestige media under these circumstances drop their preference for institutional voice and criticize policies on grounds that they misrepresent the public interest? If there is no systematic cultural bias toward marginalizing popular opinion on key policy questions, we would expect the media to elevate some expression of public interest or popular voice (PV) to the level of institutional voices (IV) in the time intervals following (tf) the disappearance of strong institutional opposition and the simultaneous appearance of evidence that the policy process may have been corrupted by poor information or political intimidation:

$$H_o: PV_{tf} = IV_{tf}$$

This null hypothesis would be rejected if institutional voice continued to dominate popular voice in media coverage of policies that run counter to popular preference and that were reportedly contaminated by poor information or political intimidation intended to suppress institutional opponents. If we reject the null hypothesis in cases that satisfy the conditions of the critical test, then we have a very strong case for the existence of a standing cultural disposition toward marginalizing popular opinion.

If cultural pressures for a "neutral" media have become dominant, then the political system is left without a critical voice when institutional critics become silenced. When neither institutions nor the media speak with a popular voice, the people are faced with the difficult challenge of gaining access to the policy process when the two gates regulating the flow of voices in that process have been shut. If critical tests indicate that the emerging cultural assumption of media neutrality is adopted by the media even in extreme cases of institutional malfunction, then we will have diagnosed an important problem in the American democracy. Put simply, we are talking about a tendency for the political system to be geared almost entirely toward the prevention of one type of policymaking error while being dangerously vulnerable to another type of policymaking error. The type of error the system is predicted to guard against is the possible contamination of institutional rationality by the whims and ignorance of an incoherent popular majority. The error to which the system would be vulnerable, if the null hypotheses are rejected, is the potential risk that corruption in the institutional policy process will trigger no critical mechanism for bringing public accountability to bear as a corrective to bad policy (save the unwieldy, untimely, and often insensitive mechanism of retrospective voting). The remainder of the analysis is devoted to an empirical test of the hypotheses that bear on the validity of the marginalization thesis.

U.S. POLICY TOWARD NICARAGUA: A TEST CASE

The struggle between the White House and Congress over funding the "Contra" rebels fighting the Sandinista government in Nicaragua displayed all the elements necessary to test the above hypothesis. The policy struggle was a long one, with many voices and shifting institutional opinion formations. The issue was prominent on the national agenda for a full three years from 1983–86 before turning into a major crisis of state following discoveries that the White House had been running a secret foreign policy operation unbeknownst to Congress. Shortly before the crisis surfaced, the House of Representatives had been red-baited into supporting White House policy—a policy that for three years had been opposed by a large and stable majority in the polls. Chart 15–1 provides an overview of congressional policy activity for the period in question, broken into 17 periods of time, defined by: lack of policy activities; episodic policy activities (e.g., investigations, hearings, funding votes); and periods in which policy activities followed red-baiting and electoral intimidation from the White House. Note: The dates in this and other charts correspond to the day the event was reported in the *New York Times*, normally one day after the event occurred.

In the beginning, there was considerable factual confusion among poll respondents, as indicated by the infamous *New York Times/CBS*

CHART 15–1   Description of Major Congressional Policy Activities Bounding the Time Intervals Used in Nicaragua "Contra" Funding Study

Dates	Activity Level/Description of Activities
Jan. 1, 1983– Mar. 31	NO ACTIVITY (NA): No reported hearings, votes. • *New York Times* runs major series (Jan. 23–Jan. 25) explaining wars in region and Reagan administration policies.
Apr. 1–May 5	ACTIVITY (ACT): Hearings, committee votes. • Sen. Moynihan: Congress may restrict CIA in Nicaragua (Apr. 1). • Rep. Boland: Reagan Contra aid violated law (Apr. 14). • Pres. Reagan declares security of Americas at stake (Apr. 28). • House Select Intelligence Committee votes cut off CIA covert funds (May 4).

Chart 15–1   Congressional Activities (continued)

Dates	Activity Level/Description of Activities
May 6–Aug. 2	*ACT*: Hearings, committee votes, House vote. • Senate Intelligence Committee divided on aid (May 6). • House Foreign Affairs Committee votes to cut off covert aid (June 8). • House votes to cancel all secret aid to Contras (July 29). • News on vote continues through Aug. 2.
Aug. 3–Nov. 19	*ACT*: House, Senate funding votes. • U.S. Navy hails Soviet freighter off Nicaragua coast (Aug. 4). • Congress questions administration goals in Nicaragua (Aug. 6). • Reagan/Shultz press for aid to Contras (Oct. 20). • House votes for second time to cut off Contra aid (Oct. 21). • Senate approves aid to Contras (Nov. 4). • House, Senate approve $24 million covert aid (Nov. 19).
Nov. 20, 1983– Jan. 7, *1984*	*NA*: No reported votes, hearings. • Democratic presidential candidates speak against administration Nicaraguan policies.
Jan. 8–May 29	*ACT*: House, Senate: hearings, funding votes. • Kissinger Commission calls for aid program (Jan. 8). • Senate approves $21 million Contra aid (Apr. 6). • House votes against further funding for Contras (May 25).
May 30–Aug. 5	*ACT*: Senate, House votes. House intelligence budget. • Administration says CIA plans operations until October, hopes Congress will renew aid (May 30). • Reagan calls Nicaragua "totalitarian dungeon" (July 19). • House approves intelligence budget with no Contra aid (Aug. 3).
Aug. 6–Oct. 14	*ACT*: House/Senate hearings; funding votes. • Administration under congressional pressure talks with Sandinistas (Aug. 23). • House, Senate, White House break deadlock on $470 billion spending bill with no aid to Contras (Oct. 11).
Oct. 15, 1984– Jan. 4, *1985*	*ACT*: House, Senate: hearings, investigations. • Reports of CIA secret training manual for Contras (Oct. 15). • Hearings, investigations: manual illegal, Contra abuses against civilians (Dec. 27). Articles on abuses through Jan. 4.

Chart 15–1 Congressional Activities (continued)

Dates	Activity Level/Description of Activities
Jan. 5–Feb. 24	*NA*: No reported votes or hearings.
Feb. 25–Apr. 29	*ACT*: House, Senate: funding votes. • Administration opens campaign for new aid (Feb. 25). • House rejects aid request (Apr. 24). • Senate adopts aid request (Apr. 24). • Congress in all-night sessions, no compromise; House vote cuts off aid (Apr. 28).
Apr. 30–July 26	*ACT*: House, Senate funding votes. • Reagan announces embargo against Nicaragua (May 1). • Nicaraguan President Ortega visits Soviet Union (May 5, 7). • House, Senate conference votes non-military aid for Contras (July 26).
July 27–Nov. 4	*NA*: No reported hearings, votes. National Security Council (NSC) Contra aid reported (Aug. 8).
Nov. 5, 1985– Apr. 15, *1986*	*ACT*: Committee hearings, House vote. • Administration asserts heavy Soviet arms buildups (Nov. 5). • House rejects military aid request (Mar. 21). • Red-baiting reports against vulnerable House members (Apr. 15).
Apr. 16–June 30	*ACT*: New House voting after red-baiting (ARB). • *NYT* editorial: "No case for war against Nicaragua" (Apr. 16). • Reagan renews aid drive—escalates rhetoric (June 7–25). • House votes for Reagan military-aid request (June 26).
July 1–Aug. 17	*ACT*: Senate funding vote after red-baiting (ARB). • *NYT* editorial: "Stalinism in Nicaragua" (July 7). • Senate approves military aid (Aug. 14).
Aug. 18–Oct. 15	*NA*: No reported votes, hearings. • Reagan plans to send U.S. advisers to train Contras (Aug. 21). • Reagan trial balloon: withdraw recognition of Nicaragua, grant recognition to Contras (Oct. 5). • Cargo plane shot down in Nicaragua (Oct. 7)—links to CIA (Oct. 14). • First report by Senate staff that Oliver North, NSC, set up private network to aid Contras (Oct. 15).
Oct. 16. 1986– Summer *1987*	Iran–Contra arms scandal emerges.

News poll showing that only 13 percent knew that the United States was supporting the rebels in Nicaragua, and only 8 percent knew what side the United States was supporting in both El Salvador and Nicaragua (see Clymer 1983). Although the ranks of the "knowledgeable" in these terms had risen to only 38 percent by 1986 (see Shipler 1986), it appeared that the unwavering majority based its opposition all along on other, more basic facts and values. From the beginning, the majority of respondents knew two things: first, the United States was pursuing a military course of action against Nicaragua and elsewhere in Central America, and second, this military policy entailed intervention into the affairs of sovereign nations. In dozens of polls taken over the period, stable opposition to policy was based on concerns that a military course of action would result in "another Vietnam" and that military intervention in the affairs of small sovereign states would "turn much of Latin America against us." (Compare, for example, responses in the *Harris Survey* on: El Salvador, March 13–16, 1981; Nicaragua, March 18, 1985; and Nicaragua, April 14, 1986).

Response patterns were virtually identical on questions of military intervention whether the polls asked about Nicaragua, El Salvador, or Central America in general. This generalized response led both Harris and Gallup to conclude that the issue of concern to the public was the general fact of military intervention—an issue that transcended details of what local factions the United States supported in its various intervention strategies. The standing concerns about "another Vietnam" and loss of U.S. respect in the hemisphere thus seemed to constitute reasonable, coherent, and stable grounds for interpreting opinion—the kind of opinion structure that would have to exist if policymakers could be expected to interpret and incorporate popular voice into their deliberations.

Another characteristic that gave popular opinion some qualification for inclusion in the policy process was the increasing importance attributed in the polls to the problem of military intervention in Central America in general, and Nicaragua in particular. After two years of public debate, military intervention in Central America rose from third place on the list of foreign policy concerns, behind Soviet downing of a civilian airliner and U.S. involvement in Lebanon (see Shribman 1983), to third place on the list of most important issues, behind the U.S. budget deficit and arms control with the Soviet Union, and ahead of foreign trade problems and tax reform (Clymer 1985). Both in terms of coherence and salience, popular voice on Nicaragua *could* have been given a prominent place in the policy process. The first empirical question that the Nicaragua case raises sharply is what place *was* given to popular voice in relation to institutional voices in the overall press and institutional records?

Also relevant to our criteria for a test case is the fact the Reagan administration waged an intense public opinion campaign on behalf of its Nicaragua policies. The campaign was aimed first at manipulating opinion, or, as Reagan put it, "educating" the public about the real situation. From early on, Reagan attributed popular confusion and opposition to "careless reporting" and "a concerted propaganda campaign" waged against his policies (Weisman 1983). After two years of intense rhetoric, the manipulation strategy had not made a dent in popular opposition to his policies, while making only a 10-point gain in the small minority supporting those policies. As a result of the failure of manipulation to erode the opposition or create a notable support base, the administration shifted to a marginalization strategy.

Washington Post political analyst Lou Cannon noted the new strategy in his column on June 10, 1985, with the observation that: "White House spokesmen gush with reports from pollster Richard B. Wirthlin showing favorable public sentiment for the [tax reform] proposal. . . . But the White House does not rush forward with public opinion polls on [Nicaragua] . . . because it does not want to advertise widespread public opposition to the Reagan policy in Nicaragua" (Cannon 1985: A2). Cannon noted that the administration had conceded failure in its two-year effort to manipulate opinion—a concession suggesting that opinion manipulation strategies have their limits even when a popular president proclaims the objects of his policy (i.e., the Contras) to be "the moral equivalent of the Founding Fathers." Rather than bend to popular will, Reagan and his allies in the administration chose, instead, to shift to a marginalization strategy and simply ignore popular opinion.

Cannon also noted that at this key moment in the policy process, Reagan and allies like CIA Director William Casey chose to ignore in-house (CIA) intelligence reports that undermined Reagan's fears of communist subversion on the American mainland (Cannon 1985: A2). This case of marginalization thus includes the possibility that unpopular policy was based on bad information. Also qualifying this as a critical test case is the fact that the administration pursued its unpopular policies through political intimidation of the institutional opposition. A key element of the marginalization campaign that replaced the manipulation campaign was rhetoric based on ever more grandiose images of communist menace to the hemisphere. These images were increasingly aimed at silencing opposition in Congress through a red-baiting campaign aimed at vulnerable House members during the 1986 elections—a campaign to be analyzed shortly.

Throughout the entire three-year propaganda barrage, the administration got its message across often: of the 604 story-dominating opinions voiced by institutional actors in the news, the administration, alone, voiced more than half (316) of them in defense of its policies. An overwhelming 406 out of 604 total policy opinions emanating from institutions were voiced in support of administration Nicaragua policy. Yet until the red-baiting campaign effectively silenced congressional opposition and produced a major administration victory on a $100 million Contra-aid package in 1986, there was a vocal institutional opposition (primarily in Congress), and the administration suffered a number of defeats on key policy votes. The empirical question here is the extent to which *New York Times* editorials and op-ed pieces keyed on this congressional opposition in the process of charting the historical record. Even more critical empirically is what happened to *Times* editorials after Congress fell silent, and finally supported the Contra policy after having been intimidated. How did the *Times* respond to this disingenuous shift in institutional voice that put Congress in clear opposition to popular opinion? Did *Times* editorial opposition continue, or did it fall silent along with the institutional opposition voice of record? Moreover, at the point of this dubious policy reversal in opposition to popular opinion, did any amplification of popular voice appear in the news, or was popular voice ignored when institutional opposition was silenced? The Nicaragua case provided critical tests of all the key hypotheses underlying the marginalization thesis—tests that were constructed through the following research design.

Research Design

The basis hypotheses about marginalization involve predictions about the ratios of different voices at different time periods in news reporting on Nicaragua. Both the voices and the time periods for comparisons were constructed from news text abstracts in the *New York Times Index* and from the complete texts of *Times* coverage stored in the *Lexis/Nexis* data archive.

The *Times Index* proved a reliable source from which to code institutional voices and organized interest group opinions. Not only does the *Index* provide fairly detailed abstracts of the actual news stories, but the abstracts are keyed to the very concern of this study: who said what about the policy that drives the ongoing news story. Not only is the mass media in general keyed to personalities in the news (Paletz and Entman 1981; Bennett 1988: chap. 2), but the *Times* is the paper of record for institutional policy deliberations and the actors who weigh into those decisions. Cross checks between the *Index* and *Nexis* text data showed that the only voice, ironically, to be omitted regularly from the *Index* abstracts was popular voice expressed in the polls (another general face validation measure for the assumption of cultural bias against popular voice). A systematic *Nexis* search was conducted for all references to opinion polls in *Times* coverage of Nicaragua.

The Sample.   The sample consisted of all indexed stories about Nicaragua, and for supplementary analyses, all stories in which polls on Nicaragua or Central America military policies were mentioned. Between

January 1, 1983 (when Congress began to challenge the legality of covert CIA funding of Contra activities), and October 15, 1986 (when Reagan had secured his major overt funding victory and, ironically, the Iran-Contra scandal began to unravel), there were 2,148 articles and editorials written on all aspects of the Nicaraguan situation from policy debates in Washington, to war stories from the Honduran border, to reports on conditions inside Nicaragua. Out of these 2,148 stories in the *Times Index,* there were 1,177 voiced opinions on the Contra policy. There were 184 articles containing more than one voice, and 1,155 articles were non-opinionated descriptions of the war, the players, and background information. There were a total of 288 editorials and op-ed pieces included within the 2,148 articles.

Coding the Opinion Voices.   Two coders were assigned the tasks of independently reading the story abstracts in the *Index* and making three simple judgments:

1. Whether or not an opinion was voiced on the Contra policy.
2. If an opinion was voiced, who voiced it.
3. What the direction of the opinion was.

The first task was a simple, mechanical one, with correct decisions being made by both coders in 98 percent of the cases, resulting in an allocation of 1,155 articles into the category nonopinionated, or "descriptive." Most of the coder disagreement in the 23 discrepant cases was due to simple clerical error. In a few cases, disagreement centered on whether to count as "opinion" passing references to political debates at home in long articles describing events in the field.

The second task entailed assigning opinions to various categories of "voice": editorial and op-ed/administration source/congressional source/judicial source/popular source, including interest groups and polls/foreign opinion from U.S. allies. Opinions from Sandinistas and Contras were not coded; they were assigned "no valence" codes on grounds that we are looking at a domestic U.S. opinion process aimed at evaluating the relative supportability of Sandinistas and Contras. There was no theoretical reason to think that opinion from the foreign targets of U.S. policy would be given equal weight with U.S. institutional actors, popular voices, or the voices of trusted allied leaders. Hence, Sandinista and Contra opinions were "canceled out." Since their numbers were approximately equal, this canceling out would not have affected the results of hypothesis tests, anyway.

For purposes of this first crude test of the model, *all coded voices were weighted the same.* Thus, President Reagan was given the same weight as an undersecretary of state and a grass-roots opposition group.

A speech by a senator was coded as a single "voice," as was a Senate roll-call vote deciding a funding bill (as long as the vote was summarized in the *Times* in terms of its policy outcome as a "victory" or a "loss"). An article describing different policy positions in Congress either in terms of emerging voting "blocs" or in terms of representative individual voices was coded as multiple voices. For example, an article documenting a battle between President Reagan and House Speaker O'Neill was double-coded as "administration voice" and "congressional voice" (see Chart 15–2 for sample codes).

Valence was assigned $+$, $-$, or $\pm$, depending on whether the opinion expressed by the voice in question was supportive of administration Contra policy ($+$), opposed to Contra policy ($-$), or ambivalent or divided about it ($\pm$). For example, when an article reported that a House vote to provide "humanitarian aid" to the Contra army gave the Reagan administration a major policy victory, the coding was: Voice: (Congress); Valence: ($+$). When Congress was reported as "divided" or "embattled" over Contra funding, the valence was coded as ($\pm$) (see Chart 15–2 for examples of voice and valence codes).

The intercoder reliability on the 1,177 opinion voice and valence codes was .94, with many cases of disagreement representing clerical error (e.g., "Congress" mistakenly coded as "popular") and easily corrected. The remaining disagreements tended to involve differing interpretations of opinion valence, with one coder scoring $\pm$ and another scoring $-$ or $+$. These few discrepancies were resolved by mutual agreement. Decisions to keep the codes simple paid off in high reliability, and offered a good first test to see if more sophisticated coding or weighting schemes are required. As the results indicate, the equal weighting seems appropriate in light of the striking support for the hypotheses.

Data Analysis.   Having access to the entire population of *New York Times* stories for the period in question provides considerable luxury in data analysis. Since we have gathered all the cases, there is no call for statistical estimation. In some comparisons the Ns are so large and the differences or trends so striking that significance tests are unnecessary as an aid to the naked eye. In other analyses the three-year time interval is broken down to a small number of intervals ($N = 17$) corresponding to episodes punctuated by key policy votes in Congress. Although the number of cases pooled within the intervals is large, the small N makes significance testing pointless. The emphasis in the following analyses will be to explore structural and graphically visible patterns in the data. In most cases, the patterns are quite dramatic as they bear on the key hypotheses. "Confidence" in this sort of exploratory analysis is obtained by building up "layers" of consistent patterns based on multiple indicators for each hypothesis and the accumulation of support for all hypotheses.

CHART 15-2   Coding Categories

Opinion Source in News

E = Executive branch	N = *New York Times* editorial
C = Congress	P = Popular domestic opinion (polls, groups, authorities)
J = Courts	F = Foreign leaders, groups, authorities, except Sandinista and Contra
Op = OP-ED column	leaders

(Multiple sources in the same article receive multiple codes)

Opinion Valence

+ = Opinion supporting Reagan administration Nicaragua policies

− = Opinion opposing Reagan administration Nicaragua policies

± = Mixed: partial support, partial opposition, evenly divided

0 = No opinion expressed in descriptive article on Nicaragua. Also, Sandinista and Contra leaders not given valence scores.

Sample Codes

C±   U.S. House Intelligence Committee is split, mostly along party lines, over whether to recommend cutting off funds for covert support of rebels seeking to overthrow Sandinista government in Nicaragua . . . *NYT,* Apr. 23, 1983; sec. I, 5:1.

E±   Policy struggle within Reagan administration over whether the United States can accept existence of a Nicaragua aligned with Soviet Union and Cuba . . . Nov. 12, 1984; I, 8:1.

N±   Editorial commends Pres. Reagan's premise for opposing Sandinista government in Nicaragua; notes Americans are also displeased by betrayals of democracy in other countries, but holds waging war is not way to help . . . Feb. 13, 1985; I, 26:1.

Op-   OP-ED by John B. Oakes scores rhetoric by Pres. Reagan . . . July 9, 1984; I, 19:2.

O   Article on how residents of Limay, Nicaragua, have coped with tides of war that have swept through their town . . . Mar. 24, 1985; I, 11:1.

Note: Intercoder reliability: .94 for 2,312 codes.
SOURCE: *New York Times.*

The Results

The first element of the marginalization thesis, the ***popular inferiority assumption***, refers to a standing cultural bias against introducing popular voice directly into the policy process, particularly on state interest issues.

A review of the voice data suggests a broad range of support for this prediction. Let us begin by taking opinion polls as a measure of popular voice and assess the frequency and nature of their introduction into the public record on Nicaragua policy. A number of obvious questions bear on the relationship between polls and the popular inferiority hypothesis: With what frequency relative to other voices are polls introduced? When polls are mentioned by journalists or political actors, are they taken at face value or explored for flaws and weaknesses? Who introduces polls into policy discussions? To what extent are references to polls linked to decision makers and policy outcomes in news accounts of the policy process?

All of the indicators point to a huge systemic bias against the introduction of popular opinion into the public dialogue on Nicaragua policy. A search of the *Nexis* index revealed only 30 references to the polls in a total of 2,312 articles on Nicaragua, which means that only 1.3 percent of news stories in the *Times* made even passing reference to polled opinion on the subject of Nicaragua. And only 2.6 percent of voiced opinions on Nicaragua policy involved either direct citations of the polls, or citations of other actors responding to the polls. These figures become even more striking when one considers that most references to the polls were brief mentions by reporters and officials buried in the bodies of new stories. Only seven poll references (.6 percent of voiced opinion) were deemed important enough to be included in the *Times Index* abstracts of stories. Only five references to the polls made it into the headlines of the 2,312 articles on Nicaragua, meaning that popular opinion was the lead issue in only two-tenths of one percent of the coverage of one of the biggest and least popular policy campaigns of the Reagan administration.

It is surprising how seldom policymakers mention the polls, or are even mentioned in the same context as the polls. Only 7 times was the president or one of his advisers or a member of Congress attributed as the source of a statement about polls, and only on 18 occasions did a journalist refer to polls in the context of remarks about Congress or the administration. Along these lines of linkages between polls and the policy process only 7 statements were made in *Times* coverage that could be construed as in any way holding congressional actions accountable to poll results, and a larger number of references (9) could be construed as suggesting that congressional actions were not bound by opinion due to the alleged confusion among the public. Indeed, a reader seeking any sense that popular opinion might feed meaningfully into the policy process would have been hard-pressed to find it.

Polls were mentioned in the news at least once during 9 of the 13 time periods in which important hearings and Contra funding votes were on the agenda in Congress. However, links within news stories between polls and congressional decisions were drawn during only 5 of these key periods, and only in 4 of the 13 congressional "policy periods" did the links drawn between polls and Congress suggest that Congress might be following popular sentiment or might have grounds for doing so. The bottom line here is that in three years of extensive policy coverage a reader seeking images of positive links between popular voice and institutional policy outcomes would have found them in only three-tenths of one percent of the news stories (that is, 7 out of a total of 2,312 stories).

An even more telling pattern in the data is that fully half of the references to the polls (and most of the prominent references) attacked the quality of popular thinking either directly (reporters pointing out areas of confusion) or indirectly (the president attempting to educate a misguided public). The important question here is whether the polls were thoroughly unworthy of more favorable and more serious attention, or whether cultural dispositions against popular voice lead analysts and politicians to seek out areas of weakness and to ignore areas of coherence and stability. To be sure, the polls did reflect great factual confusion about who the players were in Central America in the first year or so after the issue of U.S. military intervention hit the national policy agenda. However, in the next two years, levels of factual confusion steadily declined and the popular importance of the issues increased. Despite these trends, attention to the polls was far greater during the period of greatest popular ignorance than during later periods of lesser popular confusion: half of the poll references appeared during the first year of the Contra controversy, and most of these references were to the single, worst case, *NYT*/CBS poll showing popular confusion at the outset of public debate on Nicaragua policy. More significant than the emphasis on popular confusion, however, was the nearly total neglect of potential areas of popular certainty and legitimate concern. Only three times did reporters or opinion experts emphasize the stable (and seemingly reasonable) popular concerns about "another Vietnam" and about U.S. disregard for Nicaraguan sovereignty. As mentioned earlier, these seemed to be the best grounds for interpreting the remarkably stable pattern of popular opposition to U.S. policy—a pattern that withstood an intense propaganda campaign for three years (see Figure 15-1). When weaknesses in the polls are systematically emphasized and strengths are systematically ignored by journalists and politicians alike, we would seem to be operating in the realm of strong cultural bias.

A fascinating comparison case strengthens the cultural bias hypothesis. In the midst of the Nicaragua policy struggle the Democrats attacked Reagan's Contra policy as a major campaign issue during the 1984 election. All the presidential candidates took stands against administration policy, and Democratic Party polling showed Nicaragua to be a hot issue for congressional races around the country. It is ironic that the polls were taken seriously in one arena of the political culture (elections) while being

FIGURE 15–1   Opposition to Nicaragua Policies, 1983–1986

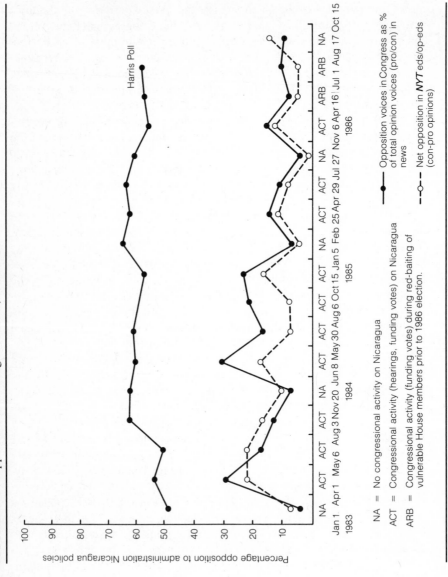

discredited or ignored at the same time in another (state foreign policy deliberations). In *none* of the 18 references to polls on Nicaragua in coverage of the 1984 elections did a reporter or a candidate discredit popular opinion as a valid basis for defining campaign issues or casting votes. For some reason the people are perceived by elites and journalists to be less confused as voters than as policy evaluators. It is also worth noting that every reference to the polls in electoral coverage established a positive linkage between the public and a political outcome, namely, the election of representatives.

It seems clear that we are talking about selective cultural bias when polls on an issue are interpreted in ways that legitimize popular involvement in one political process while at the same time being interpreted in contradictory ways that marginalize popular involvement in another political process. When it comes to policy, a different ideological program seems to govern the thinking of the gatekeepers of the press and the institutions about the legitimacy of popular involvement.

The *institutional superiority assumption* is the cultural complement of the popular inferiority assumption. Even if popular will cannot be trusted, so the assumption goes, the combination of electoral discipline and countervailing powers within institutions constrain public officials to exercise reason and represent the broad public interest. If the institutional superiority assumption prevails in the culture, we would expect to find that representatives of public institutions are granted the lion's share of opinions on state policy issues.

In searching for measures of extra-institutional opinion to compare to the frequency of institutional (i.e., Congress, executive, judicial) voice on Nicaragua, it is clear that there are many sources of extra-institutional domestic opinion besides the polls: citizens' groups, candidates for office, experts and authorities, community leaders, etc. By the broadest measure of domestic, noninstitutional opinion (any domestic poll or group, or agent who wasn't a public official), there were 139 opinions voiced on Nicaragua policy compared to 604 opinions expressed by institutional agents and factions. Institutional voices expressed more than four times the number of policy opinions expressed by extra-institutional voices. Even if we take the 288 editorials and op-ed pieces in the *Times* to be part of a broad, noninstitutional popular voice, the margin of institutional dominance is still an overwhelming 604 to 427.

The critical measure of marginalization is not just whether institutional voices outnumber other voices in the public policy debate, but whether publicity given to extra-institutional voices in the news somehow depends on the presence or absence of institutional conflict over policy. Recall our prediction that even the responsible press like the *New York Times* depends on the existence of institutional opposition, not popular opposition, to sustain its own editorial opposition voice on policies such as the Nicaraguan Contra case. The prediction is that when institutional voice patterns shift, so will patterns of editorial opinion. If this prediction holds, it would suggest both that institutions have a measure of license to ignore standing patterns of popular opposition of the sort found in Figure 15–1, *and* that the responsible press plays an active role in granting institutional actors their immunity from popular accountability.

It is unlikely that the relationship between institutions and press opinion has a one-way causal flow. More likely, there is a two-way relationship, with certain elites providing grist for editorialists, and editorial voices, in turn, shaping elite thinking and vision. It is the case, after all, that members of Congress, the courts and the executive branch wake up every morning and read the prestige press before going to work and entering their own voices into the same public record. The key theoretical question is not which way the causality flows, but whether there *is* a correlation and, in limiting cases, whether the media silence themselves when opposition voices fall silent in institutions. The null hypothesis based on commonsense ideas about press editorial policy is that the ideological stance of editorials should remain constant as a disciplining agent on institutions, even when patterns of institutional agreement with editorial stance begin to erode (H_0: $EV_{t1} = EV_{t2...tn}$).

Testing this hypothesis involved coding the opinions in *NYT* editorials and op-ed pieces, as well as coding the opinions voiced by institutional actors. The codes followed the scheme outlined in Chart 15–2. The first measure of *NYT* opposition was the net editorial and op-ed opinion valence as defined by the difference between the number of "con" editorials and the number of "pro" editorials within each of the policy periods described below. (Bivalent editorials received double codes.) Institutional opposition included dissenting voices in: the executive branch (e.g., unnamed State Department officials objecting to the CIA making foreign policy); the judiciary (e.g., federal courts hearing charges of presidential violations of the Neutrality Act of 1794); and of course, Congress (e.g., suggesting diplomatic rather than military solutions, objecting to presidential disregard of congressional foreign policy prerogatives, viewing Contras as undesirable allies, majority voting against Contra funding, etc.). *All dissenting institutional voices went into this measure.* However, since the policy struggle hinged primarily on congressional investigations and funding votes over three years, it is not surprising that the vast majority of opposition voices came from Congress. The breakdown of opposition voices is as follows: Congress (180), executive branch (15), courts (2). On other issues we might expect the institutional patterns to be quite different. For example, on civil rights issues such as desegregation policy, we might find a more even distribution of opposition voices across the institutions. The key theoretical question (at this stage, at least) is not which institutions generate policy opposition, but whether there is some general relationship between levels of opposition from any and all institutional sources and levels of editorial opposition in the prestige press. Figure 15–1 shows a clear three-year pattern of covariation between levels of institutional opposition and *NYT* net editorial opposition. Both institutional and editorial opposition are expressed in Figure 15–1 as percentages of all opposition voices in the news for each of the 17 time intervals noted. The number of all opposition voices over the entire 17-interval range is 1,177.

The time series of 197 institutional and 288 editorial dissents over three years has been collapsed into 17 intervals for this analysis. Each interval corresponds to a bounded episode of policy activity or inactivity in Congress where the policy struggle was centered institutionally and where the overwhelming majority of opposition voices emerged. At this stage of theory-building, grounds do not exist for creating more numerous intervals. The 17 intervals into which the opposition voices have been collapsed are defined substantively by the policy decisions toward which both institutional and editorial voices were addressed. These intervals are not equal in terms of calendar time (e.g., number of days); rather, they are episodic intervals set by a "decision clock" that ran on the timing of key hearings, committee and floor votes, and House-Senate conferences punctuating the policy process. The reader may wish to consult Chart 15–1 again to get a sense of how these policy intervals were chosen from the cycles of congressional activity and inactivity over the three years of Contra funding debates.

If Figure 15–1 suggested a general relationship between institutional opposition and media opposition, it did not reveal the strength of that relationship. In order to assess the correlation between the two variables, it is necessary to take the data out of time and look at them in terms of the degree to which they share a common "property space." Figure 15–2 provides related ways of viewing the strength of relationship between levels of institutional opposition (primarily congressional opposition in this case) and editorial opposition in the *Times*. Both A and B use the same measure of institutional opposition expressed as a percentage of total opposition voices in the news in each time interval. The two diagrams employ different *NYT* opposition measures. Figure 15–2A presents *NYT* opposition by using the same "net opposition" measure as in Figure 15–1, namely the number of opposing editorial and op-ed opinions minus the number of supporting opinions, expressed as a percentage of all opinions voiced in the news for the period in question. The strength of association between institutional and *NYT* opposition as presented in Figure 15–2A is described by a Pearson correlation coefficient ($r = .63$).

It might be argued that a better measure of *Times* editorial and op-ed opposition is simply the number of editorial and op-ed opposition voices expressed as a percentage of all opposition voices in the news during each period. This measure is shown in Figure 15–2B. The relationship between

FIGURE 15–2   Institutional and *New York Times* Opposition to Nicaragua
Policy, 1983–1986

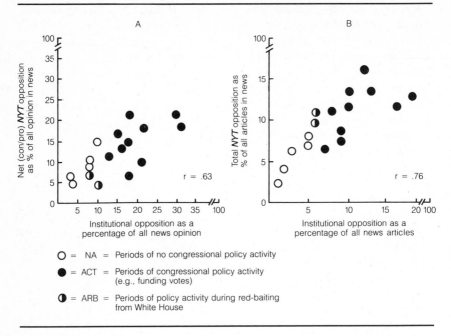

O = NA = Periods of no congressional policy activity

● = ACT = Periods of congressional policy activity
(e.g., funding votes)

◑ = ARB = Periods of policy activity during red-baiting
from White House

Times opposition and institutional opposition by this measure is an even
stronger Pearson *r* of .76. We can summarize both figures by noting, simply, that when institutional opposition goes up, so does *Times* editorial
opposition, and when institutional opposition dies, so does *Times* opposition.

Looking at the limiting case of what happened when the Reagan
administration launched an intimidation campaign based on red-baiting
vulnerable members of Congress will help determine whether Congress
or the media is the "driver" in this relationship, and whether the media
are active players in the process of opinion marginalization. This brings
us to the evaluation of the third component of our thesis. The *passive
media assumption* predicts that the media, bound by cultural pressures to
be neutral, cannot sustain criticism of government policies in the absence
of supporting institutional criticism. This leaves the policy process vulnerable to cases in which institutional critics may be silenced through
political intimidation and misinformation, resulting in ill-considered policies and threats to democratic representation.

Preliminary support is found in Figure 15–2 for the prediction that
when institutional opposition falls silent, so will the "liberal" *New York*

Times. Notice that the relationship between congressional and *Times* opposition following the red-baiting campaign (indicated by the two half-filled dots) fall toward or below the lower end of institutional/editorial opposition levels for all previous periods of congressional policy activity (indicated by completely filled dots). Moreover, the post red-bait opposition actually falls to within the range of institutional/editorial opposition levels observed during periods of congressional inactivity on Nicaragua policy (indicated by the open dots in the figures). *In other words, the levels of opposition in both Congress and the* New York Times *at the time of the most consequential vote in three years of policy struggle fell within the range of opposition levels observed during periods when no policy decisions were on the institutional agenda!*

This relationship between *Times* and congressional opposition after red-baiting (compared to levels of opposition during earlier policy periods and during "no-policy" periods) is shown more clearly in Figure 15–3. Figure 15–3A depicts levels of congressional opposition in periods of no activity (NA), normal policy activity (ACT), and policy activity after the red-baiting campaign (ARB). Figure 15–3B shows *NYT* opposition levels over the same three periods. Figure 15–3 suggests that both opposition levels fell dramatically following the red-baiting campaign, and opposition levels in Congress fell toward the bottom end of the range of opposition registered during periods when no policy decisions appeared on the congressional agenda. Yet the $100 million Contra funding votes during the summer of 1986 were the largest and most consequential of the entire policy struggle.

To what extent was congressional opposition silenced by the red-baiting campaign leading up to the crucial votes? Turning to Figure 15–3A, we see that during the first ARB period culminating in the final House vote, opposition voices in Congress represented only 5 percent of *all opinion* (pro and con) in the news, compared with an average of 19 percent over the 10 previous normal-policy-activity periods, and 17 percent in the immediately prior period. This 5 percent figure falls well outside the range (low of 12 percent, high of 31 percent) for all the other policy periods. The same pattern emerges if we look at congressional opposition as a percentage of just the *opposing opinion* voiced in the news. Congressional opposition during the first red-baiting period dropped to just 17 percent of all opposing opinion voiced against administration policies compared to an average of 36 percent over the 10 previous normal periods. Again, this drop in congressional opposition falls well outside of the range for normal (ACT) periods, a range with a low of 23 and a high of 51.

To summarize the pattern in Figure 15–3A, we see that congressional opposition to the Contra war policy all but disappeared following electoral red-baiting. This occurred despite strong opposition throughout the two and one-half years immediately prior to the red-baiting, and despite

FIGURE 15-3   Congressional and *New York Times* Opposition to Nicaragua
Policies in Relation to Policy Context

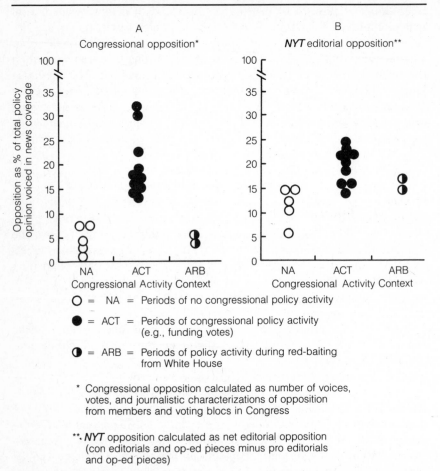

A
Congressional opposition*

B
NYT editorial opposition**

O = NA = Periods of no congressional policy activity

● = ACT = Periods of congressional policy activity
(e.g., funding votes)

◐ = ARB = Periods of policy activity during red-baiting
from White House

* Congressional opposition calculated as number of voices,
votes, and journalistic characterizations of opposition
from members and voting blocs in Congress

**. *NYT* opposition calculated as net editorial opposition
(con editorials and op-ed pieces minus pro editorials
and op-ed pieces)

the magnitude of the policy decision that was before Congress at the time.
Indeed, anyone using official opposition voices in the news as a gauge of
the importance or divisiveness of an issue might have received the impression that this was not an issue worth worrying about. As Figure 15–3A
shows, opposition during the ARB policy period fell to levels characteristic of periods in which there was no issue before Congress at all.

Even more distressing is the pattern in Figure 15–3B showing that
the *New York Times*, knowing full well what was going on, followed Congress into silence on the Contra funding issue. *Times* editorial and op-ed

opposition to the consequential funding votes of 1986 fell to the bottom of its range of previous opposition, even though prior news articles suggested considerable cause for concern about the corruption of the policy process that was going forward. If ever there was reason for the *Times* to object forcefully, it was during these ARB periods. Yet, *Times* opposition fell close to levels registered during NA periods in which there was nothing pertaining to Nicaragua policy on the institutional decision agenda. The *Times* pattern in Figure 15–3B is not as extreme as the congressional pattern in Figure 15–3A, but any expectations about a "watchdog press" would lead us to expect a *Times* response in just the opposite direction, with editorial opposition rising beyond "normal" levels to draw attention to clear corruption in the decision process on a major policy question that the *Times* had opposed consistently in the past. It is clear that *Times* editorial policy on Nicaragua was cued by Congress, not by its own political agenda or sense of journalistic responsibility. The "new professionalism" of the press would seem to operate on the assumption that "the system works," despite any evidence to the contrary, and that the "responsible press" keeps its criticisms within the bounds of institutional debate, however narrow or distorted those bounds may become.

The key interpretive questions pertaining to the evidence of Figure 15–3 are: (1) Did a serious red-baiting campaign clearly occur during the two policy periods defined as ARB periods? (2) Did the *NYT* and members of Congress recognize the existence and impact of the intimidation campaign, and, if so, did they make an issue of it? (3) Did *Times* editorial opposition decline before or after congressional opposition declined? and (4) Did members of Congress (e.g., the losers) or representatives of the media raise objections after the funding votes on any of the following grounds: that the policy ran counter to popular opinion; that it was based on poor information; or that it was passed on the strength of an intimidation campaign against electorally vulnerable House members?

1. Did the red-baiting campaign clearly occur during the two final policy vote periods as claimed? And, we might also ask, just how intimidating was this campaign? A casual inspection of White House propaganda over the entire three-year period suggests that anticommunism was a theme from the beginning. However, links between communism, un-Americanism, and congressional opposition were not drawn until the end of the last "normal" policy period culminating in an initial House rejection of the $100 million Contra aid plan on March 21, 1986.

There are two reasons why this period of November 15, 1985–April 15, 1986, was scored as the last "normal" activity period rather than the first red-baiting (ARB) period. First, the three red-baiting incidents during this period came toward the end (February 21, March 7, March 17 in Chart 15–3) of the period, and were relatively minor compared to the in-

CHART 15–3 Buildup to 1986 Red-Baiting Campaign against Congress

Dates	Source	Message/Event
May 5, *1983*	Reagan	Calls Contras "Freedom Fighters."
July 19, *1984*	Reagan	Calls Nicaragua "totalitarian dungeon."
Feb. 20, *1985*	Shultz	Nicaragua "has fallen behind iron curtain."
Apr. 16	Reagan	Warns Congress that vote against Contra aid is "literally a vote against peace." (*First direct threat against Congress.*)
Feb. 21, *1986*	*NYT*	White House to release document linking members of Congress to "Nicaraguan lobbying." (*First linkage of Congress to enemy.*) Denounced by Sen. Durenberger as "outrageous" attempt to portray any opponent of Contra aid as "stooge of communism."
Mar. 7	Reagan	Says members of Congress must choose between supporting his administration or supporting communists: "I've had enough experience with communist subversion back in my former profession to know that a great many people are deceived, and not aware that what they're doing is inimical to the interests of the United States." (*First linkage of opponents in Congress to communists and un-Americanism.*)
Mar. 7	*NYT*	Unnamed members of Congress say administration is "red-baiting."
Mar. 9	National Conference Political Action Committee	Announces $1.5 million campaign to "sell" Americans on aid to Contras.

CHART 15–3   Buildup to 1986 Red-Baiting Campaign against Congress
(continued)

Dates	Source	Message/Event
Mar. 10, 15	*NYT*	OP-EDs say Contra aid is defining issue of the era reminiscent of McCarthyism.
Mar. 17	Reagan	Calls on Americans to demand that Congress endorse aid package to stop communism.
Mar. 21	Reagan	Terms first House vote a "dark day for freedom."
Apr. 15	*NYT*	OP-ED fears House may support aid plan rather than face charges of being "soft on communism" in upcoming election campaigns.
Apr. 16	*NYT*	Citizens for Reagan conduct phone, mail, media ad blitz of 39 key congressional races.
June 25	Reagan	National speech on eve of final House vote: U.S. faces "Soviet military beachhead" in Nicaragua. The failure of the House to support Contras would "dash prospects for democracy in the region" and create a communist threat to United States.
June 26	*NYT*	House, by 221–209 vote, gives Reagan administration major victory: approves military aid to Nicaraguan rebels.
June 26	Tip O'Neill	Reagan pressure "no doubt" had effect.
July 7	*NYT*	Editorial: "Stalinism in Nicaragua."

SOURCE: All statements, articles appeared in the *New York Times* on date cited.

tensive media campaign launched by the White House over the subsequent Easter recess and prior to the final House vote. In my judgment, these three instances of red-baiting (out of 249 articles in the period) did not constitute a serious, full-fledged "campaign," but were more a "trial balloon" to assess the potential for bad publicity that might accompany a more systematic campaign. Although the three incidents were noted both in the *Times* and by members of Congress (see February 21, March 7, March 10 in Chart 15–3), the level of outcry was remarkably low-key.

The second reason why the period was coded as a normal activity period is that House Speaker O'Neill effectively granted members of the House "immunity" from any pressure they might have experienced at this stage by promising that there would be a second funding vote after the House Easter recess. This parliamentary move effectively turned the March 21 vote into a straw vote because the decisive vote of record was postponed until June 1986.

A serious intimidation *campaign* emerged only after the Reagan administration lost the straw vote on March 21 and went into the field on April 15 with a systematic and well-prepared campaign, targeting electorally vulnerable House members with mail and media blitzes in their local districts when they went home for recess. The first indication of this full-fledged red-baiting campaign came from the *New York Times* in an editorial on April 15 (see Chart 15–3). The editorial expressed fears that charges of being "soft on communism" in upcoming election campaigns might lead House members to shift their votes. A news analysis article on April 16 reported that "Citizens for Reagan," a "grass-roots" organization, was conducting a phone, mail, and media ad blitz in 39 key congressional districts. These indicators suggest that something reasonably described as a red-baiting *campaign* began at the outset of the April 16–June 25, 1986 period—the first of two periods labeled ARB.

Subsequent revelations from the Iran-Contra arms sale investigations suggest that the media campaign, alleged at the time to have been run by "grass-roots" Reagan supporters, was actually planned by Lieutenant Colonel Oliver North more than a year earlier in coordination with Carl Channell, a key "private sector" Contra fund raiser. The campaign was run through International Business Communications, Inc., one of several companies involved in North's illegal National Security Council operation on Nicaragua. Part of the funding for the campaign was funneled through a State Department contract "signed" on September 2, 1986 (after the House and Senate votes), but "put into effect" on October 1, 1985 (in preparation for a final assault on Congress should such intimidation be necessary). A State Department official was quoted in the AP wire story of February 6, 1987, from which these data are drawn as saying that discrepant dating of such contracts was "unusual" but "not illegal." The million-dollar ad campaign linked communism, Nicaragua, Colonel

Muammar el-Qaddafi of Libya, and terrorism to targeted congressmen who opposed Contra aid.

Another important indicator that the red-baiting campaign both began in earnest after the middle of April and had serious effects is the jump in pro-policy voices that began to dominate the policy debate at that point (see Figures 15–4A and 4B). Even though the percentage of news articles containing policy opinions rose only slightly in the first ARB period (.72) compared to the last normal period (.67), the increased domination of executive branch and other pro-administration policy voices was overwhelming. The inference here is that administration domination of the "public opinion space" at the time of its policy victory was not due to an increase in the sheer volume of White House messages, but due to the virtual silencing of opposition voices in Congress. A silenced Congress, followed by a silenced press, created, by default, an overwhelming dominance of pro-administration voices in the public policy debate.

Figure 15–4 shows clearly that silencing the opposition (shown in Figure 15–3) created the illusion of overwhelming support for administration policy. With the impact of the red-baiting campaign, a new universe of public opinion was created to ease the passage of the $100 million military aid package through Congress. Even more impressive is that this illusion of support for the policy was not created by the White House trumpeting its own cause more loudly than it had done in the past. Note in Figure 15–4A that levels of White House self-promotion during the ARB (red-baiting) periods of the decisive Contra vote fall around the middle of its three-year overall range of contribution to the total public voice on the subject. (It is worth noting in passing that White House and other supporters of Contra policy made their voices felt loudly during NA or nonactivity periods in Congress simply because there was no decision pending in Congress and the opposition both in Congress and in the *New York Times* dropped its voice. This suggests that it is relatively easy for an administration to keep its issue alive and make its points more salient even when its favored issues are not currently on the institutional "front burner.")

The really dramatic finding is in Figure 15–4B, which shows that red-baiting created a de facto climate of support for Contra policy, and this climate of support appeared to come from outside the White House to a considerable degree. What happened of course is that existing pro-policy voices simply grew "louder" due to the artificially diminished levels of opposition. The resulting illusion, nonetheless, is one of the strongest levels of policy support expressed in public in three years.

It is important to bear in mind this important corollary of marginalization: *As the majority voice is silenced, the minority voice becomes the majority.* If, as Noelle-Neumann (1984) suggests, people funnel their own expressed reactions to policy through the climates of opinion that form

FIGURE 15–4   Support for Nicaragua Policies from White House and All News Sources during Periods of Congressional Inactivity, Congressional Policy Debate, and Policy Debate during White House Red-Baiting Campaign

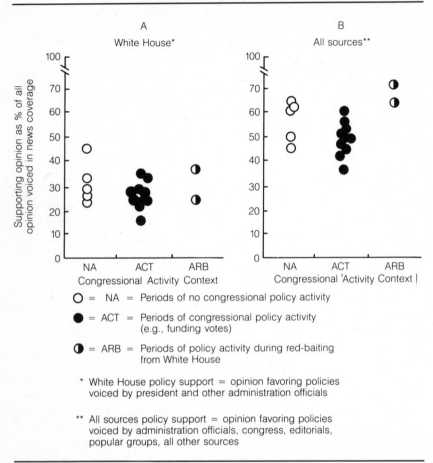

and dissolve around them, the whole public opinion process changed dramatically during that month of red-baiting in the spring of 1986. And so, climates of opinion, policy outcomes, and legitimation all can be constructed by marginalizing various public voices and allowing others to take the fore. By the time the Reagan administration finally secured its long-sought policy goals, virtually every sector of possible public opposition had been marginalized, from the majority of the public in the polls, to the majority in Congress, to the voice of the *New York Times,* the historical record.

2. Did members of Congress and editorials in the New York Times recognize the impact of the intimidation campaign on the character of the policy debate and on the resulting policy?   The answer is "yes," it was an acknowledged factor, but "no" it was not made into a salient issue as it happened. As suggested above, the *Times* documented the existence of the intimidation campaign and noted editorially that it could have an unfortunate effect on the integrity of the policy process. Moreover, House Speaker O'Neill observed for the record that the intimidation campaign "no doubt" had an effect in turning the straw vote of March 21, with its 222–210 margin of opposition, into the Reagan victory margin of 221–209 on June 26.

Although the gatekeepers noted the existence of the intimidation campaign and its impact, none of them made an issue of it by pursuing allegations of unfairness or corruption of the normal policy process. In fact, only a total of three news articles and editorials addressed the subject of red-baiting out of a total of 192 articles on the subject of Nicaragua during the two ARB periods. When only slightly more than one percent of the coverage of an issue mentions a particular feature (in this case, red-baiting), the casual reader might receive the impression that the feature was not important. The more important point is that whatever the popular audience thought of the quality of this policy process was irrelevant, since no voice replaced the institutional opposition when it fell silent!

3. Did shifts in the Times editorial opposition clearly follow the silencing of Congress?   Reading the sequence of these editorials makes it clear that the demise of editorial and institutional opposition was something of a "spiral of silence," with the *Times* following the lead of Congress. At the opening of the final House vote period, the *Times* warned of the evils of red-baiting (April 15). Moreover, the major policy editorial at the beginning of the ARB period condemned the White House for failing to make a case for waging war on Nicaragua. Yet six weeks later on the day of the final vote when it had become clear that the opposition coalition in the House was crumbling, *Times* editorial resolve began to crumble, too. Rather than exhort lawmakers to hold their ground on the morning of the fateful House vote, the paper ran an ambivalent editorial paving the way for the impending Reagan victory of that afternoon to enter the historical record smoothly. If the institutions were about to speak with a united voice, far be it from the *Times* to echo a false note of division. The editorial in question of June 25, 1986, turned on the perplexing statement that "Neither side in Nicaragua is worth a wrenching, red-baiting war of recrimination in the United States" (*NYT*, June 25, 1986: 22). The bottom line gave lukewarm encouragement to the possibility that Congress might "give the President some of what he asks."

In light of earlier *Times* objections to red-baiting and to the policy itself, the best explanation for this reluctant turnaround is that the editors sensed a shift in the institutional political currents and responded with a cautious shift in editorial policy, keeping the editorials within the bounds of institutional debate. The sensed shift in congressional opposition was validated that afternoon when the House gave Reagan all of what he wanted.

Once congressional opposition had crumbled decisively, the *Times'* cautious opinion shift turned into a clear reversal. The next round of the policy process would culminate in a Senate vote, and the Republican-dominated Senate would surely deliver the votes to seal the White House victory. There was no misreading the signal in the *Times* editorial opening this final round of the policy process. The editorial of July 7, 1986 (p. 22), was titled: "The Sandinista Road to Stalinism." Reagan couldn't have said it better! Whereas Congress had been intimidated by the red-bait, the *New York Times* had swallowed it. The irony, of course, is that the paper was neither the target of the harassment nor unaware of the reasons for the turnaround in Congress. Despite these factors, the *Times* dutifully wrote itself into the emerging political record rather than rise above the scene to register strong objections. Rising above the institutional fray would have made the *Times* a player in history rather than the keeper of the historical record.

4. The final question is whether anyone took up the cause of "the people" once their institutional representatives had been intimidated into silence. The answer is a qualified "no": the few voices raised on behalf of popular objections to the outcome were too few in number to give popular voice any standing in the emerging record of public opinion. For example, in the period between the House and Senate votes, only two voices introduced poll data as grounds for opposing the pending policy: one voice was that of Senator Alan Cranston who announced the possibility of a Senate filibuster on July 17, and the other was that of former Senator George McGovern who wrote an op-ed piece noting strong popular opposition to the House action.

After the Senate predictably supported the Contra plan, only two more voices were raised noting the discrepancy between the policy and popular opinion. One of these voices was *Times* columnist Tom Wicker who had opposed administration policy consistently from the beginning and was one of the few voices allowed to register opposition of the op-ed pages during the several preceding months of *Times* self-imposed silence. The other post-policy voice was—you guessed it—the *Times* editorial voice itself. Following the Senate vote, the *Times* mysteriously recovered its lost opposition voice and noted for the record that the "bipartisan" support for Reagan Nicaragua policy was opposed by a majority of Americans. That was it; the record was complete for the future scholar who wished to assemble the facts of institutional life as they pertained to Reagan Nicaragua policy.

Yet for the citizen interested in a contemporary sense of what was going on, the voices speaking for popular opinion were few and far between. Indeed, a citizen seeking an impression of public opinion on Nicaragua policy might have concluded by the summer of 1986 that, somehow, Ronald Reagan had won a margin of legitimate public support for his policies. In a sense, that impression would have been correct: the Reagan administration did *construct* a record of public support for its policies.

CONCLUSION

As it should be clear by now, public opinion is defined by the distribution of voices in institutions as they are recorded in the press. By this definition, public opinion *was* behind administration Nicaragua policy and, insofar as the media record showed it, the support was strong and legitimate. It all has to do with how public opinion is constructed politically in a given situation. Perhaps on other issues at other times, the institutional opposition would not have been so vulnerable, or the administration so willing to intimidate, and the press would have entered a slightly different distribution of institutional voices into the public record. But this time, the process joining institutions and the media in the construction of the American public displayed some of its potential for serious error.

This case study has provided a critical test for the basic assumption that ignoring or marginalizing majority opinion is a culturally viable option in the policy process. The relative mix of marginalization, manipulation, and "bottom-up" representation in the political system over time can be determined by the evaluation of other critical cases selected to test differences in issue type, historical context, and political circumstance.

This theory-building process need not entail the accumulation of hundreds of cases. If cases are chosen with an eye to maximizing their critical features, theoretical generalizations can be obtained from a relatively small number of critical tests. The case of Nicaragua policy, for example, illustrates a set of general conditions under which stable, long-standing popular majorities can be ignored in the policy process with little immediate risk. More important, the case illustrates the process through which a "public opinion" is constructed—constructed in this case without much reference to the polls. We can begin to imagine other cases in which the polls would play a larger part, either as dependent variables or independent variables in the construction of other patterns of "public opinion." Through the careful study of how cultural assumptions are used by institutional and media gatekeepers, we can begin to build a general theory of public opinion and American democracy.

Conclusions

CHAPTER 16

Public Opinion as a Dependent Variable: An Empirical and Normative Assessment

Michael Margolis
Gary Mauser

OVERVIEW

The essays in this book illustrate that placing the primary analytic focus upon the initiatives of political elites leads to the conclusion that public opinion is not the moving force in any of the three areas of analysis: elections, public policy, or long-term political socialization. This is demonstrated both at the macro level by analyzing long-term trends and at the micro level by analyzing specific cases. Nonetheless, public opinion does not emerge as totally dependent either. The "public will" is not so malleable that political elites can act with impunity, regardless of the circumstances. Indeed, a major task for empirical political science is to specify those circumstances when public opinion leads or circumscribes elite initiatives, when it is driven by such initiatives, and when it is marginalized, or simply ignored by political elites.

Regardless of the pattern of influence in any particular circumstance, the mass media provide the principal means of linking the ideas and opinions of elites with those of various segments of the public. That linkage is not unbiased. It is clear that the ideas and policies promoted by established elites—business leaders, public officials, televangelists and the like—have greater access to the media than do those of others and that they receive more favorable coverage than do those of dissident elites or of the public. Even so, the fact that the established elites do not win every time indicates the limitations of the media's power to sway public opinion. Again, specifying the circumstances in which the media are more likely or less likely to persuade the public to accept concepts and policies advocated by established groups becomes the task of political science.

What do the preceding essays suggest concerning these circumstances? And what are their implications for the conduct of democratic
politics? In this concluding chapter we pull together the main arguments
and findings of our contributors, and we attempt to sketch the outline of
a democratic theory of public opinion that takes them into account. We
begin with an examination of the role of the various media in communicating political ideas and proceed to an examination of the roles of leadership elites in various contexts. In these examinations we consider both
the extent and the limitations of the influence over public opinion exerted
by the media and the elites. We finish with a sketch of our theory of the
role of public opinion in modern mass democracies.

MEDIA, POLITICS, AND THE LIMITS OF PERSUASION

The mass media play a pivotal role in what we referred to in our
introduction as "popular notions of liberal democracy." In modern societies these media comprise the primary source of information about public affairs received by most citizens. In theory, they also serve to monitor
and criticize the actions of government and social groups and to relate
information about the state of public opinion both to decision makers and
the general public. In practice, however, they tend to reflect, rather than
monitor, the actions of government and private institutions.

As Qualter and Parenti point out, in most Western democracies the
mass media are largely profit-making businesses whose long-term interests and abilities to survive are, for better or for worse, intimately related
to the success of established institutions. Where democratic theories cast
the media in an independent role, the realities of the market normally tend
to position them on the side of the established interests. The media may
criticize the conduct of a particular public or private official or the policies of a particular governmental or private institution, but rarely do they
place such criticism into a broad systematic framework. Did Admiral
Poindexter and Lt. Colonel North surreptitiously arrange to sell arms to
the Iranians? Did they then use portions of the proceeds to supply the
Contras illegally? These actions are portrayed in the media as errors by
overzealous patriots: the president wasn't aware of the details. Did Ash-
land Oil's neglect of licensing procedures and safety requirements lead to
the spill of over 700,000 gallons of diesel fuel into the Monongahela River
near Pittsburgh? Some engineers and supervisors cut corners or got careless: the accident hardly reflects the standards of the industry. Typically,
the underlying message is: "the 'system' works, except in the relatively
few instances we have exposed."

Moreover, the voices that gain access to the media predominantly
belong to those groups already established. Besides the class bias that
~rises from the affinity of the media and other established businesses,

messages put forth in the media are further biased by the costs of purchasing advertising time or space. Even though minority candidates, such as George Wallace in 1968 or John Anderson in 1980, or unconventional causes, such as the advocation of "nuclear freeze" referenda in the early 80s, sometimes capture the attention of the mass media, only limited amounts of "free" time and space are available for news coverage of elections and public affairs. Candidates and causes with money to purchase time or space to put forth their messages normally get better coverage. The essays in Section One uniformly indicate that chances of electoral success are enhanced by money. Money can buy polling data and expertise to devise powerful strategies for marketing candidates (Mauser; Kayden) or electoral propositions (Magleby). Money can also purchase data bases and software to facilitate "narrowcasting," or targeting of messages to specific populations. It can be used to hire speech writers or media coaches to improve candidates' execution of those strategies (Windt). And regardless of how it is used, the overall impact of spending money tends to enhance candidates' performances at the polls (Chapman and Palda).

When the focus shifts to policy in Section Two, the bias in favor of established groups remains. The media tend to emphasize those issues which established groups wish to promote and to deemphasize those which such groups prefer to suppress or to ignore (Qualter). Complete suppression or total ignorance, however, are rarely achieved. Exceptions, such as successful media campaigns by environmental groups to curtail the expansion of nuclear power in the United States, can readily be cited. Indeed, in recent decades enterprising protest groups have captured media attention with skillfully staged demonstrations. Coverage of the activities of Reverend Martin Luther King, Jr., and the Southern Christian Leadership Conference helped to transform American attitudes toward segregation during the 1960s; similarly, coverage of the protests of antiwar students and their allies in the late 60s and early 70s eventually led Americans to question their country's involvement in Vietnam; and currently, the protests by anti-apartheid students are designed to focus media attention upon how their universities' investments support the Republic of South Africa's economy. Such exceptions sometimes become the wellsprings for long-term reforms, but as the essays by Bosso and by Margolis and Burtt illustrate, "resource-poor" groups normally face considerable difficulty in getting their concerns before the public. Moreover, even when these latter concerns do receive attention, they are often presented in ways that place their proponents in unfavorable light. Thus, much of the early news about famine in Ethiopia characterized it not as a natural disaster, but as a political catastrophe brought on by the selfish actions of a Marxist government (Bosso). And while the Denominational Ministry Strategy in Pittsburgh achieved a modicum of success in getting the mass media to call public attention to the problems of the unemployed, much of the actual coverage was devoted to condemnation of the militant tactics the group chose to employ (Margolis and Burtt).

Over and above the bias toward favorable coverage they already enjoy, established groups and institutions usually can muster more resources than can their opponents to propagate an argument via the mass media. The televangelists use their pulpits to raise money to spread their versions of the gospel. They face no comparable opposition in the media from less-well-funded groups such as atheists, agnostics, or secular humanists (Johnston). Public officials—even presidents of the United States—may fail to persuade the citizenry to follow their lead, but they ordinarily have little trouble gaining access to the mass media to present their case (Hurwitz). Indeed, as Bennett shows both here in Section Three and elsewhere (Bennett 1988), the news media tend to amplify the voices of institutional elites, both public and private, and to marginalize or ignore other expressions of opinion.[1]

Finally, the essays in Section Three suggest that far from playing an independent role in checking the influence of government and private groups on public attitudes over the long term, the mass media tend to serve as conduits for established values. As we noted, the mass media normally portray the established institutions and orders as benign, and portray critics and dissenters as unreasonable or destructive (Parenti). The media legitimate the notion that responses of representative samples to polls comprise a more valid expression of public opinion than do public actions by individuals or groups; and this legitimation undercuts the influence of individual leaders and pressure groups who dissent (Ginsberg). Most damningly, the mass media tend to publish the information provided by established sources with little alteration. They rarely seek independent confirmation; nor do they place the information into broader contexts to facilitate independent interpretation. Instead, the media tend to "balance" their coverage by reporting alternative viewpoints drawn mostly from the diversity among already established groups. When institutional voices cease to disagree in public, the media usually cease to report controversy over policy (Bennett; Page and Shapiro).

---

[1] It must be noted, however, that on certain controversial issues the mass media do exhibit an independent influence. On gun control, for example, the National Rifle Association, which might well be counted among "established elites" and which is certainly well funded, must rely largely on paid advertisements and lobbyists to promote its position, for it gets little editorial support in the media and even finds that many publications won't accept its advertisements. Moreover, the NRA claims that many supposedly objective news reports are biased, particularly television news, reflecting the media's support for stricter controls on gun ownership.

Yet despite the citizenry's reliance upon the mass media for most information about public affairs, the influence of the dominant viewpoints expressed in the media remains limited. This seems associated with two factors: first, to maintain credibility the mass media periodically must show obeisance to the role of independent critic called for in popular democratic theories (Parenti); second, citizens who are socialized to a particular set of fundamental values or viewpoints tend to be resistant to change despite massive pressures from established elites (Hurwitz; Page and Shapiro; Bennett). And beyond these factors, the public's relative indifference to politics in comparison to personal concerns such as family or work slows the penetration of altered political values (Qualter; Johnston). Let us examine how several of the essays illustrate these generalizations.

Even though the media tend to fault particular offenders rather than the political system, the necessity to criticize creates an opportunity for elite reformers and resource-poor groups, alike, to gain access to large audiences to present their arguments and interpretations. For example, Bosso shows that once famine was "discovered" in Ethiopia, the appeals of relief agencies, which played to humanitarian rather than ideological values, suddenly could command prominent news coverage. By having programs ready to go, the agencies were able to exploit the favorable climate of opinion. By contrast, Margolis and Burtt point out that while the DMS helped to stimulate the mass media's discovery of the plight of the unemployed, its lack of a coherent program to relieve unemployment (other than a militant insistence on reinvestment in obsolete factories) gave the news media no guidance. As a result, the media elites could freely portray the established groups' sponsorship of programs that retrained skilled workers for lower-paying jobs as an attractive public policy. For a protest group to succeed it must either solicit the support of dissident elite groups directly, or else it must use the (often unfriendly) media attention gained from its outrageous behavior to attract potential allies from among otherwise uninvolved elites (Lipsky 1970; Schattschneider 1960).

The series of congressional reforms instituted in the wake of the Vietnam war were designed to deter presidents from using their superior information about foreign affairs to manipulate Congress into precipitous support of using American troops to intervene in civil wars abroad. The American public evidently accepted these reforms as legitimate limitations on presidential power. Bennett argues that much of the resistance to the Reagan administration's efforts to generate popular support for the Contras was grounded in concerns that military aid could result in "another Vietnam." Hurwitz finds similar resistance to the use of American troops "to stop the spread of Communism in Central America." Despite the legitimacy and prestige that the presidential office holds for almost all Americans, the president cannot necessarily convince public opinion to support his policies just because he declares there is a danger (the deference hypothesis). On a broader basis Page and Shapiro demonstrate that trends in public opinion often "are best understood in terms of gradual political, economic, or social changes," not as responses to current public policy initiatives. They do note, however, that public opinion is usually responsive to dramatic events, especially those involving the threat of war or the actual outbreak of hostilities, so that within these circumscribed areas, the potential for outright manipulation remains.

Before public opinion can be influenced, however, the persuasive communciations must be received. The low ratings of public affairs programming and the low circulation of serious newspapers and journals of public affairs relative to lighter, more entertaining fare, are indicative of the minor interest most citizens take in public affairs. Even though the public gradually becomes socialized to ideological viewpoints and stereotypical images congenial to the general interests of established groups, it is, for better or for worse, correspondingly difficult to disabuse the public of these viewpoints and images when political elites desire a change. Mauser points out that political marketers advise clients to adopt strategies that respect the public's "perceptual maps," that is, strategies which conform to public expectations and beliefs, which appear consistent with the candidates' previous records, and which do not attempt to alter the public's basic viewpoints. Johnston observes that in liberal democratic societies, private values—be they God's or mammon's—tend to overshadow public ones. Thus televangelists, no less than party leaders, have great difficulty in mobilizing their ostensive followers to support their public agendas. In general, the media's influence is limited by "Other structures and socio-political variables, set in the established norms and traditions of society, . . . Family, school, church, peer group, and local information networks all add items to the agenda of each individual's concerns, and reorder the priorities of existing items" (Qualter).

In summary, audiences are not merely passive receptacles into which the media pour information about public affairs. People have relatively fixed values that are rooted in their social affiliations. Interest in public affairs tends to be low, but people screen and interpret the political information to which they decide to expose themselves. Moreover, when they do become interested in particular public issues, they actively seek out information (Bauer 1972). Determining the extent that political information in the media influences public opinion, therefore, entails not merely unraveling the psychological processes involved but also understanding the socialization processes that condition the reception and absorption of such information (McLeod and O'Keefe 1972).

INSTITUTIONAL ELITES: REALMS OF INFLUENCE AND AREAS OF CONSTRAINT

The central contentions of this book have been that the preponderance of influence over electoral politics, policymaking, and long-term political socialization rests with established institutional elites, not the general public, and that opinions expressed in the mass media tend to reflect these institutional voices, not those of independent analysts, resource-poor groups, or the citizenry in general. The analyses our authors present go beyond simple confirmation of these general claims: they provide some evidence of the specific circumstances that favor or hinder the ability of elites to influence public opinion.

In summarizing their study of the relationship between responses to public opinion polls and the formulation of public policy over nearly a half century, Page and Shapiro conclude that the American public is regularly exposed to biased information that tends to reinforce the values of dominant institutions in the nationalistic, market-based, capitalist economy. Importantly, however, the impact of these influences upon public opinion varies by policy area. For instance, governmental leaders usually find it easier to focus attention upon and to provide uncontradicted interpretations of particular events regarding foreign rather than domestic affairs. And within the domestic realm, it is usually easier to gain acceptance for interpretations that are pro-capitalist, pro-incumbent, and/or supportive of the traditional two-party system.

The underlying propositions suggested here are that the ability of elites to influence public opinion will be proportionate to (1) their control of the relevant information necessary for the public to define the terms of discourse (often easier regarding foreign affairs); and (2) the fit of their arguments and interpretations to images and categories that the public already finds compelling. The two conditions complement one another, and their specification in each particular circumstance can help us to explain the extent to which elites succeed or fail to influence public opinion.

The essays by Magleby, Bosso, Hurwitz, Bennett, and Ginsberg all stress the importance of various forms of information control. Magleby points out that the key campaign battle in complex ballot questions centers around gaining public acceptance of a favorable definition of the questions at issue. Established interests with the wherewithal to publicize their definitions effectively usually gain the advantage. For example, if corporations opposed to a referendum's proposed regulations can successfully define them as threats to "jobs and energy," rather than as efforts to curb the abuses of particular utilities, then they have a much better chance of defeating the referendum. Bosso shows that the mass media began to give the Ethiopian famine widespread attention only after normal procedures for filtering foreign news broke down. A few members of the media elite—English affiliates of NBC and then national news anchorman, Tom Brokaw—saw some particularly vivid footage of starving Ethiopians, and Brokaw used his discretion to run the footage in place of some previously scheduled election campaign stories. Hurwitz demonstrates that not only is presidential influence stronger on foreign than domestic issues, but it is more likely to affect those in the public with the least amount of information. Bennett demonstrates that the Reagan administration's "marginalization" of public opposition to military support for the Contras was made easier not only because of adroit manipulation of the mass media, but also because of the media's own assumptions—"popular inferiority" and "institutional superiority"—that led them to deemphasize information about public opinion polls demonstrating such opposition. But should polls be identified with "public opinion"? Chapman and Palda stress the reliability of measures based upon "revealed preferences," such as actual votes or other overt actions, as opposed to those derived from responses to polls. Ginsberg also cautions against equating public opinion with survey results. He argues that polling tends to distort public opinion by enhancing elite control over the subject matter of public discussion. Polling transforms public opinion from a spontaneous expression of groups to a tabulation of individual responses to a constrained set of alternatives, most of which have been preselected by the elite.

Complementing this first theme, the essays by Mauser, Windt, Qualter, Parenti, Johnston, and Margolis and Burtt all point to the importance of casting arguments and interpretations within familiar, simple, and relatively fixed images. Mauser and Windt both stress the need for professional campaign organizations to apprise themselves of how the electorate views the relevant candidates, parties, and issues and to devise strategies that are compatible with these views. Campaigns that do not respect the electorate's categories and images do so at their own peril: the electorate cannot readily comprehend nor readily respond to such arguments. At a broader level Qualter shows how the news media help define events by classifying news items into familiar categories in the newspaper: business, sports, or entertainment sections; local, state, national, or international news. No sections are normally devoted to the interests of labor, and news items of particular interest to women still tend to be deemed less important. Moreover, by patronizing dissenters as harmless oddities, the media discourage the public from taking such dissent seriously. Parenti further generalizes about the overall pattern of ownership and control: the vested class interests promote the established capitalistic order through advertising and the prerogatives of ownership. The FCC rules that count the paid programs by right-wing religious groups as public service exemplify the favoritism granted to those groups whose interests are supportive of the established order (Johnston). Conversely, the media's harsh treatment of the DMS typifies the coverage afforded to groups whose tactics challenge that order (Margolis and Burtt).

Nonetheless, the established elites do not have a free hand to develop public policy as they please. To begin with, elites often disagree among themselves regarding the best ways to deal with public problems and policies. And when elites do disagree, those who see themselves losing the back-room battle are strongly motivated to bring the debate out in the open in order to ask the public to play the role of arbiter (Schattschneider 1960). Moreover, the elites' actions are constrained by their own socialization to democratic norms (Dye and Zeigler 1987) and by the necessity of being perceived to observe democratic forms. Even though elites have the power to ignore the niceties of democracy in particular cases, observing them lends a much desired legitimacy to policy outcomes, which arbitrary actions would inevitably destroy. Appeals to democratic symbols and values, therefore, can still make a difference. Whatever the ultimate verdicts regarding their failure or success, the job programs for retraining citizens in the Pittsburgh area did receive substantial monies from U. S. Steel, governmental sources, and other established interests (Margolis and Burtt). Similarly, a large portion of the money collected for Ethiopian famine relief did reach programs that supplied food and shelter for those who were starving (Bosso). In both cases the established elites acted in part to avoid the public anger and chagrin that might follow if people perceived them to have violated democratic norms by failing to respond to human suffering.

It would seem, then, that public opinion sets constraints, which, though flexible, require political elites to rationalize their actions in terms of commonly shared notions of the public interest. And while elites often have both sufficient control of information and sufficient cooperation from the news media to make even selfish actions appear supportive of that interest, their ability to influence public opinion remains incomplete. As long as the mass media retain a measure of critical autonomy and the elites continue to profess to democratic norms, dissenters will escape systematic suppression, and the bulk of the constraints will remain in place.

PUBLIC OPINION AND MASS DEMOCRACY

To proclaim that public opinion constrains but does not direct political decision makers is to say nothing new. Political scientists, such as V. O. Key, E. E. Schattschneider, and David Truman, have already made this point and have even suggested processes—socialization of leaders, competition among political parties, or actualization of potential interest groups—through which such constraints come into play (Key 1961; Schattschneider 1942; Truman 1951). Indeed, as we pointed out in Chapter 1, a long tradition of democratic theory has held that the public's essential role is to provide retrospective rather than prospective judgments on policy. (See pages 7–9.)

Notwithstanding their faith in the power of public opinion to act as a democratic constraint, theorists have been slow to account for how new developments in communications technologies have affected the processes through which this constraint is supposed to operate. When central party organizations and major party candidates have become proficient at targeting persuasive messages to preselected groups of electors (Kayden; Mauser; Windt), has the power of voters to judge political leaders thereby weakened? When established interests have become more adroit at getting both the mass media and the parties to adopt their viewpoints (Qualter; Johnston; Parenti; Bennett), has the potential for the emergence of new, and dissenting, interest groups diminished? When the long-term impact of major agencies of socialization in Western democracies—family, school, church, and particularly the mass media—is to reinforce the legitimacy and permanence of nationalistic values and capitalistic economies (Qualter; Margolis and Burtt; Parenti; Ginsberg; Page and Shapiro; Bennett), does the political socialization of leaders tend to undercut democratic values that emphasize openness to change and the ongoing reexamination of current policy? The answers to all these questions still remain open. Even though the new technologies and resources have been employed mostly to the advantage of elites, they also can be utilized to strengthen the role of the general public.

If the essays in this book document the growing extent to which elite manipulation of mass opinion has eroded democratic contraints, they also contain clues as to how such constraints could be strengthened. After all, the fruits of the information revolution, which thus far have been employed mostly to serve the interests of the elite, provide the mass public with access to new resources as well. The new technologies available to citizens of Western democracies include devices and facilities that increase the diversity of accessible sources for information, that afford greater control and selection over the incoming messages, and that provide individuals with the means to originate one-to-many communications. How ordinary citizens might employ these new technologies to impose constraints upon the elites deserves examination.[2]

When we think of mass media as sources of information, printed media such as books, newspapers, magazines, or the mail, and electronic media such as radio and television ordinarily come to mind. Such information usually originates from or is published by established institutions:

---

[2]For a systematic evaluation of various efforts to employ these technologies to enhance citizen control, see Arterton, 1987.

broadcast networks, large publishing houses, news services, or advertising firms. Developments such as cable television, satellite dishes, audio and video cassette recorders (VCRs), however, now provide citizens with the power to diversify the sources from which they receive electronic communications. For example, Americans with satellite dishes can now capture Moscow prime time television. The key development here is access to sources that do not repeat the same old stuff. Citizens have not only a greater choice of sources, but they also have access to a greater variety of perspectives as oligopolistic control of national network news and public affairs programming is weakened (McQuail and Suine 1986). Similarly, the advent of microcomputers with communications and publications software has weakened the information oligopoly of large publishing houses, print news services, and newspaper chains. Individuals can access alternative news services via electronic bulletin boards. Moreover, they can use their personal word-processing and publication software to originate high quality "print" documents, which in turn can be distributed personally, via electronic bulletin boards or electronic mail, or by ordinary post. Distribution via both electronic and ordinary post can be facilitated by powerful mail-merge programs, as users employ either their own organizations' mailing lists or those available from commercial sources.[3] Computer disks, audio and video cassettes, and printed facsimiles can also be rented, sold, copied, or exchanged. Finally, numerous data bases, even whole libraries, can be accessed interactively and at an affordable price.

Many of the same advances that afford citizens a greater choice of information sources also afford them more control over the conditions under which that information is received. For a start, by early 1988 over one-half of all households in the United States owned a VCR. Ownership of a VCR permits people to record programs for viewing according to their own schedules rather than those of network executives. Additionally, the "fast forward" button on the hand-held VCR controller provides the power to zip through those messages, often commercials, that users deem superfluous. Turning to "print" media, the menus available on electronic bulletin boards or through services such as "teletext" or "videotex" allow readers to focus upon desired information without being distracted by competing messages, commercial or otherwise (McQuail and Suine 1986: 100–105). Finally, the receipt of electronic mail may afford the addressees more control than mail delivered by ordinary post: physi-

---

[3]For example, companies like Aristotle Industries; Campaign Software, Inc.; or Russo, Watts and Rollins currently offer sophisticated computer packages that will identify target voters or groups and then deliver direct-mail or recorded telephone messages to them (Heller 1987; Brown et al. 1987).

cally, it is easier to "toss away" an electronic message than a paper envelope unopened.

That the new technologies provide ordinary citizens with practical means to send messages to many others simultaneously, however, has the most profound implications for democratic theory. The potential to reach large audiences is no longer restricted to those with massive amounts of capital to control the established mass media: the capital needs have been vastly reduced. Moreover, the recipients of messages via these new technologies—at least those using electronic media—often have the ability to reply and to question the source directly, sometimes even interactively. In any case, thanks to the new technologies, citizens desiring to acquire or impart opinions or information on problems of public concern have the opportunity to seek such opinions or information from a broader variety of sources and to communicate their own opinions or information easily to others with similar concerns. All this involves not only greater access to data banks that can supply the public with information relatively free from control by political elites, but also cheap and efficient means for new unorthodox groups to organize, to persuade, and to initiate action on behalf of whatever goals they wish to pursue.[4]

When writers such as Key, Schattschneider, and Truman cited socialization of leaders, competition among political parties, or actualization of potential interest groups as mechanisms for effecting democratic control, they presumed the presence of "slack resources" in the political system. That is, they presumed that individuals or groups who were dissatisfied with present policies had access to sufficient unused resources to organize and mobilize support for their own favored alternatives (Dahl 1956). Powerful new interest groups could form; new political parties or new factions within parties could arise; dissenters could access the mass media to argue their cases and appeal to the democratic values held by decision makers. In the wake of political unrest in the late 60s, however, critics charged that these mechanisms no longer provided adequate means for dissent. The pluralism they presumed had become too biased in favor of those in power. Large private corporations had acquired such great wealth, income, and concentration of employment opportunities that their ostensibly private decisions in basic matters like economic investment and planning often became de facto public policy, regardless of groups formed in opposition or dissent. Political executives, not legislators, dom-

---

[4]An example of the latter is the opposition in fall 1987 by a loose coalition of users of electronic bulletin boards and information networks to the proposed FCC regulations that would have dramatically increased the costs of accessing such services. Indeed, inexpensive electronic teleconferencing was successfully employed to delay indefinitely rules that threatened to destroy it by making such conferencing too expensive to use!

inated the leadership of political parties, and business executives and public bureaucracies (including the military) controlled sufficient amounts of sensitive and technical information to effectively manipulate legislatures in critical areas of public policy. Lastly, the mass media, by and large, provided access for the rationalizations of leaders of established public and private institutions, not to the arguments of spokespersons for dissenting groups (Connolly 1969; Margolis 1983).

The new communications technologies described above provide a means for overcoming these alleged shortcomings. By lowering the organizational costs for potential interest groups, new political parties, or dissenting factions within established groups or parties, they bolster traditional mechanisms of democratic control that theorists have cited. They also serve to break the established groups' near monopoly over the generation and distribution of relevant information, and they thereby strengthen the ability of dissenters—both within and without the dominant public and private elites—to bring their cases before the public. In short, the new communications technologies serve to revitalize and to enhance the ability of ordinary citizens to circumscribe the powers of decision-making elites in manners prescribed in traditional democratic theories.

We believe that in order to realize public opinion's role of constraining policymakers, it is necessary that citizens make active use of these new communications technologies. If citizens do not take advantage of independent sources from which to access information about matters of public concern, their opinions become even more susceptible to manipulation by the established elites who already generate much of the information that gets reported in the mass media (Bennett 1988) and who own or control the current means, including the mass media, through which most information about public affairs is made known. We stress, however, that access to such information is a necessary, but not sufficient condition for democratic governance.

As Ginsberg argues in his essay above, public opinion, properly conceived in accordance with democratic theory, is the collective expression of groups, not the aggregate expressions of individuals who respond to polls. This opinion can be articulated by leaders or spokespersons in an orderly fashion, or it can be demonstrated through direct, and sometimes disorderly, actions of groups themselves. Either way, the accumulated opinions of individuals who have developed their ideas in splendid isolation—even those who have informed themselves using the new communications technologies—do not correspond to this theoretical conception of public opinion. A nation of well-informed "couch potatoes" does not a democracy make (see Arterton 1987: chaps. 2–3).

At its core, democratic politics involves *collective* decision making about problems of public concern. In a similar vein, public opinion involves the collective expression of citizens' considerations about public problems, where those considerations take place within democratic political (*i.e.*, collective) contexts (see Margolis 1979: chap. 7; Barber 1984: chap. 10). Some theorists have already noted that the new communications technologies make possible the regularization of collective decision making via "electronic" town meetings (Hollander 1985; Pool 1983). We believe, however, that the more promising use of teleconferencing is to conduct electronic pressure-group meetings, not town-hall discussions. Teleconferencing provides a practical way for groups to organize via modern communications to put pressure on leaders in Washington, D. C., Ottawa, London, or in other national, regional or local decision-making sites. Other promising possibilities include providing for resource-poor groups access to information that was formerly available only to institutionalized elites. Political actions by multiplicities of interest groups, well-informed through access to communication technologies, may actuate the democratic expression of public opinion in modern societies.

To recapitulate: the effects of the new communications technologies on the conduct of democratic politics cut two ways. On the one hand, they enhance the political elites' capabilities of influencing public opinion; on the other, they afford citizen groups new opportunities to develop facilities to acquire and exchange information independent of the media that elites generally control. The essays in this volume indicate that despite the enhancements of the manipulative capabilities of the elites, the public has at times exhibited remarkable tenacity in resisting the elites' influence. We have argued that if citizen groups take proper advantage of these new technologies, the constraining influence of public opinion over the decision making of political elites, as envisioned by democratic theorists, can be realized.

The development of independent communications networks for citizen use would make it possible for public opinion to serve "as a guideline, an indicator of people's interests and desires that representatives and other political decision makers . . . take into account" (Chapter 1, p. 1). To effect this democratic role for public opinion, however, we must fall back upon the traditional liberal democratic faith in the virtuousness and ultimate rationality of the citizens themselves, and upon the Aristotelian faith that in the long run ordinary citizens acting together will prove wiser than any political elite. Communications networks through which citizens can access information about public affairs are not sufficient: citizen groups must organize themselves to make use of these capabilities to constrain political elites.

The editors hope that the essays in this volume have served to highlight not only the conditions that favor elite manipulation of public opinion but also the opportunities for citizens to limit such control. In our view, the critical question concerns the development and maintenance of easy access to the new communications media for origination, exchange, and consumption of information. If established elites are allowed to dominate these media to the same extent that they dominate traditional sources of information, we can expect their manipulation of public opinion to become ever more successful. But if citizen groups use these media to develop their own information networks and to organize politically, they will enhance their capacity to constrain or control those elites. Public opinion really will make a difference.

Bibliography

Aaker, David A., and John G. Myers. *Advertising Management*. Englewood Cliffs, N.J.: Prentice-Hall, 1975.

Aaron, Henry J. *Politics and Professors*. Washington, D.C.: Brookings Institution, 1978.

Abramson, Paul R. *Political Attitudes in America*. San Francisco, CA: W. H. Freeman, 1983.

Achen, Christopher. "Mass Political Attitudes and the Survey Response." *American Political Science Review* 69 (1975):1218–31.

Acheson, D. *Present at the Creation*. New York: W. W. Norton, 1969.

Adamany, David. "Political Parties in the 1980s." In *Money and Politics in the United States: Financing Elections in the 1980s*, ed. Michael J. Malbin. Chatham, N.J.: Chatham House, 1984:70–121.

Adams, William C. "As New Hampshire Goes. . . ." In *Media and Momentum: The New Hampshire Primary and Nomination Politics*, ed. Gary R. Orren and Nelson W. Polsby. Chatham, N.J.: Chatham House, 1987:42–59.

Adorno, T. W.; E. Frenkel-Brunswick; D. J. Levinson; and R. N. Sanford. *The Authoritarian Personality*. New York: Harper & Row, 1950.

Alexander, Herbert. *Financing Politics*. 3rd ed. Washington, D.C.: Congressional Quarterly Press, Annenberg School of Communication, 1984.

Alinsky, Saul D. *Rules for Radicals: A Pragmatic Primer for Realistic Radicals*. New York: Vintage Books, 1972.

Allegheny County Coroner's Office. *Report of the Coroner: 1986*. Pittsburgh: Coroner's Office, 1986.

American Marketing Association. *Marketing Definitions: A Glossary of Marketing Terms*. Chicago, Ill.: American Marketing Association, 1960.

Anderson, Totten V., and Eugene C. Lee. "The 1962 Election in California." *Western Political Quarterly* 16 (1963):396–420.

Aronson, James. *The Press and the Cold War*. Boston: Beacon Press, 1970.

Arterton, F. Christopher. *Teledemocracy: Can Technology Protect Democracy?* Newbury Park, Calif.: Sage Publications, 1987.

Asher, Herbert. *Presidential Elections and American Politics*, 4th ed. Chicago, Ill.: Dorsey Press, 1988.

Assael, Henry. *Consumer Behavior and Marketing Action*. Boston, Mass.: Kent, 1981.

Bachrach, Peter and Morton Baratz. "Decisions and Non-Decisions: An Analytical Framework." *American Political Science Review* 57 (September 1963): 632–42.

Bachrach, Peter and Morton Baratz. "Two Faces of Power." *American Political Science Review* 56 (December 1962): 947–52.

Bagdikian, Ben. *The Media Monopoly*. Boston: Beacon Press, 1983.

Bagdikian, Ben. *The Effete Conspiracy*. New York: Harper & Row, 1974.

Baker, Gordon E. "American Conceptions of Direct vis-à-vis Representative Governance." *Claremont Journal of Public Affairs* 4 (1977):5–18.

Ball, Desmond. *Politics and Force Levels*. Berkeley, Calif.: University of California Press, 1980.

Barber, Benjamin. *Strong Democracy*. Berkeley, Calif.: University of California Press, 1984.

Barnard, Chester. *Public Opinion in a Democracy*. Princeton: Herbert L. Baker Foundation, Princeton University, 1939.

Barnet, R. J. *Roots of War*. Baltimore, Md.: Penguin Books, 1972.

Barron, J. A. *Freedom of the Press for Whom? The Right of Access to the Mass Media*. Bloomington, Ind.: University of Indiana Press, 1973.

Barton, Allen H., and R. Wayne Parsons. "Measuring Belief System Structure." *Public Opinion Quarterly* 41 (1977):159–80.

Barzel, Yoram, and Eugene Silberberg. "Is the Act of Voting Rational?" *Public Choice* 16 (Fall 1973):51–58.

Bauer, Raymond A. "The Audience." In *Handbook of Communication*, ed. Ithiel de Sola Pool, Wilbur Schramm, Nathan Maccoby, and Edwin B. Parker. Chicago: Rand McNally, 1972:141–52.

Beard, Charles A. *President Roosevelt and the Coming of the War 1941: A Study in Appearances and Realities*. New Haven, Conn.: Yale University Press, 1948.

Becker, Lee B. "Two Tests of Media Gratifications: Watergate and the 1974 Election." *Journalism Quarterly* 53 (1976):28–33.

Bellah, Robert N. "Civil Religion in America." In *American Civil Religion*, ed. R. E. Richey and D. G. Jones. New York: Harper & Row, 1974.

Bennett, W. Lance. *News: The Politics of Illusion*, 2nd ed. New York: Longman, 1988.

Bennett, W. Lance. "Marginalizing the Majority: Conditioning the Public to Accept Managerial Democracy." Paper presented at the annual meeting of the Midwest Political Science Association, Chicago, Ill., April 9–11, 1987.

Berger, P. L., and T. Luckmann. *The Social Construction of Reality*. New York: Doubleday Publishing, 1966.

Bergholz, Eleanor. "Church 'disinvestment' along the Mon decried." *Pittsburgh Post-Gazette,* May 1, 1987.

Berke, Richard L. "GOP seeks to improve its spending habits." *New York Times,* March 22, 1987; IV, e5:1.

Berlin, B.; D. E. Breedlove; and P. H. Raven. *Principles of Tzeeltal Plant Classification*. New York: Academic Press, 1974.

Berman, Harold. "The Devil and Soviet Russia." *American Scholar* 27 (1958): 144–49.

Bessette, Joseph M. "Deliberative Democracy: The Majority Principle in Republican Government." In *How Democratic Is the Constitution?* ed. Robert A. Goldwin and William A. Schambra. Washington, D.C.: American Enterprise Institute, 1980, pp. 102–116.

Birch, A. H. et al. *The Popular Press in the British General Election of 1955. Political Studies* 4 (1956):297–306.

Blumenthal, Sidney. *The Rise of the Counter-Establishment.* New York: New York Times Books, 1986.

Blumler, J. G., and Michael Gurevitch. "The Political Effects of Mass Communication." In *Culture, Society and the Media,* ed. Michael Gurevitch et al. London: Metheun, 1982.

Blustein, Paul. "Supply-Side Theories Became Federal Policy with Unusual Speed: Politicians and Journalists, Rather than Academics, Played a Crucial Role." *Wall Street Journal,* October 8, 1981:1, 20.

Bock, R. D., and L. V. Jones. *The Measurement and Prediction of Judgment and Choice.* San Francisco: Holden-Day, 1968.

Bogart, Leo. *Press and Public: Who Reads What, When, Where and Why in American Newspapers.* Hillsdale, N.J.: L. Erlbaum Associates, 1981.

Bonner, Raymond. *Waltzing with a Dictator: The Marcoses and the Making of American Policy.* New York: Times Books, 1987.

Boorstin, Daniel. *The Image.* New York: Atheneum Publishers, 1962.

Boot, William. "Ethiopia: Feasting on Famine." *Columbia Journalism Review* (March/April 1985):47–48.

Borman, Ernest G. "The Ethics of Ghostwritten Speeches." *Quarterly Journal of Speech* 47 (October 1961):262–67.

Botein, Michael, and D. M. Rice. *Network Television and the Public Interest.* New York: Holt, Rinehart & Winston, 1980.

Bottome, Edgar M. *The Missile Gap.* Rutherford, N.J.: Fairleigh Dickinson University Press, 1971.

Bowles, Chester. *Promises to Keep.* New York: Harper & Row, 1971.

Bowles, Samuel, and Herbert Gintis. *Schooling in Capitalist America.* New York: Basic Books, 1976.

Breckinridge, Adam C. *The Executive Privilege.* Lincoln, Neb.: University of Nebraska Press, 1974.

Brewster, Lawrence G. *The Public Agenda: Issues in American Politics.* New York: St. Martin's Press, 1984.

Broder, David S. *The Changing of the Guard: Power and Leadership in America.* New York: Simon & Schuster, 1980.

Brokaw, Tom. Remarks at a breakfast seminar, University of Washington, September 15, 1986.

Brown, C. J., et al. *The Media and the People.* New York: Holt, Rinehart & Winston, 1978.

Brown, Les. *Television, the Business behind the Box*. New York: Harcourt Brace Jovanovich, 1971.

Brown, Tom; Joe Cowart; Beth Provinse; and Sally Sadosky. "Campaign Software Reviews." *Campaigns and Elections* (May/June 1987):22–29.

Brownstein, Ronald. "On Paper, Conservative PACs Were Tigers in 1984—But Look Again." *The National Journal*, June 29, 1985:1504–09.

Buchanan, James M. "Public Finance and Public Choice." *National Tax Journal* 28 (December 1975):383–94.

Buckalew, J. K. "The Local Radio News Editor as Gatekeeper." *Journal of Broadcasting* 18 (1974):211–21.

Burdick, Eugene. *The 480*. New York: McGraw-Hill, 1964.

Burns, Tom. "The Organization of Public Opinion." In *Mass Communication and Society,* ed. James Curran et al. London: Edward Arnold, 1977:44–69.

Burstein, Paul A. "Public Opinion, Demonstrations, and the Passage of Anti-Discrimination Legislation." *Public Opinion Quarterly* 43 (Summer 1979):157–72.

Calvert, Randall L. "The Value of Biased Information: A Rational Choice Model of Political Advice." *Journal of Politics* 47 (1985):530–55.

Campaign Finance Study Group. "Financing Presidential Campaigns: An Examination of the Ongoing Effects of the Federal Election Campaign Laws upon the Conduct of Presidential Campaigns." Cambridge, Mass.: Institute of Politics, John F. Kennedy School of Government, Harvard University, 1982.

Campbell, Angus. "A Classification of Presidential Elections." In *Elections and the Political Order,* ed. Angus Campbell et al. New York: John Wiley & Sons, 1966:63–77.

Campbell, Angus; Philip E. Converse; Warren E. Miller; and Donald E. Stokes. *The American Voter*. New York: John Wiley & Sons, 1960.

Cannon, L. "Two objectives, polls apart." *Washington Post,* June 10, 1985:A2.

Cantril, Hadley. "The Intensity of an Attitude." *Journal of Abnormal and Social Psychology* 41 (1946):129–35.

Cantril, Hadley, and Lloyd A. Free. *The Political Beliefs of Americans: A Study of Public Opinion*. New Brunswick, N.J.: Rutgers University Press, 1967.

Capon, Noel, and Gary Mauser. "A Review of Non-Profit Marketing Texts." *Journal of Marketing* 46 (Summer 1982):125–29.

Carnahan, Ann. "Organizer." *Pittsburgh Press,* April 7, 1985.

Carson, Rachel. *Silent Spring*. Boston: Houghton-Mifflin, 1962.

Chakotrin, Serge. *The Rape of the Masses*. New York: Alliance Books, 1940.

Chapman, Randall G., and Kristian S. Palda. "Electorate Turnout in Rational Voting and Consumption Perspectives." *Journal of Consumer Research* 9 (March 1983):337–46.

Chapman, Randall G., and Kristian S. Palda. "Assessing the Influence of Campaign Expenditures on Voting Behavior with a Comprehensive Electoral Market Model." *Marketing Science* 3 (Summer 1984):207–26.

Chapman, Randall G., and Kristian S. Palda. *An Econometric Analysis of the*

1984 Canadian Federal Election. Department of Marketing, Boston University, 1987.

Childs, Harwood. *Propaganda and Dictatorship.* New York: Arno Press, 1972.

Childs, Harwood. *Public Opinion.* Princeton: Van Nostrand Reinhold, 1965.

Childs, Harwood L., ed. *Pressure Groups and Propaganda. The Annals* 179 (May 1935).

Chomsky, Noam. "All the News That Fits." *Utne Reader* 14 (1986):56–65.

Chomsky, Noam. *Towards a New Cold War: Essays on the Current Crisis and How We Got There.* New York: Pantheon, 1982.

Chomsky, Noam. "The U. S. Media and the Tet Offensive." *Race and Class* 20 (1978):21–39.

Chomsky, Noam. *Syntactic Structures.* The Hague: Mouton, 1957.

Cirino, Robert. *Don't Blame the People.* New York: Vintage Books, 1972.

Clark, Peter B., and James Q. Wilson. "Incentive Systems: A Theory of Organizations." *Administrative Science Quarterly* (September 1961):129–66.

Clausen, Aage R.; Philip E. Converse; and Warren E. Miller. "Electoral Myth and Reality: The 1964 Election." *American Political Science Review* 59 (June 1965):321–32.

Clymer, A. "Majority in poll looks to Congress to cut spending." *New York Times,* November 17, 1985: I1.

Clymer, A. "Poll finds Americans don't know U.S. positions on Central America." *New York Times,* July 1, 1983:A1.

Cobb, R. W., and C. D. Elder. *Participation in American Politics: The Dynamics of Agenda Building.* Boston: Allyn & Bacon, 1972.

Cockburn, Alexander. "Silence Is Golden." *Nation* 242 (May 1986):638.

Cockburn, Alexander. "Remember El Salvador?" *Nation,* June 1, 1985.

Cohen, Bernard C. *The Press and Foreign Policy.* Princeton: Princeton University Press, 1963.

Cohen, Carl, ed. *Communism, Fascism, and Democracy,* 2nd ed. New York: Random House, 1972.

Cohen, Manuel F., and George J. Stigler. *Can Regulatory Agencies Protect Consumers?* Washington, D.C.: American Enterprise Institute for Public Policy, 1971.

Committee on Political Parties of the American Political Science Association. "Toward a More Responsible Two Party System." Washington, D.C.: Supplement to *American Political Science Review* XLVIII (1950).

Compaine, Benjamin, ed. *Who Owns the Media?* New York: Harmony Books, 1979.

Conlan, Timothy J. "Federalism and American Politics: New Relationships, a Changing System." *Intergovernmental Perspective* 11 (Winter 1985):38.

Conner, Walter D., and Zvi Gitelman. *Public Opinion in European Socialist Systems.* New York: Praeger Publishers, 1977:314.

Connolly, William, ed. *The Bias of Pluralism.* New York: Atherton, 1969.

Converse, Philip E. "Attitudes and Non-Attitudes: Continuation of a Dialogue." In *The Quantitative Analysis of Social Problems*, ed. Edward Tufte. Reading, Mass.: Addison-Wesley, 1970:168–69.

Converse, Philip E. "The Problem of Party Distances in Models of Voting Change." In *The Electoral Process*, ed. M. K. Jennings and L. H. Zeigler. Englewood Cliffs, N.J.: Prentice-Hall, 1966:175–207.

Converse, Philip E. "The Nature of Belief Systems in Mass Publics." In *Ideology and Discontent*, ed. David Apter. New York: Free Press, 1964:206–61.

Creel, George. *How We Advertised America*. New York: Harper & Row, 1920.

Crick, Bernard. *In Defense of Politics*, 2nd ed. New York: Penguin Books, 1982.

Cronin, Thomas E. *The State of the Presidency*, 2nd ed. Boston: Little-Brown, 1980.

Cunningham, Jim, and Pamela Martz eds. *Steel People: Survival and Resilience in Pittsburgh's Mon Valley*. Pittsburgh: Rivers Communities Project, School of Social Work, University of Pittsburgh, 1986.

Curran, James, and Jean Seaton. *Power without Responsibility: The Press and Broadcasting in Britain*. London: Fontana, 1981.

Currim, Imran. "Predictive Testing of Consumer Choice Models Not Subject to Independence of Irrelevant Alternatives." *Journal of Marketing Research* 19 (May 1982):208–22.

Dahl, Robert A. *After the Revolution?* New Haven: Yale University Press, 1970.

Dahl, Robert A. *A Preface to Democratic Theory*. Chicago: University of Chicago Press, 1956.

Darr, Thomas B. "On Electing a Governor: Notes on a Political Internship." Master's thesis, Graduate School of Public and International Affairs, University of Pittsburgh, 1978.

Davis, Phillip. "Anti-Mellon activist fired by Lutherans." *Pittsburgh Post-Gazette*, April 11, 1983.

Davison, W. Phillips. "Public Opinion Research as Communication." *Public Opinion Quarterly* 36 (Fall 1972):314.

Deacon, Robert T. "Individual Preferences and Public Policy." In *Advances in Consumer Research* 8, ed. Kent B. Monroe. Ann Arbor, Mich.: Association for Consumer Research, 1980:517–22.

Denton, Robert E., Jr., and Gary C. Woodward. "Ghostwriters, The Presidency, and The Bureaucracy." In *Political Communication in America*, New York: Praeger Publishers, 1985:234–73.

Dewey, John. *The Public and Its Problems*. New York: Holt Rinehart & Winston, 1927.

Diamond, Edwin, and Stephen Bates. *The Spot: The Rise of Political Advertising on Television*, rev. ed. Cambridge, Mass.: MIT Press, 1988.

DMS. *Newsletters*. Pittsburgh: DMS, East Liberty Lutheran Church, 1986, 1987.

Domhoff, G. William. *The Powers That Be: Processes of Ruling Class Domination in America*. New York: Vintage Books, 1979.

Domhoff, G. William. *Who Rules America?* Englewood Cliffs, N.J.: Prentice-Hall, 1967.

Donahue, G. A., et al. "Gatekeeping: Mass Media Systems and Information Control." In *Current Perspectives in Mass Communication Research,* ed. F. G. Kline and P. J. Tichenor. Beverly Hills, Calif.: Sage Publications, 1972:412–69.

Donner, Frank J. *The Age of Surveillance: The Aims and Methods of America's Political Intelligence System.* New York: Random House, 1981.

Dorman, William A., and Mansour Farhang. *The U.S. Press and Iran: Foreign Policy and the Journalism of Deference.* Berkeley, Calif.: University of California Press, 1987.

Downs, Anthony. "Up and Down with Ecology: The Issue-Attention Cycle." *Public Interest* 28 (1972):38–50.

Downs, Anthony. *An Economic Theory of Democracy.* New York: Harper & Row, 1957.

Drew, Elizabeth. *Politics and Money: The New Road to Corruption.* New York: Macmillan, 1983.

Drier, Peter, and Steve Weinberg. "Interlocking Directorates." *Columbia Journalism Review* (November/December 1979):51–68.

Duverger, Maurice. *Political Parties.* New York: Wiley & Sons, 1954:426.

Dye, Thomas R. *Who's Running America? The Conservative Years,* 4th ed. Englewood Cliffs, N.J: Prentice-Hall, 1986.

Dye, Thomas R., and Harmon Zeigler. *American Politics in the Media Age,* 2nd ed. Pacific Grove, Calif.: Brooks/Cole, 1986.

Dye, Thomas R., and H. Zeigler. *The Irony of Democracy,* 3rd ed. Pacific Grove, Calif.: Brooks/Cole, 1975.

Dye, Thomas R., and H. Zeigler. *The Irony of Democracy,* 7th ed. Pacific Grove, Calif.: Brooks/Cole, 1987.

Edelman, Murray. *The Symbolic Uses of Politics,* rev. ed. Urbana, Ill.: University of Illinois Press, 1985.

Edelman, Murray. *The Symbolic Uses of Politics.* Urbana, Ill.: University of Illinois Press, 1964.

Edsall, Thomas B. "The Republican well is running dry these days: But the party still outdraws the Democrats." *Washington Post, National Weekly Edition,* May 4, 1987:15.

Edsall, Thomas B. *The New Politics of Inequality.* New York: W. W. Norton, 1984.

Edwards, George C. "The Two Presidencies: A Reevaluation." *American Politics Quarterly* 14 (1986):247–434.

Edwards, George C. *Presidential Influence in Congress.* San Francisco: W. H. Freeman, 1980.

Ehrmann, Henry W. *Politics in France,* 4th ed. Boston: Little, Brown, 1976.

Einhorn, Lois J. "The Ghosts Unmasked: A Review of Literature on Speechwriting." *Communication Quarterly* 30 (1981):41–47.

Eldersveld, Samuel J. *Political Parties*. Chicago: Rand McNally, 1964.

Ellul, Jacques. *Propaganda: The Formation of Men's Attitudes*. New York: Alfred A. Knopf, 1965.

Engel, James, and Roger Blackwell. *Consumer Behavior,* 4th ed. Hinsdale, Ill.: Dryden Press, 1982.

Epstein, Edward Jay. "The Selection of Reality." In *What's News: The Media in American Society,* ed. Elie Abel. San Francisco: Institute for Contemporary Studies, 1981:119–32.

Farney, Denis. "Coelho makes money, and waves, for the Democrats." *Wall Street Journal,* June 14, 1983.

Federal Election Commission. *The First 10 Years, 1975–1985.* Washington, D.C.: Federal Election Commission, 1985.

Federal Election Commission: *FEC Releases Political Party Spending Figures through October 17, 1984; Independent Expenditure Index by Committee/Person Expending.* Washington, D.C.: Federal Election Commission, March 1985.

Ferguson, Thomas. "Party Alignment and American Industrial Structure: The Investment Theory of Political Parties." In *Research in Political Economy* vol. 6. Greenwich, Conn.: JAI Press, Inc., 1983:1–82.

Ferguson, Thomas, and Joel Rogers. *Right Turn: The Decline of the Democrats and the Future of American Politics.* New York: Hill & Wang, 1986.

Festinger, Leon. *A Theory of Cognitive Dissonance*. Stanford, Calif.: Stanford University Press, 1965.

Fiorina, M. P. *Retrospective Voting in American Politics*. New Haven, Conn.: Yale University Press, 1981.

Fitzgerald, Frances. "A Disciplined, Charging Army." *The New Yorker,* May 18, 1981.

Flanigan, William H., and Nancy Zingale. *Political Behavior of the American Electorate,* 6th ed. Boston: Allyn & Bacon, 1987.

Fletcher, Frederick J. "Media Elections in Canada: Trends and Portents." Presentad at the 1985 annual meeting of the American Political Science Association, held in New Orleans, La., August 29–September 1, 1985.

Flexner, James Thomas. *George Washington: Anguish and Farewell (1793–1799).* Boston: Little, Brown, 1972.

Fodor, J. A., and Katz, J. J., eds. *The Structure of Language: Readings in the Philosophy of Language.* Englewood Cliffs, N.J.: Prentice-Hall, 1964.

Fogelson, Robert M. *Violence as Protest*. New York: Doubleday Publishing, 1971.

Ford, Daniel. *The Cult of the Atom: The Secret Papers of the Atomic Energy Commission.* New York: Simon & Schuster, 1984.

Fowler, Robert Booth. *Religion and Politics in America.* Metuchen, N.J.: Scarecrow Press, 1985.

Freiberger, Paul, and Michael Swaine. *Fire in the Valley, the Making of the Personal Computer.* Berkeley, Calif.: Osbourne/McGraw-Hill, 1984.

Friesema, H. Paul, and Ronald D. Hedlund. "The Reality of Representational Roles." In *Public Opinion and Public Policy*, 3rd ed., ed. Norman Luttberg. Itasca, Ill.: F. E. Peacock, 1981:316–20.

Frolich, Norman; Joe A. Oppenheimer; Jeffrey Smith; and Oran R. Young. "A Test of Downsian Voter Rationality: 1964 Presidential Voting." *American Political Science Review* 72 (March 1978):157–62.

Gallup, George. *Public Opinion in a Democracy*. Princeton: Stafford Little Lectures, Princeton University Press, 1939.

Gallup, George. *The Pulse of Democracy*. New York: Simon & Schuster, 1940:266.

Gallup, George. *The Gallup Poll: Public Opinion 1935–71*, 3 vols. New York: Random House, 1972.

Gallup, George. *The Gallup Poll: Public Opinion 1972–77*. Wilmington, Del.: Scholarly Publications, 1978.

Gallup, George. *The Gallup Poll: Public Opinion* (1979–85, annual vols.). Wilmington, Del.: Scholarly Publications, 1979–85.

Gallup Organization. *The People, Press and Politics*. Los Angeles: Times-Mirror Publishers, 1987.

Gamson, W. A. *Power and Discontent*. Homewood, Ill.: Dorsey Press, 1968.

Gans, H. *Deciding What's News: A Study of CBS Evening News, NBC Nightly News, Newsweek, and Time*. New York: Vintage Books, 1979.

Gaynor, Pamela. "Analysts see fewer USX jobs." *Pittsburgh Post-Gazette*, January 20, 1987.

Gelb, Leslie H. "Arms control and the Russians: Battle on compliance heats up." *New York Times*, June 7, 1985:1, 4.

Gervasi, Tom. *The Myth of Soviet Military Supremacy*. New York: Harper & Row, 1986.

Gieber, Walter. "News Is What Newspapermen Make It." In *People, Society, and Mass Communications*, ed. L. A. Dexter and D. M. White. New York: Free Press of Glencoe, 1964:173–82.

Giertz, J. Fred, and Dennis H. Sullivan. "Campaign Expenditures and Election Outcomes: A Critical Note." *Public Choice* 31 (Fall 1977):157–62.

Gilsdorf, R. R. "Public Opinion and Participation." In *Liberal Democracy in Canada and the United States*, ed. T. C. Pocklington. Toronto: Holt, Rinehart & Winston, 1985.

Ginsberg, Benjamin. *The Captive Public: How Mass Opinion Promotes State Power*. New York: Basic Books, 1986.

Ginsberg, Benjamin. *The Consequences of Consent*. New York: Random House, 1982.

Gitlin, Todd. *The Whole World Is Watching*. Berkeley, Calif.: University of California Press, 1980.

Glasgow University Media Group. *More Bad News*. London: Routledge & Kegan Paul, 1980.

Glasgow University Media Group. *Bad News*. London: Routledge & Kegan Paul, 1976.

Goldenberg, Edie N. *Making the Papers: The Access of Resource-Poor Groups to the Metropolitan Press*. Lexington, Mass.: Lexington Books, 1975.

Golding, Peter. *The Mass Media*. London: Longmans, 1974.

Goldstein, Robert J. *Political Repression in Modern America*. New York: Two Continents, 1978.

Goodin, Robert E. "Voting through the Looking Glass." *American Political Science Review* 77 (1983):420–34.

Gosnell, Harold. *Machine Politics: Chicago Model,* rev. ed. Chicago: University of Chicago Press, 1968.

Goulden, Joseph C. *Truth Is the First Casualty: The Gulf of Tonkin Affair—Illusion and Reality*. Chicago: Rand McNally, 1969.

Graber, Doris A. "Say It with Pictures: The Impact of Audio-Visual News on Public Opinion Formation." Paper presented at the annual meeting of the Midwest Political Science Association, Chicago, Ill.: April 9–11, 1987.

Graber, Doris A. *Mass Media and American Politics,* 2nd ed. Washington, D.C.: Congressional Quarterly Press, 1984.

Grassmuck, George, ed. *Before Nomination: Our Primary Problem*. Washington, D.C.: American Enterprise Institute, 1985.

Gravel, Mike, ed. *The Pentagon Papers: The Defense Department History of United States Decisionmaking on Vietnam,* 4 vols. Boston: Beacon Press, 1971.

Green, Mark, and Gail McColl. *There He Goes Again: Ronald Reagan's Reign of Error*. New York: Pantheon Books, 1983.

Green, Paul E., and Frank J. Carmone. *Multidimensional Scaling and Related Techniques in Marketing Analysis*. Boston, Mass.: Allyn & Bacon, 1970.

Green, Paul E., and V. Srinivasan. "Conjoint Analysis in Consumer Research: Issues and Outlook." *Journal of Consumer Research* 5, no. 2 (December 1978):103–23.

Greider, William. "The Education of David Stockman." *The Atlantic* (December 1981):27–54.

Guterman, Norbert, comp. *A Book of Latin Quotations*. Garden City, N.J.: Doubleday Publishing, 1966.

Hadden, Jeffrey. *Prime-Time Preachers*. Reading, Mass.: Addison-Wesley, 1981.

Hall, Robert N. "Lyndon Johnson's Speech Preparation." *Quarterly Journal of Speech* 51 (1965):168–76.

Hallin, Daniel C. *The "Uncensored War": The Media and Vietnam*. New York: Oxford University Press, 1986.

Hallin, Daniel C. "The Media, the War in Vietnam, and Political Support: A Critique of the Thesis of an Oppositional Media." *Journal of Politics* 46 (1984):2–24.

Halloran, Richard, and Leslie Gelb. "CIA analysts now said to find U.S. overstated Soviet arms rise." *New York Times,* March 3, 1983:1.

Hamilton, Alexander; James Madison; and John Jay. *The Federalist.* New York: Random House Modern Library (follows original Mclean edition of 1788).

Hamilton, Howard D. "Direct Legislation: Some Implicataions of Open Housing Referenda." *American Political Science Review* 64 (1970):124–38.

Harrington, Michael. *The Other America.* New York: Macmillan, 1962.

Harris, Louis. *The Anguish of Change.* New York: W. W. Norton, 1973.

Hart, Vivien. *Distrust and Democracy: Political Distrust in Britain and America.* Cambridge: Cambridge University Press, 1978.

Hartley, Robert R. *Marketing Mistakes.* Columbus, Ohio: Grid, 1976.

Hastie, Reid. "A Primer of Information-Processing Theory for the Political Scientist." In *Political Cognition,* ed. Richard Lau and David Sears. Hillsdale, N.J.: Erlbaum, 1986.

Heider, Fritz. *The Psychology of Interpersonal Relations.* New York: John Wiley & Sons, 1958.

Heller, David J. "Mail, Money and Machiavelli." *Campaigns and Elections* (November/December 1987):32–45.

Helpline. *Help Is a Four Letter Word,* 5th ed. Pittsburgh: United Steelworkers of America, 1985.

Hendel, Samuel, ed. *The Soviet Crucible,* 5th ed. North Scituate, Mass.: Duxbury Press, 1980.

Hendon, Donald W. *Battling for Profits.* Jonesboro, Ark.: Business Consultants International, 1986.

Hennessey, Bernard. *Public Opinion.* North Scituate, Mass.: Duxbury Press, 1975.

Henry, William A., III. "News as Entertainment: The Search for Dramatic Unity." In *What's News: The Media in American Society,* ed. Elie Abel. San Francisco: Institute for Contemporary Studies, 1981:133–58.

Hensler, Deborah R., and Carl P. Hensler. "Evaluating Nuclear Power." Manuscript. Santa Monica, Calif.: Rand Corporation, 1979.

Herman, E. S. "Diversity of News: 'Marginalizing' the Opposition." *Journal of Communication* 35 (1985):135–46.

Hersh, Seymour M. "Target Qaddafi." *New York Times Magazine,* February 11, 1987:17.

Hersh, Seymour M. *"The Target Is Destroyed": What Really Happened to Flight 007 and What America Knew About It.* New York: Random House, 1986.

Hersh, Seymour M. *The Price of Power: Kissinger in the Nixon White House.* New York: Summit, 1983.

Hochschild, Adam. "A Tale of Two Exposes." *Mother Jones* (September/October 1981):10.

Hodiak, Bohan. "Protest at Lutheran service." *Pittsburgh Post-Gazette,* October 27, 1986.

Hodiak, Bodan, and Andrew Sheehan. "Insight: Stategist for protestors keeps low profile." *Pittsburgh Post-Gazette,* May 2, 1983.

Hofstadter, Richard. *The American Political Tradition and the Men Who Made It.* New York: Vintage Books, 1973.

Hoggart, Richard. *The Uses of Literacy: Aspects of Working-Class Life, with Special Reference to Publications and Entertainments.* London: Chatto & Windus, 1971.

Hollander, Richard S. *Video Democracy: The Vote From Home Revolution.* Airy, Md.: Lomond Publications, 1985.

Honeywell, Charles. "Self-Ministry: The Attraction Goal of the American Church." Pittsburgh: A DMS Paper, September 15, 1985.

Hovland, Carl I. "Reconciling Conflicting Results Derived from Experimental and Survey Studies of Attitude Change." *American Psychologist* 14 (1959):8–17.

Hunt, Shelby. "The Nature and the Scope of Marketing." *Journal of Marketing* 40 (July 1976):17–28.

Hunter, Floyd. *Community Power Structure.* Chapel Hill, N.C.: University of North Carolina Press, 1953.

Hursh, Burton. *The Mellon Family: A Fortune in History.* New York: William Morrow, 1978.

Hurwitz, Jon, and Mark Peffley. "How Are Foreign Policy Attitudes Structured? A Hierarchical Model." *American Political Science Review* 81 (1987):1099–1121.

Ippolito, Dennis; Thomas G. Walker; and Kenneth L. Kolson. *Public Opinion and Responsible Democracy.* Englewood Cliffs, N.J.: Prentice-Hall, 1976.

Iyengar, Shanto, and Donald R. Kinder. *News That Matters.* Chicago: University of Chicago Press, 1987.

Iyengar, Shanto; Mark D. Peters; and Donald R. Kinder. "Experimental Demonstrations of the 'Not-So-Minimal' Consequences of Television News Programs." *American Political Science Review* 76 (1982):848–58.

Jacobson, Gary C. "Money in the 1980 and 1982 Congressional Elections." In *Money and Politics in the United States: Financing Elections in the 1980s,* ed. Michael J. Malbin. Chatham, N.J.: Chatham House, 1984:38–69.

Jacobson, Gary C. *Money in Congressional Elections.* New Haven: Yale University Press, 1980.

Jakobson, Roman, and M. Halle. *Fundamentals of Language.* The Hague: Mouton, 1956.

Jakobson, Roman; G. M. Fant; and M. Halle. *Preliminaries to Speech Analysis: The Distinctive Features and Their Correlates.* Cambridge, Mass.: MIT Press, 1952, 1963.

Javits, Jacob. "How I Used a Poll in Campaigning for Congress." *Public Opinion Quarterly* (Summer 1947):220–26.

Jensen, C. "The Ten Best-Censored Stories of 1985." *Utne Reader* 18 (1986):84–91.

Jensen, Richard. "American Election Analysis." In *Politics and the Social Sciences,* ed. Seymour Martin Lipset. New York: Oxford Press, 1969:226–43.

Johnson, Richard M. "Tradeoff Analysis of Consumer Values." *Journal of Marketing Research* 11 (May 1974), pp. 121–27.

Johnson, Stephen D. "The Political Impact of the Christian Right in Middletown." Presented at the annual meeting of the American Political Science Association, Washington, D.C., 1986.

Johnson, Stephen D., and Joseph Tamney. "The Christian Right and the 1984 Presidential Election." *Review of Religious Research* 27 (1985):124–33.

Johnson, Stephen D., and Joseph Tamney. "The Christian Right and the 1980 Presidential Election." *Journal for the Scientific Study of Religion* 21 (1982):123–31.

Johnston, Michael. "The New Christian Right in American Politics." *Political Quarterly* 53 (1982):181–99.

Jones, Charles O. *An Introduction to the Study of Public Policy,* 2nd ed. North Scituate, Mass.: Dorsey Press, 1977.

Jones, Charles O. *Clean Air: The Policies and Politics of Pollution Control.* Pittsburgh: University of Pittsburgh Press, 1975.

Jones, Ruth S. "Financing State Elections." In *Money and Politics in the United States: Financing Elections in the 1980s,* ed. Michael J. Malbin. Chatham, N.J.: Chatham House, 1984:172–213.

Joslyn, Richard. *Mass Media and Elections.* Reading, Mass.: Addison-Wesley, 1984.

Joyce, Ed. *Prime Times, Bad Times.* New York: Doubleday Publishing, 1988.

Kaplan, Fred. *The Wizards of Armageddon.* New York: Simon & Schuster, 1983.

Karson, Marc. *American Labor Unions and Politics.* Boston: Beacon Press, 1965:chap. 9.

Katz, Daniel et al., eds. *Public Opinion and Propaganda: A Book of Readings.* New York: Holt, Rinehart & Winston, 1954.

Kayden, Xandra. *Campaign Organization.* Lexington, Mass.: D. C. Heath, 1978.

Kayden, Xandra, and Eddie Mahe, Jr. *The Party Goes On.* New York: Basic Books, 1985.

Kearns, D. *Lyndon Johnson and the American Dream.* New York: Harper & Row, 1976.

Keeter, Scott. "Public Opinion in 1984." In *The Election of 1984: Reports and Interpretations,* ed. Gerald Pomper et al. Chatham, N.J.: Chatham House, 1985.

Keith, Bruce E., et al. "The Partisan Affinities of Independent 'Leaners'." *British Journal of Political Science* 16 (1986):155–85.

Kellman, H. C. "Compliance, Identification, and Internalization: Three Processes of Attitude Change." *Journal of Conflict Resolution* 2 (1958):51–60.

Kennan, G. *Memoirs (1925–1950).* New York: Bantam Books, 1969.

Kernell, Samuel. *Going Public: New Strategies of Presidential Leadership.* Washington, D.C.: Congressional Quarterly, 1986.

Kernell, Samuel. "The Truman Doctrine Speech: A Case Study of the Dynamics of Presidential Opinion Leadership." *Social Science History* 1 (1976):20–45.

Kessel, John H. *Presidential Campaign Politics,* 2nd ed. Homewood, Ill.: Dorsey Press, 1984.

Kessel, John H. *The Goldwater Coalition: Republican Strategies in 1964.* Indianapolis, Ind.: Bobbs-Merrill, 1968.

Key, V. O. *Public Opinion and American Democracy.* New York: Alfred A. Knopf, 1961.

Kilpatrick, James J. "Tempest on the Hilltop." *Washington Post,* February 18, 1983:A21.

Kirkpatrick, Ivone. *Mussolini, A Study in Power.* New York: Hawthorne, 1964.

Kotler, Philip. *Marketing Management,* 2nd ed. New York: Prentice-Hall, 1972.

Kotler, Philip, and Sidney Levy. "Broadening the Concept of Marketing." *Journal of Marketing* 33 (January 1969):15.

Kotz, David M. *Bank Control of Large Corporations in the United States.* Berkeley, Calif.: University of California Press, 1978.

Kropotkin, Peter. *Fields, Factories and Workshops; or Industry Combined with Agriculture and Brain Work with Manual Work.* New York: G. P. Putnam & Sons, 1909.

Landau, Lev D., and E. M. Lifshitz. *Quantum Mechanics,* trans. J. B. Sykes and J. S. Bell. Reading, Mass.: Addison-Wesley Publishing, 1958.

Lane, Robert E., and David O. Sears. *Public Opinion.* Englewood Cliffs, N.J.: Prentice-Hall, 1964:105.

Lang, G. E., and K. Lang. *The Battle for Public Opinion: The President, the Press, and the Polls during Watergate.* New York: Columbia University Press, 1983.

Langer, Walter. *The Mind of Adolf Hitler.* New York: Basic Books, 1972.

Lash, Cindi. "Columbus police here to develop DMX plan." *Pittsburgh Press,* December 13, 1986.

Lasswell, Harold. *Politics: Who Gets What, When, and How.* Cleveland: Meridian, 1951.

Lazarsfeld, Paul; Bernard Berelson; and Hazel Gaudet. *The People's Choice: How the Voter Makes Up His Mind in a Presidential Campaign,* 3rd ed. New York: Columbia University Press, 1968.

Le Monde. "L'election presidentielle, 26 avril–10 mai 1981." *Supplement aux dossiers et documents du monde,* May 1981.

Lichter, R. S.; S. Rothman; and L. S. Lichter. *The Media Elite.* Bethesda, Md.: Adler & Adler, 1986.

Lindblom, Charles. *Politics and Markets.* New York: Basic Books, 1977.

Lindblom, Charles. *The Policy-Making Process.* Englewood Cliffs, N.J.: Prentice-Hall, 1968.

Lippmann, Walter. *Public Opinion.* New York: Free Press, 1965.

Lippmann, Walter. *Essays in the Public Philosophy.* New York: Mentor Books, 1962.

Lipset, Seymour M. "The President, the Polls, and Vietnam." *Transaction* (September/October 1966):19–24.

Lipset, Seymour M., and William Schneider. *The Confidence Gap: Business, Labor, and Government in the Public Mind.* New York: Free Press, 1983.

Lipsky, Michael. *Protest in City Politics: Rent Strikes, Housing and the Power of the Poor.* Chicago: Rand-McNally, 1970.

Lipsky, Michael, and D. J. Olson. *Commission Politics.* New Brunswick, N.J.: Transaction Books, 1977.

Long, Philip D. *The Book on Pittsburgh: The Other Side of the Story.* Pittsburgh: DMS, East Liberty Lutheran Church, 1985.

Luce, Duncan. "The Individual Choice Axiom after Twenty Years." *Journal of Mathematical Philosophy* 15, no. 3 (June 1977):215–33.

Luce, Duncan. *Individual Choice Behavior.* New York: John Wiley & Sons, 1959.

Lutheran Church in America, Division for Mission in North America, Christian Associates of SWPA, Mellon Bank, University and City Ministries. *The People's Guide to Human Services.* Pittsburgh: United Steelworkers of America, 1986.

Lutrin, Carl E. "The Public and Ecology: The Role of Initiatives in California's Environmental Politics." *Western Political Quarterly* 28 (1975):352–72.

MacNeil, Robert. *The People Machine: The Influence of Television on American Politics.* New York: Harper & Row, 1968.

Magleby, David B. "Participation in Initiative and Referendum Elections in Switzerland and the United States." Paper presented at the XIII World Congress of the International Political Science Association, Paris, 1985.

Magleby, David B. *Direct Legislation: Voting on Ballot Propositions in the United States.* Baltimore, Md.: Johns Hopkins University Press, 1984.

Main, Jeremy. "The Tax Revolt Takes Hold." *Money* (February 1980):52.

Malbin, Michael J. "You Get What You Pay For, But Is It What You Want?" In *Before Nomination: Our Primary Problems,* ed. George Grassmuck. Washington, D.C.: American Enterprise Institute, 1985: 72–86.

Malbin, Michael J., ed. *Money and Politics in the United States: Financing Elections in the 1980s.* Chatham, N.J.: Chatham House, 1985.

Mansbridge, Jane J. *How We Lost the ERA.* Chicago: University of Chicago Press, 1986.

Marchetti, Victor, and John D. Marks. *The CIA and the Cult of Intelligence,* (exp. ed.: orig. pub. 1974). New York: Dell, 1980.

Margolis, Michael. "Public Opinion as a Dependent Variable." Paper delivered at the 1985 annual meeting of the American Political Science Association, New Orleans, La., 1985.

Margolis, Michael. "Democracy: American Style." In *Democratic Theory and Practice,* ed. Graeme Duncan. New York: Cambridge University Press, 1983, 115–32.

Margolis, Michael. "From Confusion to Confusion: Issues and the American Voter, 1956–1972." *American Political Science Review* 71 (March 1977):31–43.

Margolis, Michael. "The New American Government Textbooks." *American Journal of Political Science* 27 (1973):457–63.

Margolis, Michael. *Viable Democracy.* New York: Penguin, 1979.

Margolis, Michael; Robert Burtt; and Jeffrey McLaughlin. "The Impact of Industrial Decline: Braddock, North Braddock, and Rankin." In *Steel People: Survival and Resilience in Pittsburgh's Mon Valley,* ed. Jim Cunningham and Pamela Martz. Pittsburgh: River Communities Project, School of Social Work, University of Pittsburgh, 1986:9–32.

Martin, William. "The Birth of the Media Myth." *The Atlantic,* June 1981.

Marx, Karl, and Frederick Engels. *The German Ideology.* New York: International Publishers, 1947.

Mauser, Gary. *Political Marketing: An Approach to Campaign Strategy.* New York: Praeger Publishers, 1983.

Mauser, Gary. "Positioning Political Candidates—An Application of Concept Evaluation Techniques." *Journal of the Marketing Research Society* 22 (July 1980):181–91.

Mauser, Gary. "A Structural Approach to Predicting Patterns of Electoral Substitution." In *Multidimensional Scaling, Theory and Applications in Behavioral Sciences,* ed. A. Kimball Romney, Roger N. Shepard, and Sara Beth Nerlove. II/Applications. New York: Seminar Press, 1972.

McCabe, Peter. *Bad News at Black Rock: The Sell-Out of CBS News.* New York: Arbor House, 1987.

McCamy, James L. *Government Publicity.* Chicago: University of Chicago Press, 1939:chap. 5.

McCarthy, E. J. *Basic Marketing.* Homewood, Ill.: Richard D. Irwin, 1960.

McCombs, M. E., and D. L. Shaw. "The Agenda-Setting Function of the Mass Media." *Public Opinion Quarterly* 36 (1972):176–87.

McDonald, Fred J. "Television and the Red Menace: The Video Road to Vietnam." New York: Praeger Publishers, 1985.

McFarland, Gerald W. *Mugwumps, Morals, and Politics 1884–1920.* Amherst, Mass.: University of Massachusetts Press, 1975:92.

McGinniss, Joe. *The Selling of the President, 1968.* New York: Trident, 1969.

McKay, Jim. "Pension agency blocks LTV talks, union says." *Pittsburgh Post-Gazette,* March 25, 1987.

McKay, Jim. "Pickets allow razing of Dorothy." *Pittsburgh Post-Gazette,* September 10, 1986.

McLeod, J. M. et al. "Another Look at the Agenda-Setting Function of the Press." *Communication Research* 1 (1974):131–66.

McLeod, Jack M., and Lee B. Becker. "The Uses and Gratifications Approach." In *Handbook of Political Communication,* ed. Dan D. Nimmo and Keith R. Sanders. Beverly Hills, Calif.: Sage Publications, 1981.

McLeod, Jack M., and Garrett J. O'Keefe, Jr. "The Socialization Perspective and Communication Behavior." In *Current Perspectives in Mass Communication Research,* ed. F. Ferald Kline and Phillip J. Tichenor. Beverly Hills, Calif.: Sage, 1972:121–68.

McQuail, Denis, and Karen Suine. *New Media Politics: Comparative Perspectives in Western Europe.* London: Sage Publications Ltd., 1986.

Meadow, Robert G., ed. *New Communication Technologies in Politics.* Washington, D.C., 1985.

Mellon Bank Corporation. *1985 Community Report.* Pittsburgh: Mellon Bank Corporation, 1985.

Mellon Bank Corporation. *Annual Reports for 1984 and 1985.* Pittsburgh: Mellon Bank Corporation, 1984, 1985.

Meuller, John E. *War, Presidents and Public Opinion.* New York: John Wiley & Sons, 1973.

Meuller, John E. "Trends in Popular Support for the Wars in Korea and Viet Nam." *American Political Science Review* 65 (1971):358–75.

Miliband, Ralph. *The State in Capitalist Society.* New York: Basic Books, 1969.

Mill, John Stuart. *Considerations on Representative Government.* Southbend, Ind.: Gateway Editions, Henry Regnery, 1962.

Miller, Arther S. "Do We Want to Know?" *Progressive* (April 1986):41–2.

Miller, G. A. "The Magic Number Seven, Plus or Minus One." *Psychological Review* 63 (1956):81–97.

Miller, W. E., and T. E. Levitin. *Leadership and Change: The New Politics and the American Electorate.* Cambridge, Mass.: Winthrop, 1976.

Miller, Warren E., and Donald E. Stokes. "Constituency Influence on Congress." *American Political Science Review* LVII (1963):45–56.

Mills, C. Wright. *The Power Elite.* New York: Oxford University Press, 1956.

Minsky, M. "A Framework for Representing Knowledge." In *The Psychology of Computer Vision,* ed. Patrick H. Winston. New York: McGraw-Hill, 1975.

Monroe, Alan D. "Consistency Between Public Preferences and National Policy Decisions." *American Politics Quarterly* 7 (1979):3–19.

Monroe, Alan D. *Public Opinion in America.* New York: Dodd, Mead, 1975.

Moody's Investors Service. *Moody's Bank and Financial Manual,* vol. 1. New York: Moody's Investors Service (annual), 1984, 1985.

Muldern, Ronald. "Media Credibility: A Use-Gratifications Approach." *Journalism Quarterly* 57 (1980):474–77.

Myrdal, Gunnar. *An American Dilemma,* 2 vols. New York: Random House, 1944.

Nader, Ralph. *Unsafe at Any Speed: The Designed-In Dangers of the American Automobile.* New York: Grossman, 1965.

Nader, Ralph, and William Taylor. *The Big Boys: Power and Position in American Business*. New York: Pantheon, 1986.

Nader, Ralph; Clarence Ditlow; and Joyce Kinnard. *The Lemon Book*. Ottawa, Ill.: Caroline House, 1980.

National Advisory Commission on Civil Disorders. *Report of the National Advisory Commission on Civil Disorders*. New York: Bantam, 1968.

Neustadt, Richard E. *Presidential Power: The Politics of Leadership from FDR to Carter*. New York: John Wiley & Sons, 1980.

Newman, Bruce I., and Jagdish N. Sheth. *A Theory of Political Choice*. New York: Praeger Publishers, 1987.

New York Times. "Survey finds many skeptics among evangelists' viewers." March 31, 1987:A1, B8.

Nichols, Marie Hochmuth. "Ghost Writing: Implications for Public Address." In *Rhetoric and Criticism*. Baton Rouge: Louisiana State University Press, 1963.

Nie, Norman; Sidney Verba; and John R. Petrocik. *The Changing American Voter*, enlarged ed. Cambridge, Mass.: Harvard University Press, 1979.

Niemi, Richard G. "The Future of Public Opinion Research: Theory and Methods." Paper delivered at the annual meeting of the American Political Science Association, Chicago, Ill., September 1983.

Nimmo, Dan, and R. L. Savage. *Candidates and Their Images: Concepts, Attitudes and Findings*. Santa Monica, Calif.: Goodyear Publishing, 1976.

Nisbett, Robert. "Public Opinion versus Popular Opinion." *Public Interest* (Fall 1975):166–92.

Noelle-Neumann, E. *The Spiral of Silence: Public Opinion—Our Social Skin*. Chicago: University of Chicago Press, 1984.

Novak, Michael. "Television Shapes the Soul." In *Television as a Social Force: New Approaches to TV Criticism*, ed. D. Cater and R. Adler. New York: Praeger Publishers, 1975:9–21.

Nunnally, Jum. *Psychometric Theory*, 2nd ed. New York: McGraw-Hill, 1978.

Oravecz, John D. "Mellon pulling back from foreign aid." *Pittsburgh Press*, March 8, 1987a.

Oravecz, John D. "Mellon to spread cuts, analysts say." *Pittsburgh Press*, March 20, 1987b.

Ordeshook, Peter C. "The Spatial Theory of Elections: A Review and Critique." In *Party Identification and Beyond*, ed. Ian Budge, Ivor Crewe, and Dennis Farlie. London: Wiley, 1976:285–314.

O'Shaughnessy, John, and Michael Ryan. "Marketing, Science and Technology." In *Conceptual and Theoretical Developments in Marketing*, ed. O. C. Farrell, S. W. Brown, and C. W. Lamb. Chicago: American Marketing Association, 1979:577–89.

Osolnik, Bodgan. "Socialist Public Opinion." *Socialist Thought and Practice* 20 (October 1955):20.

Page, Benjamin I., and Robert Y. Shapiro. "The Rational Public: Fifty Years of Opinion Trends." Manuscript, 1987.

Page, Benjamin I., and Robert Y. Shapiro. "Presidents As Opinion Leaders: Some New Evidence." *Policy Studies Journal* 12 (1984):649–61.

Page, Benjamin I., and Robert Y. Shapiro. "Effects of Public Opinion on Policy." *American Political Science Review* 77 (1983):175–90.

Page, Benjamin I., Robert Y. Shapiro, and Glen R. Dempsey. "What Moves Public Opinion?" *American Political Science Review* 81 (1987):23–43.

Palda, K. Philip, and Kristian S. Palda. "Ceilings on Campaign Spending: Hypothesis and Partial Test with Canadian Data." *Public Choice* 45 (Summer 1985):313–31.

Paletz, David L., and Robert M. Entman. *Media Power Politics.* New York: Free Press, 1981.

Paletz, David et al. "How the Media Support Local Government Authority." *Public Opinion Quarterly* 35 (1971):80–92.

Palmgreen, Phillip; Lawrence A. Wenner; and J. D. Rayburn II. "Relations between Gratifications Sought and Obtained: A Study of Television News." *Communication Research* 7 (1980):161–92.

Paltsits, Victor Hugo, ed. *Washington's Farewell Address.* New York: Arno Press, 1971.

Parenti, Michael. *Inventing Reality: The Politics of the Mass Media.* New York: St. Martin's Press, 1986.

Paris, Barry. "Church diners 'bombed' with skunk water." *Pittsburgh Post-Gazette,* December 17, 1984.

Patterson, Thomas E. *The Mass Media Election.* New York: Praeger Publishers, 1980.

Patterson, Thomas E., and Robert D. McClure. *The Unseeing Eye: The Myth of Television Power in National Elections.* New York: G. P. Putnam's Sons, 1976.

Pearstein, Steven. "Hot Spots: INC's list of 50 fastest growing U.S. cities." *INC.* 9, no. 4 (April 1987):50–52.

Peffley, Mark A., and Jon Hurwitz. "A Hierarchical Model of Attitude Constraint." *American Journal of Political Science* 29 (1985):871–90.

Pennsylvania Department of Commerce. *1983 Pennsylvania Statistical Abstract,* 25th ed. Harrisburg, Penn.: Bureau of Statistics, Research and Planning, 1983.

Petty, Richard E., and John T. Cacioppo. *Attitudes and Persuasion: Classic and Contemporary Approaches.* Dubuque, Iowa: William C. Brown, 1981.

Petty, Richard E.; T. M. Ostrom; and T. C. Brock. *Cognitive Responses in Persuasion.* Hillsdale, N.J.: Lawrence Erlbaum, 1981.

Piechowiak, Cynthia. "Breaking bread: USX touts future at 'pep rally' for workers." *Pittsburgh Press,* March 17, 1987.

Pittsburgh Press. "Steel to lose more jobs in 1987. [Chase Econometrics] study says." *Pittsburgh Press,* December 22, 1986:B4.

Pitz, Marylynne. "Roth sues pastor, police chief." *Pittsburgh Post-Gazette,* March 18, 1987.

Political and Economic Planning. *Report on the British Press.* London: PEP, 1938.

Pomper, Gerald. "From Confusion to Clarity: Issues and American Voters, 1956–1968." *American Political Science Review* 66 (1972):415–29.

Pool, Ithiel de Sola. *Technologies of Freedom.* Cambridge, Mass.: Belknap Press of Harvard University, 1983.

Portz, John. "Politics, Plant Closings and Public Policy: The Steel Valley Authority in Pittsburgh." Paper delivered at the annual meeting of the Midwest Political Science Association, Chicago, Ill., April 9–12, 1987.

Pressman, Jeffrey, and Aaron Wildavsky. *Implementation,* 2nd ed. Berkeley, Calif.: University of California Press, 1979.

Price, Ray. *With Nixon.* New York: Viking Press, 1977.

Rados, David. *Marketing for Non-Profit Organizations.* Boston, Mass.: Auburn House, 1981.

Ranney, Austin. *Channels of Power: The Impact of Television on American Politics.* New York: Basic Books, 1983.

Rathburn, Flora. "Solberg to fight decision on defrocking." *Pittsburgh Press,* February 1, 1986.

Ray, M. L.; A. G. Sawyer; M. L. Rothschild; R. M. Heeler; E. C. Strong; and J. R. Reed. "Marketing Communications and Hierarchy of Effects." In *New Models for Mass Communications Research,* vol. 2, ed. P. Clarke. *Sage Annual Review of Communications Research.* Beverly Hills, Calif.: Sage Publications, 1973.

Republican National Committee. *Chairman's Report.* Washington, D.C.: Republican National Committee, 1984.

Rice, Msgr. Charles O. "An apology to Lutheran clergy." *Pittsburgh Catholic,* March 1, 1985.

Rice, Msgr. Charles O. "Burr in steel industry saddle." *Pittsburgh Catholic,* January 15, 1985a.

Rice, Msgr. Charles O. "DMS attack unwarranted." *Pittsburgh Catholic,* January 29, 1985b.

Rice, Msgr. Charles O. "On the Easter incident." *Pittsburgh Catholic,* May 18, 1984.

Richards, J.; Gary Mauser; and R. Holmes. "What Do Workers Want? Attitudes towards Collective Bargaining and Participation in Management." *Relations Industrielles* 43 (1988):133–52.

Ricks, David A. *Big Business Blunders: Mistakes in Multinational Marketing.* Homewood, Ill.: Dow Jones-Irwin, 1983.

Rishell, Grace, and Gabriel Ireton. "200 LTV retires rally inside plant." *Pittsburgh Post-Gazette,* March 25, 1987.

Rishell, Grace, and Bill Moushey. "LTV retirees push for pension money." *Pittsburgh Post-Gazette,* March 30, 1987.

Robinson, Claude. *Straw Votes.* New York: Columbia University Press, 1932: chap. 4.

Rogers, Everett. *Diffusion of Innovations.* Glencoe, Ill.: Free Press, 1965, 1971.

Roll, Charles W., and Albert H. Cantril. *Polls: Their Use and Misuse in Politics.* New York: Basic Books, 1972.

Rosen, Corey M. "A Test of Presidential Leadership in Public Opinion: The Split-Ballot Technique." *Polity* 6 (1973):282–90.

Rosenberg, Tina. "How the Media Made the Moral Majority." *Washington Monthly* (May 1982).

Rossiter, Clinton. *The American Presidency,* rev. ed. New York: Harcourt Brace Jovanovich, 1960.

Rothman, Stanley, and Robert Lichter. "Personality, Ideology, and World View: A Comparison of Business and Media Elites." *British Journal of Political Science* 11 (1985):29–49.

Rousseau, Jean Jacques. *The Social Contract (1762)* and *Discourses (1754).* New York: E. P. Dutton, 1950.

Sabato, Larry. *PAC Power: Inside the World of Political Action Committees.* New York: W. W. Norton, 1984.

Safire, William. *Safire's Political Dictionary.* New York: Ballantine Books, 1978.

Safire, William. *Before the Fall.* New York: Belmont Press, 1975.

Salisbury, Robert. "Interest Representation: The Dominance of Institutions." *American Political Science Review* 78 (1984):64–76.

Salmore, Stephen A., and Barbara G. Salmore. *Candidates, Parties, and Campaigns: Electoral Politics in America.* Washington, D.C.: CQ Press, 1985.

Saloma, John S., III. *Ominous Politics: The New Conservative Labyrinth.* New York: Farrar, Straus, 1984.

Sanders, Jerry W. *Peddlars of Crisis: The Committee on the Present Danger and the Politics of Containment.* Boston: South End Press, 1983.

Sapir, Edward. "Symbolism." In *Encyclopedia of the Social Sciences.* New York: Macmillan, 1934:494–95.

Scammon, Richard M., and Ben J. Wattenberg. *The Real Majority.* New York: Coward-McCann, 1970:49.

Schattschneider, E. E. *The Semisovereign People: A Realist's View of Democracy in America.* Hinsdale, Ill.: Dryden Press, 1960.

Schattschneider, E. E. *Party Government.* New York, Rinehart, 1942.

Schiffman, Susan, M. Lance Reynolds, and Forrest W. Young. *Introduction to Multidimensional Scaling: Theory, Methods, and Applications.* New York: Academic Press, 1981.

Schiller, Herbert. *Communication and Culture Domination.* New York: Pantheon Books, 1978.

Schiller, Herbert I. *The Mind Managers.* Boston: Beacon Press, 1973:108–10.

Schlozman, Kay L., and John T. Tierney. "More of the Same: Washington Pressure Group Activity in a Decade of Change." *Journal of Politics* 45 (May 1983).

Schlozman, Kay L., and Sidney Verba. *Injury to Insult: Unemployment, Class, and Political Response.* Cambridge, Mass.: Harvard University Press, 1979.

Schmalensee, Richard. *Perceptual Maps and the Optimal Location of New Products.* Cambridge, Mass.: Marketing Science Institute, report no. 86–103, 1986.

Schram, Martin. "Why can't Democrats be more like Republicans? They're Trying." *Washington Post,* March 21, 1982:A2.

Schulte, Henry F. "Mass Media as Vehicles of Education, Persuasion, and Opinion Making in the Western World." In *Comparative Mass Media Systems,* ed. L. John Martin and Anju Grover Chaudhary. White Plains, N.Y.: Longman, 1983:133–46.

Schumacher, E. F. *Small Is Beautiful: Economics as If People Mattered.* New York: Harper & Row (Perennial Press), 1975.

Schumpeter, Joseph. *Capitalism, Socialism, and Democracy.* New York: Harper & Row, 1942.

Schwartz, Tony. *The Responsive Chord.* Garden City, N.J.: Doubleday Publishing, 1974.

Schwarz, John E. *American's Hidden Success: A Reassessment of Twenty Years of Public Policy.* New York: W. W. Norton, 1983.

Shapiro, Robert Y., and Benjamin I. Page. "Foreign Policy and the Rational Public." *Journal of Conflict Resolution,* 1988.

Shaw, D. L., and M. E. McCombs. *The Emergence of American Political Issues: The Agenda-Setting Function of the Press.* St. Paul, Minn.: West Publishing, 1977.

Shawcross, William. *Sideshow.* New York: Simon & Schuster, 1979.

Shepherd, Jack. "Ethiopia: The Use of Food as an Instrument of U.S. Foreign Policy." *Issue: A Journal of Opinion* 14 (1985):4–9.

Shipler, D. K. "Poll shows confusion on aid to contras." *New York Times,* April 15, 1986:A6.

Shocker, A., and V. Srinivasan. "Multiattribute Approaches for Product Concept Evaluation and Generation: A Critical Review." *Journal of Marketing Research* 16 (May 1979):159–80.

Shribman, D. "Foreign policy costing Reagan public support." *New York Times,* September 30, 1983:1.

Sigal, Leon V. *Reporters and Officials: The Organization and Politics of Newsmaking.* Lexington, Mass.: D. C. Heath, 1973.

Sigel, Roberta. "Images of the American Presidency." *Midwest Journal of Political Science* 10 (1966):123–37.

Sigelman, Lee. "The Commander in Chief and the Public: Mass Response to Johnson's March 31, 1968, Bombing Halt Speech." *Journal of Political and Military Sociology* 8 (1980):1–14.

Sigelman, Lee, and Carol K. Sigelman. "Shattered expectations: Public Responses to 'Out-of-Character' Presidential Actions." *Political Behavior* 8 (1986):262–86.

Sigelman, Lee, and Carol K. Sigelman. "Presidential Leadership of Public Opinion: From 'Opinion Leader' to 'Kiss of Death'?" *Experimental Study of Politics* 7 (1981):1–22.

Silver, Alan. "The Demand for Order in Civil Society." In *The Police*, ed. David Bordua. New York: John Wiley & Sons, 1967:17–18.

Smith, Arthur L. "Life in Wartime Germany: Colonel Ohlendorff's Opinion Service." *Public Opinion Quarterly* 36 (Spring 1972):1–7.

Smith, Geoffrey. "Can Marxism Stand Prosperity?" *Forbes*, July 1, 1977:41–46.

Smith, M. B.; J. S. Bruner; and R. W. White. *Opinions and Personality*. New York: John Wiley & Sons, 1956.

Spragens, William C. "Kennedy Era Speechwriting, Public Relations, and Public Opinion." *Presidential Studies Quarterly* 14 (1984):78–84.

Stefflre, Volney. *Developing and Implementing Marketing Strategies*. New York: Praeger Publishers, 1986.

Stefflre, Volney. "Multidimensional Scaling as a Model for Human Information Processing." *Proceedings of the 1978 Marketing Educators Meeting*. Chicago, Ill.: AMA, 1979.

Stefflre, Volney. "Market Structure Studies: New Products for Old Markets and New Markets (Foreign) for Old Products." In *Applications of the Sciences in Marketing Management*, ed. F. Bass, C. W. King, and E. A. Pessemier. New York: John Wiley & Sons, 1968:251–68.

Steinberg, Charles. *The Information Establishment*. New York: Hastings House, 1980.

Sterling, Christopher, and Timothy Haight. *The Mass Media*. New York: Praeger Publishers, 1978.

Stigler, George J. *The Citizen and the State: Essays on Regulation*. Chicago: University of Chicago Press, 1975.

Stockman, David A. *The Triumph of Politics: How the Reagan Revolution Failed*. New York: Harper & Row, 1986.

Stockwell, John. *In Search of Enemies: A CIA Story*. New York: W. W. Norton, 1978.

Stokes, Donald E. "Spatial Models of Party Competition." *American Political Science Review* 57 (June 1963):368–77.

Stouffer, S. A. *Communism, Conformity, and Civil Liberties*. New York: Doubleday Publishing, 1955.

Talbott, Strobe. *Deadly Gambits: The Reagan Administration and the Stalemate in Nuclear Arms Control*. New York: Random House, 1984.

Tax Review. *State Tax Prospects, 1979*. vol. 40, 1979.

Tesser, A. "Self-Generated Attitude Change." In *Advances in Experimental Social Psychology*, vol. 11, ed. L. Berkowitz. New York: Academic Press, 1978.

The Economist. "Taxes Overboard," 17: June 1978:11.

Thurstone, L. L. "The Prediction of Choice." *Psychometrika* 10 (December 1945):237–53.

Tichenor, P. J. et al. *Community Conflict and the Press.* Beverly Hills, Calif.: Sage Publications, 1980.

Time. "Power, Glory and Politics." February 17, 1986:62–69.

Tocqueville, Alexis de. *Democracy in America,* 2 vols. Ed. Phillips Bradley, trans. Henry Reeve. New York: Alfred A. Knopf, 1948.

Truman, David. "Public Opinion Research as a Tool of Public Administration." *Public Administration Review* 5 (Winter 1945):62–72.

Tuchman, G. *Making News.* New York: Free Press, 1978.

Tulis, Jeffrey. *The Rhetorical Presidency.* Princeton, N.J.: Princeton University Press, 1987.

Tversky, Amos, and Shmuel Sattath. "Preference Trees." *Psychological Review* 86, no. 10 (November 1979):542–73.

Tyler, S. A., ed. *Cognitive Anthropology.* New York: Holt Rinehart & Winston, 1969.

U.S. (The Tower Commission) *Report of the President's Special Review Board.* Washington, D.C.: USGPO, 1987.

U.S. Senate, Select Committee to Study Government Operations with Respect to Intelligence Activities. *Alleged Assassination Plots Involving Foreign Leaders* (The Church Committee Interim Report). Washington, D.C.: USGPO, 1975.

University Center of Social and Urban Research. *The State of the Region: Recent Economic, Demographic, and Social Trends in Southwestern Pennsylvania.* Pittsburgh: University of Pittsburgh, September 1984.

Urban, Glen, and John Hauser. *Design and Marketing of New Products.* Englewood Cliffs, N.J.: Prentice-Hall, 1980.

Utne Reader. Minneapolis: Lens Publishing Co. (March/April 1987):19.

Verba, Sidney, and Norman H. Nie. *Participation in America: Political Democracy and Social Equality.* New York: Harper & Row, 1972.

Wade, Chet. "Special report: How things went awry at Mellon." *Pittsburgh Post-Gazette,* July 4, 1987.

Wallace, Henry A., and James L. McCamy. "Straw Polls and Public Administration." *Public Opinion Quarterly* 4 (June 1940):221–23.

Warren, Robert Penn. *All the King's Men: A Play.* New York: Random House, 1960.

Washington Post. "Born-Again Politics." March 30, 1980:C1.

Weaver, D. H. et al. "Watergate and the Media: A Case Study of Agenda-Setting." *American Political Quarterly* 3 (1975):458–72.

Webb, Eugene. *Unobtrusive Measures.* Chicago: Rand McNally, 1966.

Weisberg, H. F., and J. Rusk. "Dimensions of Candidate Evaluation." *American Political Science Review* 64 (1970):615–28.

Weisman, S. R. "President, in Texas, stresses Central America." *New York Times,* May 6, 1983:A17.

Weissberg, Robert. *Public Opinion and Popular Government.* Englewood Cliffs, N.J.: Prentice-Hall, 1976:12–16.

Wekkin, Gary D. *Political Parties and Intergovernmental Relations in 1984: The Consequences of Party Renewal for Territorial Constituencies.* Unpublished draft, 1984.

Welch, W. P. "Money and Votes: A Simultaneous Equation Model." *Public Choice* 36 (Summer 1981):209–34.

Wheeler, Michael. *Lies, Damn Lies and Statistics.* New York: Liveright, 1976: chap. 12.

White, Theodore. *The Making of the President, 1972.* New York: Atheneum Publishers, 1973.

Wilcox, Walter. "The Congressional Poll and Non-Poll." In *Political Opinion and Electoral Behavior,* ed. Edward C. Dreyer and Walter Rosenbaum. Belmont, Calif.: Wadsworth, 1966.

Wildavsky, Aaron. "The Two Presidencies." *Transaction* 4 (1966):7–14.

Wildavsky, Aaron. "The Goldwater Phenomenon: Purists, Politicians, and the Two Party System." *Review of Politics* 27 (July 1965):386–413.

Wilson, James Q. *Political Organizations.* New York: Basic Books, 1973.

Wilson, James Q. *The Amateur Democrat: Club Politics in Three Cities.* Chicago: University of Chicago Press, 1962.

Wilson, Linda S. "County to buy idled mills." *Pittsburgh Post-Gazette,* March 26, 1987.

Windchy, Eugene G. *Tonkin Gulf.* New York: Doubleday Publishing, 1971.

Wise, David. *The Politics of Lying: Government Deception, Secrecy, and Power.* New York: Random House, 1973.

Wise, David, and Thomas B. Ross. *The Invisible Government.* New York: Random House, 1964.

Wolfinger, Raymond E., and Fred I. Greenstein. "The Repeal of Fair Housing in California: An Analysis of Referendum Voting." *American Political Science Review* 62 (1968):753–70.

Young, Richard P. *Societal Change and the Evolution of American Race Relations.* Ph.D. dissertation, Stanford University, 1979.

List of Interviews

Bergholz, Elizabeth. Religion beat reporter, *Pittsburgh Post-Gazette*. Telephone conversation, October 5, 1986.

Bonn, Mike. Former president of USW Local 2227, Irwin Works. Active in DMS in 1983 and 1984. February 11, 1987.

Broderick, Mary Ann. Internal consultant—employee relations, USX Corporation. Telephone conversation. February 11, 1987.

Brown, Lois. Displaced Workers Program/Bridge to Recovery, McKeesport. January 16, 1987.

Clark, Sylvia. Vice president, Mellon Foundation. March 10, 1987.

Cochran, Wayne. Former president, Trinity Lutheran Church, Clairton [DMS]. August 25, 1987.

Confidential, Anonymous. State legislative leader. April 1985.

Craig, John. Editor-in-chief, *Pittsburgh Post-Gazette*. October 21, 1986.

Curcio, Marion. Displaced Workers Program/Bridge to Recovery, McKeesport. January 16, 1987.

Dorsey, Fr. Garrett. Priest, St. Stephen's Catholic Church, Hazelwood. August 5, 1986.

Fahrenkopf, Frank J., Jr. Chairman, Republican National Committee. April 25, 1985.

Farley, David. Head of City of Pittsburgh JTPA programs. February 13, 1987.

Fleming, Dorothy. Director of Lutheran Synod Coordinating Committee on Unemployed. August 21, 1986.

Fletcher, Charles ("Chuck"). Vice President for Community Affairs, Mellon Bank. February 19, 1987.

Foster, Rev. Kristin. Pastor, St. James' Lutheran Church, Emsworth [DMS]. August 26, 1986.

Fritz, Mike. Head, Small Business Loan Department, Mellon Bank. March 10, 1987.

Gropp, Rev. John J. Pastor, St. John's Lutheran Church, Duquesne [DMS]. July 23, 1986.

Haulk, Jake. Staff economist, Mellon Bank. March 10, 1987.

Hefner, Jim. News director, KDKA (CBS). Telephone conversation. October 3, 1986.

Hoffman, William. General Manager for Public Affairs, USX Corporation. Telephone conversation. January 30, 1987.

Honeywell, Charles. DMS trainer and consultant. September 17, 1986.

Long, Rev. Philip. East Liberty Lutheran Church, DMS headquarters. July 26, 1987.

Looney, Joseph. Head, Veterans Job Search Committee, East Liberty Lutheran Church [DMS].

Manatt, Charles T. Chairman, Democratic National Committee. April 1985.

McCauley, Katherine. Director of staff, JTPA Private Industry Council. March 18, 1987.

McClellan, Ross. Head of community services, Member of Legislative Committee, USW, Local 2227, Irvin Works. February 5, 1987.

McGough, Michael. Editorial page editor, *Pittsburgh Post-Gazette*. Telephone conversation. October 3, 1987.

Mitchell, William ("Rickey"). Veterans' Job Search Committee, East Liberty Lutheran Church. March 4, 1987.

O'Brien, Frank. Director of direct-mail fundraising, Democratic National Committee. May 7, 1985.

Peterson, Francis. Mon Valley Unemployed Committee, McKeesport Office. February 5, 1987.

Quinn, Ron. Assistant director, Allegheny County JTPA Programs. January 28, 1987.

Rice, Msgr. Charles Owen. Activist labor priest. July 21, 1986.

Ross, Madelyn. Managing editor, *Pittsburgh Press*. Telephone conversation. October 6, 1986.

Roth, Rev. D. Douglas. Former minister, Trinity Lutheran Church, Clairton [DMS]. September 9, 1986.

Rouvalis, Christina. General assignment reporter, *Pittsburgh Post-Gazette*. October 16, 1986.

Rovitto, Joe. News director, WTAE (ABC). October 9, 1986.

Schrensky, Isador. Editorial page editor, *Pittsburgh Press*. Telephone conversation. September 29, 1986.

Solberg, Rev. Daniel. Assistant pastor, East Liberty Lutheran Church; formerly pastor of Nativity Lutheran Church, Allison Park [DMS]. July 23, 1986.

Stewart, Wyatt. Republican Congressional Campaign Committee. November 24, 1984.

Warner, David. Former city editor, *Pittsburgh Post-Gazette*. October 2, 1986.

Werner, The Very Reverend George S. Dean, Trinity Cathedral [Episcopal]. October 27, 1986.

Williams, V. Byron. News director, WPXI (NBC). October 23, 1986.

Young, Bobbie. Veterans' Job Search Committee, East Liberty Lutheran Church. March 4, 1987.

Zundell, Rev. Donald. Chairman, Lutheran Synod Coordinating Committee on Unemployed. August 7, 1986.

Names Index

Subject Index